MAN O' WAR

A Legend Like Lightning

DOROTHY OURS

St. Martin's Griffin
New York

MAN O' WAR. Copyright © 2006 by Dorothy Ours. All rights reserved. Printed in the
United States of America. For information, address St. Martin's Press, 175 Fifth Avenue,
New York, N.Y. 10010.

www.stmartins.com

Design by Ruth Lee-Mui

Library of Congress Cataloging-in-Publication Data

Ours, Dorothy.
 Man o' War : a legend like lightning / Dorothy Ours.
   p. cm.
 ISBN-13: 978-0-312-34100-8
 ISBN-10: 0-312-34100-8
 1. Man o' War (Race horse) 2. Race horses—United States—Biography. I. Title.

SF355.M3 O97 2006
798.400929—dc22

                                                              2006041631

10 9 8 7 6 5 4 3 2

To all of my teachers, human and otherwise

CONTENTS

MAN O' WAR

PROLOGUE

The Legend of Man o' War

THE HORSE REMINDED his owner of lightning, but not ordinary streak lightning that flashes once and rolls away. This horse seemed to set off a chain of strikes that raced across the entire landscape and lit up the whole sky. He filled his handlers with exhilaration and fear, as if they were swept up in a rare form of electrical storm. His impact, in fact, would never leave them. As long as these insiders lived, people would stop and ask them for the real story of the Thoroughbred racehorse named Man o' War.

The horse had become world-famous in 1920, while Babe Ruth revolutionized baseball and Louis Armstrong began reinventing jazz. His genius, like theirs, would intrigue each new generation. Eight decades after Man o' War retired from racing, the sport's world-class Keeneland Library in Kentucky still received more questions about him than any other subject. In 1999, a panel of experts assembled by racing's prestigious *The Blood-Horse* magazine voted Man o' War the number-one American racehorse of the twentieth century, with the magnificent Triple Crown champion Secretariat at number two. The majority had answered an unanswerable question—Who is the greatest of all time?—by honoring the equine equivalent of the Sultan of Swat and Satchmo.

Like any lasting legend, Man o' War combined unique quality with perfect timing. Setting an unprecedented number of speed records, he became old-fashioned horse racing's modern response to automobiles and flying machines. Wowing crowds with his majestic good looks, he shared photo spreads and newsreels with top-ranking politicians and movie stars.

Newspapers described him as a "super-horse" who never reached the limit of his abilities.

A few people close to Man o' War knew the more complicated truth. His owner, trainer, and jockeys learned how partnering with a Thoroughbred hero could raise a person to intoxicating heights and curse a person with accusations that would never die.

I

TWO WARS BEGIN

IN THE GREEN hills of Kentucky, nine days after riding his first winner, an apprentice jockey named John Patrick Loftus got an offer to sell his soul. Fourteen years old, still wearing knee pants when not in jockey uniform, he entered the fifth race at Latonia on Friday, June 24, 1910, with an angel on one shoulder and a devil on the other. His mount, a classy colt named Boola Boola, could win easily. But Johnny would be far richer if he made Boola Boola lose. Thursday night, during a streetcar ride, a stranger had propositioned him: two hundred dollars to pull Boola Boola, and make long shot First Peep a "sure thing."[1]

Two hundred dollars. In 1910, that would buy ten ounces of gold or a thousand large cans of Van Camp's pork and beans. Whatever Johnny wanted, that quick money might be the highest peak he would ever reach. Many apprentice jockeys outgrew the job within months. Johnny weighed less than 100 pounds right now, but with his stocky build, he wouldn't stay light for long. Also, as long as he remained a jockey, he performed a very dangerous job. On June 8, the day after Johnny debuted at the Latonia meet, a veteran jockey named George Glasner had suffered life-threatening injuries when his horse fell during a Latonia race. When Johnny got offered two hundred dollars to pull Boola Boola, Glasner remained hospitalized and seemed unlikely to ride ever again.

Now, for losing one race, Johnny Loftus could pocket a fortune that his growing body and risky job might keep him from earning honestly . . . if he was willing to betray the trainer who believed that Johnny *could* be a successful race rider, and the racehorse-owning senator who trusted him with Boola Boola.

Riches, or respect? As Johnny reined Boola Boola onto the track, his life balanced over a tiny saddle about four inches wide. His career balanced between truth and deceit.

Thunder, lightning, and drenching rain broke the oppressive heat at Latonia—known to sweating horsemen as "Death Valley"—midway through the program on that Friday afternoon. Casual fans fled. Only horsemen and devoted gamblers stayed, and a reporter noticed the diehards "wagering heavily on their choices."[2] Steering Boola Boola through the monsoon, Johnny Loftus made his choice. At the finish, he held the lead by an easy length. Only one horse launched a serious rally: First Peep, gaining like mad through the homestretch, rushing up into second place.

Having kept his soul, Johnny could have kept quiet. Instead, he talked about the bribe. That should have shown what an honest boy Johnny Loftus was, letting people know that they could trust him with their good horses. Their actual response must have been a shock.

Latonia laughed it off. Johnny couldn't have been tempted on Thursday night, they said, because he hadn't been hired to ride Boola Boola until *Friday morning*. "Loftus and those responsible for bringing the matter to the attention of the [racetrack] judges are being held to ridicule," the Louisville *Courier-Journal* declared. ". . . The lad's misrepresentation of facts may cause him to lose his license."[3] But he did not.

At second glance, logic supported Johnny's story. By Thursday morning, Boola Boola's people had known that their colt would carry only 92 pounds in Friday's race. Few jockeys could ride that light. Ted Rice, the veteran who had finished fourth with Boola Boola in the Kentucky Derby, couldn't do it. Loftus was Latonia's leading lightweight. In the sharp-eyed small town of racetrack life, a generous "stranger" easily could figure the probabilities, or even pay for not-yet-public information—and, in a public place, catch up with the new young rider who didn't know all of the serious gamblers by sight.

Crooked gamblers enjoyed another sweet advantage. Although newsreels flickered in every neighborhood nickelodeon, racetracks didn't film horse races. If Johnny decided to take a dive, his trip with Boola Boola—lost in mud and rain and time—couldn't be reviewed. But immediate impressions written down by professional chart makers did remain. While Boola Boola beat First Peep by one body length, a horse named Charles F. Grainger finished third, only a half length behind First Peep. "Charles F. Grainger, weakly handled, ran a good race," the *Courier-Journal*'s result chart noted, "and might have won with a stronger ride."[4] No one asked whether Grainger's rider had dealt with a streetcar stranger.

Surviving the ridicule, Johnny Loftus learned a lesson. It wasn't "Don't make up stories." It was "Keep your mouth shut."

He would live by that lesson nine years later, when he rode the horse named Man o' War.

Latonia's leading trainer during the summer of 1910 was an almost mummy-thin thirty-four-year-old veteran of Western cattle drives, livery stables, and county fair races. His name was H. G. Bedwell. Officially, the H.G. stood for Harvey Guy. Bedwell insisted—and liked to prove—that it stood for "Hard Guy."

He had grown up very poor, in the Pacific Northwest, a region where many dreams had died. Bedwell came from parents who had followed a dream, the 1849 gold rush, across the prairies into Oregon. Like most other pioneers, they discovered there was no such thing as easy money. Late in 1876, when Harvey Guy was eighteen months old, his father died and his mother found herself with four boys to raise. Gold was a long-gone fantasy. By the time more privileged children were attending eighth grade, Harvey Guy was out on the Oregon range, living as a cowboy. In remote territory, where his life literally depended on his horsemanship, Harvey Guy Bedwell became "Hard Guy."

"Hard Guy" Bedwell was not sentimental about horses, but he learned how they worked. He learned from the cow ponies that carried him through four seasons outdoors, and he learned from the riding and driving horses he rented out to travelers after establishing a livery stable in Grand Junction, Colorado. He learned how to soothe sore legs and feet, and he learned to provide his horses with plenty of good grain, hay, water, and fresh air. Somewhere along the line, he also learned about racetracks and decided that Grand Junction's fair grounds needed one. Succeeding there, he stretched his tether from fair to fair, winning more than his share. But the prize money wasn't much. And so, in his thirty-fourth year on Earth, "Hard Guy" Bedwell hatched a bold plan. Thoroughbred racehorses—the world's elite running-horse breed—would become his gold rush, and they would lead him East.

Bedwell surprised Eastern horsemen in 1909 with sixteen victories during fourteen days of his first New York meet. A year later, as New York racing shuddered to a stop because of antigambling laws, Hard Guy didn't wait for the death throes. He invaded Kentucky. This should have been another golden move, but instead, Bedwell ran into trouble. The racetrack officials at Latonia had made a revolutionary decree that doping horses was a punishable offense.

This was a high-minded public-relations tactic for the track, but for horsemen and handicappers, it was a startling cultural change. Horsemen had experimented with speed potions for centuries, as trainers learned that many racehorses, sooner or later, needed artificial inspiration. Some horses were scared to race; others became tired or sore. Faced with endless bills to pay, horsemen developed temporary ways to distract a horse from his troubles. Heroin earned the nickname "horse" because it kicks equines into overdrive. Morphine and other opiates, which lull humans to sleep, also trigger this ancient equine flight response. In the wild, pursued by predators, a horse runs as fast as it can or dies. Given narcotics, a horse feels unnatural sleepiness creeping into its nervous system—sleepiness like the shock caused by a carnivore's fatal bite. And so the hopped horse runs without reserve. If kept in his stall, he trots in circles until the dose finally ebbs. Let loose on a racetrack, he outruns any normal inhibition.

When Bedwell came to racing, everybody knew that many horses ran "hot" and "cold." For the betting public, the main problem was noticing if a cold horse going off at long odds suddenly heated up—or vice versa. A classic example happened in 1897 at Elkton, Maryland, when a poky mare named Sister Myra suddenly won by ten lengths. Owner John Ryan, who cashed a healthy bet, admitted that it was her first time on "hop." The presiding steward, Judge Bowie, gave him strict orders: From now on, every time she runs, make sure she gets the same dose.

By the time Johnny Loftus got his jockey license, recipes for hop were as plentiful as recipes for corn bread and coming by ingredients wasn't hard. Caffeine could be boiled out of black coffee. Strychnine (also used by human athletes for speeding up muscle contractions) was a common rat poison. Even cocaine, heroin, and morphine were legal for anyone with a doctor's prescription to buy from a drugstore, until prohibited by the Harrison Act of 1914—and could be bribed from pharmacists long after that. But using those mixtures effectively was a fine art. Prudent trainers experimented during morning workouts, discovering the right dope and dose for each horse. Still, anything could happen at racing time.

Early in the summer of 1910, as Guy Bedwell moved from New York to Kentucky, Latonia exposed dope's dangers in the worst way. During the last race on July 1, while leading the field into the homestretch, a chestnut gelding named Charley Hill abruptly fell, slamming into the inside fence on his way down. Broken beyond repair, Charley was dragged to a far edge of the course and, in the words of a local reporter, "put out of his misery by a friendly bullet, when the main crowd had left the grounds."[5] A more widely heard shot followed. "It is charged that the animal had been given a stimulant," the *New York Times* reported, "and the [Latonia] officials were told by a veterinarian that the effects of the drug caused the horse to fall."[6] All of a sudden, a dope case was national news. Within twenty-four hours, horsemen Kay Spence and J. S. Merchant were ruled off the track. Now Latonia's eyes were open wide, but some horsemen still thought they could hide in plain sight.

Three days after Charley Hill died, an experienced racer named Nadzu reached Latonia's saddling paddock in a "frenzied condition."[7] Drug tests for racehorses had not yet been invented, but the paddock judge, veterinarian William Keogh, believed that he could read the body language. Taking Dr. Keogh's advice, the judges scratched Nadzu and summoned the man who owned and trained him: "Hard Guy" Bedwell, the most successful trainer on the grounds.

Their decision didn't take long. On July 6, Bedwell was officially ruled off the turf. Banned from racing, he couldn't even sell his horses for their $70,000 market value. Presumably tainted by dope, they were banned, too.

Latonia's righteous action surprised most racetrackers. Though impressed that mighty Bedwell was suffering the same as humble Kay Spence, horsemen doubted he would be outlawed for long. With twenty-two Thoroughbreds in his string and a high percentage of in-the-money finishes, Bedwell's presence meant a quality racing product. Didn't the game need him? Spence, meanwhile, took no comfort in the impartial punishment. "I was doing my best to win and I can see no crime in that," he told the Louisville *Courier-Journal*, "and with my horse dead and then be handed a package like was given me, I think is pretty hard."[8]

Ten days later, the Kentucky Racing Commission reinstated Kay Spence, who benefited from a procedural lapse: "the failure of Dr. Keogh . . . to examine the horse [Charley Hill] for evidence of doping either before or after his death."[9] Bedwell, however, couldn't overcome the raw truth that Nadzu had been hopped. He claimed that one of his grooms had taken a gambler's bribe to dose Nadzu with cocaine, and he presented telegrams of support from several of racing's most prestigious men, including Jockey Club chairman August Belmont, Jr. The commission was unmoved. For several months, they firmly backed Dr. Keogh's testimony. But Dr. Keogh died that autumn. Bedwell kept agitating. Early in 1911, he regained his license and promptly became the nation's leading trainer by number of wins.

There was more to his success than dope. Any fool could get his hands on that. Veterinarian Frank M. Keller would recall, "The best trainer I've ever seen with bad-legged horses was H. Guy Bedwell."[10] Those bad-legged runners owed some of Bedwell's magic to clever blacksmithing and pharmacy, and even more to the galaxy of limitations he had managed with the cow ponies, livery stable nags, and county fair racers. They also benefited from the skilled help Bedwell chose to employ.

Early in 1912, with Kentucky racing closed for the winter, Bedwell migrated to a Charleston, South Carolina, track so new that its dirt was still settling. From prominent trainer Rome Respess, he borrowed Kentucky's most promising young jockey: sixteen-year-old Johnny Loftus.

For Johnny, this assignment couldn't have been easy. A fierce perfectionist, Bedwell liked to keep his employees living in fear. But for a few weeks at Palmetto Park, he and Loftus exploited each other's abilities to an improbable degree. Eleven days into the meet, Bedwell had won every stakes race offered. A month into the meet, the Louisville *Courier-Journal* proudly noted that, "Loftus stands head and shoulders above all the other jockeys . . ."[11] Bedwell was giving him sharp horses, and Loftus was making the most of them.

After Johnny's contract obligations pulled them apart, respect for each other's skill remained. Reunited seven years later, they would develop a champion colt who would rival Man o' War.

First, however, August Belmont had to prepare the way.

Man o' War's life, and Thoroughbred racing's survival in the eastern United States, depended on a short and suave Manhattan-based financier named August Belmont, Jr.[12] He presided over a select society called The Jockey Club.

Despite his jockeylike height and his skill as a polo player, Belmont never had been a professional race rider. Despite its name, The Jockey Club of New York was never open to professional jockeys. Only socially prominent racehorse *owners* were invited to join. They didn't make their living on the back of a galloping horse, but they did make racing's rules. Formed in 1894 to fight corruption, The Jockey Club vowed to make certain that each horse entered in every race was the same runner actually brought to the starting post, and to investigate whenever a horse performed much better or much worse than its known ability. Trainers or jockeys caught using foul tactics were quickly suspended or banned.

But by 1910, The Jockey Club was losing its fight. That summer, as Johnny Loftus clung to his new career, most racetracks in the United States had been closed or were closing. State after state had banished Thoroughbred racing because too many people would do almost anything to try to win a bet. Crooked bookies, gamblers, and horsemen could make more money when favorites didn't win, and they knew how to stop favorites in any number of ways: Keep the horse thirsty, then offer a pail of water shortly before the race and watch the horse struggle along with water sloshing in its gut; sit on the horse's back for a few hours in its stall, during the night before a race, and quietly tire it out; "roll" the horseshoe toes with a blacksmith's file to reduce traction and then watch the horse try like mad while going nowhere; put a sedative in a tempting snack; find a slow horse that closely resembled the favorite and run the slow horse in the fast horse's name (then run the actual fast horse several days later, at much higher odds); pay an assistant starter to release the horse too slowly at the break; or pay a jockey not to find the quickest way home.

Racetrack wisdom said that most people didn't care if a race was fixed, so long as they found out who was supposed to win. But across the United States, thousands of antigambling reformers trumpeted a vision of how pure and honorable America should be. It didn't matter to them that a great many races yielded reasonable results. Risking dollars on horse races was a sinful shortcut to the poorhouse; robbing the public through unfair gambling was damnable; and racing's common swindles gave antigambling reformers political leverage. As politicians fell in line, betting on horse races became illegal in state after state. By April of 1911, only three states—Kentucky, Maryland, and Virginia—kept government-sanctioned racing with wagering alive. New York, which had sponsored America's richest prizes, was completely shut down.

While Guy Bedwell was becoming the nation's winningest trainer and Johnny Loftus was raising his own winning rate to more than 20 percent,

August Belmont tackled an enormous task: restoring racing to New York. Top stables were relocating to Europe or selling out entirely. Belmont, who had played a crucial role in developing New York City's subway system, understood big business—and New York's racetrack properties occupied prime real estate worth more than $12 million. But instead of selling to developers, Belmont focused on saving his favorite sport.

Ever since his father launched a Thoroughbred farm on Long Island in 1867, racehorses had been Belmont's refuge. He fulfilled family demands by graduating from Harvard and taking over his father's financial firm, but fine horses gave him joy. Belmont didn't only want to own them; he wanted to create them. Fascinated with pedigrees, he studied Thoroughbred bloodlines for more than four decades and bred dozens of stakes winners. Then the New York legislature tried to tell him that Thoroughbred racers had no place in his home state.

Giving up would have been simple. Belmont already operated a breeding farm in France and raced elite horses at the best European meets. He easily could have deserted the troubled United States scene. Instead, he rounded up friends to build a stylish new track at Havre de Grace, Maryland—just in case restoring the New York tracks took awhile—and began digging for a loophole in New York's antibetting law. Meanwhile, he insisted that Thoroughbred racing served a patriotic duty: testing the courage, endurance, and early maturity of cavalry stock so badly needed by the U.S. Army. Few racers actually left the track to carry officers into battle, but Belmont persuaded army generals to tell the *New York Times* that race-proven Thoroughbred stallions made the most useful contributions to the cavalry horse gene pool.

While Bedwell and Loftus roamed the racing circuits in Kentucky, Canada, and Mexico, August Belmont searched for some way that gambling at his home tracks could exist. After all, betting brought in the crowds. Legal or not, most patrons would have their friendly wagers whenever horses had a contest—and that was it! Did the law prohibit casual bets among friends? No, it did not. And so New York racing reopened on May 30, 1913, courtesy of a legal compromise that earned this era the nickname of "the Oral Days." Instead of paying one hundred dollars per day to the racing association and selling betting tickets to clients, each bookmaker at the track made verbal agreements with hundreds of "friends."

August Belmont hated to see the general public waste their money by wagering on horse races—only the rich could afford that, he thought—but now his lifelong love had meaning again. Once again he presided over racing at Belmont Park, the giant Long Island course named for his father. Once again he ran his homebred horses in the classic Belmont Stakes, a demanding race that showcased what greatness should be.

Winning a single race is hard enough. More than half of all racehorses never reach the winner's circle. But the rarest of champions achieve the ultimate domination: winning *every time.*

During 1907 and 1908, Americans watched a handsome young horse unroll a seamless carpet of wins. Foaled from an English-born mare named *Pastorella (who, like all foreign-born Thoroughbreds imported to America, sported an asterisk next to her name), he was named for a lovesick lad in a pastoral English poem: "Poor Colin sat weeping and told them his pain."[13] The reference was far too fitting. Colin the colt was born with an enlarged hock—the central joint in his hind leg—which had to be numbed with ether before each race. But as a two-year-old in 1907, Colin entered twelve sprints and won every one.

August Belmont bred and owned Colin's chief rival, a high-headed golden colt named Fair Play, who chased Colin home several times but never got close to beating him. Colin seemed to have an effortless extra gear that he employed when threatened. He also had the cleverest of trainers: a former star jockey, ex–circus rider, and future Hall of Famer named Jimmy Rowe, Sr. As a trainer, Rowe had won eighteen consecutive races with a champion colt named Hindoo. In 1904 and 1905, he had won 14 of 15 starts with the sensational Sysonby. But Rowe thought Colin could be the best of all.

At Belmont Park, in the 1908 Belmont Stakes, Fair Play made him fight for it.

Colin started as the favorite on that stormy June afternoon, despite grave concerns about the tendons in his front legs. Two days earlier, after a brilliant workout, his front pasterns (the springy slope joining ankle to hoof) had swollen to "nearly double their normal size."[14] Thinking that Colin had broken down, Jimmy Rowe telephoned owner James R. Keene with the terrible news, then collapsed on a couch and cried.

But on Belmont Stakes day, Colin appeared in the saddling paddock after all. Hundreds of men and women pushed through the wind and rain to see for themselves whether Colin was all right. Thick bandages wrapped around all four of his lower legs, not stripped off until Colin was about to leave the paddock, kept them guessing. Jimmy Rowe swore that Colin was not sore. The track veterinarian, Dr. R. W. McCully, swore that this was true. But had the historic Belmont Stakes, worth $21,765 to the winner, plus a thousand-dollar trophy, tempted owner Keene and trainer Rowe to take a chance with Colin not completely fit?

Pouring rain turned the track surface to deep mud. Beneath the saddling shed, Fair Play hammered his heels against the stall sides, making one reporter think of gunshots. Then the four contestants jogged roughly three-quarters of a mile away from the crowd, down to the Belmont Stakes' special starting place at the far side of Belmont Park's training track (a one-mile oval lying perpendicular to the 1 1/2-mile main course). Patterned after idiosyncratic European classics, the Belmont Stakes course made a fishhook shape: curving around the training track, then joining the main track for a long, straight run to a special finish line.

Obscured by driving rain, the start was virtually invisible from the grandstand. Even as the racers entered the main track, halfway around its turn for home, spectators saw no more than a moving blur. Only as the galloping shapes straightened into the stretch could they pick out the white silks with blue polka dots carried by the leading horse. Then thousands yelled, "It's Colin!"[15] Tearing through the curtains of rain, it was Colin in front, Colin leading by an indistinct three or five lengths over the determined Fair Play. A quarter mile out, even as Eddie Dugan urged Fair Play to run for real, Colin looked like an easy winner. An eighth of a mile from the regular finish line, as Fair Play drew near, Joe Notter waved his whip and Colin bounded away. A sixteenth of a mile from the regular finish line, splashing past the grandstand, Colin seemed to be in control. Notter sat still as Fair Play trailed the champion by a length. Cruising past the regular finish line, Colin had comfortably won. But the Belmont Stakes still had fifty yards to go.

Some observers would say that Notter eased Colin up as they passed the regular finish post, forgetting the special finish line still ahead. Others said that Colin began to falter, either tiring from his effort or feeling pain in his forelegs. This much was certain: All of a sudden, the Belmont Stakes was not safely won.

While thousands cheered, forgetting that Colin still had 150 feet between himself and victory, Colin's owner pitched a fit. Across from the true winning post, Mr. Keene was roaring, wildly waving his gold-handled umbrella. Fair Play was still driving, closing *fast* now, and in a flash Notter began riding hard again. Fair Play was lapped on Colin, at his girth, at his neck. Colin struggled to regain lost momentum, and Fair Play would *not* go away. Rain-soaked but tenacious, they passed the special finish line with Colin—who led the field by a few easy lengths entering the homestretch—beating Fair Play by no more than three or four feet.

James R. Keene hurled his umbrella across the lawn.

Colin's triumph was not a pure joy. Keene and Rowe quickly blamed Notter for misjudging the finish line. Notter claimed that Colin had faltered, probably feeling pain in his legs. But there were no motion pictures of the race and no photographs of the final fifty yards. The dispute about why Colin had slowed down never died.

Unquestioned was the brave performance of the runner-up. "Fair Play ran a wonderfully game race," *Daily Racing Form* noted, "and stood a long stretch drive in the most resolute fashion imaginable."[16] Even winners rarely receive such superlative praise.

Colin managed only one more start, beating a tepid group of fellow three-year-olds without Fair Play. His record reached a perfect 15 for 15, but his condition was falling apart. Fair Play tangled with all comers, even the best older horses in training, won seven times, and earned more praise for bravery. Late that October, both colts boarded a ship for England. Royal Ascot offered a 2 1/2-mile race known as the Gold Cup—to connoisseurs, the most prized trophy in the world. August Belmont believed Fair Play could win. Jimmy Rowe, staying home in the States, regretted that James Keene was making Colin try. Rowe doubted Colin's legs could stand the stress, and he was right. After besting English star Jack Snipe in a dazzling workout, Colin strained a tendon so badly that he had to retire. He never raced on an English track.

Fair Play remained physically healthy, but his attitude went foul. Son of an evil-tempered stallion named Hastings, Fair Play began acting more and more like his uncooperative sire. Six times he went out in English races, important races, but did not finish in the top three. "He was sound and had speed," wrote American handicapper Walter Vosburgh, "but he would not try. . . ."[17] It was a sorry comedown for the horse that had run Colin to within a few feet of defeat.

Colin and Fair Play, America's best colts, had gone abroad and failed to show the world how good they were. England, where Thoroughbred race-horses had emerged in the mid-1700s, still could take credit for producing the world's finest champions. England had created such titans as Isinglass, the world's leading money earner; St. Simon, who won the famous Ascot Gold Cup by twenty lengths and retired undefeated in ten races; and Ormonde, who won England's Triple Crown and retired undefeated in sixteen starts. Colin had come close to proving that he belonged in their exclusive company. Fair Play had not threatened them at all.

But the next great challenger to English supremacy would emerge from Fair Play, whose international foray had flopped. Early in 1910, while Thoroughbred racing collapsed in most of the United States, Fair Play returned to August Belmont's Nursery Stud near Lexington, Kentucky. There he would father a colt more brilliant than himself, who might succeed where Colin had finally failed.

Fair Play's most famous mate never got near England, but her sire, *Rock Sand, won the 1903 English Triple Crown. August Belmont plucked him out of a 1906 estate sale, for the giant price of $125,000, and sailed him to Kentucky. Some of *Rock Sand's sons showed tremendous racing talent, and Belmont sold them for grand prices. Many of *Rock Sand's daughters he kept for his broodmare band. A filly foal of 1910, from an undistinguished mare named *Merry Token, would become known as "Fair Play's wife."[18]

Although an Arabic greeting meaning "May good things be with you" inspired her name, Mahubah,[19] good things took awhile to find her. As a two-year-old, she ran second in her first start, then moved from Maryland to a nongambling meet sponsored by Long Island's Piping Rock hunt club. There she finished fifth, thoroughly beaten by a Harry Payne Whitney–owned filly cleverly named Pankhurst. Christened after British suffragette Emmeline Pankhurst and her activist daughters, leading crusaders for a woman's right to vote, Pankhurst had been sired by Voter and foaled by Runaway Girl. Continuing the line of political names, she would later produce a colt named Upset, who would lock horns with Mahubah's most famous son.

Had she been human, Mahubah would not have made a hardy suffragette. Tending to fret and lose weight, she was soundly beaten in her third race and earned a winter vacation. She did improve after her trainer put a goat in her stall. Whenever the goat dived for Mahubah's feed, the filly drove her companion away and ate every morsel, apparently from sheer possessiveness.

Mahubah's one moment of racetrack glory came in her three-year-old debut. At Baltimore's Pimlico racecourse on May 8, 1913, she met a field of other nonwinners and thoroughly outclassed them. Her time was not fast, but the *Daily Racing Form* noted, "Won cantering"—a racetrack expression for the easiest kind of victory. Maybe that graceful performance gave Mahubah's handlers too much confidence. Five days later, she raced again. Facing other winners, including males, she ran fifth of six. And that was all. Deciding that Mahubah wouldn't sustain a distinguished racing career, August Belmont retired her to the Nursery Stud. He preferred to save her energy for her foals.

Mahubah began having babies while the world waged war. Her first, a bay daughter of Fair Play, was born in 1915, while the United States gave material support to Great Britain but did not join in the battles overseas. Her second, a chestnut son of Fair Play, was born in 1917, exactly one week before the United States officially entered the Great War. Because the recent antiracing movement had decimated the American bloodstock business, he was one of only 1,961 Thoroughbred foals registered in the United States that year. It would be the fifth-smallest crop of the entire twentieth century.

He was born at the Nursery Stud, shortly before midnight on March 29. He resembled Fair Play, with a similar white star on his forehead and a narrow, slightly crooked white streak racing down the ridge of his nose. He was very tall for a newborn. Once he managed to stand, foaling attendants measured him as forty-two inches—three and a half feet—from the top of his shoulder blades (known as the withers) to the ground. His girth—the circumference of his body just behind the shoulder blades, crucial to heart and lung capacity— was a sturdy thirty-three inches.[20] Farm manager Elizabeth Kane sent a telegram to August Belmont: "Mahubah foaled fine chestnut colt."

At home in New York, Belmont shared the good news with his wife. Twenty-five years younger than her husband, Eleanor Robson Belmont had retired from starring roles in New York and London theater to marry Augie (as he was known to family and close friends) on February 26, 1910. A widower since 1898, Belmont already was a grandfather. Eleanor never had married before. But despite their age difference and dissimilar social backgrounds, they found genuine companionship. Augie appreciated the intelligence behind Eleanor's striking blue eyes. Eleanor described her publicly aloof husband as "a veritable Peter Pan in youth of mind" with "a priceless sense of fun. . . ."[21]

During the spring of 1917, however, the Belmonts were becoming preoccupied with war. Eleanor soon would be crusading for the Red Cross, while

Augie offered his service to the army. Still, before those new obligations took hold, the Belmonts finished an annual task that Eleanor called a " 'What shall we name the baby?' pastime"[22]: christening their new Thoroughbred foals.[23] For this, the Belmonts pooled their powers. Augie, the banker, provided a system: using the first letter of the dam's name, to keep the families organized. Eleanor, the actress, inspired by the meaning of both parents' names, added drama.

The *M* name for Mahubah's second foal saluted August Belmont and his active new role in the Great War. Even though he was sixty-five years old, Belmont had quickly volunteered to serve his country, been commissioned a major in the Quartermaster Corps, and accepted assignments overseas. When Eleanor imagined names for the colt by Fair Play from a mare whose name meant "May good things be with you," her husband came to mind. In tribute to Major Belmont, she named Mahubah's colt *Man o' War*.

2

AUCTION AT SARATOGA

WHEN HE WAS sixteen months old, the colt named Man o' War arrived in Saratoga Springs, New York. He wasn't there for racing, not yet. He was there because August Belmont chose to sell him off.

Belmont almost never sold yearlings. He preferred to race his horses first and then sell any that didn't meet his standards. In 1918, however, money, war, and a problematic trainer forced Belmont's hand. Deeply in debt from financing the Cape Cod Canal, with no buyer willing to pay its worth, he needed cash. Even so, Belmont dropped his personal business for patriotic duty. By October 1917, he had arrived in France and begun procuring mules for the American Expeditionary Forces. Although he returned to the United States four months later on "detached duty" and continued as chairman of The Jockey Club, Major Belmont didn't have time to monitor his racing stable closely. Determined to master every detail of any project he undertook, Belmont couldn't stand to let his racing stable operate without his own careful supervision. This personality trait—combined with his cash-flow problems and wartime workload—would strip him of Man o' War.

By June 1918, Major Belmont had closed his own racing stable and transferred his trainer, Sam Hildreth, to his son Raymond's outfit. Then, not knowing how much longer the war would last, he offered most of his yearlings for sale. He would keep five fillies for his broodmare band, plus two colts, including Man o' War. But by mid-July, Belmont had reconsidered. He would get better prices if buyers didn't think that he was keeping the best colts for himself. Man o' War would have to go.

Exactly when Belmont decided to give up Man o' War remains a mystery. Traveling to Kentucky during the first week of July, he had seen his yearlings and made his decisions based on up-to-date observations. Then, less than a week after returning to New York, he underwent an operation that left him hospitalized until at least July 27—a period of at least twelve days.[1] It is possible that Belmont made the decision to sell Man o' War from his hospital bed. If so, the lead time needed for printing a weekly magazine proves that he made it early in his stay. *The Thoroughbred Record* for the week of July 20 noted twenty-five Nursery Stud yearlings to be auctioned at Saratoga Race Course under the auspices of the Powers-Hunter Company on August 17. Eleventh on the list—with a typographical error or misunderstanding in the printing of his name—was "My Man o' War."[2]

And although he didn't plan it that way, August Belmont opened another door for a young trainer named Louis Feustel.

There was something not quite smooth about Lou Feustel, as if the sculptor who had molded him got distracted before giving him a final polish. In his early thirties, Feustel would be fairly tall and strong but a tiny bit chunky, always neatly dressed but never quite chic. Even his face seemed slightly askew, with the pupil of his right eye wandering to the right. But he would earn the trust of August Belmont, one of the world's most highly polished men.

Born on January 2, 1884, to a Saxon father and Austria-Hungarian mother, Louis Feustel entered his life only twelve furlongs from Belmont's New York training center. In going to work there, he entered a different galaxy. Louie spent his first ten years in Breslau, a Long Island community settled in the early 1870s by immigrant German farmers.[3] In nearby Babylon, Belmont's Nursery farm, with its deer park, pedigreed livestock, and trout-stocked lake, resembled an English squire's estate. Apprenticed there, Louie Feustel would grow up literally tipping his hat to August Belmont and losing his own family history. In middle age, when applying for a Social Security card, Feustel wouldn't know his own mother's maiden name.

By 1918, Louis Feustel had spent more than twenty years in Belmont's orbit. He had felt Belmont's pull as a boy, drawn down the road to watch other boys ride Belmont Thoroughbreds. He had felt it at age ten, when Belmont's farm became his workplace and boarding school. He had felt it as an exercise boy, a groom, a night watchman. He had felt it when, unhappy as night watchman, he asked for Belmont's help in joining the police force. He had felt it when Belmont pointed out that his farm wages were better and reassigned him to training yearlings. Looking back, Feustel would say, "I was really happy doing this."[4] Belmont had noticed.

During the precarious years from 1910 to 1913, Lou Feustel became August Belmont's head trainer in America. Even when New York racing revived and Belmont hired Sam Hildreth for that job, he kept paying Feustel's salary. Feustel eventually moved out on his own with a former Belmont horse, then landed the job of head trainer with a Philadelphia textile mogul named Samuel Doyle Riddle. But Belmont's influence was never far away.

Early in the summer of 1918, one of Feustel's childhood friends from Belmont's farm approached him to talk about Belmont's yearling sale. Dapper little Adolphe Pons, now Belmont's secretary, knew that Feustel would appreciate such well-bred youngsters and worked for an owner who could afford them. "He come to me one day at Belmont Park," Feustel remembered decades later, "and he says, 'Louie,' he says, 'are you going to buy any yearlings this year for Mr. Riddle?' I said, 'Yeah, we're gonna buy two or three or four, I don't know.' 'Well, why don't you buy this whole bunch of twelve colts, you know. . . .'"[5] What Feustel did know was that August Belmont's breeding program belonged with the world's best and Sam Riddle was getting a rare chance to benefit.

Cameras liked Samuel Doyle Riddle—or at least found him interesting. When amused, he charmed them with a bright, toothy smile, made all the more engaging by the slight gap between his front incisors. When annoyed, he challenged them with piercing eyes that could freeze anything crossing their path. In almost any mood, he shared some of his energy with them. Riddle was rarely noncommittal.

Cameras could not explain that Samuel Doyle Riddle had grown up facing an enormous challenge: keeping up with his father. The elder Samuel Riddle had succeeded at an epic quest. Sailing to America with only "four Spanish dollars"[6] to his name, he had transformed himself from a worker in a cotton factory near Belfast, Ireland, to the founder of a thriving factory town near Philadelphia, Pennsylvania. Honoring his Celtic roots, he named the town Glen Riddle. Well into middle age, after marrying a young woman named Lydia Doyle, he started a family.[7]

When Samuel Doyle Riddle was born in Glen Riddle on July 1, 1861, the United States was embroiled in civil war and his father's two cotton mills were spinning cloth for Union army uniforms. By the time Sam turned fifteen years old, his father owned five factories, which made up "perhaps the largest textile manufacturing plant"[8] in the United States. Bearded like Zeus and built like a heavyweight wrestler, the elder Riddle also emanated personal power. "A great man, my father," Samuel Doyle Riddle would recall. "Weighed 265 and he was under six feet. Had arms like my legs. In the old country, he had a standing bet that he could throw any three men—any size."[9]

Samuel Doyle Riddle did not need to imagine material success. He did need to develop his own power. Athletic animals helped him. Although he attended Pennsylvania Military College for a couple of years,[10] Sam Riddle was a much more eager student of fast horses and hunting dogs. He would become president of his father's company after his father's death in 1888, overseeing the international enterprise that his father had created and benefiting from its wealth. But he would concentrate his own creative energy on horses and hounds, filling his stables and kennels, gravitating to racecourses and hunts. As a young man, he would ride in amateur steeplechase races. In middle age, he would become president of the prestigious Rose Tree Hunt Club, a few miles up the road from Glen Riddle, and campaign prizewinning show horses. Along the way, he would sing humorous songs at Rose Tree meetings, travel across the United States and abroad, become fast friends with a northern Virginia huntsman famous for his all-night poker parties, and marry an heiress who insisted that he build a ballroom into their Glen Riddle home. He excelled in the art of having fun.

"The trouble with the world is that everybody is chasing the dollar," Riddle once declared. "What's the use of piling up a lot of money after you've made enough to make you happy? All everyone does is try to take it away from you."[11]

Buying untested Thoroughbred yearlings, Samuel Doyle Riddle would prove his disdain for piling up a lot of money. Horse racing is so famous for rapid reversals of fortune that a track proverb warns, "Chicken today, feathers tomorrow." But for a lucky few, the racetrack could turn a passing entertainment into immortality. As Riddle would note toward the end of his life, "I think a man's name lives longer on the track than anywhere else."[12] He could not know, during 1918, that a rebellious colt would give the name Samuel D. Riddle more renown than old Samuel Riddle's factory town.

* * *

About one week into July, Lou Feustel, his friend Adolphe Pons, and a veteran trainer named Mike Daly arrived at the Nursery Stud in Kentucky to inspect August Belmont's yearlings.[13] Daly was there because he'd met Sam Riddle at small-time racetracks in New Jersey nearly thirty years before. He was still training in 1916, when Riddle began campaigning horses in major races, and in 1918, when Riddle decided to hire his own private trainer instead of sharing a public trainer with other horse owners. At this point, Daly could have taken over the Riddle racing stable. Employing Feustel instead, Sam chose something else: a well-connected horseman who was young enough to be his own son and might follow his ever-ready advice. Riddle had relatives, however, who also needed a trainer and appreciated Daly's seniority.

Scouting the Belmont yearlings, Mike Daly represented Riddle's independently wealthy niece-in-law, Sarah Dobson Fiske Jeffords, and her banker husband, Walter. Sarah, a dynamic lady in her early thirties, was the closest thing that Sam Riddle and his wife had to a child of their own. Orphaned as a young woman, she had moved in with her aunt Elizabeth and uncle Sam. When she married Walter M. Jeffords in 1914, Sam Riddle had given her a nearby estate. Soon afterward, she and Walter, longtime foxhunters and steeplechasing enthusiasts, had grown serious about owning high-class flat racers. Ambitious in her own right, Sarah Jeffords even purchased her own horses and competed them in her name and silks instead of sharing her husband's runners and colors. Elizabeth Dobson Riddle, more old-fashioned, took an active interest in the sport but let her husband take center stage at the track. (Their horses raced, however, in the all-purpose name of Glen Riddle Farm.)

And so, when Feustel and Daly arrived at Nursery Stud, they were charged with satisfying four strong-minded owners. Their first impressions may have been disappointing. The Belmont yearlings, recently sick with distemper, were still underweight. At least their pedigrees were excellent, and several had the basic build of promising athletes.

Separated from his fellow yearlings was the tall chestnut colt by Fair Play out of Mahubah. Man o' War, one of the last to get sick, was the last to recover. After he grew famous and the story was worth embellishing, a tale that Daly and Feustel didn't see him at the Nursery would become widely accepted as fact. Sam Riddle, wanting credit for discovering the wonder horse, would spread that version of events. But farm manager Elizabeth Kane insisted that Man o' War had not been hidden from prospective buyers, only kept in a paddock by himself because he was not yet fully well. Feustel confirmed that he and Daly saw Man o' War in Kentucky—and also said Adolphe Pons told him that Man o' War was August Belmont's pick of the crop.

Pons knew that Feustel would understand how important Belmont's estimation was.

Needing owner approval for any purchase, Feustel and Daly left the Nursery with Mrs. Kane's offer of $42,000 for twelve colts hanging in the air. This opportunity quickly collapsed. Telephoning Feustel, Sam Riddle announced, "The sale is off." "Why?" Feustel asked. And Riddle explained that Mike Daly didn't like the group: "He's an older man than you, and he's had more experience, and you've gotta listen to him."[14]

Feustel still tried to make his boss take one colt: Man o' War. "I begged the old man to buy him separately," Lou recalled more than forty years later. "He wouldn't do it." Looking back, Feustel sighed, "He was a funny man, I'll tell ya. Mrs. Riddle was *aces* high, but Riddle, he was, oh—"[15]

Riddle's reluctance to buy twelve colts for $42,000—an average price of $3,500 each—made financial sense. The group included too many colts that wouldn't cost $3,500 if sold individually. But if one or two excelled at the track, their racing earnings and stud value could make $42,000 seem cheap. And at auction, with competition from many millionaires, prices for the best Belmont colts might rise beyond Riddle's comfort zone.

As buyer after buyer refused his high group rates, August Belmont realized that he would have to auction his yearlings and hope that the market recognized their worth. The best market would appear during August in Saratoga Springs, where the nation's wealthiest horse owners gathered for an elite racing meet and patronized several yearling sales. The Saratoga clientele, combined with Belmont's superb reputation as a racehorse breeder, offered his best chance for maximum revenue.

Now Belmont's big gamble began. Transportation to the sale bumped up his overhead and risked his yearlings' health. Venturing outside the Nursery fences for the first time in their lives, Man o' War and his comrades would travel several hundred miles by train. Grooms wrapped the yearlings' lower legs in thick cotton bandages and dosed them with mineral oil, hoping to prevent digestive troubles. Then stable boys led the colts and fillies to the waiting train, loaded them into straw-bedded cars, and settled in with them for the ride. All hands watched for signs of "shipping fever"—a respiratory illness that could cause death.

Another hurdle of the journey was psychological: enduring many hours of strange noises and motion, while confined to the vibrating, rattling railroad car. Finally, after a gradual halt, the wide-eyed yearlings clattered down the ramp and cut across the southern end of town. They had about one mile to walk, from the train depot on West Circular Street to Belmont's private training center, known as The Surcingle, behind Saratoga Race Course.[16]

Weaning not from his dam this time but from the Kentucky fields that had been all he had known, Man o' War moved into a new stall. Like all horses, his senses of hearing and smell were more sensitive than any human's. Like all horses, he depended on those senses for warnings or comfort. He heard his confused companions whinny and shuffle nearby in their straw beds—restless, then gradually still. He inhaled the scent of evergreens and crisp Adirondack air. During the nights, he heard a new kind of hush, sprinkled with unfamiliar sounds from the nearby town. During most afternoons, six times his ears picked up a muffled roar from the racecourse, roughly a quarter mile away. It was throatier than the tree-shaking, grass-rustling winds at the Nursery . . . sudden as a barking dog, but deeper, and wide . . . like the train he had recently ridden within, gathering speed and volume . . . unlike the steady rattle within the train, a swelling, then abruptly dropping sound. Unlike the train, alive.

On August 8, 1918, while watching yearlings glisten under the electric lights at the Fasig-Tipton Company's innovative evening sale in Saratoga Springs, Sarah Jeffords found a treasure. He was a lucky refugee from France, shipped across the U-boat-infested Atlantic in early April and sheltered in New Jersey at Harry Payne Whitney's Brookdale Stud Farm. His dam, Zuna, had been born at Brookdale. His sire, Sweeper—winner of England's classic 2,000 Guineas—had been sired by Whitney's illustrious stallion Broomstick.

Sarah knew what this breeding could produce. She had won minor stakes races with another Zuna son, Red Sox. But this Sweeper-Zuna colt was even more impressive: a strapping golden chestnut with four white stockings flowing up to his knees and hocks, and a broad white blaze shining the length of his face. Beneath his flashy colors, his close-coupled body with well-bunched muscles said *speed, speed, speed.*

The crowd shared Sarah's opinion, quickly pushing his price to ten thousand dollars. Sam Riddle watched but made no move. The Sweeper-Zuna colt had caught his eye, but Riddle knew that his niece was set on this one. He had agreed to stay out of her way.

Suddenly, the bidding flurry stopped. It was a match race now, between Sarah Jeffords and prominent owner P. A. Clark. Mrs. Jeffords and Mr. Clark raced up to eleven, twelve, thirteen thousand and more, closing in on a season-record price while the golden colt quivered in the artificially bright nighttime light, seeing and smelling a far larger crowd than he had ever known at close quarters. Mr. Clark reached $15,500. Mrs. Jeffords raised the bid by $100, daring him to a long siege.

At Saratoga two summers before, Sarah Jeffords had paid more than $16,000 for a yearling filly named Smoky Lamp. Clearly, she wouldn't flinch. The hammer fell at $15,600, and Mike Daly's work with a golden colt registered in France as Caughnawaga—but listed in the next day's *Saratogian* newspaper as Switch—began. (Though the name change wasn't noted or explained in news reports, stable hands may have been tired of pronouncing Caughnawaga. Sarah Jeffords soon rejected both Caughnawaga and Switch, officially renaming her golden colt Golden Broom.)

Expert observers noted that Sarah Jeffords, paying so much money for a handsome but unproven baby, was assuming a considerable financial risk. "I wonder, oh, I wonder, if this high-priced fellow is to earn distinction on the race course," a columnist known as "Exile" confided to *The Thoroughbred Record*'s clientele. "I wish I could bring myself to think so."[17] But at Thoroughbred auctions during this summer of 1918, high prices fueled by war-supplier fortunes were becoming commonplace. The evening after Sarah Jeffords bought the colt that would race for her as Golden Broom, three other choice babies sold for $9,000, $10,000, and $14,500. *The Saratogian* noted that ". . . those who for a moment had doubted the future of racing and horse breeding in the United States declared that there was nothing wrong with either the sport or industry where the average per head approached $3,000."[18]

"Jim, won't you help me pick some colts this year?"[19]

Many times, northern Virginia native James Kerfoot Maddux had heard similar words from friends and clients in the foxhunting set who believed him "unexcelled as a judge of horse flesh."[20] On this mid-August morning in Saratoga Springs, his hunting and poker buddy Sam Riddle requested his advice.

"By the way, Mr. Belmont is in the Army and he's sent his yearlings up here for sale," Riddle continued. "Let's get in the car and go over to his stable."[21] With those instructions, one of America's most perceptive horse traders joined Riddle in shopping from America's most classic racehorse breeder.

Comparing sales catalog data with the yearlings in the flesh, Riddle and Maddux joined a swarm of hopeful owners. They saw Fair Gain, a handsome chestnut half brother to Fair Play; Rouleau, a streamlined brown colt sired by Belmont's European sensation, Tracery; youngsters named Sentry, Battalion, Trench Mortar, Mess Kit, Tourniquet; and Fair Play daughters and sons named Violet Tip, Northward, Man o' War.

Though Man o' War's pedigree sparkled with classic winners, purists could rightfully complain about Mahubah's mediocre maternal line. But most buyers actually were put off by the red colt's appearance and attitude. Man o' War's coat, though polished as fine as the grooms could make it, was not show-sleek. His distemper had been too recent, and his ribs still showed. But far worse was his behavior. Shortly before this Saratoga trip, he had been living mostly outdoors, running semiwild. For Man o' War, the presale routine meant many hours of stall confinement, plus a hellish number of people coming to examine him and his neighbors. His spirit flared at the commotion surrounding him and chafed against restriction to the stall—a restriction that, as a racehorse living at a racetrack, he would have to endure for more than twenty hours every day.

Inspecting Man o' War, potential buyers saw a thin, rough-coated, anxious colt that might not be completely healthy and might not adjust to the daily boredom and occasional high excitement of racetrack life. Trainer Max Hirsch, a future Hall of Famer much praised for picking yearlings, said years later that he didn't buy the yearling Man o' War because, "He was too nervous. He had pawed a deep trench in the dirt underneath the webbing of his stall door."[22]

Four people concerned with Glen Riddle Farm—Lou Feustel, Jim Maddux, Sam Riddle, and his wife, Elizabeth—debated buying the stir-crazy Fair Play colt. After Man o' War became famous, each of the men would stress his own importance in making the choice. Elizabeth Dobson Riddle, assertive but soft-spoken, a supremely gracious hostess, did not go on record with her own description of events. Only Feustel, among the men taking credit for finding Man o' War, would also credit Mrs. Riddle with a decisive role. This much is certain: Each of them saw a groom open a stall door and lead out a tall, tense red chestnut colt, the brother of a fast but flighty three-year-old filly named Masda.

Sam Riddle always described this moment as a revelation: "While he wasn't in as high condition as the others, one good look told me that here was a colt in a million."[23] Riddle insisted he had immediately declared to Feustel and Daly that this was the best colt he had *ever* seen. But his story was not accurate.

Jim Maddux, for one, would hear Riddle's extravagant claims too many times. Late in 1920, he would sign an affidavit, witnessed by members of the Fauquier Club in Warrenton, Virginia, describing elements of the sale that his friend consistently overlooked. "They led out about sixteen yearlings, but I didn't see anything I liked," Maddux maintained. "A Negro groom told me there were some others, however, and although we were just getting ready to leave, we decided to stay and have a look." Last in line came "a great big upstanding chestnut colt," and a smile had spread across Maddux's face. Riddle had asked him why. "When anything pleases me, I smile," Maddux had declared. "Look at that one, Sam. That's the best colt I've ever seen at Saratoga, not excepting any. . . ."[24]

Maddux claimed that Riddle had then rustled up Feustel and told him to go see Man o' War. But catching up with Maddux that afternoon, Riddle had given him a ribbing. One source recalled that, "Mr. Riddle, in a bantering way, reproached Mr. Maddux that he should ask him to bid on a colt that needed a crutch. . . ."[25] In his affidavit, Maddux left out the joke and claimed that Riddle said, "Why, Jim, that good-looking colt you were so crazy about I wouldn't give a dollar for. He has a crooked foot. Louis went down there with me and showed it to me."[26]

Maddux misrepresented Feustel's words. Man o' War did not have a crooked foot, but his left forefoot was a bit narrower than normal.[27] Riddle misinterpreted Feustel's action. Pointing out the mismatched hoof hadn't meant that Feustel didn't like Man o' War. In fact, his reputation as a trainer depended on his being straightforward with his boss. What if someone else came along and said, "Why, Sam, that colt has a funny foot. Doesn't your trainer know any better?" Feustel needed to be careful. But he hadn't ruled out Man o' War. Not yet.

* * *

"Very tall and gangling, he was thin and so on the leg as to give the same un-gainly impression one gets in seeing a week-old foal."[28] That was how Lou Feustel described his first impression of the yearling Man o' War, in a pad-dock by himself at Nursery Stud. Six weeks later at Saratoga, there was no great difference. And still, among the twenty-two Belmont sale yearlings, Man o' War made Feustel's top four.

Four was the buying limit that Sam Riddle established. And although the four that Feustel liked best included Man o' War, he didn't seem over-whelmed by the thin red chestnut who could hardly stand still. "Feustel, to his honor, confessed that he thought some of the other Belmont colts might be better," *Blood-Horse* magazine editor Abram Hewitt confided. "Man o' War was somewhat Roman-nosed and short in the neck."[29]

And yet, while guessing that Sam Riddle might not pay the price that Man o' War could bring, Lou Feustel wanted the big red colt. Decades later, Feustel recalled, "Finally, in desperation, I turned my sales talk on Mrs. Riddle."[30]

It was well worth a try. The former Elizabeth Dobson came from a Philadelphia textile-manufacturing fortune even larger than Sam Riddle's. She was one of the richest women in America.

After Man o' War became famous, Sam Riddle would claim that the mar-velous yearling inspired him to accost trainer Sam Hildreth for the lowdown on older sister Masda. Hildreth gave Riddle a dramatic image: "He said she was one of the fastest fillies that ever lived."[31] Although his own memoir didn't mention Riddle's query, Hildreth offered a similar evaluation: "Several times when I had held the stop-watch on Masda she had run so fast that I thought there must be some mistake and I had asked others to verify what my own watch told me. But they caught her in the same time. In her works she was one of the fastest tricks I've ever trained. . . ."[32] Always willing to make a good story even better, Riddle promoted Hildreth's "ever trained" to the supreme "ever lived."

But both men knew the coin's other side. Ornery and high-strung, Masda was inconsistent in actual races. Hildreth eventually persuaded Belmont to sell her. Man o' War might prove similarly disappointing. "But I listened to Maddux and not to Hildreth," Riddle said later, proud of his choice.[33]

When he published his memoirs, Sam Hildreth had his own reputation to uphold. "If it hadn't been that I wanted to get horses in training instead of yearlings Man o' War might have worn my own racing colors. . . . I thought of Masda when I first heard of Man o' War," Hildreth noted—proving to the public that, yes, he knew that the colt might be very fast—"but I let it stop with thinking. Riddle didn't."[34]

Of course, if you listen to almost everyone but the man himself, Riddle very nearly did.

"If I'd gone home that night, I don't believe Sam Riddle would have ever bought Man o' War," Jim Maddux proclaimed. "I couldn't help thinking about that colt, though, and told him so. The next morning we went and had another look at him." This was auction day: Saturday, August 17.

The second look made Maddux adamant. "Sam, there's nothing in the world the matter with this colt's foot; and I've not changed my opinion one bit. I want you to promise me not to let your trainer or anyone else persuade you out of buying him."[35]

Neither Riddle nor Maddux seemed to understand Feustel's true intentions. "In going back to the automobile," Maddux continued, "I met Louis Feustel, and I asked him why in the world he was trying to persuade Mr. Riddle from buying that nice chestnut colt. He said, 'Mr. Maddux, I like him now, after seeing him the second time.'"[36] Again, Maddux underestimated Feustel. At this point, Feustel certainly had seen Man o' War more than twice.

Even so, according to Maddux, Feustel wasn't satisfied. The young trainer consulted New York's primary racetrack vet, Dr. R. W. McCully, who decreed, "There's nothing wrong with that colt's foot. He's a nice colt."[37] Reassured, Lou Feustel set his mind on Man o' War.

If timing is everything, the day that August Belmont chose for selling his yearlings came out exactly right. Perfectly clear, warm, but cool-breezed weather and a top-notch racing card drew the meet's largest crowd—roughly twenty thousand—to Saratoga Race Course. That afternoon they would see Kentucky Derby winner Exterminator, Preakness winner War Cloud, Belmont Stakes winner Johren, and Hopeful Stakes winner Sun Briar vying for the classic Travers Stakes. That day, Saratoga truly became a hub of racing dreams.

The first race would start at 3:05 P.M. Early that afternoon, the outdoor auction began. One by one, twenty-two yearlings ventured into the tall-treed paddock where their older cousins would be saddled for the races, jigging wide-eyed through the crowd, circling in front of brassy-voiced[38] auctioneer George A. Bain. Dozens of straw-hatted men, and several women draped in "summer furs and knitted silk sweaters of varied hues,"[39] angled for advantageous views, knowing their favorites and watching to see what one another would do.

The sale started favorably for August Belmont as the first baby led between the trees, a chestnut colt named War Map, brought a healthy fifteen hundred dollars. Next, the chestnut colt Peccant went for $750. Then came a string of bargain-basement prices: bay filly Drumfire for $400, bay filly Destruction for $450, chestnut colt Lieutenant for $600, and brown filly Oleaster for $450. Three colts had sold for from six hundred to fifteen hundred dollars, and three fillies for less than five hundred dollars each.

Man o' War became the seventh yearling, the fourth chestnut colt, guided through the crowd. Shining red in the sunshine, no electric lights needed, natural.

A groom turned him in tight circles, hemmed in by humanity. Here was another jarring experience for a young horse on his first trip away from his birth farm. "Man o' War showed plenty of spirit in the sales paddock," Kentucky Derby promoter Matt Winn observed, "and many horsemen, aware of the tempers possessed by some of his forbears [sic], wanted no part of him. He was tall, long of body, a fine looker—but, in the eyes of many, too good to be true."[40]

While the red colt startled and sweated, Sam Riddle's friend Ed Buhler, a New York trainer, signaled Riddle's bids. Quickly, they had competition from prominent businessman Robert L. Gerry, encouraged by his wife and sister-in-law. Jim Maddux's 1920 affidavit would feed a lingering legend that the Gerrys, expert equestrians, wanted to buy Man o' War as a good mount for foxhunting.[41] This may have been their backup plan or may have become their joke after Man o' War's fame made the thought of foxhunting him delightfully ridiculous. In fact, Robert L. Gerry, eager to improve his racing stable, had heard about Man o' War during a telephone call from August Belmont himself.[42]

Encouraged by his wife and by Belmont's advice, Gerry offered $4,500. Years later, a slew of horsemen swore they had bid more. A sweet-tempered young trainer named "Sunny Jim" Fitzsimmons—who would go on to develop five Hall of Fame horses, including two Triple Crown winners— claimed that he himself had stopped at four thousand dollars. Fitzsimmons regretted that his deep-pocketed patron, James F. Johnson of the Quincy Stable, wasn't there to approve a far larger amount. Looking back from the 1940s, veteran turf writer Joe Palmer winked at the tangle of testimonies. "If you trust stories, some 15 persons bid $4,900. . . ."[43]

As the bidding climbed toward five thousand dollars, Sam Riddle looked ready to let Masda's brother go. Feustel hadn't swayed his opinionated boss. One hope remained. Elizabeth Dobson Riddle had reached the auction knowing that their trainer wanted Man o' War. Perhaps his earnestness touched her. He was young enough to be her son, if she'd had one.

As auctioneer Bain stalled and prodded, waiting for top dollar before pounding his hammer down, Mrs. Riddle came through. "Just buy him for Lou's sake if nothing else,"[44] she urged Sam, according to Feustel's much later memory. In another of Feustel's reminiscences, her words to her husband were more firm and challenging: "Louie wants him, and I am going to buy him."[45]

There was only an instant for Sam Riddle to decide: Should he let his wife overrule his judgment, in front of everyone?

"He was a difficult man," Lou Feustel recalled from the safety of the 1950s and retirement, "but he knew when he was licked. He put up the $5,000." And then Feustel offered a final accolade, not to his own insight as a trainer but to the resourceful woman who stepped up at the crucial moment: "Man o' War was really more Mrs. Riddle's horse than Sam's."[46]

It shouldn't surprise anyone that Samuel D. Riddle eventually hired horse racing's most respected historian, John Hervey, to record his version of events, or that Jim Maddux let a roomful of witnesses sign his affidavit, which said, "If I'd gone home that night, I don't believe Sam Riddle would have ever bought Man o' War." Both would have lost face for overlooking the "horse of the century"—Riddle, prominent in clubhouse society and proud of his lifelong horsemanship, Maddux with an exalted horse-trading reputation to uphold. Some men would have chosen to laugh and say, "You know, I wasn't eager to pay as much as five thousand dollars for the horse, but my wife was determined to do it so that our trainer would be happy." Instead, Sam Riddle convinced himself that he would have paid $20,000 or more to make Man o' War his own.

And Elizabeth Dobson Riddle, with nothing to prove in public, no clients she needed to impress, kept the peace in her marriage and let it go.

* * *

"Remarkable prices were realized for the Nursery Stud yearlings owned by August Belmont," the next day's *New York Times* reported.[47] Getting $52,250 for twenty-two youngsters, Belmont won his gamble.[48] Philadelphia multi-millionaire Joseph E. Widener paid $14,000 for Fair Gain, a half brother to Fair Play. Sam Riddle bid eagerly for Rouleau—"a fine-looking animal," said the *New York Times*—but Frank M. Taylor prevailed at $13,600. Riddle did buy Gun Muzzle, one of Feustel's recommendations, for a moderate twelve hundred dollars. And that leggy, sweaty, ditch-digging colt that the Gerrys had pushed up to five thousand? Man o' War had brought the third-highest price of the Belmont lot.

Leaving his elite breeder, Man o' War had landed with promising new-comers. Before leaving Saratoga Springs that summer, the Riddles bought a "cottage"—actually a columned mansion—at the corner of Union and Nelson avenues, near Saratoga Race Course. Not quite three years after launching their racing stable, they were cementing their presence in the upper reaches of society. Reporting the purchase, the *New York Herald* noted that, "The Riddles' stable, Glen Riddle Farm, is one of the best known at the Saratoga track, and the owners are very popular among the racing set here."[49] Becoming so prominent without any champion carrying their colors was powerful proof of their social success, and their extremely visible and convenient summer home reflected that status. Traveling little more than two city blocks from their front door, the Riddles could reach their clubhouse box seats and watch their horses run.

Though the world at large didn't realize it, this purchase defied social norms. Elizabeth Dobson Riddle, not her husband, Sam, had signed on the dotted line—and she bought their grand new house from the Leslie Woman Suffrage Commission.[50] Mrs. Riddle's money, her choice and voice, supported the proposed constitutional amendment legalizing a woman's right to vote.

3

LICENSE TO FLY

I HAD MENTAL problems with him from the very beginning,"[1] Lou Feustel would recall. This time, he wasn't talking about Sam Riddle. At Saratoga, Feustel and his crew had begun training each of Riddle's yearlings to carry a rider. The one giving them "mental problems" was Man o' War.

Like many offspring of Fair Play, this colt would fight anything that bothered him. He also seemed ready to take it to extremes—a trait inherited from his paternal grandsire, Hastings. In fact, back in 1894, Hastings had been such a problematic yearling that his owner wanted him gone. He was so awkward-looking that a farm visitor remarked, "I've seen better looking creatures under wet stones."[2] But his appearance was a minor issue. Hastings also had thrown every exercise boy who sat on him. As J. Simon Healy, the eighteen-year-old assistant trainer charged with getting the yearlings fit, observed, "Not only was he as ugly as a gargoyle, but as mean as a scorpion, to boot."[3]

Fair Play and Man o' War would owe their existence to Healy's persistence. Colts as hazardous as Hastings often were gelded, in a last-ditch effort to improve their attitude. Gelding, the ancient practice of castrating male horses that were to be used for work rather than breeding, could be highly effective. When testosterone stopped surging through the young horse, often he would drop or reduce his wild behaviors and focus on what people wanted him to do. Many male racehorses that did not show exceptional ability in their early training or spring from exalted bloodlines became geldings—especially if they endangered human beings.

But Healy, impressed by Hastings' excellent pedigree, refused to castrate or cull him. "That defiant spirit persuaded me that maybe he wasn't as bad as he appeared," Healy recalled, "and I was determined not to get rid of him until I had at least given him a fair trial."[4] The fair trial came with a large boy named Red, who didn't know the colt's horrible reputation. He and Hastings got along. Before long, Hastings proved to be the fastest colt in the barn. He remained unfriendly, even dangerous, but became a high-class racehorse. By July of his two-year-old season, he showed so much promise that August Belmont bought him for an extravagant $37,000.

Winning several important races, including the classic Belmont Stakes, Hastings earned his place as a stallion at Belmont's farm. There, his belligerence got him nicknamed "the bull."[5] To discourage attacks, his grooms always displayed a sturdy stick.

Fortunately for young Man o' War, Lou Feustel had handled Hastings and many of his descendants. He knew them as ferocious, high-spirited, and sensitive. He understood that fighting these horses, trying to overpower them, would only reinforce their resistance and ruin them.

Feustel saw that Man o' War resented each new intrusion: the metal bit resting on top of his tongue, several pounds of saddle resting on his back, and the hug of a saddle girth just behind his forelegs. He especially hated the girth squeeze. Feustel knew that the only successful approach would be to "try to out-guess him . . . figure things out with him and let him believe he'd done it for himself."[6] However long Man o' War remained in training, this approach would not change. But the first question was, Would he accept a rider at all?

The person Feustel trusted with this delicate task was a slim young man named Harry Vititoe, a former jockey with a kinship for wild creatures. Vititoe had ridden many a bucking horse and was even said to have tamed the occasional bear or timber wolf obtained on one of his hunting trips.[7] But Vititoe's patience didn't make this colt trust a squeeze around his middle, a breathing weight behind his shoulders, and a human voice three feet behind his ears. When Vititoe settled into the saddle, Man o' War exploded. Vititoe, shaken, picked himself up from the ground. Breaking free, Man o' War roamed the stable area for about fifteen minutes before being caught.[8]

To his human handlers, the red colt's explosive energy would remain a constant threat. "He never actually hurt anyone unless it was the exercise boy he threw off the first time anybody ever got on his back," Feustel would recall. "But all of us working with him realized that he might try it at any time."[9]

Perhaps because he couldn't take credit for the hands-on work, Sam Riddle's descriptions of breaking Man o' War to saddle would echo Feustel's. "There was not just one battle—there were several," Riddle told historian John Hervey. "He didn't want to be broken, didn't intend to, and when he found out that we intended to break him the war was on. Did he fight? He did—like a tiger! And, as he was a big, stout colt, quick as chain-lightning in all his movements, and also just as quick an actor mentally, the battles he put up were big ones."[10]

Grandsire Hastings was living on.

Looking back, Riddle appreciated Feustel's calm approach. "I think there's no doubt he would have been ruined, right then and there, by anybody that was rough or cruel, or short-tempered, that fought him back and used brute force."[11] But the big colt probed everyone's patience, perhaps his owner's most of all. "No wild animal ever fought its captors more desperately or tried harder to get free from them," Riddle declared. "Once or twice I really began to wonder just when and how it was going to end."[12]

August neared September. Saratoga racing concluded for the year. The Riddle yearlings boarded railroad cars bound for Maryland's Eastern Shore, where they would stay until spring. Man o' War, still resisting his rider, remained a problem.

Meanwhile, as stable hands became familiar with Riddle's new yearlings, names registered with The Jockey Club had given way to barn names. Man o' War was a racing name full of fire, but a handler couldn't bother with it every time he wanted the colt to move over in his stall, lift a foot for cleaning, cut out a dangerous behavior *right now*, or come forward for a treat. The men developing rapport with Man o' War quickly dropped any extra syllables. Impressed with the colt's bright chestnut coat, they simply called him "Red."[13]

Red's railroad car squeaked to a halt at Holly Grove Road, about four miles west of Ocean City, Maryland. This stop sprang from Sam Riddle's influence: There was no railroad station here, only the roadside and swishing trees. Grooms urged the skeptical young horses down slanted ramps, out of their wooden boxes, and into open air that smelled of salt water and pine trees. They walked about half a mile, across the narrow Ocean City "boulevard," then through a field to the palatial stable that would be their winter home.

Late in 1915, as Sam Riddle prepared to develop a first-class racing operation, he had bought an off-season training site little more than one hundred miles from Glen Riddle, Pennsylvania. The location was temperate enough that even in December, nearby farms would grow green with wheat. The creekside property that the Riddles transformed into a winter training center would become known as "one of the wonders of the farming world on the Eastern Shore. . . ."[14] They built a twenty-five-room manor house, which Mrs. Riddle, a pioneering collector of American antiques, filled with local finds. They built a large kennel for foxhounds and a berth for their yacht. In 1916, they spent $6,000 on shrubberies to line the estate's main driveway. They also built a training track as big as most major racetracks, one full mile around. While racers in the winter quarters of leading owners Harry Payne Whitney and J. K. L. Ross cantered under covered sheds in New Jersey and mainland Maryland, the Riddle horses trained at racing speed, outdoors.

Here, away from the crowded, distracting Saratoga track, Feustel and his crew coaxed Man o' War into cooperating. "What made him finally submit?" Sam Riddle mused. "Brains. There never has been a more brainy horse. . . . He saw that it had to be—that we were too many and too strong for him and that he would gain more by submitting than he would by fighting. So he submitted. But like all good horses, he had a long memory. He never forgot."[15]

Man o' War teased his people with the delicacy of their bargain, as if the ink on his armistice agreement would never completely dry. Feustel looked for ways to steady him. He found relief with an unflappable equine chaperone named Major Treat.

A Lincolnesque brown gelding, Major Treat had survived several careers. He may have come from Tennessee, where a brown Thoroughbred colt his same age was registered with The Jockey Club as *Major Street.* That colt never raced. Maybe, relocated to Glenara Stock Farm in northern Virginia and relieved of his stud-colt status, he became Major Treat. What is certain is that early in 1911, the four-year-old gelding Major Treat placed second at Washington, D.C.'s National Horse Show in a military class called "Horses Suitable to Become Chargers." Then Samuel Doyle Riddle's show-ring ambitions saved him from a cavalry career.

Jim Maddux, horse trader supreme, may have steered Riddle to this promising hunter prospect. A powerful animal with a beautifully sloping shoulder, Major Treat proved to be an exceptional jumper. He won ribbons for Riddle at the most prestigious East Coast shows. In 1917, he formed part of the winning team in the "Hunters—three abreast" class at Devon, vaulting over large obstacles side by side with two other champions from Riddle's barn. Then something went wrong. Or—for Man o' War—something went right.

When 1918 rolled around, eleven-year-old Major Treat disappeared from the horse shows. Leg problems had ended his jumping days. Sam Riddle decided to give Major Treat a traditional hunter's send-off: shooting him and feeding him to the foxhounds.

But Lou Feustel intervened.[16]

Standing 16.3 hands tall (five feet seven inches at the withers), Major Treat could make a useful mount for the hefty Feustel when he led his charges to the track for training. Also, his mature presence might stabilize the fretful yearling Man o' War. It worked. Accepted by Man o' War, Major Treat began living in a neighboring stall. Shielded by Major Treat, Red began focusing much of his energy where it mattered most: bursts of speed down the training track.

At full gallop, within a single second, a Thoroughbred racehorse can travel 55 feet or more. In a race, if one horse finishes a full second faster than another, the contest isn't even close. To racehorse owners, a full second's difference between horses is like a handful of thousand-dollar bills.

During the autumn of 1918, Lou Feustel and Mike Daly began measuring the Riddle and Jeffords yearlings' speed. Their first test lasted only one furlong, the racetrack term for one-eighth of a mile[17] and the building block for race distances. Sprinting for a furlong, then two and more, yearlings began revealing their potential. They were learning to "breeze," the racetrack term for galloping at or near racing speed. When the Glen Riddle yearlings performed these bursts of fast work, Lou Feustel held a stopwatch that timed their progress down to one-fifth of a second. A horse that could breeze two furlongs in less than 12 seconds each—a quarter mile under 24 seconds—was a real runner. In mid-autumn, Man o' War reportedly galloped a quarter in :23 2/5 with his rider holding him back.[18]

After accidentally uncovering this raw brilliance, Feustel did not need to push. Instead, he let Red's immature body and mind catch up with his natural talent. Even so, he had given Sam Riddle something to brag about while Sarah Jeffords bragged about Golden Broom.

From autumn through early spring, the Riddles and Jeffordses spent many weekends at the Maryland farm and watched their young stock in several trials. With their owners making friendly bets, the farm's fastest colts began building a rivalry. Exact records of these events would not survive, but general impressions remained. Golden Broom, launching his compact body like a cannonball, could hit top speed prodigiously fast. Man o' War needed more time to coordinate his long legs. At distances up to three furlongs, Red eventually ranged up alongside Golden Broom but did not take the lead. Sarah Jeffords pictured the same result when the colts entered real races. Sam Riddle pictured success at greater distances as Man o' War settled into his bounding stride and made up for his slower start.

Years later, exercise rider Paul Cervin would claim there was an additional explanation. The Jeffords juveniles weren't developing as quickly as the Riddle ones that year, and both trainers wanted to please their employers. According to Cervin, the riders for both barns agreed to keep each contest close.[19] If either Golden Broom or Man o' War was clearly better than the other, the riders may not have been letting the owners know.

After Man o' War joined Glen Riddle Farm, Lou Feustel honed an exercise program to fit his physical needs and personality. Harry Vititoe balanced on Red's back for fifteen or twenty minutes almost every day, educating Red with each tug on a rein, shift of weight, and verbal command. But someone else monitored this strong and fragile animal through the hours of confinement before and after his daily exercise. His name was Frank Loftus, and he was a groom.

Although jockey Johnny Loftus had a brother named Frank, the young man who tended Man o' War came from a different family. Born in Waterford, Ireland, in 1892, Frank Loftus had arrived in America when he was six years old. At age eleven, tired of working on his uncle's Hartford, Connecticut, farm, Frank "went with horses"[20]—to the track. He was small enough to be a jockey but outgrew riding after brief experience as an exercise boy. Instead, he looked after racehorses' most basic needs. Wild horses, living in herds, scratch one another's itches and forage for their own food; domesticated horses depend on human care. Frank Loftus, barely tall enough to look over Man o' War's back while brushing him, kept the volatile colt clean, fed, and entertained. Frank delivered meals, which Red wolfed down. He also let Red play a harmless game: grab the cap off his head and walk around holding it in his mouth.

Frank Loftus kept Man o' War grounded. Another Loftus would teach him to fly.

During the summer of 1918, while Man o' War began learning a racetrack routine, Johnny Loftus had nearly lost his jockey career. But it was remarkable that he had a career to lose. He had been born too big for the job, and just in time to watch racing die.

When Irish immigrant Frank Joseph Loftus and his wife Margaret O'Dowd welcomed their second son on October 13, 1895, their adopted home of Chicago, Illinois, hosted some of Thoroughbred racing's most lucrative events. But by the time John Patrick Loftus grew old enough to ride racehorses, the nationwide antigambling movement had prevailed in Illinois. Chicago racing had closed.

History would not record what drew Johnny to the races. His father worked as a stationary engineer—that is, designing or maintaining heavy equipment such as boilers—rather than working with horses. The racetrack's lure could have been money and also prestige. Irish women in America were stereotyped as household servants, Irish men as manual laborers or police officers. A few of the men ran powerful political machines. Their success mixed with stigma—but at the racetrack, Irish boys could find fortune and fame. When Johnny Loftus came of age, the world's most successful jockeys included Winnie O'Connor, top U.S. rider by number of wins in 1901 and a pacesetter in Europe for years afterward; Danny Maher, who parlayed his American success to England and won the 1903 Triple Crown there with *Rock Sand; and Frank O'Neill, who partnered 1904 Horse of the Year Beldame and vaulted from New York to a distinguished career in France. Even the arguably best rider of all, 1890s African-American superstar Isaac Murphy, happened to carry an Irish name.

But perhaps the most vital factor was that horses fascinated Johnny Loftus. "He has the natural interest in a horse," noted Rome Respess, who eventually acquired the apprentice jockey's contract, "and he'd sleep [in the stall] with one, if I would let him. He is always the first up in the morning and ready to take them out for their airing and he displays a wonderful memory of which horses were worked and what they did. . . ."[21]

Like most other aspiring jockeys, Johnny Loftus would start working at the track while barely into his teens. Unlike O'Connor, he did not have a baby face. From his high forehead to his rugged chin, his head formed a long but strong triangular wedge that looked like it would only harden under pressure. His tapered eyes hid under narrowed lids, shielding his inner being from public scrutiny.

In 1909, leaving his family and following the winter circuit to Jacksonville, Florida, fourteen-year-old John Patrick Loftus rode in his first official race. The omens were not good. He finished last, on a 100–1 shot named Bitter Miss, and the *Daily Racing Form* chart maker misspelled his name as "Oftis."

A month later, Johnny rode his second official race and finished last again. For two months after that, he rode no races at all. Johnny's contract holder, trainer George Moreland, said that the boy had "calves like a wrestler"[22] and never would succeed as a race rider. He would outgrow the job before developing sufficient skill. But another trainer, John M. Goode, decided to risk it. Many of the best jockeys *were* wrestlers, of a sort. In a tight finish, they would catch another jockey's leg behind their own, keeping the rival horse from forging ahead or scraping the rival jock out of the saddle if he dared drive his horse forward. Johnny's bulky calves could become a blessing, because—more important than his extra pounds—he was *determined*. On January 1, 1910, Goode signed Johnny to a three-year contract.[23] His livelihood became a balancing act: suspended over a galloping horse, matching its motion at up to forty miles per hour. His life centered over a thin pad of leather just wide enough to cover a horse's spine.

Johnny Loftus learned the give and take of his own muscles supplementing a racehorse's strength: steady feet, legs, hands, and arms that a horse could balance against. A horse's head is a heavy weight for neck muscles to carry, especially late in a race. Johnny became more than a passenger. He added support.

While training his body, Johnny also became what is called "a practical horseman," understanding equine gestures and needs. He learned how to persuade or intimidate his mounts, soothing the uncertain ones, stirring up the blasé. Loftus had confidence, and more than enough for himself—it splashed over into his horse.

The spirit of race riding couldn't be learned, only unloosed. The spirit, he already had.

Six years after the Wright brothers' first successful airplane tests, Johnny Loftus earned his own license to fly. Long before he became old enough to vote, Johnny transformed himself into a slightly bowlegged powerhouse, surviving without safety helmets or goggles and quickly outgrowing any weight advantages. Safety gear simply didn't exist, and excessive weight chased many young riders out of the game. Racehorses often carried 110 pounds or less, and only a few of the very best jockeys could win enough races to sustain a career while weighing more than that. Johnny Loftus soon left 110 behind and rarely made 112.[24] Trainers wishing to hire him often had to accept a few pounds of "overweight." Time and again, they did. Ever more frequently, Johnny pushed their horses to victory.

Early in his career, however, Loftus drew a few suspensions for getting left at the start. Inexperienced jockeys often struggled to develop good timing of this chaotic and crucial moment. There was no such thing as a starting gate, with each horse standing in a separate metal stall. Instead, the racers milled around behind a narrow elastic webbing—known as "the barrier"—that stretched across the track like a badly frayed badminton net. Horses showed little respect for this flimsy webbing, sometimes rushing through it, and sometimes while scuffling for position, they kicked one another. Assistant starters, strong men with whips in hand, tried to herd the anxious Thoroughbreds into place and sometimes held the bridle of a "bad actor." The official starter shouted orders from his platform just behind the track's inner rail, watching for all of the tossing heads and fidgeting hooves to face forward and stand roughly in line before pulling the lever that sent the barrier springing into the air. Through it all, each jockey had to pay attention to his horse, his advantage-seeking fellow riders, and the shouting man who would tell them when to go—and, as Johnny Loftus quickly learned, a tiny incoordination could lose the race as it began.

While Loftus mastered the start and the other facets of race riding, the racetrack offered him a vivid, wandering life. Before turning eighteen, he rode races from New York to Florida, Canada to Mexico. As 1912 bridged into 1913, Johnny spent his first complete Mexican meet at the wild young track in Juárez. Directly across the Rio Grande from El Paso, Texas, Juárez had replaced the shut-down California and Florida tracks and become a beloved winter haven for American horsemen. Johnny lived with racetrackers, cattlemen, and conventioneers in a town where games of chance spun round the clock and the whorehouses were palaces. The best stories never would be written down.

But something steady lived in Johnny's soul. When New York racing reopened in 1913, the Saratoga jockeys revived their annual ball. Fifteen committee members, elected from the Saratoga jockey colony, organized the extravaganza. Seventeen-year-old Johnny Loftus stood out as a reliable character who could manage money. His peers trusted him with the job of financial secretary.

Early in 1914, while eighteen-year-old Loftus was winning 33 percent of his starts, Philadelphia multimillionaire Joseph E. Widener scooped him out of the Juárez jockey colony and shipped him to France. Enjoying Europe's higher weight assignments, Loftus won his share. He also became the father of a daughter, born on July 3 and named Elinor Marie. Then war erupted. Loftus escaped to the United States and then migrated to Juárez. Waiting there was a four-year-old Texas-bred filly nicknamed "Old Grandma." Her registered name—honoring the Juárez police chief's daughter, Pansy—was Pan Zareta. She would become one of the few sprinters voted into Thoroughbred racing's Hall of Fame.

Pan Zareta blossomed into such a speed sensation that track handicappers, giving other contestants incentive to face her, rarely assigned her less than 130 pounds. Johnny Loftus, reducing to American riding weight, formed a pattern that winter of steering Pan Zareta to victory under 132 pounds, 136 pounds, 140 pounds, then taking a few days off. On March 26, 1915, Pan Zareta carried the staggering load of 146 pounds—Loftus plus roughly thirty pounds of lead—and gamely won her six-furlong race.

While Pan Zareta was his refuge, most mounts made Loftus ride at 114 pounds or less. A famous photo shows the robust filly and her hollow-cheeked jockey, a deep shadow running beneath his cheekbone. He looked like a starving young man, and yet he seemed completely at home. A 1915 photo of the Juárez jockeys caught Johnny Loftus in the middle of a laugh, his left arm hooked around the shoulders of 1914 Kentucky Derby–winning jock Johnny McCabe. Dressed in a stylish suit, tie, and fedora, McCabe stood out among the solemn boys in silks, wearing their employers' uniforms. Something else set Loftus apart from most. He was photographed bareheaded, glowing with informality—brazen as a butler leaving his collar unbuttoned while answering the door.

He would reinforce his improbable success the next year, on a day exactly six months before his birthday. On May 13, 1916, with fifty or sixty thousand patrons crowding Churchill Downs, twenty-year-old Johnny Loftus delivered "the best race of his career."[25] While Harry Payne Whitney's speedy Dominant set a sizzling pace, Loftus reserved his mount, George Smith, for a homestretch burst. The favorite, A. K. Macomber's Star Hawk, broke poorly and took too long to find his stride. Through the homestretch Star Hawk charged ferociously, biting into George Smith's lead, but Loftus had the finish measured. George Smith won by a neck. And before the summer ended, A. K. Macomber[26] had Johnny Loftus under contract.

This latest deal with a multimillionaire was especially welcome, because Loftus was now married to the former Eleanor Gallagher, daughter of a Kentucky racing official, and was supporting his two-year-old girl.[27] While

Macomber's large stable of fancy runners kept Loftus profitably occupied, his career seemed to be locked into high gear.

Then Macomber tried to bring it to an end.

During the summer of 1918, while war clouds darkened Europe, A. K. Macomber's three-year-old colt War Cloud looked like a rising champion. Ridden by Johnny Loftus, he started as favorite in a muddy Kentucky Derby but got bumped around and faded to fourth place. A 30–1 shot named Exterminator, piloted by veteran jockey Bill Knapp, splashed to victory.

Four days later, the $15,000 Preakness Stakes at Baltimore, Maryland, attracted so many entries that it was split into two divisions. Quickly shipping over from Kentucky, War Cloud won his division. But luck deserted him in the classy Withers Stakes at Belmont Park. As the barrier rose, War Cloud stumbled terribly. "Loftus told me he didn't know how he retained his seat in the saddle," Macomber later explained. "He had never before come so near falling off a horse without doing it. When he recovered his seat the colt had no chance."[28]

Two weeks after the Withers, War Cloud got another chance. Going off at even money—only one dollar of profit for each dollar bet on him to win—War Cloud was supposed to romp in the June 15 Belmont Stakes. But no one told that to Harry Payne Whitney's massive colt Johren, recent vanquisher of older horses in the Suburban Handicap. And few riders could match skills with Johren's jockey, Frankie Robinson.

Johren hooked War Cloud about three furlongs from the finish line. They veered into the homestretch side by side, War Cloud swerving wide, taking Johren out with him. Correcting course, Loftus steered War Cloud too far the other way. A *Thoroughbred Record* reporter saw Macomber's colt "floundering a bit over where Loftus had placed him near the inside rail, where the track was far deeper than the course Robinson was taking with the leader."[29] Johren sailed down the firmer middle of the track. And even so, for nearly a furlong, War Cloud stayed on even terms.

Bounding past the infield stand, giant Johren edged into the lead. Johnny Loftus—"probably the best whip rider and finisher among all the jockeys," a reporter noted[30]—swatted War Cloud once, twice, and War Cloud surged forward. Then Johnny's hand swung empty. His whip slipped free, landing in the dirt.

Kicking War Cloud's sides, slapping War Cloud's neck with his right hand while reining with his left, Loftus rode a furious finish. Johren easily pulled away. "My colt stuck right at War Cloud's head until Loftus had to go to the whip," Frankie Robinson declared. "When Loftus saw I had him he lost his whip and everything else."[31]

Loftus was about to lose much more than a race. Trainer Walter Jennings blamed him for a bad ride—maybe a deliberately bad ride—and Macomber agreed. Maybe it took a deep inside track and a fallen whip to help the even money favorite lose. Loftus objected, but he had no leverage. Macomber not only held his contract; he also was a rich gentleman. As a jockey, a mere hired hand, Loftus had no right to contradict the boss. Within hours, Macomber had grounded him indefinitely.

In public, Loftus kept his mouth shut. Racetrackers gossiped, of course, about his bad ride on a short-priced favorite. Macomber told friends that he would never let Loftus ride his horses again. That didn't mean cutting him loose, however. "Although Loftus will be prohibited from riding for anybody, he will receive his contract salary until released or until the contract expires," the *New York Herald* reported.[32] But Macomber didn't want to release his high-priced jockey. Paying Loftus not to race also meant not competing against him.

Weeks passed. Racing moved to Saratoga. Johnny Loftus, working horses in the mornings but still not allowed to jockey them in the afternoons, went with it. Among the promising two-year-olds that August at the Spa, he may have noticed a stocky chestnut colt with a white-blazed face, not yet in winning form but bred to do almost anything. High-profile breeder John E. Madden, known as "the Wizard of the Turf," was offering him for sale. In time for Saratoga racing, an ambitious Canadian sportsman took the bait. Commander J. K. L. Ross—a war-decorated navy destroyer captain, whose own son called him "something of a swashbuckler"[33]—paid $10,000 for the colt named Sir Barton and gave him to "Hard Guy" Bedwell to train.

While Sir Barton learned basic racing lessons, Loftus galloped horses in the mornings and played baseball in the afternoons, patiently staying in shape. "This is no easy or enjoyable task," a journalist remarked, "for a boy of his weight whose conduct since his suspension has aroused the admiration of his many admirers."[34] One admirer finally persuaded Macomber to let him borrow the sidelined star. On Friday, August 23—six days after Samuel D. Riddle bought the yearling Man o' War—Johnny Loftus appeared in Saratoga's Sagamore Handicap, wearing the colors of his former patron Joseph E. Widener and guiding a fast but temperamental gelding named

Naturalist. What followed would prove that Loftus, riding his first race in ten weeks, hadn't lost an ounce of nerve.

Breaking well, Naturalist slid into second place. Along the backstretch and around the far turn, Loftus sat chilly, conserving energy until it counted most. With three-sixteenths to go and the leader getting tired, the race was Naturalist's to lose. And lose he did—spectacularly. Refusing to surge forward, Naturalist pronged like an antelope and swerved toward the inner rail. Loftus reacted instantly, lurching in sync with his horse. Respect permeated a *New York Herald* reporter's summary: "Loftus whipped him off the rail and eventually made him finish third."[35]

Afterward, Loftus showed reporters his welcome-back souvenir: a cut hand. He also showed a ready sense of humor about Naturalist's acrobatics—and his own high weight—joking, "That fellow thought I was a steeplechase rider and wanted to take me over the fence."[36] For newspaper purposes, someone surely substituted "fellow" for a term far less polite.

Winning 30 percent of all races he rode during 1918, Johnny Loftus wrapped up the year as the best all-around jockey in the United States. He had fresh competition, however. During July, Commander Ross had bought the contract of a nineteen-year-old riding sensation whose last name rhymed with *handy*: Earl Sande.

A Norwegian farm boy from Idaho, Sande had run away from home to become a jockey. He practiced his craft at Western bush-league tracks, then popped up in New Orleans during January 1918 and won his first big-league start. Already a skilled "hand rider," Sande didn't like to whip his mounts. Believing that most horses resented being hit, he preferred to "jolly" them along.[37] By year's end, he had jollied up more than 100 wins.

Sande earned special notice in the annual *American Racing Manual,* which also saluted Johnny Loftus, Bill Knapp, and Andy Schuttinger for riding "with skill, vigor and good judgment." Praising Loftus at year's end, *The Thoroughbred Record* remarked, "He possesses more than ordinary intelligence when on a horse, and has proved time out of number his ability to outride a threatening opponent when on probably the second best horse. Hardly has there been an instance where he has been beaten on the best horse. No specific case can be recalled."[38]

Eight months later, Loftus would ruin that forever.

4

WAKE UP, SHAKE UP

ON MARCH 29, 1919, Man o' War reached his actual second birthday and August Belmont, Jr., suffered a terrible loss: the eldest of his three sons, thirty-six-year-old August Belmont III, died two days after undergoing an operation for intestinal trouble. Deep mourning, as well as postwar business obligations, would keep Major Belmont from racing his own horses that year. Even if he had not sold the yearling Man o' War in 1918, Belmont would have leased or sold the colt in 1919.[1] Not once, but twice, extraordinary events had pulled Man o' War away from his breeder's control.

Belmont did, however, still control The Jockey Club. He would miss the April 3 License Committee meeting but would preside over a vital follow-up meeting on April 10. There he would pass judgment on Johnny Loftus, setting guidelines for the star jockey's most eventful year.

It was hard to be a jockey without getting in some kind of trouble. The starter could ground you for taking unfair advantage at the barrier. The stewards could ground you for fouling other riders and their mounts. If you were caught betting on other riders' horses, your license would be immediately revoked. If you were deeply unlucky, you could die. But if you were deeply lucky, you could earn a fortune.

As 1919 arrived and Man o' War reached racing age, many people were awed by the big money pouring into professional sports. A shady stockbroker named Charles Stoneham bought the New York Giants baseball team for $1,030,000, a record price. Baseball sensation Babe Ruth wrangled with the

Boston Red Sox for a raise—demanding one year at $15,000 or three years at $10,000 each—while average citizens lucky to take home $1,000 a year howled with amazement or disgust. But Ruth only wanted a salary like leading jockeys drew.

During 1919, Johnny Loftus could earn far more than Babe Ruth. First, however, he needed a license. The Jockey Club didn't grant permanent permission to ride or train Thoroughbreds. Instead, they made each jockey and trainer apply for a new license every year. An individual in good standing received a card; an individual in trouble got his applications delayed or denied. And that is where Loftus found himself in mid-March: seeking a hearing with the License Committee, which had put his application aside. *Daily Racing Form* reported a rumor that Loftus was involved with heavy gamblers and The Jockey Club was squeezing him for evidence of illegal betting coups. Such rumors were easy to believe. No matter what the law decreed, temptation never left the racetrack. Prominent horse owners offered substantial salaries and bonuses to their jockeys, hoping to buy honesty. The Jockey Club, however, couldn't assume that such rewards always worked. Instead, The Jockey Club kept extensive secret files on who associated with whom. Evidence came from Pinkerton detectives, hired to spy on trainers, jockeys, and big bettors. But the Pinkertons couldn't catch every illicit transaction. A huge volume of bets coursed through the racing wire: a nationwide telegraph system, centered in Chicago, that helped high rollers and bookies disguise their identities while placing wagers from remote locations.

Now Johnny Loftus was in trouble, and The Jockey Club wouldn't say why. The *New York Times* reported that A. K. Macomber had formally charged his former contract rider with "violating stable rules."[2] The public could only guess what this meant.

Traveling to The Jockey Club's Manhattan office, Loftus faced the License Committee on Thursday, April 3. Afterward the committee assured reporters that Loftus wasn't accused of criminal wrongdoing. "On the contrary," the *New York Times* noted, "it was said the committee was mindful of what Loftus had done for the racing game, and that they favored his reinstatement."[3] This prediction came true the following week, when August Belmont and his fellow officials agreed to license Loftus. *Daily Racing Form* admitted that there must have been no evidence to support the gambling rumor and reckoned that "the charges were unfounded."[4] Loftus could start riding races on May 1—with one caution. The License Committee warned him "not to get into further trouble with his employers even in minor matters."[5] Throughout 1919, in the eyes of The Jockey Club, Johnny Loftus would be riding on probation.

While Johnny Loftus galloped horses at Sam Riddle's Maryland farm, waiting for his jockey license to take effect, one of America's most successful riders left the sport forever. His absence would draw someone else into a key role in Man o' War's career.

Frankie Robinson, under contract to powerful owner/breeder Harry Payne Whitney, rode to the post for the last time in the sixth race at Bowie, Maryland, on Friday, April 4. Eight horses jumped away from the barrier and sprinted toward the clubhouse turn. Robinson's mount, Roederer, broke from post position four, sandwiched in the middle of the pack. Three paths to his outside, a gelding named Garbage broke with slightly greater speed. Anxious not to lose any ground around the turn, jockey Willie Doyle gunned Garbage forward and cut sharply toward the inner rail. At the same moment, Roederer bid for the lead.

Mindless momentum took over as Garbage bumped past Roederer's forelegs. In a flash, while Garbage grabbed the inside track, Roederer was flipping to the ground. Three horses close behind him, unable to dodge, tripped and crashed. As Garbage gained a comfortable lead, half the field sprawled on the ground.

Four horses peeled away from the mess on the turn, cruising off into the backstretch. Incredibly, all four fallen horses regained their feet and ran riderless after the pack. Two of the fallen jockeys got up and walked away. A third lay in the dirt, stunned, suffering two fractured ribs. Frankie Robinson lay nearby. A flying hoof had smacked into his head. People rushing to his aid found "a gaping hole torn in his skull."[6] Attendants hurried Robinson, the highest-paid jockey in America, to University Hospital in Baltimore. But there was nothing anyone could do.

Racetrackers mourned the "clean-cut, quiet boy,"[7] then gasped at the size of his estate. The *New York Herald* marveled in a six-word headline: ROBINSON, JOCKEY, LEFT HALF A MILLION.[8] For a typical United States worker, that looked like enough salary for at least five hundred years. But was this just another racetrack rumor bolting out of control? Two months later, *Daily Racing Form* would grumble, "The fool story about jockey Frank Robinson leaving an estate of $500,000 is traveling all over the world and causing illy-founded wonder in the minds of various turf critics."[9] To suspicious souls, a jockey *that* rich meant dishonesty. If Robinson had really had it, he'd been more than the gentlemanly lad everyone thought they knew. It would have meant he "did business"—took bribes.

But even if the reported fortune was real, there was another explanation. Unlike many jockeys, Frankie Robinson had lived conservatively. "He was well off in this world's goods," noted the *New York World*, "for . . . he had saved his big salary and riding fees and invested the greater portion of it in apartment houses in Cleveland."[10] Robinson the alleged bribe taker may have been only Robinson the successful landlord. His true character would fade from sight, while storytellers reinforced their own beliefs.

Robinson's departure also brought an aging comrade closer to Man o' War. Harry Payne Whitney, whose precocious two-year-olds would challenge Red, now needed a new contract rider. Whitney soon hired a veteran who had been an elite jockey when Frankie Robinson was still a child. Back in 1901, "Big Bill" Knapp had begun blooming from a 56-pound apprentice into a riding star. By the spring of 1919, he was ancient for a jockey: pushing thirty. Most boys grew too heavy before their mid-twenties. Blessed with a wiry frame, Knapp still hovered near the top of the game and tolerated a new nickname: "Old Man."

Working for Whitney, "Old Man" Knapp might turn 1919 into one of his most profitable years. Johnny Loftus, emancipated from Macomber, had equally bright prospects. Loftus had signed contracts with two owners, giving one "first call" and the other "second call." When the first-call owner didn't have a horse running or needed a lighter jockey, the second-call owner got a chance. When neither contract holder required Loftus, he could freelance. The way he managed these choices was financially shrewd.

Loftus gave second call to Commander J. K. L. Ross, whose large and phenomenal stable included 1918's champion older horse, Cudgel, and two-year-old sensation Billy Kelly. Ross, whose first-call rider was young Earl Sande, offered big bonuses and often needed more than one top-class jockey. But Loftus would ride first call for a smaller outfit, paying serious money yet racing too few horses to tie him up all the time. First call belonged to Glen Riddle Farm.

Early in April, Lou Feustel and Mike Daly shipped the Riddle and Jeffords horses across the Chesapeake Bay to mainland Maryland's northeast corner, disembarking at a town racetrackers called "Haver duh Grace" or "Haver duh Grass" and high society called "Hahrv d'Graw" or simply "the Graw." At Havre de Grace, Man o' War began learning a real racetrack routine. Feustel helped him by lodging the tranquil Major Treat in a neighboring stall.

Although giving two-year-olds short races in April wasn't unusual and a few Riddle juveniles would win races at "the Graw" that month, Feustel let Red develop at a slower pace. Mike Daly set a more ambitious schedule with Golden Broom. One morning, he sent the Jeffords colt a quick five furlongs, the full length of a baby race. A five-furlong breeze in sixty seconds would have thrilled trainers of proven stakes horses. Golden Broom, still unraced, dashed the distance in :59 3/5. But he emerged from his sensational work with a vertical crack in the rear quarter of his left front hoof.

Ignored, a quarter crack could lead to a split hoof, serious infection, or a galloping misstep that fractured a leg bone. Before stressing Golden Broom again, Daly had to let the damaged hoof grow out. But that wasn't all. The colt's left front ankle puffed up, threatening to calcify. His body was simply trying to reinforce a hard-worked joint, but calcification could stiffen the ankle too much for racing. *:59 and three*.[11] Golden Broom might never go that fast again.

And so, numbed with a local anesthetic, Golden Broom met a firing iron. Red-hot metal pinpoints quickly pressed into his injured ankle, punching tiny holes into the upper layer of bone. Medical theory said that firing, by increasing blood circulation to a wounded area, made the body intensify its repair process. Even so, recovery took several weeks. A few horsemen suspected that the vacation from training did at least as much good as the firing itself. "My friends give me credit for having restored a lot of famous cripples," future Hall of Fame trainer Sam Hildreth would recall, "and if I've had more than my share of success in this line I reckon it's because I let nature help do the mending. I don't like firing-irons any more than the horses themselves do. Plenty of rest, liniments, patient handling, and the proper amount of work are a pretty good cure in themselves. Of all these I recommend patience. You can't make horses recover any quicker than nature will permit. But you can form a partnership with nature."[12]

While Golden Broom wore a wooden neck cradle so that he couldn't chew his doctored ankle, Man o' War's feet and legs stayed remarkably strong. Most sources would state that he never developed any unsoundness. Frank Loftus would claim that Red briefly suffered from one typical baby problem:

bucked shins in his front legs.[13] In a galloping racehorse, the long bones known as the cannon bones, connecting ankle to knee, must withstand 10,000 pounds or more of force with every stride. During his early high-speed training, as his bones adapted to this stress, Man o' War's shins may have become inflamed. If so, Feustel would have let him stop and heal before returning to work and new bursts of speed.[14] According to Frank Loftus, Red recovered in only a week.

One undisputed ailment interrupted Red's progress. In early May, after Maryland racing moved from Havre de Grace to Baltimore's Pimlico track, influenza broke out in the racehorse colony. While his neighbors fell sick with fever and congestion, Man o' War at first stayed well. But he was not immune. Late one night, Red's temperature soared to almost 106 degrees. Normal for a horse at rest averages 100.5.

There was no veterinarian available until morning. Several Riddle horses that caught the same bug never regained racing strength. But when morning arrived, Red's fever was gone. He was galloping again in less than a week.

While Man o' War and Johnny Loftus both trained into racing shape, "Hard Guy" Bedwell cranked up a three-year-old colt who seemed cut out to be both a hero and a villain. This was Sir Barton, a handsome athlete with an aloof personality, uninterested in people and hostile toward barn pets. The grooms called him "Sammy" for short. If he could have understood the nickname, Sir Barton might have made them stop. He hated familiarity. As a young foal, he had been kept in a small paddock alone with his dam, Lady Sterling, because she was old and blind. While other babies became part of a herd, Sir Barton strengthened his independent nature. After being put into racehorse training, he did not bond with his human caretakers.

Tender feet made his unfriendly attitude even worse. Like many offspring of the popular stallion *Star Shoot, Sir Barton had brittle hoof walls and thin soles. The stinging impact of galloping full out on a hard dirt track could cause him to shorten stride. Bedwell helped by having the blacksmith place a layer of piano felt between Sir Barton's steel horseshoes and sensitive hooves. But sometimes when Sir Barton ran, horseshoe nails broke loose from his fragile feet, sending one or more shoes flying, removing some of his cushion and balance.

Brought along gradually, two-year-old Sir Barton hadn't even come close to winning in his first five starts. But his sleeping talent had awakened in America's most important juvenile race, the Futurity at Belmont Park. Breaking awkwardly, then caught in traffic, Sir Barton had seemed well beaten. Suddenly, with less than a furlong left, he found running room—and, as Commander Ross's teenaged son Jim remembered, "zoomed at the leader like a comet." It was too late—Dunboyne, with a perfect trip, won by two lengths—but it was remarkable. "And my father," said Jim Ross, "even though Sir Barton had failed to win, seemed more pleased with the result than I had ever seen him."[15]

Soon afterward, Sir Barton nearly died. A cut ankle led to blood poisoning. For several days, Bedwell basically lived in the colt's stall, offering all possible help. Jim Ross claimed that Bedwell pulled Sir Barton back to life. Bedwell insisted all credit belonged to Sir Barton's stubborn spirit and hardy constitution.

Despite his adventures, Sir Barton wasn't the Ross horse making headlines. That was Billy Kelly, a deceptively sleepy-looking gelding who had dominated Saratoga's two-year-old stakes. But Billy hadn't faced an impressive colt named Eternal. Responding to public demand, their owners agreed to a special match race, with the prize money going to charity. In the paddock, Bedwell gave Earl Sande explicit orders: Let Eternal take a short lead at the start—but if the pace is slow, take the lead with Billy Kelly. And no matter how wide Eternal runs around the turn, stay *outside* of him.

Strategy, it turned out, was everything. Veteran jockey Andy Schuttinger, riding Eternal, lulled Sande with a slow first furlong, then sped into a three-length lead. Turning for home, Eternal veered wide—and Sande forgot Bedwell's warning. Instinctively aiming to save ground, he drove Billy Kelly toward the open inner rail. Schuttinger instantly pulled Eternal inward, blocking Billy's path. Now Sande had to check his horse and swing outside. Lost momentum made all the difference. Billy Kelly rallied with heartbreaking determination. Eternal won by half the length of his head. "In the next stride past the post," said Jim Ross, "Billy Kelly passed him."[16]

Showing only good sportsmanship, Commander Ross leapt forward to congratulate the winners. "There was a smile and pat on the shoulder for Sande, too," Jim observed. "The youngster was visibly pale and trembling. . . . He went from my father to Bedwell and 'Hard Guy' did not hesitate to scold him furiously." Bedwell had plenty of company. "In the press and in the discussions that prevailed for weeks after the race . . . ," Jim recalled, "the majority opinion was that Billy Kelly had not lost to Eternal; rather, Sande had lost to Schuttinger."[17]

Bedwell didn't forget Sande's lapse, but over the winter he cooled down. The boy had rare ability and always tried to win; he just needed seasoning. Bedwell would trust Sande with Billy Kelly in the 1919 Kentucky Derby—a race in which the high-rolling Commander Ross had a fortune at stake.

John Kenneth Leveson Ross, like Samuel Doyle Riddle, came from a Scottish family that developed great wealth in the New World. His father, James Ross, had been a leader in various industries and helped to pioneer the Canadian Pacific Railroad. Like Sam Riddle, Jack Ross was an athletic young man who prepared for the elevated place waiting for him in the business world but found his true passion in sports. While Riddle immersed himself in foxhunting, Ross excelled in football and tuna fishing. In 1911, the six-foot-two-inch Ross, who weighed about 210 pounds, caught a tuna weighing a world-record 680 pounds. In those days, harnesses to give a fisherman additional leverage in the boat did not exist.

James Ross's death in 1913 left thirty-eight-year-old Jack Ross with several million dollars to invest and enjoy. The heir acquitted himself well, continuing the family tradition of philanthropy and comporting himself with "great dignity."[18] He also gave vent to what his own son, Jim, called "a great splash of daring in his nature."[19] Part of this he exercised by yachting on the high seas, a pursuit that his father had loved. Another part he exercised in a place that his father had scorned: the racetrack. James Ross had been, as a turf writer explained, "a dour Scotsman of the old school to whom gambling was anathema."[20] Jack Ross, however, yearned to own a top-class racing stable. He also hired a trainer, in Guy Bedwell, who exploited many gambling angles in the sport of kings.

In some ways, Jack Ross seemed like a more obviously noble citizen than Sam Riddle. After all, he had earned distinction while captaining a Royal Canadian Navy ship in the Great War. His demeanor—"Unassuming, a gentleman in every meaning of the word, a man who is ready at all times to shake the hands of the most diminutive stable boy or the hand of kings"[21]— constantly drew favorable comment in the press. And yet, Commander Ross used part of his inheritance to stray dramatically from his father's values. The contradiction flickered every time he appeared at a racetrack proudly wearing his navy uniform and ribbons, as he was well entitled to do, and began wagering thousands of dollars. Sam Riddle, despite his love for racing and ample wealth, would not risk more than fifty bucks.[22]

During the winter of 1919, when gamblers started making future wagers on the Kentucky Derby, the Commander's sporting reputation drew him into interesting company. While dining in a Manhattan restaurant, Ross had been approached by a pale, measly-looking man with a proposition. The stranger believed that Eternal would beat Billy Kelly in the Derby and wondered if the Commander would take that wager. With typical speed, Ross asked how much the stranger had in mind. Not more than $100, he thought. But the unimpressive man was impressive after all. "Would fifty thousand dollars suit you, Commander?" First-place money for the Derby was thirty thousand less.[23]

"That would suit me well, sir," Ross replied, rebounding from his surprise. "Provided you can produce some guarantee of payment should you lose." Somewhat miffed, the stranger introduced himself as Arnold Rothstein. He was the underworld financier who had helped Charles Stoneham raise more than $1 million to buy the New York Giants—a racketeer known to New Yorkers as "the Big Bankroll" and "the Brain."

Billy Kelly shipped to Kentucky as the Derby favorite, though needing only to outfinish Eternal to win the Commander's bet. Billy Kelly's trainer, willing to make his own bets, formed a further plan. Winter wagering on the Derby offered generous odds for a horse that had never won a race. Bedwell placed a bundle on Sir Barton.

On Saturday, May 10, preparing to ride Sir Barton in the Kentucky Derby, twenty-three-year-old Johnny Loftus found himself vigorously fighting his own physique. With Derby weights based on each horse's previous victories, winless Sir Barton had been assigned only 110 pounds. Reducing from his usual riding weight of 115 pounds, Loftus made 112 1/2. His unnaturally thin body had been able to lose only two and a half pounds.

Surrounded by at least fifty thousand track patrons despite soggy weather, Loftus met Bedwell and Sande in the Churchill Downs paddock. Bedwell—completely in charge because the Ross family had rushed to Canada on Derby eve to be near Mrs. Ross's ailing father—told Loftus to take the lead and set an honest pace with Sir Barton while Sande saved Billy Kelly's best run for the stretch. He would need it to beat Eternal and win Commander Ross's extravagant bet. Loftus followed orders perfectly. Sir Barton ticked along like a metronome, his first quarter in :24 1/5, a half-mile in :48 and two—good speed through driving rain on a heavy track. Loftus snagged a

breather in the third quarter, six furlongs in 1:14. That slowdown brought
Eternal to Sir Barton's side.

Two master strategists, Johnny Loftus and Andy Schuttinger, dueled
around the far turn. Sande and Billy Kelly shadowed them. A quarter mile
from the finish line, Sande secured his revenge for the previous year's embar-
rassing match race: Billy Kelly had opened three lengths on Eternal. Cooked
by Sir Barton's quick pace, Eternal floundered backward, finishing tenth of
twelve. But with a quarter mile left, Sir Barton stayed two lengths ahead of
Billy Kelly. Dashing for home in America's most famous race, Sir Barton and
Johnny Loftus weren't ready to give in.

"I got around the last turn in front, stood up in my stirrups, but failed to
see Sande and Billy Kelly," Loftus professed in later years. "I thought, 'What
a shame. If this little horse had been rated and saved, he would have come back
the winner.' Seeing nothing of Billy Kelly, I gave Sir Barton a cut of the whip
and he jumped off as if it were the start. Then I rode him the rest of the way,
figuring to hell with Bedwell, Sande, and Billy Kelly. . . ."[24] At the finish line,
with Loftus easing up on him, Sir Barton had trounced Billy Kelly by five
lengths.

Shortly after the race, Loftus practically apologized for Sir Barton's upstart
performance. "When it looked like I was shaking him up in the stretch I was
only stalling," he told *The Thoroughbred Record,* "as I knew that his stablemate, Billy Kelly, was closest to him, and you know it did not make any difference to me which one of the entry won, as long as one of them got home
in front."[25]

The truth was more complex. Trumping Billy Kelly with Sir Barton, Loftus had beaten the only horse actually dear to Bedwell's hard-boiled heart. At
the same time, Bedwell did not look displeased. A winner's circle photo
showed his closed lips forming a straight line but his face somehow conveying
a smile. Beside him, Sir Barton stared, his ears swiveling sideways at the clam-
oring crowd and slobber showing on his lower lip. In the saddle, Loftus sat
with the blanket of roses pushed in front of his knees rather than draped over
his lap, wearing a stern expression despite his triumph. His cheeks were hollow, his eye sockets deep and dark. In that moment, glancing toward the photographer, his face seemed like a NO TRESPASSING sign.

Summing up the day, Loftus would credit his Derby success to simple
good fortune. "The Kentucky Derby is my lucky race, as I won it two years
ago with George Smith, and I will be happy if Sir Barton turns out to be as

good a horse as George Smith is when he is at his best."[26] Bedwell, for his part, gladly collected his winter book bet. He didn't say whether he gave a cut to Johnny Loftus.

Mere hours after wearing Derby roses, Sir Barton rode more than 650 miles in a railroad car from Louisville, Kentucky, to Baltimore, Maryland. Only four days after his first victory, he would race in the $25,000 Preakness Stakes at Pimlico. Sir Barton would be favored this time, but forced to carry 126 pounds against ten lively opponents. Seeking an advantage, Bedwell added Commander Ross's fleet filly Milkmaid to the field. Bedwell ordered Sande to watch Sir Barton. If Mars Cassidy seemed ready to trigger the barrier with Sir Barton unprepared, Sande would wheel Milkmaid out of line and cause a recall. Trusting Sande with this ruse, Bedwell recognized the young rider's superior skill. Breaking a horse out of line without letting it look intentional and getting penalized by the starter required finesse.

Bedwell was right: Chaos reigned. For five minutes, the Preakness field jostled back and forth. Three times, false starts tore the barrier from its posts. Twelve keyed-up racers fretted while assistant starters tied the webbing back in place. The official start, at last, was good for most. Only Harry Payne Whitney's Vindex, with Bill Knapp up, was left at the post. Milkmaid broke sixth, exactly in mid-pack. Sir Barton was off flying.

Angling inward from post eight, Loftus steered Sir Barton to the front and grabbed the rail position as they rounded the clubhouse turn. He was seeking an uncontested lead, the easiest way for a free-running horse to succeed. Stay in front, kicking dirt back at your pursuers instead of catching dirt in your own face. Hug the inner rail, for the shortest trip around the track. Speed up if anyone tries to overtake you and slow down when challengers get discouraged. A brisk first quarter of :23 2/5 and rapid half in :47 1/5 sealed Sir Barton's dominance. All along the backstretch, no one dared run with him. They couldn't match his ambitious pace and still have enough energy left for the last phase of this 11/8-mile race. Meanwhile, having subdued his pursuers, Sir Barton enjoyed a breather. With his third quarter slowing abruptly to :25 and four, he held the lead by one comfortable length while cruising around the far turn. Then he entered the homestretch and Loftus turned him loose.

Now Sir Barton's opponents uncorked their remaining speed, but it was useless. Sir Barton had gotten the jump on them and pulled away with plenty of energy. Eternal, driving in second place, couldn't get any closer than four lengths—that near only because Loftus eased up Sir Barton during the final yards.

The Thoroughbred Record pointed out a brand-new distinction, noting that Loftus "set a mark for other riders to shoot at in future years by riding the winner of both the Kentucky Derby and the Preakness. . . ." Taking notice, Commander Ross gave Loftus a $2,000 check: one grand for each classic win. Meanwhile, two sterling efforts had convinced Loftus that his Derby/Preakness partner was something special. As *The Thoroughbred Record* reported, "Loftus says Sir Barton is the best horse he ever rode and this is a plenty, as Johnnie [*sic*] has kicked many a good one in his time. . . ."[27]

Another good one, too young to challenge Sir Barton, was gaining a place in Johnny's life. As Man o' War grew increasingly fit, he needed a racing-sharp rider's guidance. One May morning, someone boosted Johnny Loftus onto his back and Red felt a new kind of energy. Loftus didn't ride in slow training gallops. His body and mind were tuned to competition pitch. In a few morning breezes, Loftus taught Man o' War the tempo of the afternoons. He also went out of his way to develop rapport with the big bold colt. Years later, a journalist would recall that Loftus "grew very fond of the horse, used to come down to the stable and fool with him."[28] A busy jockey would only invest such time with a promising prospect.

The jockey's tempo lingered while Man o' War learned to break from the barrier. Harry Vititoe steadied Red behind the bouncing net, teaching him to vault underneath and sprint down the track. One morning at Pimlico, several horsemen who were watching a mob of two-year-olds practice group starts began betting which one would get away first. Prominent owner Ral Parr noticed that a black colt and a certain chestnut always broke in front. Their riders wore the black-and-yellow-striped sweaters of Glen Riddle Farm. His curiosity excited, Parr tracked down Sam Riddle. Noting that he owned many colts and hadn't seen the trials, the master of Glen Riddle refused to guess which individuals had performed best. But Parr kept investigating until he learned the truth. The black colt was Dream of the Valley. The chestnut was Man o' War.

On May 15, the day after Sir Barton's Preakness, the racing season opened in New York. When ten thousand patrons flowed into Brooklyn's Jamaica racecourse, the *New York Herald* proclaimed it a very encouraging sign. "Fully twice as many persons were present as at the opening last year," the *Herald* noted, "and though the afternoon was chilly, dark and threatening, everybody seemed to be in a gala mood, in striking contrast with the unmistakable depression at the opening a year ago, when the Germans were just launching their last great offensive, and the fate of something more than horse racing hung in the balance."[29] The *Herald* did not mention what The Jockey Club feared: the fate of New York racing was still unclear.

Although August Belmont and The Jockey Club in New York claimed racing's highest prestige, Maryland and Kentucky racing enjoyed a large financial advantage. In Kentucky and Maryland, each racetrack received a percentage of the money that patrons lost in pari-mutuel wagering sponsored by the track. This revenue boosted prize money. In New York, where racetracks could not endorse gambling, bookmakers offering barely legal "oral" wagering attracted patrons to the tracks but could not pay any fees to the racing associations. Instead, New York racing depended on horsemen's entry fees and patrons' admission fees for its prize money. Survival was possible, but this was no way to prosper.

Of course, anything that raised track attendance significantly could help.

Bringing the newly famous Sir Barton to race at Belmont Park, Commander Ross would help. Sam Riddle hoped for similar success with his talented three-year-old filly Colinella, but his dream collapsed in the worst way. While galloping over Belmont's training track, Colinella broke a leg and could not be saved.[30] Riddle's disappointed ambition for Colinella showed through her name and pedigree. Her sire, *Star Shoot, also had sired Sir Barton. Her dam, *Pastorella, was the mother of Colin himself.

While Colinella's potential disappeared, Sir Barton's appeal increased with every race. Moving from the Kentucky Derby to the Preakness to Belmont Park's prestigious Withers Stakes, he followed a demanding trail blazed in 1918 by War Cloud and Johnny Loftus. Already, he was more successful than Macomber's colt. When Sir Barton appeared for the Withers only ten days after his Preakness win, the crowd response showed that he was becoming a celebrity. Commander Ross's son Jim, on holiday from school and joining his father at the races, saw so many people mobbing Sir Barton in the saddling paddock that Pinkerton guards had to form a human barrier around the horse. The colt's behavior also intrigued Jim. "Sir Barton was placid until he heard the first notes of the bugle calling the horses to the track," he observed. "Then he pricked his ears, and, after Johnny Loftus had been given a leg up into the saddle, he grew alert and became so eager to reach the track that

Loftus had difficulty restraining him from cantering through the crowd. Bedwell himself had to take hold of his bridle and lead him out."[31]

While Sir Barton paraded past the grandstand, inspiring a continuous ripple of applause, Jim Ross anticipated tactical magic. During morning training hours, Bedwell had noticed which horses had trouble navigating the right-handed turns on Belmont's clockwise course. He alerted Loftus, and sure enough—when pacesetting Eternal drifted wide on the homeward turn, ground-saving Sir Barton powered through to his inside. Sir Barton won so emphatically that he didn't need the shortcut, but for Jim Ross, this smooth maneuver made Bedwell a racing prophet.

Sir Barton would keep his momentum rolling in the June 11 Belmont Stakes. He would be the first horse to enter the Belmont after winning the Kentucky Derby and Preakness Stakes, but this daring interstate sortie had no official status. England, however, had long since organized three classic races at three different tracks into a "triple crown" for three-year-olds. (Back in 1853, a colt named West Australian had become the first Triple Crown winner; he later would become Man o' War's great-great-great-grandsire.) While the United States did not offer any national series, Belmont Park followed the English pattern in promoting its own so-called triple crown: the Withers in May, the Belmont Stakes in June, and the Lawrence Realization in September. As of 1919, no horse had swept all three. Sir Barton, heavily favored for the Belmont Stakes, might glamorize the New York triple. Even better, he might do it in record time.

Most American racegoers weren't attuned to triple crowns, but they *were* marveling at speed. In August of 1918, Saratoga Race Course had debuted a fast new racing surface and gained sensational publicity: During Saratoga's twenty-seven-day meet, winners broke or equaled twenty-two track records.[32] This attraction soon spread to Long Island. During the winter, track superintendent H. I. Pels treated Belmont Park's racing surface like Saratoga's, installing a state-of-the-art drainage system, mixing loads of sand into the top layer of dirt, and rolling the upper "cushion" thin and tight. When Belmont Park reopened in mid-May 1919, speed records began to fall. By early June, *Daily Racing Form* reported that Belmont's main track was becoming "the fastest in the country . . . and what is more it is getting faster every day now that the soil is becoming settled. Nearly all horsemen declare it is faster than Saratoga. . . ."[33] At this point, seemingly bouncy Belmont Park earned a new nickname: the "rubber track."[34] But its hard base, which increased the concussion absorbed by horses' bones, also caused new problems. As *Daily Racing Form* explained, "Just how many horses have pulled up lame after works and races cannot be correctly enumerated."[35] On this newsworthy surface, Sir Barton would attempt his Belmont Stakes and Man o' War would run his first race.

If Lou Feustel had any fears about Red's racing debut, however, reporters didn't print them. Instead, morning regulars at Belmont Park's training track saw what Maryland horsemen had been boasting about: a spirited red colt, under heavy restraint, breezing half miles in :47. Two-year-old Man o' War was running faster than three-year-old Sir Barton's rapid early pace in the Preakness Stakes—and on a surface substantially slower than Belmont's revamped main course.

Despite Red's exceptional speed, Feustel would introduce him to racing very carefully. He ignored the May 30 Juvenile Stakes, a five-furlong dash with a tempting $7,500 purse. With sixteen starters scrambling for its riches, the Juvenile would be too chaotic and intense. Instead, Feustel entered his star pupil in another five-furlong event, a $700 purse on Friday, June 6, for two-year-olds that had not yet won a race. Near the Long Island plains where America's first official racing meets had been held in 1665, at the grand track that upheld his breeder's ideals, Man o' War would begin making his own name in a nameless race.

5

LAUNCHED

For anyone who wanted honest racing, Lou Feustel was the perfect man to train heavy favorites. Following August Belmont's example, he did not try to make fortunes by betting on his horses. Therefore, not caring what odds his winners paid, Feustel didn't mind letting short-priced favorites win. And so, as his fastest two-year-old became ready to race, Feustel didn't try to hide Man o' War's speed. He only worried about getting him fit and keeping him well.

Sharpening Red for his Friday-afternoon racing debut, Feustel gave him a Thursday morning "blowout"—sprinting just far and fast enough to exercise his lungs. He sent Red three furlongs with the chestnut gelding Dinna Care, another two-year-old who had not raced yet but was nearly ready. As the pair breezed past the finish line, Feustel couldn't believe what he saw: Dinna Care beating Man o' War by half a length.

When Harry Vititoe offered no excuse for Red, Feustel began worrying. "I couldn't sleep all night wondering what was wrong," he would recall. "The next day Man o' War's exercise boy came to me and said, 'Boss, bet my month's wages on our horse.' I said, 'Harry, you better hang onto your money. He may not be right.' You know, that kid just busted out laughing at me. He'd done everything he could to get him beat in that workout, thinking he'd get a price on him the next day."[1] But clockers, bookmakers, and horseplayers put more stock in Red's previous fast workouts than Vititoe's last-minute charade. Man o' War would enter his first race as the odds-on favorite. Anyone risking five dollars on him to win could get eight dollars back—the original five, plus three dollars' profit. Those short odds would keep bookies from going broke and Man o' War supporters, like Harry Vititoe, from getting rich.

Man o' War, meanwhile, experienced a change in his routine. There was less food today, and someone sewed his mane into a row of small neat braids.[2] He heard the usual cycle of racetrack sounds, rising to a peak one, two, three, four, five times. Then a handler led him away from his barn and into the paddock behind Belmont Park's grandstand, a green oval dotted with stately trees, ornamental shrubs, and chatting spectators.

Sam and Elizabeth Riddle watched Man o' War, the tallest contestant in this baby race, take his place in the paddock. Their friends, admiring Man o' War's size, kidded Sam about sneaking a four-year-old into a two-year-old event. Red felt a tiny racing saddle being strapped to his back.

Johnny Loftus appeared from the jockey house, bloused in Glen Riddle Farm's yellow-and-black silks. His challenge would be keeping Man o' War out of trouble at the start, then unleashing his speed at the right time. Feustel told Loftus to be patient and build momentum gradually. "Wait until they get out of your way, Johnny, then let him go after them. He'll catch them at the furlong pole and win galloping."[3] Then Feustel gave the traditional orders from a trainer anticipating victory—"Hurry back"—and boosted Loftus onto Red's back.[4]

Five colts and two fillies followed outrider "Red Coat" Murray onto the track for the last race at Belmont Park on Friday, June 6, 1919. First in line came the long-legged, high-headed red colt with the meet's most popular jockey on his back, the good thing known as Man o' War.

From their clubhouse box seats, the Riddles and Jeffordses looked to their right, along the homestretch and down the long chute known as Belmont Park's straight course. Many patrons pulled out binoculars, trying to watch the activity at the barrier more than half a mile away. For about two minutes, seven baby racehorses bounced in and out of line. Then suddenly, at 5:10 P.M., the barrier lifted and Man o' War's racing career began.

Following orders, Loftus let Red leave slowly. Starter Mars Cassidy later would tell Feustel, "Either the rest of those colts are bums, or you've got the fastest horse that ever lived. He broke so far out of it that for a split second I was going to recall 'em."[5]

But no one waved the recall flag, and within moments it clearly didn't matter. Man o' War found his stride. Within about six seconds of running, he ran neck and neck on the lead with the filly Retrieve while Loftus reined him in. Such quick progress seemed barely possible. With knees bouncing chest high and neck thrust up like a submarine periscope, Red's motion didn't look fast. The best racehorses, grabbing every inch of ground, were supposed to stretch out long and low. But Man o' War sprang up and onward like a boulder from a catapult. His high knee action, which looked like wasted energy, was a seamless phase of this powerful arc.

Man o' War did not look fast, but he soared forward in giant bounds. Completing the first furlong, still under restraint, he led Retrieve by half a length. After a quarter mile, he had opened daylight, galloping two lengths in front. One furlong from the finish line, he had doubled that margin, leading Retrieve by four. Then Loftus, following orders, let him loose.

For a few seconds, Man o' War kicked into high gear. Almost immediately, Loftus began stopping him from doing too much. About 100 yards from the finish line, the crowd saw Man o' War's jockey looking "in all directions"[6] for any challengers. There were none.

Man o' War crossed the finish line with Loftus "standing straight up in the stirrups,"[7] trying to save Red's excess energy for another day. Despite slowing down in the final strides, he beat Retrieve by six lengths. The official timer stopped his watch at :59 flat—the second-fastest five-furlong win at Belmont Park that spring. Only Sam Hildreth's two-year-old colt Dominique had beaten that time, romping by six lengths in :58 and three.

Journalists did not interview Lou Feustel or Sam Riddle after Red's nameless race. They did, however, notice Man o' War. The *New York Herald* described the new winner as, "either a very smart colt or else there was an awfully bad lot behind him, for he won pulled up after running off and losing his competitors in the first half mile."[8] The *New York Tribune* called Man o' War "one of the finest-looking two-year-olds seen in some time."[9] The *New York Telegraph* deemed Man o' War's performance "so impressive that he will be a hard colt to beat in the rich stakes to come, if he doesn't go wrong."[10]

After Man o' War's easy leap from morning practices to afternoon performance, Feustel made a confident move. Only three days after earning $500 for his maiden victory, Red would run in Belmont Park's $5,000 Keene Memorial Stakes. Because stakes races represented racing's highest level and few horses could dominate them, this was a steep step up in class. Only one in every twenty Thoroughbreds foaled in 1917 ever would win a stakes race.

Five of the six 1919 Keene Memorial contestants, however, eventually would earn that honor. Their handlers had evaluated them well.

Starting Man o' War in the Keene Memorial, Sam Riddle found himself in competition with his niece. Although Golden Broom wasn't fit to race yet, Sarah Jeffords entered another burly chestnut colt. He had yet to win a race, but the Jeffordses had given him a perfect name. This colt was a grandson of the famous speedster Domino. One meaning of *domino* is an eye mask worn at a costume party. Saluting his ancestry, Sarah's colt bore the name Hoodwink. An old-fashioned meaning of the verb *hoodwink* is "to blind by covering the eyes."[11]

Hoodwink fitted his name in another way: He came to the races wearing a blinker hood, with leather crescents blocking his peripheral vision. Whether frightened, lazy, or easily distracted, Hoodwink needed help in focusing his attention on the track ahead instead of the activity in the grandstand. Blinkers also adorned two other Keene Memorial colts: My Laddie, unplaced in two previous starts, and On Watch, a promising son of the mighty Colin. Man o' War, Ralco, and Anniversary would race with their vision unrestricted.

A little after four o'clock on a warm, wet Monday afternoon, the six colts stepped out onto a track surface that *Daily Racing Form* officially rated "slow."[12] The air was so thick with misty rain that the six thousand spectators could barely see the starting barrier, five and a half furlongs down the straight course from the finish line. Many gamblers also were disgruntled that the gummy track had caused trainers to withdraw many horses from the afternoon's program. Two runners had been scratched in the last possible hour from the Keene Memorial: Rouleau, who had brought $13,000 at August Belmont's yearling auction, and Bonnie Mary, a notably fast filly who had already won two stakes races. Bonnie Mary would have carried 125 pounds— ten more than Man o' War. Her presence would have created a more interesting betting contest. As it was, the gamblers strongly favored Man o' War, dropping his odds to 7–10 by post time.

The start, obscured by fog, confused the distant audience. Some thought that Hoodwink took the early lead. Others, more accurately, figured that the leader was My Laddie. Barely visible from the grandstand, the galloping colts drew a smudge of movement thirty-some seconds long. At the front edge, Ralco dueled with My Laddie. Sandwiched between them, Loftus held Man o' War in check—Red's head seesawing near their girths—for more than three-eighths of a mile.

One furlong from the finish line, the field pushed into clear view with three colts bunched at the front of the pack. But it was My Laddie in the lead, Ralco next, *then* Man o' War. Wise-guy gamblers known as "sharpshooters" yelled, "They've got him!" and "The favorite's beat!" But the eighth pole meant it was time for Loftus to let Red go, "and then," the *New York Times* observed, "Loftus spoiled an interesting race. . . ."[13]

That first clear vision had been pure illusion. My Laddie, the leader, was flat out. A tired Ralco already was dropping back. On Watch overhauled them, flying up into second place. And Man o' War—supposedly beaten at the eighth pole—accelerated on cue as Loftus let loose the reins and shook the whip for him to see.[14] At the finish, Red had strolled off into his own company, leading On Watch by three full lengths and last-place Hoodwink by nearly sixteen. Horsemen with stopwatches caught his winning time as fast as 1:05, while Belmont Park's official clocker said 1:05 and three. Though not threatening the track record, 1:05 and change was pretty sharp for a two-year-old, especially over a surface rated "slow." A good horse maintaining a twelve-seconds-per-furlong pace would have finished the five and a half furlongs in 1:06. Red had beaten that effortlessly.

After two short races, Man o' War had earned $4,700 for Glen Riddle Farm—only three hundred dollars less than his purchase price—and looked like he might become America's most valuable two-year-old. One reporter guessed that Red's dominating stakes debut "probably would make him favorite for the $30,000 Hopeful Stakes at Saratoga and the $25,000 Futurity at Belmont Park if a future book were open on those juvenile classics of the autumn season."[15] Not knowing that Man o' War had been named for Major Belmont instead of a boat, sports writers began comparing him to a battleship.

The Riddles had to be pleased with young Man o' War's quick progress. But someone else was becoming America's favorite racehorse: Sir Barton.

The colt known as Sir Barton nearly had gone to the races with a much jollier moniker: Harry Hale. That name, inspired by Maj. Gen. Harry Hale of the U.S. Army, might have pleased the American public, but its hale and hearty sound did not suit an unfriendly colt with bad feet. It was fitting that breeder John Madden had changed his mind—not guided by the colt's personality but realizing that his son, who worked on General Hale's staff, might be accused of brownnosing if the horse ran well.[16] And so, paying tribute to the colt's champion older brother, Sir Martin, Madden came up with Sir Barton.

Instead of honoring an American general, the future Kentucky Derby winner would be named after an incorrigible Scottish pirate.

The substitute name, Sir Barton, did suit the colt's soul. Legend had it that Sir Andrew Barton, mortally wounded in a showdown at sea, declared, "I'll lay me down and bleed awhile, and then I'll rise and fight again."[17] As he rose to fame, the equine Sir Barton showed similar stubbornness and vulnerability.

The general public did not know that Sir Barton's speed was threatened by fatigue and pain. Fatigue came from winning three classic races hundreds of miles apart within five weeks. Pain came from Sir Barton's delicate feet. Many horsemen, facing similar obstacles with their own racers and knowing what treatments were available, believed that Bedwell resorted to a common racetrack remedy. The backstretch grapevine insisted that, before a race, he dosed Sir Barton with cocaine.

Race-day stimulants supposedly were illegal, but Americans rarely enforced the ban. A veterinarian who regularly treated Sir Barton later recalled, "Hell, back in those days everybody hopped their horses. You couldn't stay alive if you didn't do what the others were doing."[18] U.S. racetracks wouldn't phase in drug tests—required in France since 1912—until the mid-1930s. Meanwhile, Bedwell belonged to the unapologetic tradition of giving sore or reluctant racers something to take their minds off their troubles. "If a fellow who's working for you has got a headache, you give him an aspirin tablet so he'll feel better and earn his money," trainers reasoned. "Or maybe if you want to brace yourself for some special occasion you swallow a big belt of whiskey. What's wrong with that?"[19]

Horses varied, however, in their response to hop. As Kentucky horseman Johnny Clark noted, "Some it helped, some it did not."[20] A helpful response could run in families, and trainers often tried similar tactics with closely related horses. Prominent turf reporter Neil Newman spotlighted Sir Barton's mother in 1931 by writing, "If there ever was a 'hop' mare, Lady Sterling was one."[21]

Many fans who showed up at Belmont Park on Wednesday, June 11, however, knew little or nothing about racehorse drugs. They simply wanted to see a sports celebrity. Hundreds of spectators pressed into the saddling paddock to view Sir Barton up close, for Belmont Park's "rubber track" had fueled expectations about the Belmont Stakes. "A new record for the event and track is looked for," the *New York Times* had told them, "if Sir Barton is pressed."[22]

Only two opponents would try their luck. Triggering the barrier, Mars Cassidy caught the tiny field standing in a perfect line and Johnny Loftus caught his rivals off guard. While Natural Bridge and Sweep On stood still, Sir Barton leapt underneath the rising net. "From away down at the grand stand," a reporter said, "it looked as if he had beaten the barrier by two or three lengths."[23]

In a long race of a mile and three-eighths, however, Sir Barton could play a waiting game. Occupying a perfect spot, Loftus now held him back. Natural Bridge inherited the lead, with Sir Barton hanging about two lengths behind him and two ahead of Sweep On. Their symmetrical formation held all around the training track, with Loftus sitting quiet, waiting to launch Sir Barton's move.

It happened where the training track and main course joined, nearly half a mile from the Belmont Stakes finish line. "A slight motion of Loftus's hands and a little kick provided all the urging needed for Sir Barton," a sharp-eyed reporter noted.[24] Sir Barton roared away, opening such a gap that Loftus began slowing him down before they reached the finish line and still won by six lengths. It wouldn't be recognized for years yet, but Sir Barton and Johnny Loftus—victorious in the Kentucky Derby, Preakness, and Belmont Stakes—had launched America's Triple Crown.

They were heroes anyway. Sir Barton's official time, 2:17 2/5, set a new American record. While an ebullient Commander Ross shook hands with Loftus and patted Sir Barton, veteran turfmen dubbed the winner everything from "horse of the decade" to "horse of the century." Although cautious about the century title, the *New York Times* declared, "One thing is certain—of all the good horses which have won this classic for three-year-olds at Belmont Park only James R. Keene's Colin, the victor in 1908, will bear comparison with yesterday's winner."[25] The *Herald* was less reserved: "That he may be a better horse than Colin or Sysonby or any thoroughbred [*sic*] of the present century in American racing looked more than ever possible after the fifty-first Belmont had been run."[26]

No one could get over the ease of it all. "During the last eighth Loftus sat still as a statue," the *Times* observed, "holding his mount back as well as he could, but the beautiful chestnut could not be restrained entirely. He was endowed with the spirit of competition and ran straight and true to the end, pulling up without showing the least trace of weariness."[27] A few insiders knew that this eagerness belied Sir Barton's actual condition. Unexpectedly candid but characteristically honest, Jim Ross would write in his memoir that Sir Barton was "quite sore" when he went to the post for the Belmont Stakes. He did not mention Bedwell's remedy.

The public saw only a phenomenon. A reporter asked Loftus, "Did you have to ride him [hard] at any spot or place?"

"Not a foot of the way," Loftus replied. "I never rode one like him, and I doubt whether there is a horse in the world that can beat him."[28]

Of course, Loftus had felt only a hint, in sprints, of baby Man o' War.

Less than twenty-four hours after the Belmont Stakes, New York racing moved a few miles west from Hempstead, to the township of Jamaica. While Sir Barton rested his sore feet, Johnny Loftus easily led the nation's jockeys in winning percentage and acclaim. "Racegoers call upon him by name instead of his mount when rooting," a reporter noted. "That is about the highest height of popularity a jockey can attain."[29]

Such popularity made reporters curious about Loftus, but one who turned out a long feature article for a New York paper found his subject tough to interview. "Extracting the story of his life and early struggles from Johnny Loftus is not a productive task," Dan Lyons wrote. "He is modest almost to the degree of bashfulness. He shuns publicity and the limelight. He answers questions readily and frankly enough, but he volunteers very little information about himself."[30] Lyons did discover that "Loftus is a real horse lover. He lives horse, sleeps horse, and thinks horse, but he does not talk horse. That is, not to outsiders. Among his own it is his chief topic."

When asked about Sir Barton, Loftus did not hold back. "Sir Barton is a great horse," he told Lyons. "In fact, he is one hell of a horse. That's the only way I can express it." (In deference to its gentle readers, the newspaper printed the letter *h* followed by a dash, instead of the word *hell*.)

The public learned that Loftus, when not riding in a race, often could be found in the paddock helping trainers get their horses ready. He figured that he would become a trainer after his jockey days ended, but also said, "I'll stay in the saddle as long as there is a demand for my services."

The demand seemed likely to remain high, as long as Loftus could keep his weight down. Horsemen praised him with comments such as, "He is a jockey of well-nigh perfect judgment."[31] The public had latched on to him, making many of his mounts the betting favorites simply because he was aboard. Loftus encouraged them with days such as June 18, when he won with three favorites in three rides. *Daily Racing Form* reported that "Loftus stands out so prominently compared with the majority of jockeys these days that even the next best is not within hail. It is true that he has good horses to ride, his services being in great demand, but he rarely makes a mistake once a race is started. In fact, it would be difficult to point out a race in which he has ridden this year that he has not won when on the best horse. Some riders can get beaten on the best horses. Frequently Loftus has won on the second best and even has brought the third best home on one or two occasions."[32]

When riding the best horse, Loftus often cut the finish close to save his mount's energy for future races. He understood the algebra of stretch runs, how fast his opponents were traveling and how much—or little—his own mount could give to get there first. Riding against a better horse, Loftus often used these calculations to win the race anyway. Of course, not every race could be perfect. To Loftus followers, it only seemed that way. As of June 23, he had won with 43 percent of his rides: the equivalent of a baseball player batting .430. Earl Sande, the nation's second-most-frequent winner, trailed with 27 percent.

But Loftus did not quote any statistics when Dan Lyons interviewed him about his life and career. At the end of their talk, the almost bashful jockey volunteered a bit of personal rather than professional information. "You might say in your article that I am Irish," he told Lyons before heading for the jockey house to get dressed for his job.[33] This showed pride in his heritage but also let the public know that he was not German, as some assumed. It could not hurt to distance himself from America's recent deadly enemy.

Lyons did not ask Loftus about young Man o' War, unbeaten in two starts. With much probing, he might have learned that the star jockey was making a special project of the excitable colt. Another turf writer had noticed that Man o' War, in his first two starts, "seemed frightened by the webbing [of the barrier] and his flock of opponents and did everything he could to throw Loftus and injure the other contestants."[34] Clearly, this behavior could end up hurting Man o' War and his rider. And so Loftus schooled Red at the barrier, teaching him the "flying start" that Sir Barton used so well. So far, Man o' War had caught his opponents within a few seconds, unloosing his catapult strides—but why give anything away? The flying start meant the best choice of position, like Sir Barton had enjoyed in the Belmont Stakes. Watching the starter for a subtle movement that meant *"Go,"* Loftus cued Man o' War to jump ahead as the barrier rose. But while learning this game and sometimes hitting the net, Red also learned he didn't have to respect the ragged strip of elastic. It would yield to him.

While becoming more finely trained, Man o' War remained not quite tame. "I don't think we saddled him once," Sam Riddle mused, "during his races as a two and three-year-old, that he didn't show, by his actions, that he remembered his breaking."[35] Red's favorite ploy was to take a deep breath and hold it while the saddle girth tightened around his ribs. When Red breathed out, the girth became slightly loose. This happy principle of mechanics, exploited by horses everywhere, also worked for the era's most successful human escape artist. Harry Houdini gained a similar edge whenever a stunt called for tying ropes around his arms, flexing his considerable muscles and then relaxing them to quietly slip free.

Houdini was fortunate that Lou Feustel never rose from an audience to inspect his bonds. Unfortunately for Man o' War, Feustel always fixed the equipment. He let Red walk for a few minutes, then tightened the girth every necessary notch.

On June 21—twelve days after the Keene Memorial—Feustel started Man o' War in his third race. Red would experience a different environment in this 5 1/2-furlong test, running around the wide end of the egg-shaped Jamaica track. His target: the $5,000 Youthful Stakes.

Only three opponents would challenge him. Not only did Man o' War have two easy wins in two starts; he continued training impressively.[36] The weight assignments, however, gave his rivals a speck of hope. Because of his stakes win, Man o' War had earned a significant weight penalty.

Weight served as one of racing's most basic yet complicated factors. In some events, every horse carried the same impost. In others, each runner earned extra pounds for recent victories or received allowances for lack of success. The Youthful Stakes used this allowance system. Penalized for having won a stakes race, Man o' War would carry 120. On Watch, who had run second to Bonnie Mary in the $7,500 Juvenile Stakes before losing to Man o' War in the Keene Memorial, had only 108. The less accomplished Lady Brummel and *St. Allan carried 105. Man o' War, therefore, would be giving his rivals from 12 to 15 pounds.

"Weight will stop a freight train," an old racetrack saying goes. While 120 pounds wasn't excessive for a big healthy youngster such as Man o' War, the weight spread—the difference between his burden and those of his opponents—might be meaningful. According to the traditional theory that each four-pound increase handicapped a horse by one length in a sprint race, Red would spot his opponents the equivalent of three or four lengths. Furthermore, he would have to handle a track officially rated "good"—a little too deep to be really fast, and presumably more tiring for the high-weighted runner. One reporter noted that during the Youthful Stakes most of the track surface was "cuppy"—drying out and crumbling away underfoot—but the going was "deep and sticky" near the inner rail.[37] Even so, bookmakers doubted that these conditions would discourage Man o' War. They sent him off at 1–2 odds.

Lou Feustel's unfettered comments in the saddling paddock drove the odds. "This colt is the fastest two-year-old I ever saw," Feustel proclaimed. "In his trial for this race he stepped five furlongs in the remarkably fast time of 58 seconds. If I had a million dollars I would bet half of it that he would win. Even if he gets a bad break he has enough speed to beat this field."[38]

For four minutes, the baby racers agitated behind the barrier—*St. Allan next to the inner rail, then On Watch, Lady Brummel, and Man o' War—while each jockey aimed for the inside path into the long half-circle turn. Lady Brummel, too keyed up, ruined her start with a vertical leap as the barrier finally rose. At the same moment, Loftus gunned Man o' War to the front, outsprinting his three rivals and cutting toward the inner rail, securing the shortest trip for Red's first race around a turn. Red entered the bend at what *Daily Racing Form* called "a great pace,"[39] getting the first quarter mile in :23 1/5. An unofficial clocker, catching Red's first quarter in :23 flat, reported his first three furlongs as a dazzling :34 and three. Lady Brummel, flying up into second place, still ran four lengths behind Red as they entered the homestretch. Still averaging less than twelve seconds per furlong, Red officially sped the half in :47 and three. Lady Brummel fell back. Man o' War easily beat On Watch by two and a half lengths. "In the last quarter of a mile he was only romping," a *New York Herald* reporter observed.[40] Despite the not-quite-fast track and leisurely finish, Red's official winning time of 1:06 3/5 was only 2/5 slower than the stakes record set by a colt carrying 15 pounds less.

Expert horsemen now reckoned that something special was unfolding. The *New York Times* reported a widespread opinion that Man o' War "would go through the season unbeaten and turn out a better horse than his sire, Fair Play."[41] Andrew Jackson Joyner, who had trained Fair Play, led the praise chorus. "He is the only great two-year-old shown this year," Joyner asserted. "We have seen no other like him."[42]

Newspapers didn't quote Lou Feustel after the race, but the young trainer's actions showed his confidence. Forty-eight hours after winning the Youthful Stakes, Man o' War would race again. What's more, he would run at a different track and carry more weight than ever.

Feustel entered Red for opening day at Aqueduct, a major venue about three miles from the quirky Jamaica course. The $3,500 Hudson Stakes, a five-furlong dash, looked like easy money for Glen Riddle Farm. Usually, Feustel would give a horse more than two days between races, but the Youthful had been nothing more than a public workout for Man o' War. The Hudson, however, offered a potentially serious drawback. Penalized by his impressive stakes wins, Man o' War would carry 130 pounds. Although this substantial weight assignment wasn't uncommon for top two-year-olds, very few had toted 130 as early as June 23. No Hudson winner had carried more than 125.

Man o' War's challenge wasn't enough to draw a large crowd. Despite the additional lure of the prestigious Brooklyn Handicap and a clear summer day that reached seventy-five degrees, few spectators visited Aqueduct this Monday afternoon. Something, however, put Man o' War on edge. One moment, he was waiting for his jockey to mount—the next, as Loftus settled onto the saddle, he was rearing high on his hind legs, rushing forward and overbalancing, then falling backward and slamming to the ground. In that instant, Man o' War could have broken his neck or fractured his skull and Loftus could have been crushed beneath him. Instead, sliding from the saddle in midair and hurling himself away from Red's falling body, Loftus escaped with minor problems. "The fall stunned Loftus and strained his back," a reporter noted. "The horse landed on his back very gracefully, rolled over on his side and arose without any help."[43] Another reporter said that Loftus suffered "a slightly bruised hip."[44]

This would not be the only time that summer when Man o' War gave Loftus a close call. One morning later in the Aqueduct meet, while jogging to the starting point for a workout, Red suddenly reared sky-high, teetering on his hind feet, then leaped forward one, two, three times. The first leap, Loftus insisted, seemed like it could clear the racetrack's eight-foot-high outer fence. Red breezed a quick half mile without further drama, but Loftus "was unnerved," a reporter noted, "and said he didn't want any more such experiences."[45] Feustel would have to help straighten the colt out. A racehorse as talented as Man o' War was worth extra trouble, and Loftus endured a lot. "On a dozen occasions," a reporter would recall later that year, "he came within an ace of hurling Loftus through the air."[46]

Feustel would remember such moments, in later years, when a friendly reporter asked him about the rumors that Man o' War had been the greatest hop horse of all. "Good Lord," Feustel retorted. "Why would I ever give a horse like that any dope? He was hard enough to handle without it. . . ."[47]

Feustel's response rang true. No claims that he would never do such a thing to any horse—instead, a plain reason why hopping Man o' War in particular would have been foolish. Red's naturally fiery attitude made him a poor candidate for stimulants. It also could make him resemble a hopped horse, eager to be moving. Suspicious observers or jealous competitors might draw that conclusion. Feustel, however, knew this restless energy as Red's typical state of being. "When I wanted him to walk, he jogged," Feustel recalled, "When I wanted him to jog, he cantered and when I wanted him to canter he'd breeze."[48]

Excited by his second race in three days, Red overflowed with energy before the Hudson Stakes. Johnny Loftus tried to use this to their advantage at the start. If Red broke slowly in this very short race, while giving his four opponents from 15 to 21 pounds, he might fail to make up the lost ground. So Loftus kept Red on his toes, delaying the start for three minutes while seeking the perfect break, miscalculating once and charging through the barrier.

Finally, he timed it right. Man o' War vaulted underneath the rising net, Evergay going with him. Red spotted Evergay 18 pounds. Saving energy, Loftus waited. Red led Evergay by only half a length at first, then a full length heading toward the homestretch. Violet Tip and Shoal overhauled Evergay, but Red bounded away from them. Forty yards from the finish, Loftus took a hold, gearing down through the last half a dozen strides. Red coasted under the wire one and a half lengths in front of the driving Violet Tip, who had four lengths on Shoal. In that moment, he beat a filly and a colt that had been raised with him at August Belmont's Nursery Stud.

Clockers reported times from 1:01 flat to the official 1:01 and three. In any case, the time on a fast track was leisurely—Aqueduct's record for five furlongs was :58 and one—but few trainers were guessing that any two-year-old could defeat Man o' War this year. Man o' War's most dangerous opponent seemed to be himself.

Thanks to his paddock acrobatics, Red emerged from the Hudson Stakes with bruised muscles. Letting him gently walk the soreness away,[49] Feustel told *Daily Racing Form* that Red would be ready for the Great American Stakes that Saturday, June 28. The five-day rest didn't faze him. He didn't count, however, on Red's gluttony.

Man o' War, a greedy eater, gobbled his grain. Feustel had begun making the colt wear a metal bit in his mouth at mealtimes, forcing him to slow down and thoroughly chew his oats. Soon after the Hudson, Feustel told an admiring reporter, "Now he weighs 130 lbs. more than when he left Glen Riddle for the races."[50] But Red's impressive weight gain only told the outside story. Inside, like all horses, Man o' War had a small stomach, narrow small intestine, and large colon, where gallons of food fermented every day. These proportions make horses susceptible to the bloating and blockages known as colic. Two regular parts of Red's rations, bran mashes and linseed oil, were anti-colic measures with a laxative effect. But Feustel's precautions couldn't prevent all trouble. During the morning of Saturday, June 28, Red showed signs of colic. In severe cases, horses can twist their intestines and suffer an excruciating death.

Red escaped with a mild bellyache on June 28, but he couldn't race that afternoon. Instead, the Great American Stakes showcased another sensation: the filly Bonnie Mary, who had avoided meeting Man o' War in the Keene Memorial. She ran brilliantly with 127 pounds up, setting a new stakes record by a full second. Observers could only guess what effort she might have forced from Man o' War, flying alongside her and carrying 130 pounds.

He would give them some idea on July 5.

6

PRICKLY HEAT

On FRIDAY, JULY 4, while a record crowd swarmed the popular Aqueduct racetrack in New York's borough of Queens to watch the Carter Handicap, a disappointing twenty thousand patrons, instead of the expected eighty thousand, gathered around a desperately hot canvas square in Toledo, Ohio, to watch the world heavyweight boxing match. Some boxing fans feared that the defending champion, six-foot-six Jess Willard—known as "the Pottawatomie Giant"—would literally kill his six-foot-one opponent, Jack Dempsey, whom he outweighed by fifty-eight pounds. They found a new, improbable hero when Dempsey demolished Willard in three rounds.

The highly publicized fight result resonated with racing-stable agent Frank Hackett, who worked for Commander Ross. As racehorses go, Sir Barton was not tall. In the horse world's ancient measurement system of four inches equaling one "hand" in height, he stood fifteen and a half hands[1] at the highest point of his shoulder blades—only five feet two inches from the ground. Some rivals towered over him like equine Jess Willards. Amused by how much this didn't matter, Hackett gave little Sir Barton a powerful nickname: "Dempsey."

Racing fans expected Dempsey-like punch from Sir Barton in the July 10 Dwyer Stakes at Aqueduct. First, however, they would see the young giant Man o' War, who already stood about two inches taller than Sir Barton. On July 5, Red would carry 130 pounds in the $6,000 Tremont Stakes. While making his fifth start in just under a month, he also would race six furlongs for the first time. He would do this on an afternoon when the temperature reached eighty-nine degrees, but he would face only two foes: Ralco, getting 15 pounds from Red this time, and Ace of Aces, a nonwinner added to the Tremont that morning because he could collect three hundred dollars for finishing third. Man o' War would spot him 18 pounds.

Fifteen thousand fans watched the three colts maneuver behind the barrier for roughly two minutes—about forty-seven seconds longer than the race would last. Suspense died almost immediately. Loftus let Man o' War dictate a brisk pace, staying a teasing length ahead of Ralco. Entering Aqueduct's extra-long homestretch, Red easily led by nearly two lengths as Ralco's jockey pushed like mad.

Man o' War galloped past the winning post without being asked for speed, one lazy length in front of Ralco and beating Ace of Aces by twenty-one. Red's 130 pounds became the highest weight ever carried by a Tremont winner, and yet—despite his running "all the way unextended"[2]—his time was a sharp 1:13. Impressed, the *New York Times* drew a comparison that eventually would become comical, dubbing young Man o' War "the best of the produce of Fair Play as yet to come to the races, with the possible exception of Stromboli."[3] To fans familiar with Stromboli's best efforts, ranking a juvenile winner of five races with a mature winner of such classics as the Metropolitan Handicap was a generous compliment.

Aside from his name figuring in any discussion of top two-year-olds, Man o' War would not make news during the rest of July. Anticipating rich opportunities at Saratoga in August, Sam Riddle and Lou Feustel decided not to race him any more this month. During the first five weeks of his career, their $5,000 colt had earned $16,175. They could well afford to let him freshen up for tougher races soon to come. Meanwhile, racetrack regulars had picked up the Glen Riddle crew's enhanced nickname for Man o' War. They were calling him "Big Red."[4]

Inside the racetrack world, the word *red* was still simply slang for a ruddy-coated horse. Outside the racetrack gates, Americans were preoccupied with other shades of meaning. Russia's Bolshevik Revolution in 1917 had linked red with communism—a political movement that most Americans viewed as a horrible threat. Now socialist-inspired workers' strikes and anarchist bombings were on the rise in the United States and widespread apprehension, which historians would label a "Red Scare," was increasing. Whether deliberately or subconsciously distancing Thoroughbred racing from such unpleasant imagery, reporters writing for the general public would not advertise Man o' War as Big Red during 1919.[5] They did, however, reveal unflattering news about his jockey.

Most racing fans called Johnny Loftus simply by his last name. He did not have a colorful nickname, nor did anyone at the track address him as "Mr. Loftus." Johnny Loftus had reached the top of his profession, wore expensive suits, and drove a pricey touring car, but his success didn't put him on equal terms with society men. Turf reporters still used the subordinate word *boy* interchangeably with the word *jockey*—sometimes even when writing about Loftus, who was now twenty-three years old.

Loftus did get unusual respect from Sam Riddle. Although the lord of Glen Riddle did not consider any jockey to be his social equal, he liked Loftus so well that a reporter would call Mr. Riddle "exceptionally fond"[6] of his first-call rider. The word "fond" suggests that Riddle's liking went beyond admiring his employee's riding skill. It is likely that he enjoyed the Loftus attitude: a mix of unguarded off-track playfulness and careful on-track ruthlessness.

Loftus maintained a clean reputation, but with regular hints of danger. In late June, he earned a traffic fine by careening his car wide around a curve and rear-ending a parked vehicle. A couple of weeks later, at Aqueduct, he displayed a similar technique with a filly named Ting-a-Ling, engineering a close finish by bumping her faster rival Housemaid out into the middle of the track. Again, his gamble failed. Housemaid still prevailed by a nose, and her jockey's foul tactics did not escape the stewards. They grounded Loftus for two days. Even so, they could have made his punishment far worse by adding one day. Three days after breaking rules with Ting-a-Ling, Loftus would ride Sir Barton in the Dwyer Stakes.

Time and again, Loftus pushed at rules that seemed possible to bend. He may have nudged reality in his favor during the fall of 1917, while claiming exemption from the military draft. With a wife and child to support, Loftus had a legitimate reason to stay home. Nevertheless, his birth year appeared on his registration card as 1894 instead of 1895—making him seem to be twenty-two instead of twenty-one years old. This difference pushed him slightly past the army's ideal age range.

Shortly before filing his draft card, Loftus had won a more daring gambit at Saratoga Race Course. Witnesses included Sam and Elizabeth Riddle, Sarah and Walter Jeffords, and The Jockey Club's confidential secretary, Algernon

Daingerfield. Loftus was riding a favorite, a horse named after baseball umpire Hank O'Day. As the field reached the starting post, someone placed a very large bet on him to win. Although reporters didn't name names, the big bettor may have been the equine Hank O'Day's owner, A. K. Macomber, who was watching from the Saratoga clubhouse and hoping for his first win of the meet.

Hank O'Day reached the final furlong in front, but a gelding named Quartz battled beside him, threatening to finish first. Loftus went to work. At the wire, Hank O'Day led Quartz by a neck. As the horses returned to be unsaddled, Macomber seemed to have his victory. Then Caldwell, the African-American jockey who had ridden Quartz, made a claim of foul to the track stewards. Moments later, Johnny Loftus was climbing up into the judges' stand for interrogation.

The judges didn't have the luxury of replaying films and studying the stretch run from various angles. They were forced to rely on what they had—or hadn't—seen as the horses flew by, then decide which jockey's testimony seemed most believable. They decided to believe Loftus and let the order of finish stand. Their choice rewarded Mr. Macomber but annoyed the general public. "While the explanation or denial made by Loftus was satisfactory to the stewards," the *New York Herald* reported, "it did not satisfy many spectators, who insisted that Loftus not only resorted to the almost forgotten leglock [*sic*] trick but cleverly used his whip to intimidate Quartz."[7]

Loftus had endured many close finishes without using forbidden tactics. This time, he perceived a risk worth taking. Riding for an especially powerful owner gave him leverage, and riding against Caldwell strengthened his advantage. New York racing had been discouraging black jockeys for nearly two decades. In 1900, the *New York Times* had noted that, "As a matter of fact, the negro [*sic*] jockey is down and out, not because he could no longer ride, but because of a quietly formed combination to shut him out. . . . It is a fact . . . that one Jockey Club official who had all but completed a contract with a negro jockey who rode successfully for him last season suddenly broke off negotiations and informed the rider in question that he would not be wanted."[8] When Johnny Loftus began riding in New York, he learned to exploit this prejudice. Compared with a well-connected white man like Loftus, Caldwell and the few other black jockeys still venturing North had little chance.

But despite his privileges, Loftus couldn't go easy on himself. During the midsummer of 1919, despite the heavy weights carried by Sir Barton and Man o' War, he was riding as light as 112 pounds—forcing his body under 110. When reaching his minimum weight, America's leading jockey lived on coffee, an occasional poached egg, and a daily slice of lean meat. In all respects, from selective rough riding to drastic dieting, Loftus ferociously protected his job. Ironically, his most accomplished partner had to be tricked and prodded into working at all. Sir Barton was, however, similarly fierce.

Although he respected tough characters, "Hard Guy" Bedwell did not claim that Sir Barton was a nice horse to be around. "I like Billy Kelly best, not because he is the best racehorse, but because he has the best disposition," Bedwell told the *Daily Racing Form* as the Dwyer Stakes drew near. "You can go into the stall and talk to Billy Kelly and you can go out on the track and talk to him and he will talk back to you or come as near it as a horse can. Sir Barton is different. If you go out into his stall he wants to take a bite at your arm or leg. He is full of life in the stall and a loafer on the track. I have an awful time getting him to work."[9] In fact, in workouts Bedwell got Sir Barton running fast enough to keep fit only by making two stablemates chase him in a sort of relay race. Without such provocation, Sir Barton would simply gorge on his high-energy racehorse food, work slowly, and rapidly gain weight.

Bedwell had even more trouble preparing Sir Barton for the July 10 Dwyer Stakes. On Dwyer morning, *Daily Racing Form* reported that the colt had been struggling with a bruised hoof and might not run that afternoon. Bedwell noted that although Sir Barton now was working all right, the injury had made him miss five days of training. Bedwell remained reluctant to start him in the Dwyer, but Commander Ross didn't want to miss a $6,000 race.

Rain sealed their decision. On Dwyer day, it poured so relentlessly that New York baseball parks closed in the early afternoon, washing a couple dozen star ball players and their most hardy fans over to Aqueduct. Meanwhile, the track transformed from hard to soft. Despite his recent soreness, Sir Barton should like the sloppy surface. Bedwell agreed to run him, on one condition: Commander Ross must not bet. This was a considerable reservation, because the Commander loved to wager and Sir Barton would face only two opponents: longshot Crystal Ford and Sam Hildreth's good colt, Purchase.

The Dwyer shouldn't be hard for Sir Barton, "Horse of the Decade," many fans thought. The colt they'd seen easily setting an American record in the Belmont Stakes should dominate this nine-furlong race, even carrying

127 pounds while Purchase carried 118. Sir Barton, a regular mud lark, would show them his heels from the start and they'd never catch up.

At first, expectations held true. "Splashing the water and ooze backward, as cheerily as a maiden churning butter," wrote the *New York Times*, "Sir Barton kept his pronounced lead to the mile. . . ." But then Purchase pounced. Suddenly, Purchase led by half a length while Loftus whipped Sir Barton uselessly. Four times in the past two months, Sir Barton had won "cantering," without Loftus ever waving the whip. Now that easygoing pattern shattered. Sir Barton ran flat out, but Purchase skipped away, winning by three lengths. Despite the sloppy track, his time beat Sir Barton's fast-track Preakness clocking by two-fifths. Instead of moving forward, Sir Barton was falling back.

"It was not a case of a popular idol being dethroned," the *Times* proclaimed; "it was worse than that, for no Bolsheviki could have knocked a reigning monarch from his pedestal more rudely than Purchase upset the Canadian colt."[10] Having failed as a source of American pride, Kentucky-bred and -born Sir Barton had suddenly become Canadian, like Commander Ross. The Commander, meanwhile, made no excuses for the defeat. "The horse is not quite as good just now as he has been," he admitted. "I was pleased to see him pull up sound."[11]

The Commander apparently disregarded the rail-hugging trip that Loftus had given Sir Barton—a ground-saving strategy that could backfire on a wet day. Like many racetracks, Aqueduct slanted slightly downward toward the inner rail, causing water to drain that way. Breaking quickly in the Dwyer, Sir Barton had grabbed and stuck to the extra-mucky inside path. In contrast, Purchase had made his rapid late rally on higher, drier ground.

No one punished Loftus for keeping Sir Barton near the soggy rail. He would soon come under fire, however, for his handling of a horse named Sun Briar.

Swamp Root patent medicine mogul Willis Sharpe Kilmer was notoriously fussy about his racehorses—Sun Briar, his favorite, in particular. When he was sound, this well-bred colt was one of the fastest Thoroughbreds in America. Unfortunately, however, Sun Briar had been intermittently lame for most of his life. "There was always a scent of ether when he was stripped before a race," track handicapper Walter Vosburgh recalled.[12] To unleash his speed, Sun Briar needed an anesthetic. Even that wasn't always enough. Preparing for the 1918 Kentucky Derby, he'd become too sore to run. Trainer Henry

McDaniel had persuaded Kilmer to start the lanky gelding Exterminator, purchased as a workmate for Sun Briar, instead. Exterminator won, beginning a rise to greatness that would land him—not Sun Briar—in the Hall of Fame. But Kilmer always believed that Sun Briar was the better horse, and for middle distances, he may have been right. Sun Briar won the classic Travers Stakes and ran two sizzling miles at Saratoga before going sore again.

Sun Briar spent the spring of 1919 at Kilmer's stud farm, staying in light training and breeding eighteen mares. Come summer, Kilmer and McDaniel asked a lot of him: return to his monk's cell on the backstretch and resume his racing career. Sun Briar responded remarkably well. Breezing seven furlongs at Aqueduct, he shaded 1:24. The track record was 1:23.

Bouncing out of this impressive work, Sun Briar moved to the upstart Empire City track in Yonkers. He entered the six-furlong Domino Handicap with a reputation so strong that, despite not having raced for ten months, he carried 130 pounds. Roamer, the American record holder for one mile, carried 114. The other two starters got in with 95.

At the top of the homestretch, Sun Briar broke away from the pack, living up to his star billing. Then Roamer sailed up on his outside, taunting him with fresh speed. While Loftus kicked and whipped Sun Briar, Roamer edged away. Sun Briar lost by three-quarters of a length. Roamer's winning time—on a surface rated "good," not "fast"—was only one second slower than the track record.

Reporters blamed Sun Briar's defeat on extra fat from his stud farm life. They figured that chasing Roamer had toned him up for his next race six days later, stretching out to a mile in Empire City's Mount Vernon Handicap. But afterward, a reporter wrote, "The Mount Vernon Handicap . . . will live long in the memory of the 8,000 race goers who saw the contest. . . . It will go down in turf history as one of the most unsatisfactory stake events of the decade."[13]

Strongly favored at 6–5, Sun Briar lost to Sam Hildreth's colt Lucullite by several easy lengths. The aged Old Rosebud, Kentucky Derby hero of 1914, overhauled Sun Briar for second place. The *New York Times* decreed that Sun Briar "plainly showed he needed another race or two to be fit."[14] But no one seemed certain why Lucullite had so quickly improved. Only two days earlier, racing the same distance as a 1–4 favorite, he had weakened and lost in the final fifty yards. Forty-eight hours later, Lucullite had rebounded wonderfully, and trainer Hildreth, if he had run true to his well-known gambling form, had cashed a healthy bet at 8–5 odds. Adding to the surprise, the way Johnny Loftus had managed Sun Briar looked strange.

While Lucullite set the early pace, Loftus had restrained Sun Briar in second place and held the rail position. Suddenly, entering the far turn and still keeping Sun Briar under restraint, he'd surrendered the rail advantage. Cornering wide, Sun Briar had opened the inner path for Old Rosebud. Entering the homestretch, he'd moved wider still while Old Rosebud continued straight. At the wire, Old Rosebud had led Sun Briar by one length—less ground than Sun Briar had given away. The next day, the Empire City stewards summoned Loftus to explain this generosity. They also questioned trainers Henry McDaniel and Sam Hildreth.

The stewards knew that one of racing's unspoken traditions was the "No" day and the "Go" day. Gambling horsemen might tell the jockey No if the horse was fit to win but the odds were sinking too low, then Go when the recently defeated fit horse became a longer shot. Now they had to investigate the possibility that Sam Hildreth had used this strategy with Lucullite and had induced Johnny Loftus to keep Sun Briar out of his way. They also had to consider whether Loftus, finishing a close third after floating wide, had done enough to protect bettors who had wagered on Sun Briar for second place.

Although the details of these interviews remained private, the public soon learned that the stewards had found Hildreth innocent. McDaniel apparently did not face any accusations, but he served to back up or refute what Loftus said. Loftus, meanwhile, gave no public statement about why Sun Briar had run wide. Horses sometimes drift outward when they're feeling sore or getting tired, but Loftus apparently did not blame his horse. Instead, he blamed himself for a bad ride, while adding that McDaniel had told him not to press the early pace.[15] Restraining Sun Briar for the first six furlongs, he had been following orders and honoring The Jockey Club License Committee's instructions "not to get into further trouble with his employers even in minor matters."[16]

Two days after the Mount Vernon Handicap, an exonerated Johnny Loftus was riding races again. But for the Empire City meet, trouble was just beginning. The most sensational story starred Man o' War's big sister, Masda.

Having opened her four-year-old season with two victories, Masda loomed as the likely favorite for Empire City's Primrose Handicap. When the day arrived, she couldn't run. That morning of Wednesday, July 23, a handler walked into Masda's stall and discovered blood "flowing freely"[17] down her left front leg. Apparently, someone had attacked Masda with a knife and barely missed making her permanently lame.

That Wednesday, while racetrackers spread this scary information, they also heard a Tuesday horror story. A two-year-old filly named Beck and Call had been a leading choice in Empire City's first race on July 22. "Hard ridden,"[18] she ran in second place for about thirty seconds, then dropped back abruptly and finished seventh of eight. Sister Helene, unexpectedly sent off as the 9–5 favorite, romped in front from start to finish—"showing radical improvement,"[19] according to the *Daily Racing Form*. It looked bad. More accurately, it smelled bad. By Wednesday, rumor claimed that a sponge had been found in Beck and Call's nose. This gave horsemen and the betting public plenty to fear.

Sponging was a cruel and invisible way to make a racehorse lose. Because horses can't breathe by mouth, pushing a small sponge far up into one nostril shuts off half of the horse's air supply. Often the sponged horse shows no symptoms until galloping at racing speed. Then, with the horse trying to inhale five gallons of air every second, tremendous need for oxygen hurtles the horse into distress. Some horses recover from this trauma. Others are ruined.

Threatened by sponge and knife, Empire City scrambled to safeguard horse health and public confidence. Meanwhile, Saratoga racing officials reacted like a king watching his food taster go into convulsions. It was bad enough that ordinary Empire City might be stricken with horse tampering. It would be disastrous if wrongdoers infiltrated the prestigious Saratoga meet, now barely more than a week away. Horses already stabled there included Man o' War.

Soothing their patrons and warning wrongdoers, Saratoga racing officials quickly publicized their plan. At the Spa, only registered workers with ID cards could go near the stables at night. "The lack of one of these registration cards," the local newspaper *The Saratogian* noted, "will be evidence enough to have the person locked up as a trespasser."[20] Unmentioned in publicity, and beyond ID card control, was possible sabotage by legitimately registered employees.

But were Saratoga officials getting riled up over nothing?

Three days after Masda's injury, Dr. McCully reported that her cuts weren't caused by a knife-wielding gambler but, rather, by a stray piece of baling wire in her bedding or hay. "I also examined the filly Beck and Call," McCully wrote, "and found no evidences of sponging."[21] The doc had examined Beck and Call, however, more than twenty-four hours after her poor race. Because so much time had passed, he couldn't absolutely prove that no sponge had ever been in her nose. That room for uncertainty remained Thoroughbred racing's thorniest public-relations problem. Because cheating was possible, the world could believe the worst—even without proof.

New York newspapers leaped on Dr. McCully's reassuring report. "Many ills are charged to racing which exist only in the minds of the super-suspicious," turf writer George Daley maintained. "It is easy to accuse an owner, trainer or jockey of sharp practice, but it is not so easy to prove. Horses are not machines, and the best of jockeys make mistakes."[22] The *New York Times,* while expressing relief at Dr. McCully's findings, remained uneasy. "There has not been a time in years when a watchful eye was more needed than now," an editorial writer declared. "Racing is sweeping on a new wave of popularity. . . . But it is just this state of prosperity which invites crookedness and tampering from that element which cares nothing for the sport beyond personal gain. There are always a few men of this type ready to take advantage of any carelessness on the part of the officials."[23]

Empire City's officials quickly became strict. During the meet's final three days, they would suspend three jockeys for rough riding and the *New York World* newspaper would pretend that "No" and "Go" tactics had been erased from Thoroughbred racing. "In the old days it used to be said that the horses of some stables on the parade to the post used to crane their necks giraffewise into the [bookmakers'] ring and read the prices on the slates," the *World* admitted. "But those days are dead and gone."[24]

The *World* could have borrowed a more accurate line from Mark Twain: "The report of my death was an exaggeration." Even George Daley, while cautioning against unverified accusations, also recommended vigilance. "There is need—crying need for a paid steward, a man of strong character and racing knowledge," he wrote. "But day in and day out the sport is more carefully guarded than some critics would have us believe. Many a word is spoken, many a warning given to jockey or trainer which is never published."[25]

As the Empire City meet neared its end, Johnny Loftus didn't ride as if he needed warnings. In the July 26 East View Stakes, he gave a master class with Kentucky invader Miss Jemima—a precocious filly that many Kentuckians were calling "the greatest two-year-old of the season."[26] Controlling the pace, Loftus kept Miss Jemima narrowly in front. Heading into the stretch, her early pursuer fell back, but a colt named Feodor charged forward. "Within a hundred yards of the finish Miss Jemima was doing her level best and Feodor was still coming on gamely," the *New York Times* reported. "Loftus gave his mount every assistance within the power of a jockey, and the fine ride got her home."[27]

After that bravura performance, Johnny Loftus took the rest of the week off. While Empire City battled unproven threats, Loftus had been fighting an all-too-tangible foe: his weight. His struggle resembled the mythical clash between Hercules and the monstrous multiheaded Hydra, which grew two new heads whenever Hercules chopped off one. Hercules finally killed the Hydra by burning the neck stump every time he cut off a head. Loftus could only keep his multiplying pounds at bay temporarily, soaking and resoaking them off in a desert-hot Turkish bath. But August, more than any other month, could make his fight worthwhile. At Saratoga, he would ride high-weighted horses in several of America's richest races. To win impressive prize money, he would not have to ride often.

Eleanor Loftus preceded her husband to Saratoga Springs, renting a modern house barely more than a block from the Riddles' gigantic cottage. The location was beautifully convenient to Saratoga Race Course and its adjacent training track. Other racetrackers enjoyed living farther from their workplace. Jockey Bill Knapp and his family settled into a spacious Victorian several blocks farther from the track and training grounds, near Lake Avenue, a thoroughfare named in honor of a popular retreat several miles southeast of Saratoga Springs: Saratoga Lake.

Saratoga Lake beckoned to official starter Mars Cassidy. Cassidy had been christened Marshall, but his god of war nickname was equally apt. As sportswriter Red Smith would recall, "Mars was distinguished by a high bowler hat, handlebar mustaches, a temper that boiled at 98.6 degrees and a vocabulary that would bring blushes to the foredeck of a Portuguese freighter."[28] This forceful personality helped Cassidy excel at managing the starts of horse races. His fun-loving appetite also made him an enthusiastic patron of bars and cockfights. It therefore was no surprise that during Saratoga's 1919 meet, Cassidy returned to Tom Luther's White Sulphur Springs resort on the east shore of Saratoga Lake. Although families made up a wholesome percentage of Luther's clientele, the lake area offered everything from a local snack food named "potato chips" to casinos and bordellos nestled under the evergreens. In fact, Saratoga Lake helped to inspire a party town built up by Eastern gangsters in the West: Las Vegas.

As Saratoga's 1919 race meet neared, Saratoga Lake danced around the edge of antivice laws. Officially, the United States was going dry. After circulating for only thirteen months, the Eighteenth Amendment to the U.S. Constitution had been ratified on January 29. While senators and congressmen wrestled with how to enforce the upcoming nationwide ban on transporting and selling alcohol, Mars Cassidy took up residence at Luther's lake house. He chose a hotelier resourceful enough to outfit a touring boat with a "real old time bar—everything you could want."[29] Saratoga—catering to tourists unwilling to ditch their drinking pleasures—welcomed a soon-to-be-hidden world.

For generations, Saratoga Springs had supplied guilty pleasures without apologies. The town's first racetrack, a trotting course opened beside the state fairgrounds in 1847, technically stood just outside the city line. While happy crowds that patronized the local restaurants and hotels traveled the broad avenue from downtown to the track, city government could claim to antigambling agitators that the sinful attraction operated outside its jurisdiction.

By 1863, racing flourished more brazenly as four wealthy partners sponsored a brief Thoroughbred meet at the old trotting track. The moneymaking prospects proved so promising that the partners opened a full-fledged course across the street in 1864. Over the next fifty-five years, August in Saratoga grew into American racing's most distinctive meet. The mineral-water resort founded for invalids and their attendants had become a playground for healthy adults from highest society to regular folks on holiday. Inevitably, the prodigious cash flow also attracted racketeers. In 1918, Arnold Rothstein converted a Saratoga mansion into an exclusive casino, and wealthy patrons began whispering about his underground connections. Nonetheless, his business thrived.

With the Great War ended and entertainment dollars surging into town, Saratoga expected to reach new heights for its 1919 meet. The Saratoga Association for the Improvement of the Breed of Horses told its racecourse superintendent to "spare no expense in making the track the most beautiful in the country."[30] That August, patrons would see fresh paint and additional flower beds. Racing officials would find a handsome iron fence, instead of a wire barrier, surrounding the judges' stand. And the horses—more than 2,200 of them, drawn from the best stables in Kentucky, Maryland, New York, and Canada—would serve up the best racing in America. Because the competition came from such a wide area and the audience included European tourists as well as North Americans, horse owners viewed winning a race here as a special feat.

Hoping for notable success, Glen Riddle Farm brought more than thirty runners to Saratoga Race Course. Man o' War, along with being unbeaten, stood apart from his stablemates in an even more unusual way. "As yet Man o' War has not been touched by a whip," *Daily Racing Form* noted. "In his last two races Johnny Loftus shook his whip at him to prevent him from loafing in the homestretch, but that is as near as the rawhide has come to him."[31]

But this didn't convince certain horse owners that Man o' War would not lose.

August Belmont, Jr., *left,* and his wife, Eleanor Robson Belmont, with Massachusetts governor David I. Walsh on July 29, 1914, at the opening of the Cape Cod Canal.

Fair Play, sire of Man o' War, seen here as
an aged stallion.

Mahubah, dam of Man o' War.

Trainer Louis Feustel with three-year-old Man o' War. The chain running through the colt's mouth is strong restraint.

The sometimes irascible Samuel D. Riddle and his gracious wife, Elizabeth Dobson Riddle.

Kennelard-Cook

In his prime as a jockey: Johnny Loftus.

George S. Bolster Collection, Historical Society of Saratoga Spring / C. C. Cook photograph

Starting a race, Man o' War and his opponents used the same system shown here: Assistant starters wielding long whips herded the horses into line behind a long, thin net known as the barrier. No photographs of Man o' War at the barrier have been found.

H. G. "Hard Guy" Bedwell, *left*, and Comdr. John Kenneth Leveson Ross at Saratoga in 1918.

A famously honest jockey who became a star while riding for the Ross stable: Earl Sande.

Sir Barton after winning the 1919 Kentucky Derby, with Johnny Loftus in the saddle. On the ground, trainer Bedwell holds his colt's bridle.

This excerpt from an August 10, 1919, *New York Times* photo spread juxtaposes young Man o' War, *right,* with the impressive three-year-old colt Purchase. Each has Johnny Loftus in the saddle.

August 1919: two-year-old Man o' War in the Saratoga paddock with, *from left,* groom Frank Loftus; Sam Riddle's brother, Leander; jockey Johnny Loftus; Samuel Doyle Riddle; and trainer Louis Feustel.

An early image of Man o' War in a race: romping home first in the United States Hotel Stakes at Saratoga, with Upset in second place.

Kraneland-Cook

Upset and Bill Knapp, near the rail, beat Man o' War and Johnny Loftus to the finish line in the Sanford Memorial Stakes. Golden Broom trails in third.

New York Racing Association

Following outrider "Red Coat" Murray and cranking his neck up like a periscope, Man o' War leads the post parade for the 1919 Futurity Stakes at Belmont Park. Note the signboard marking the special finish line used for the Suburban Handicap and the Belmont Stakes.

International photo / Courtesy of Colleen Andrepont

Guiding Man o' War back to the stands after winning the Futurity, Johnny Loftus indulges in a smile.

Man o' War's husky partner for the 1920 racing
season: Clarence Kummer.

A gleeful Clarence Kummer and slender Man o' War, after victory in the Belmont Stakes. Groom Frank
Loftus clips a lead shank onto Red's bridle.

At the finish of the Stuyvesant Handicap, Man o' War literally leaves Yellow Hand in the dust.

Man o' War and Kummer before the Dwyer Stakes.

Man o' War outgames John P. Grier in the Dwyer Stakes.

An alert Man o' War follows Major Treat, with Lou Feustel aboard, to the track for a workout. Other Glen Riddle runners fall into line behind Big Red.

Leaning back in the saddle and keeping a short rein, exercise rider Clyde Gordon tells Man o' War to slow down.

Sam Riddle and Lou Feustel in a contemplative moment at the barn.

Dressed up at the races, Feustel and Riddle exude confidence.

Sir Barton, with Earl Sande up, overwhelms Exterminator and
sets a track record in the 1920 Saratoga Handicap.

Man o' War and Sande after winning the Miller Stakes.

Elizabeth and Sam Riddle at Saratoga in 1920.

Bound for Canada, Man o' War settles into his special railroad car. Attendants include Lou Feustel, *second from left,* Clyde Gordon *at back of stall,* Frank Loftus *inside front of stall,* and stable foreman George Conway, *far right.*

Racing clockwise at Belmont Park, Man o' War enjoys an easy lead over Hoodwink soon after the Lawrence Realization start. About 2½ minutes later, he would reach the same spot with energy to spare and Hoodwink roughly 100 lengths behind him.

The great match race: Man o' War draws away from Sir Barton.

While Man o' War wins the match race, gearing down, many spectators look surprised at the long margin back to Sir Barton.

Feustel and Riddle hold the Gold Cup for a thirsty Man o' War.

Man o' War as a seven-year-old stallion, with groom Will Harbut. This image is acclaimed as the best conformation shot—a photograph accurately showing a horse's physical structure—ever taken of Big Red.

This widely seen *Saturday Evening Post* cover photo by Ivan Dmitri revealed the trust and affection that Will Harbut and Man o' War shared.

Regular exercise under saddle during his many years at stud kept Man o' War—shown here nearing twenty years old—in excellent condition long after his racing career was over.

Left: Early in his new career as a trainer, Johnny Loftus leans on the shoulder of his employer, Clendenin Ryan. *Middle:* During the summer of 1930, while hoping to restart his jockey career, Clarence Kummer performs the entry-level racetrack job of hotwalking a horse. *Right:* Twenty years after Man o' War's epic three-year-old season, seventy-eight-year-old Samuel Doyle Riddle regales a reporter with stories of Big Red.

Man o' War's larger-than-life-sized statue at his original burial site, in his paddock at Faraway Farm (photograph taken November 6, 1953).

7

RUNNIN' FOOLS

There are a half dozen horsemen who believe they have a colt or filly which can beat Man o' War," a *Daily Racing Form* reporter noted in mid-July.[1] These optimistic horsemen included John E. Madden, breeder of Sir Barton, and Harry Payne Whitney, perennial producer of top two-year-olds. The *Form* failed to mention the horse*woman* who believed that her colt could beat Man o' War. But Sarah Jeffords would attract attention soon enough. She shipped Golden Broom to Saratoga for his racing debut.

While Man o' War gathered five victories and increasingly high praise, Sarah had continued to believe that she owned a better horse. Until Golden Broom's hoof and ankle healed, she could only wait to prove it. But now Mike Daly indicated that her favorite colt was fit, and anyone could see that he looked like a possible champion. Although Man o' War was tall for a two-year-old, Golden Broom stood a shade taller and sported an even more muscular physique. But would he still have superior speed? And would he show the will to win?

As August approached, Sam Riddle and Sarah Jeffords began a diplomatic dance. Either Golden Broom or Man o' War might dominate Saratoga's richest two-year-old races—but why push each other competing for the same prizes? Mike Daly suggested that Golden Broom enter half of the best stakes, Man o' War the other half. Let the Jeffordses and Riddles share the wealth and prestige by staying out of each other's way.

The proposed compromise died instantly. Sam Riddle would race Man o' War anytime he wished.

Sarah Jeffords may have tried to make her uncle reconsider by demonstrating her colt's ability. On the Sunday morning of July 27, Golden Broom and Man o' War stepped together onto Saratoga's main track. For the first time since their training-farm trials, they would test each other's speed. Three furlongs would reveal who had the upper hand.

The Jeffords team knew that Golden Broom, incredibly fast at the break, could build a decisive lead in his first few jumps. Sure, Johnny Loftus had now taught Man o' War the flying start. But Loftus, who had ridden at Empire City the previous afternoon and then had a long journey to Saratoga, was not available that morning. Would Red carry Harry Vititoe instead? Apparently unconcerned, the Jeffords team entrusted Golden Broom to a stable boy known as "Whitey." Then the Riddle team delivered a masterstroke: giving the leg up on Man o' War to a brilliant rider known as "Cal," for the way his first name sounded in his Texas drawl. Carroll "Cal" Shilling's extreme talent as a jockey eventually would land him in the Hall of Fame. His extreme tactics also spawned stories that he could handle three runners in one race: "a [rival] horse in each hand, and his own."[2]

Although The Jockey Club had stripped Shilling of his jockey license in 1912, racing men reckoned that his skill remained unsurpassed. As an assistant trainer and exercise boy, Shilling still appeared on the track every morning, wrangling the toughest horses in "Hard Guy" Bedwell's stable. He also remained famous for his "almost uncanny ability"[3] to launch two-year-olds into a high-speed start.

It didn't matter that Shilling hadn't ridden Man o' War before. He knew the key to winning this three-furlong dash: start fast and keep it up. In his expert hands, Man o' War quickly collared Golden Broom despite his rival's lightning strides. "Red's got him!"[4] Frank Loftus yelled as Red edged ahead and stopwatches caught his first furlong in eleven seconds flat. Golden Broom didn't falter but couldn't gain. Holding a narrow lead, Red sped the quarter mile in :22.

And Golden Broom was still there, pressing Man o' War harder than any of his five official races had. Stretching out, Red ran his third furlong as strong as the first, leading by nearly his full body length as they flew past the finish line. Watches snapped: thirty-three seconds flat. The official world record, set by an older horse, was :33 1/2.

Even pulling up, Man o' War ran a fast half mile. While Golden Broom dropped about three lengths behind, clockers caught Red galloping out in anything from a very quick :46 2/5 to an otherworldly :45 and one.

Sam Riddle was now certain that no other two-year-old could touch Man o' War. Sarah Jeffords was not. Without racing experience or a champion rider, her colt had come *so close*. Now she would let him gain experience before challenging Man o' War in an official race. Red would start next in the August 2 United States Hotel Stakes. Golden Broom would enter an August 4 maiden race and then the August 9 Saratoga Special, which Feustel had overlooked when nominating Man o' War for Saratoga stakes. After that, the Jeffords team would choose the best time to challenge Riddle's champion. Meanwhile, *The Saratogian* gave perspective to Golden Broom's unofficial defeat: "Of course Man o' War had some advantage in that he had Carroll Shilling on his back. Shilling is credited with being able to make a horse travel faster in a workout than any other rider who ever straddled one."[5]

Two days after Man o' War dusted Golden Broom, Johnny Loftus breezed him a solid six furlongs in 1:13 4/5. *The Saratogian* reported that "this wonderful big colt was feeling fine and as playful as a kitten," and added, "Loftus thinks Man o' War the greatest 2-year-old of the year."[6] Johnny's opinion was newsworthy because there still was room for dispute. On Saratoga's opening day, Friday, August 1, Kentucky star Miss Jemima strengthened her case by beating Harry Payne Whitney's promising colt Wildair while giving him 17 pounds.

Twenty-four hours later, Man o' War started in the race that would confirm him as the rising champion or drop him behind someone else. Honoring one of Saratoga's mammoth hotels, the $10,000 United States Hotel Stakes offered twice as much money as any event Red had entered and notably stronger competition: Bonnie Mary, who had dashed five furlongs at Aqueduct in :58 2/5; Carmandale, a stakes winner at Empire City; and Upset—like Red, a winner at Belmont Park—from Harry Payne Whitney's formidable string, trained by the astute Jimmy Rowe. Upset must be the most forward of Whitney's precocious two-year-olds, the *New York Herald* deduced, to be sent after this big purse. In preparation, Upset had worked six furlongs in 1:13 flat—four-fifths of a second faster than Man o' War's breeze the same morning.

On United States Hotel Stakes day, freshly beautified Saratoga Race Course thrummed with festive energy. Not only would Man o' War race but Sir Barton was entered in the Kenner Stakes. A reporter noted that "a vast crowd of horse lovers came swarming in by road and rail from cities, villages and hamlets for one hundred miles around" and "Club house, grandstand, lawn and free field were black with people intent upon obtaining places from which to view this promised conjunction of star performers. . . ."[7] In the gala atmosphere, Sam and Elizabeth Riddle entered a new dimension of horse ownership. Never had one of their runners been favored in a major stakes in front of such a large audience, or in such a prestigious place.

Furthermore, Man o' War became the main attraction when the crowd learned that Sir Barton wouldn't race after all. "Just what ails the great colt nobody seems to know," a reporter lamented. "He is as sound as a bell of brass, his golden chestnut coat shines like satin, he eats as well as any horse in training and seems in every way himself except that he has lost his wonderful turn of speed."[8] In fact, Bedwell simply had decided to give hard-worked Sir Barton an overdue rest. Commander Ross could win the Kenner with his good filly Milkmaid instead. But Man o' War would dominate the headlines.

On a clear, warm afternoon relieved by a cool breeze, Man o' War shouldered 130 pounds for the third straight time. Not caring that Red gave his rivals as much as 18 pounds, bookmakers sent him off at odds of 9–10. Bonnie Mary, hoisting 127 pounds, started as the second choice at 4 1/2–1. Upset, getting 15 pounds from Man o' War, became third choice at 6–1. Six other lightweights completed the field.

Lining up to run six furlongs, Upset in post position one and Bonnie Mary beside him could inherit the shortest trip in the one-turn race. Man o' War, however, would start eight lanes out from the inside track. To avoid getting floated wide around the turn, he would have to break faster than the seven runners to his left, quickly outrun them, and cut in front of them. Loftus had anticipated this kind of disadvantage when he taught Man o' War the flying start. On this day, though, Red overreacted. Once, then twice, he broke through the barrier. "On one occasion he ran a hundred yards," the *New York Times* remarked, "before Loftus could pull him up."[9] Responding to his jockey's urgency, Man o' War was becoming a rogue.

Suddenly, Loftus got it right. After six minutes of turmoil, Red sailed under the barrier while most of his opponents stood flat-footed. Only Carmandale at Red's left side, with jockey Laverne Fator watching Loftus, leapt forward with him. Fator and Loftus steered Carmandale and Man o' War toward the inside, with Upset settling into third place and the other runners "some distance back and struggling along in a mass."[10] Bonnie Mary, gifted with post two, had broken last of all.

Carmandale hit high gear, but the long-legged colt to his outside rolled by him. "Getting over the ground with the same loose, slippery, reaching stride that has always enabled him to easily run away from every two-year-old he has met," a *New York Herald* reporter wrote, "Man o' War struck a clip which had the speedy Carmandale's head swimming at the end of the first quarter. . . ."[11] Opening a three-length lead, Red motored that first quarter in :23 flat. Meanwhile, Bonnie Mary, hustled away from her bad start, closed "an immense gap"[12] from tenth to fifth place. But running hard into Red's quick pace would cost her later in the race.

As the field entered the far turn, the crowd easily picked out Man o' War's black-and-yellow silks well ahead of the pack. Upset moved up from third place, overtaking Carmandale, but his light blue and brown silks remained three lengths behind the yellow and black. Bonnie Mary inched into fourth place, running extra yards in her outside position, while Red skimmed along alone by the rail, hitting the half-mile point in a brisk but personally comfortable :47 and one. He had run faster half miles over the deep surface of Belmont Park's training track.

Charging out of the turn, Eddie Ambrose urged Upset for all he was worth—"a game but hopeless effort," the *New York Times* would say. "Man o' War was running just as fast there as he had in the beginning. . . ."[13] In fact, Red was slowing down—he would saunter the last quarter mile in :25 1/5— but his rapid early pace had built a buffer zone. While Red only cruised, his opponents had pressed their limits as they tried to keep within striking distance. In the final quarter mile, no pursuer had enough energy to catch him. Upset, driving hard, stalled about three lengths behind. Nearing the wire, the Whitney colt seemed to vault forward only because Loftus began pulling Red up, winning by two most casual lengths. In a clubhouse box, a delighted Sam Riddle patted his wife's shoulder while a reporter noticed, "Tears of joy actually ran down her cheeks. . . ."[14] Elizabeth Riddle was so carried away that Sam said he "had to run away from her" to keep her from kissing him in full view of the crowd.[15]

An energetic Man o' War and eight tired opponents galloped out around the clubhouse turn, slowing gently, then coming back near the finish line for unsaddling. As Man o' War approached, Sam and Elizabeth Riddle received their greatest racetrack reward yet: applause throughout the famous Saratoga clubhouse and grandstand for their horse. The acclaim in that moment and in subsequent news reports would soak into them like a baptism, transforming

how they experienced the world. Because of this Saturday-afternoon triumph, people who rarely visited a racetrack would begin to recognize their
names. Regular racing fans would begin paying more attention to Glen Riddle Farm. And sportsmen who had won top races many times would greet the
Riddles in two special new ways: as winners of a $10,000 race, and as owners
of a colt that any one of them would have been proud to own.

Red had become the first United States Hotel Stakes winner to carry 130
pounds, and his official time of 1:12 2/5 for six furlongs tied the stakes record.
The *New York Times* noted that he won "in such a convincing manner as to
surprise even some of those who had been sounding his praise."[16] But a back-
lash accompanied his triumph.

"For some reason Mars Cassidy gives Loftus more liberties at the barrier
than any other boy," reporter George Daley announced. "At least, this is the
talk on the lawn and in the paddock."[17] Trainers and gamblers whose horses
stood flat-footed while Man o' War jump-started the race complained that
this was unfair. Why had Cassidy let Loftus break through the barrier re-
peatedly without suspending him? Why hadn't he made an assistant starter
restrain Man o' War? Why had he finally let Man o' War go when only one
other horse was ready, instead of calling a false start?

George Daley guessed that the restless Man o' War wouldn't tolerate being
handled by an assistant starter. He also noted that trainer Max Hirsch, after
seeing his filly, Homely, caught off guard at the start and beaten a single
length for second place, blamed her jockey "for not meeting the situation
which arose at the barrier, and breaking away with Loftus. With a $10,000
fixture at stake he seemed to feel with many others that Loftus had things too
much his own way."[18]

Loftus certainly had an advantage that the complainers overlooked. Having
watched Cassidy signal starts for nearly nine years, he knew something about
Mars that often helped him beat the barrier.

Two days after Man o' War's smashing Spa debut, Golden Broom raced for
the first time. He appeared in a low-profile spot, the last event on a Monday
afternoon. This modest competition would season him for Saturday's Saratoga
Special. Although physically fit, he needed to learn about the disorienting experience of running in a race.

Going out to race with fourteen other colts and fillies, Golden Broom
found himself surrounded by a hubbub. He wore blinkers—the badge of a

colt that startled easily or needed help keeping his mind on business. But despite his inexperience, Golden Broom started as third choice in the betting. "With speed enough to make Man o' War stretch his neck in their work," a reporter noted, "the tip went all around in the club house and among the box holders. . . ."[19] It also helped that he carried a skimpy 109 pounds and had capable Eddie Ambrose in the irons. It did not help that he broke from post position fifteen.

For about three minutes, fifteen two-year-olds jostled behind the barrier. Finally released, Golden Broom broke just behind Hasten On and My Laddie. Within the first furlong, he rushed up to second place at My Laddie's heels. He was easily in contention and gaining, with less than half a mile to run. But just as he began looking like a winner, Golden Broom neared a place known as "the gap," where a gate through the outer rail let horses pass back and forth between their stables and the track. The gap offered escape from the noisy, crowded race. Golden Broom bolted toward the familiar exit to his right, toward the path to his safe, quiet stall.

Ambrose managed to steady him as opponents rushed past to their inside. Whipping Golden Broom's right side, Ambrose startled him leftward and forward again, back into the shouting, crowding, riptide. Losing no ground now but gaining little, Broom finished fourth.

Sarah Jeffords wasn't giving up on the Saratoga Special, but her talented colt clearly needed more schooling. After the races on Friday afternoon, Mike Daly brought Golden Broom onto the main track to practice sprinting past the gap. He deployed Doctor Johnson, a speedy older horse, to run at Broom's right-hand side and pin him near the inner rail. Even so, Broom tried to run wide. He was looking like a poster child for insecurity.

Meanwhile, a week into the meet, Saratoga backstretch workers finally received their ID cards. "In addition to this some of the larger stables have arranged for at least two watchmen," a reporter noted, "and owners may now rest assured that their thoroughbreds [sic] will have everything done to make them safe from any attempts that might be made against them."[20] The most watchful owners included Glen Riddle Farm. Every night, stable foreman George Conway slept in a stall next door to Man o' War.

The colt who had dug trenches under his stall door as an untrained yearling had various outlets for his energy now. He had the job of exercising every morning and racing during some afternoons. He had daily companionship from Frank Loftus, Major Treat, and an Airedale terrier that spent many hours in his stall. Stable hands paid him extra attention, and Johnny Loftus had formed a relationship that went well beyond sitting in the saddle and telling him what to do. Visiting the Glen Riddle barn one day during the Saratoga meet, journalist Henry V. King saw Red's rider "boxing" with Man o' War. "The jockey shot right and left taps to his nose," King wrote, "but they didn't make the colt back away. He 'ducked' a few, took the others good naturedly and often countered with his head. Many times his head struck the jockey, but his head blows weren't any harder than were the taps he received from his rider. He knew he was playing and didn't want his 'blows' to hurt. For ten minutes the sparring bout lasted. Then the command, 'That's enough, Red,' caused the colt to back away."[21]

During quiet hours, however, Red's nervous energy wiggled out in odd ways. After lying down in the evening, he would bite his hooves. Frank Loftus had to put "a protection"[22] on each foot so that the colt wouldn't bite them "down to the quick." Also, thanks to the gap under the chest-high webbing across his door, Red broke the boundaries of his stall during his most vulnerable interludes. "When he relaxed," Frank noted, "he used to lay with his head out in the aisle."[23]

Horses do most of their sleeping while standing up, so that they can run away at the first hint of danger.[24] In a safe environment, however, they will lie down for several minutes of total relaxation. Living outdoors in a herd, horses take turns lying down to sleep while their companions stand guard against predators. While most horses feel protected living inside wooden walls, Man o' War did not perceive anyone guarding his deepest sleep. With his head resting on the ground outside his stall door—a blink away from seeing anyone who might approach—Red created his own sense of security.

Bill Knapp could have testified that there was no such thing as security at a racetrack. During the afternoon of August 1, Knapp rode Purchase to victory in the $7,000 Saratoga Handicap. The next morning, a feisty two-year-old named Leviathan bolted out of control with Knapp during a workout, breaking through a wooden fence. Both were lucky to emerge alive and without serious injuries.

One week after Leviathan could have killed him, Bill Knapp enjoyed one of the rewards that kept him race riding. He and Johnny Loftus rode the two favorites in the Champlain Handicap—and Loftus had instructions to let

Knapp win. Even better, The Jockey Club didn't mind. Their arrangement was perfectly legal under the "declaration to win" rule.

An owner running two or more horses in the same race could choose which one would finish first, after telling the racetrack officials and the public which horse the stable favored. This requirement traced to Man o' War's great-grandsire Spendthrift, who became 1879's champion three-year-old. When James R. Keene bought Spendthrift late in 1878, he already had wagered that his horse Dan Sparling would win the 1879 Withers Stakes. And win Dan did, with his stablemate Spendthrift "pulled double"[25] so as not to spoil Keene's bet. Outrage from unsuspecting Spendthrift supporters then inspired the declaration to win rule.

The declaration helped Willis Sharpe Kilmer follow his heart. If the Champlain Handicap finish came down to Sun Briar and Exterminator, Kilmer could be sure that his beloved Sun Briar would win. Their jockeys performed perfectly. With Knapp driving hard, Sun Briar finished first by one length. Exterminator finished with his neck bowed, his chin almost bumping his chest. Exterminator could have won, most observers thought, but Loftus had followed orders.

Newspapers praised Knapp for a good ride. They also reported that Mr. Kilmer gave trainer McDaniel a $1,000 bonus and $500 each to Knapp and Loftus. No one discussed how much money a jockey could get from honestly making a horse lose.

Thirty minutes before the Sun Briar and Exterminator show, close to 25,000 spectators enjoyed the Saratoga Special. Sarah Jeffords would be vindicated or deflated in front of the biggest crowd at the meet so far. Some trainers were saying that Golden Broom was ouchy, could break down at any time. The betting crowd remembered his violent swerve toward the outer rail only five days earlier, just when he'd looked ready for a winning move. Fast as anything, everyone knew—but could you trust him?

Golden Broom's demeanor didn't inspire confidence. Unlike Man o' War, enthusiastic whenever he went out to race, Broom acted reluctant. An assistant starter had to urge him up to the barrier and hold him there. Bettors who favored Harry Payne Whitney's entry of Wildair and Panoply, or the fast filly Bonnie Mary, had to be feeling confident. But Sam Riddle, learning that Golden Broom would start beside the inner rail, proclaimed, "That settles it!"[26]

"And Mr. Riddle was right," the *New York Herald* reported. "Though standing flatfooted, with a starter's assistant holding him, Golden Broom bounded away like a startled stag. . . ."[27] Within twelve seconds, he led by four lengths. "He drew away from the others so rapidly," the *New York Times* noted, "that it was apparent it would be no contest unless he ran wide."[28] Golden Broom behaved.

At the head of the stretch, Wildair loomed within a length of Golden Broom. His challenge hovered bright and brief as a soap bubble. Ambrose let out a wrap on his reins and it was all Golden Broom, unleashing a fresh level of speed that horsemen in the age of motorcars came to call "another gear." Ambrose took him to the finish line like Loftus with Man o' War, all alone, looking over his shoulder to confirm that this was no contest at all. "The victory of Golden Broom was as impressive as any Man o' War has gained," the *New York Times* declared, "and was attained in as select a field as the Glen Riddle Farm's youngster has met."[29]

A few experts remained cautious. Turf reporter "Exile" wrote, "Is he of the same class as Man o' War, this [is] the moot question [to which] time and patience must give the answer."[30]

Time and patience be damned. Sarah Jeffords's belief that Golden Broom could beat Man o' War boiled over during supper with her aunt Elizabeth and uncle Sam that night. A reporter revealed that "Mrs. Walter M. Jeffords . . . and Mr. Riddle were so divided as to the relative merits of the two colts that a match race, not for a pair of gloves or a box of chocolates, either, was almost made over the dinner tables."[31] The genteel custom of women wagering kid gloves or candy would not satisfy. Sarah Jeffords—willing to back her belief with cash—was a modern woman. And why not revel in it? Ever since Man o' War began racing, the Riddles had owned the family bragging rights and Sam had exercised them. Now Golden Broom joined Red in public acclaim and Sarah need not bow to anyone.

Instead of inventing a special match, however, uncle and niece decided to pit their colts in a regular Saratoga race. A reporter guessed that they would wait for the $10,000 Grand Union Hotel Stakes on August 23 or the $30,000 Hopeful on Saratoga's final race day, August 31. He underestimated their urgency. Only four days away was a more modest but still tempting purse: the $5,000 Sanford Memorial Stakes. Both Man o' War and Golden Broom were eligible.

Sam Riddle plucked the final straw. If Sarah wanted to win the Sanford with Golden Broom, he said, he would scratch Man o' War.

But Sarah Jeffords wanted true honor. She would not take charity. Golden Broom would race Man o' War in the Sanford, and may the better colt win. Forgotten, in her proud stand, was the quick, steep climb of Golden Broom's brand-new racing career. The Sanford would be his third race in ten days. Also, his weight assignment would jump from 122 pounds to 130. Man o' War already was accustomed to racing and winning under 130 pounds, and he would be racing after eleven days of rest.

But Sarah had such faith in Golden Broom that she would send him straight from grade school to college. She could have waited thirteen days for the Grand Union Hotel Stakes or twenty-one days for the Hopeful, but waiting could seem like a concession. Man o' War was ready *now*. Giving Golden Broom two or three weeks of rest and *then* challenging Red could seem like admitting—even temporarily—inferiority.

Some observers suspected a weak spot in Golden Broom. The day after the Saratoga Special, the *New York Herald* quoted "one who has successfully wagered millions on racing in America and England" with the observation, "Mark my word, the colt is either chickenhearted or something is hurting him. They don't run out as he did in his first race without cause. Yesterday he got off in front and was never challenged, but wait until a good one takes him by the head and see what he will do."[32] Yet Sarah Jeffords was not alone in her confidence. Astute horseman R. F. Carman exclaimed, "That colt is a runnin' fool and nobody knows yet whether anybody's two-year-old can beat him. . . ."[33]

Mike Daly went even further. Ever since Golden Broom had pushed Man o' War in their three-furlong match, Daly had been willing to bet fellow trainer Jack Joyner one hundred dollars that his colt would beat the Riddle champion when they raced under even weights. Joyner, who had trained Fair Play and admired Man o' War, watched for his chance to collect.

Two days before the Sanford, *The Saratogian* noted that "Man o' War . . . is sure to go because he has, already, accumulated about as many [weight] penalties as it is possible for a winning 2-year-old to amass in three months' campaigning. It is good business as well as good sportsmanship to keep him going for the best. Man o' War was never better than he is today."[34] Red had proved it Monday morning, working a brilliant half-mile in :46 2/5 and galloping out the Sanford distance of six furlongs in 1:12 and three.[35] Although the track was especially fast,[36] this was a rip-roaringly fine move. The Sanford record was 1:13 and two.

Jack Joyner recognized his opportunity. Seeing Mike Daly in the paddock on Tuesday afternoon, Joyner asked, "Do you want that bet to go on tomorrow's race?" Daly said, "Certainly!"[37] Anticipation ripened.

But Wednesday morning, while many viewed the Sanford as a Man o' War/Golden Broom duel, *The Saratogian* politely dismissed Golden Broom and added a third name for consideration:

> The contender in the race will undoubtably be Harry Payne
> Whitney's Upset, which ran second to Man o' War in the United
> States Hotel stakes, while the other five entries have only an
> outside chance, although they are all good stock.
>
> It is probable that Ambrose will have the mount on Golden
> Broom while John Loftus will ride Man o' War and Knapp will
> have charge of the Whitney colt. As all three are riders of
> experience the colts are practically assured of a good ride.[38]

And so some readers of Saratoga's small newspaper may have taken a tip toward Upset as Johnny Loftus prepared to ride the race that would haunt him for the rest of his life.

8

THE SANFORD

ON THE MORNING of the Sanford Memorial Stakes, a jockey told a trainer that he thought they could win a bet against Man o' War. Talking was Upset's jockey, Bill Knapp. Listening was trainer Jimmy Rowe.[1]

Wednesday, August 13, lurched to an atypical start at Saratoga Race Course when the usually tough Mars Cassidy called in sick. Readers of New York City papers were left guessing at the nature of his ailment. *The Saratogian,* in its small-town cozy manner, confided that Cassidy suffered from "a severe cold and tonsillitis. . . ."[2]

The tonsillitis surely had been aggravated by the liberal application of "medicinal" liquor. Tuesday, August 12, had been Mars Cassidy's birthday, and the entertainment held at Tom Luther's lake house to welcome Cassidy's fifty-seventh year had kept numerous horsemen up all night. Luther's hotel guest register suggested that the celebration was a humdinger. There would be no entries for August 13, as if the whole establishment was sleeping. The following day, the usual hand inscribed, "Wednesday, August 14th." Another hand, guided by a more alert mind, drew a line through "Wednesday" and wrote, *"Thursday."* Distraction spilled over another twenty-four hours, and the familiar register handwriting noted, "Thursday, August 15th." A third hand drew the necessary line through "Thursday" and printed above it, none too neatly, *"Friday."*[3]

Wednesday afternoon's racetrack show had to go on, of course, but Cassidy had no eager understudy. Instead, the Saratoga Racing Association pulled an old-timer from the audience and hoped he would remember his part. Thirty years earlier, Charles H. Pettingill had been a prominent starter. Now nearing retirement age, Pettingill still worked at the track, but as a placing judge: watching from a special stand above the finish line and announcing which horse's nose finished first. Here he suffered like any umpire. Sometimes fans disputed his decision and surrounded the judges' stand, hissing and shouting, to tell him so. But in many ways, at the track these days, Judge Pettingill stood above it all: calling a result but not herding the jockeys, and staying safely out of reach of the horses.

Even for a person in daily practice, organizing an orderly start was no simple task. As Mars Cassidy noted, "Jockeys must be controlled, but they cannot be prevented from trying their utmost to get their horses away first."[4] Unfortunately, in his heyday as a starter, Pettingill had become famous for not exercising enough control. In 1893, he had let the American Derby contestants suffer false starts for an *hour and a half*.

When Judge Pettingill substituted for Mars Cassidy on Sanford day, the jockeys ran wild. A large, lively crowd made the pressure even worse. Each time horses reached the barrier, about twenty thousand pairs of eyes turned Pettingill's way and the long-buried American Derby fiasco rattled in its grave. Only two starts from seven races that afternoon would turn out well.

Johnny Loftus got a look at the substitute starter in the third race, riding heavily favored War Pennant in the Watervliet Handicap. Unfortunately, a 6–1 shot named Hannibal grabbed a flying start. Although War Pennant rallied in the stretch, Hannibal cruised away from him, winning by four lengths.

Then came the Sanford Memorial Stakes.

Seven two-year-olds threaded into the crowded paddock, where curious spectators joined racehorses, trainers, owners, and jockeys beneath the trees. Under their numbered saddlecloths, Golden Broom and Man o' War each wore a many-pocketed leather pad holding more than 15 pounds of lead weights—bringing their burden, with saddles and riders added, up to 130 pounds each. Upset and The Swimmer would tote only 115 pounds, while three long shots escaped with 112.

Turf reporters didn't describe the horse owners in this scene, leaving historians to picture their typical attitudes. Sam Riddle and Sarah Jeffords probably were smiling through tight jaws, their rivalry now holding center stage. They could be pardoned for feeling that this was basically a two-horse race.

Bookies were making Man o' War the odds-on choice—only 1–2 at post time—and Golden Broom the runaway second choice, at 11–5.

Harry Payne Whitney probably was laughing with friends, feeling that Upset should be in the hunt, with his 15-pound break in the weights, but acknowledging it would be no disgrace if he failed to win. Upset stayed a distant third in the betting, opening at 10–1 and closing at a still-generous 8–1. Even so, he was the only Sanford starter whose odds to win dropped significantly. More than one somebody—or one big-betting somebody—liked him.

While grooms led the saddled horses in small circles, Riddle, Feustel, and Loftus talked strategy. With a decent start, Golden Broom would rush to the front. But racing six furlongs with a field of horses, Man o' War could let someone else rush early with Golden Broom, while saving his own energy. Loftus would report that Riddle told him to wait about three furlongs— halfway through the race—before letting Man o' War take the lead.[5]

Then the paddock judge called, "Riders up!" and seven two-year-olds swirled into line along the paddock path. Man o' War led the parade behind outrider "Red Coat" Murray, his customary, confident place. The crowd's second choice drew less favorable attention. Golden Broom—again wearing blinkers, and needing a stable pony like a shield by his side—conveyed the equine equivalent of sucking his thumb.

Judge Pettingill waited on his backstretch platform, almost directly across the infield from his usual place at the finish line, as the field bounced toward the barrier. Two long shots—The Swimmer, then Armistice—lined up nearest to the rail. Golden Broom took the third spot, buffered to his outside by Captain Alcock, Upset, Man o' War, and Donnacona. Facing the webbing, where he always vaulted into a dead run, Golden Broom jumped like an exposed nerve. Three times he charged through the barrier, needing to be hauled back, delaying the official break. Finally, an assistant starter grabbed his bridle to keep him in line.

Meanwhile, Man o' War stayed alert but calm.[6] The key was Loftus— not stirring Red up today, but waiting to fall in behind Golden Broom and whoever dared go with him. Judging from the advantage-seeking maneuvers of Bill Knapp, at Man o' War's left side, the other pacemaker could be Upset. Loftus usually played the flying-start game better than Knapp and the rest, but several strings bound him today. First, Riddle's orders to stay off the pace, then Pettingill's warning to settle down or he might get left behind—and finally a simple clue that Loftus exploited every day. There

was no familiar rhythm in Judge Pettingill's motions. As he restrained Man o'
War, Loftus missed a simple knee bend: Mars Cassidy's habitual unconscious
gesture before triggering the barrier.[7]

As decades passed, Bill Knapp would give various versions of the Sanford
start. Once, he said that he and Loftus turned their mounts away from the
barrier to walk up for a fresh start, but Knapp wheeled around early and got
the jump on Loftus. Another time, Knapp said, "I'm right beside Big Red,
and an assistant starter had hold of the big fellow's head. We try to line up
again and I can see that Johnny's having trouble, so I say to this assistant
starter, take him back a step. I keep looking over at the judge and telling the
assistant starter to take Man o' War back a step each time I think it's going to
be a break, and Johnny lets him do it. When the judge does let us go, Big Red
is going back and we're coming on."[8]

Clyde Gordon, an exercise rider for the Riddle barn, would offer another
view. "Loftus told me afterward that he was facing the [inner] rail, waiting
for Pettingill, the starter, to make room for him in the line at the post, when
Pet got excited and pulled it. You know," Gordon recalled, "Man o' War
would lunge when you faced him the right way of the track at the post."[9]

This much is certain: Bill Knapp eyed Golden Broom two spots to his left,
Man o' War directly to his right—and placed Upset perfectly. Suddenly, finally, Pettingill thought he saw the right alignment. His mistaken impulse
matched the momentum of colts three and five. Golden Broom flung forward first, his bridle whipping free of the assistant starter's hand. Upset broke
in nearly the same stride, at Broom's right flank as they gained racing speed.
A beat behind, Armistice and Donnacona launched into their wake. And now
Man o' War—angled toward the inner rail as Golden Broom became
airborne—pivoted on his hind legs and leaped into the fray, outfooting only
The Swimmer and Captain Alcock.

Exaggeration from many observers would come later. Because film
patrol wouldn't become even an experimental part of racing until the 1930s,
there would be no impartial movies to view and review. Years later, some stories would have Man o' War turned entirely backward when the Sanford
began. Lou Feustel would simply call the break "rather straggling."[10] He saw
Man o' War give Golden Broom a six- or seven-length head start—a full second, maybe a shade more.

No one exaggerated Golden Broom's quickness. In only 100 yards, he
opened two lengths on Upset, while the wave of stragglers rolled behind

them. Donnacona, the only runner to Man o' War's outside, charged up into second place but couldn't threaten Golden Broom. One furlong into the Sanford Memorial Stakes, the Jeffords colt led Donnacona by a length and a half, while Donnacona edged Upset by a head and Man o' War surged into fourth place, reaching Upset's girth. One furlong after his poor start, Red ran only about twenty feet behind Golden Broom—and Johnny Loftus had enough horse to turn his orders upside down.

Instead, with the second furlong, opportunity slipped away.

Riddle had said to stay behind the early pace. Following orders, Loftus waited. Golden Broom clocked the first quarter in :23 and one, one-fifth of a second slower than his winning Saratoga Special pace. Upset forged ahead of Donnacona, his head nodding to the right of Broom's heels. Man o' War hovered in third place, tucked in beside the inner rail, a single length behind Upset. Donnacona, running widest of all, fell back to fourth place, his shoulders and forelegs pumping beside the rear half of Red's body.

Suddenly, Loftus had to solve a flying problem in geometry. Entering the turn, Red was in a box.

Loftus chose to be patient. Compared with Upset and Donnacona, Red was saving ground as they curved into the far turn. Trapped inside, Loftus waited for a familiar sight: Golden Broom swerving wide. But Upset stuck tight by Golden Broom's right side all around the bend, gluing him close to the rail, blocking Red's path. And Donnacona stayed lapped on Red, gradually falling a full length back, but still too close for Red to cross in front of him. Red was saving ground all right, but with three furlongs left, he had nowhere to go.

Golden Broom and Upset controlled the race, flying four furlongs in a dizzy :46 4/5. Entering the homestretch, Upset forged in front by half a length, with Golden Broom still fighting on at the rail. Loftus was supposed to have Man o' War in front by now, but Red marked time two lengths behind Upset, stuck in his box, daylight barely flashing between his front hooves and Golden Broom's heels. To his right, a fading Donnacona stayed close enough to hit Red's heels if Loftus tried swinging out in front of him—and now Captain Alcock was coming on! Captain Alcock, overlapped at Donnacona's right. With two furlongs left and no seam near the rail, Loftus could take back *now*, steering Red to the far outside—if he cut off Red's momentum and angled wide enough to clear the rank of Captain Alcock, Donnacona, Upset, and Golden Broom.

It might be his only chance.

"But what jockey would think of trying to go out around four horses," Loftus would wonder afterward, "on a colt carrying 130 pounds?"[11]

Instead, straightening into the homestretch, stuck behind Golden Broom and Upset, Loftus yelled for Bill Knapp to give him room. Knapp sometimes would recall an order—"Move out, Willie! I'm coming through!"[12]—sometimes a plea: "Let me out, let me out Bill!"[13]

Glancing back, Knapp saw Man o' War pent up at Upset's heels. He had no reason to set him free. "Take off!" he shouted back to Loftus. "Take off me, bum, or I'll put you through the rail!"[14]

"He keeps hollering," Knapp would recall, "and I just sit there."[15]

One furlong remained for Loftus to win the race. No shortcuts. The pocket held.

Then Golden Broom fell apart. He had run five fast furlongs with 130 pounds on his back, hounded by the lighter-weighted Upset. He would slide back into third place, finishing about four lengths behind Man o' War. But Broom's courage hadn't failed him. It was his hoof. Another crack had popped open while he fought Upset into the homestretch, conceding fifteen pounds.

Golden Broom floundered backward, hugging the rail. Loftus checked Red again, keeping him from clipping heels with Golden Broom. Man o' War's inside path was hopelessly closed. And "Big Bill" Knapp, knowing that Loftus *must* send Man o' War outside, at full stride, told Upset: NOW! It's time to *move.*

Carrying fifteen pounds less than Man o' War, Upset had some speed in reserve. Knapp urged Upset for all he was worth as Loftus finally reined Man o' War to the outside, in the clear, *free.*

Upset sprinted in earnest for those final seconds, Knapp demanding everything the colt could find. To his right, Man o' War sprinted even faster, Loftus smacking his hip with the whip and pumping the reins. One horse to beat, dead aim on him. Knapp saw the empty ground to the winning post shrinking. Could it shrink fast enough?

At the finish line, Man o' War fell short by half the length of Upset's body—some said the length of his neck. Shortly past the line, some witnesses said, Red was in front. The *New York Herald* guessed that Man o' War "in a few more strides might have been the winner in spite of all the obstacles he had to overcome."[16]

Journalists would play up Upset's perfectly appropriate name.[17] Not surprisingly, no one recalled the distant prelude of Pankhurst beating Mahubah in a hunt meet race almost seven years before. Nor did they notice a third element that confused coincidence with destiny. In one of history's delicious ironies, the man who piloted Upset that day had been christened William *Sanford* Knapp.

The crowd cheered Upset into the winner's circle. They cheered Man o' War equally hard. They had watched wooden blocks on an infield board spell out the official time: 1:11 1/5. Until Upset hit the finish line, the Sanford record had been 1:13 and two. By the conventional rule of thumb, Upset had beaten the old record by eleven lengths—and, of course, Man o' War had lost several lengths at the start. To nearly catch Upset, Red must have run his six furlongs, despite carrying 130 pounds and being delayed in traffic, well under 1:11. The track record was 1:10 2/5. Lou Feustel's stopwatch, which he clicked as Red started and finished, said 1:10 and one.[18]

In the first shock of defeat, Sam Riddle focused on Red's brilliance. Attributing the loss to bad racing luck that strikes everyone sometimes, he did not complain about Judge Pettingill or Jockey Loftus. Instead, a *Daily Racing Form* reporter noticed that "Mr. Riddle seemed as proud as ever of his colt and enthused over his great race. He told all of his friends Man o' War would have established a new [track] record if he had received a good start."[19] Lou Feustel also drew praise for good sportsmanship, blaming nothing except bad luck. If Feustel held any suspicions about Red's misfortune, he was keeping them to himself.

Beyond managing their own disappointment, Riddle and Feustel faced another woeful task: consoling their jockey. "They praised Loftus," a reporter noted, "and did their mightiest to cheer him up."[20] They didn't succeed. After stripping his tiny saddle from Red's back and weighing in at the scales, Johnny Loftus tried to avoid everyone. "The defeat of Man o' War in the Sanford Memorial hit jockey Loftus hard," the *Daily Racing Form* would report. "It stung him to the core and made him the most downhearted person at the course. For half an hour after the race he sat by himself in the jockey room moaning over the colt's defeat, and it was with difficulty that anyone, even Mr. Riddle, could get him to comment on the race."[21]

At first, Loftus would only say, "I'm too mad to talk about it."[22]

Finally, he began describing what had gone wrong. "Man o' War was beaten at the start, but he would've overcome that defeat if I had had better luck," Loftus declared. He began explaining the mistakes: an assistant starter taking hold of Red before the break; getting boxed in; waiting too long for space to open up at the rail. "I ran him into a pocket and because of his heavy burden of 130 pounds I was afraid to take him back and around the outside," Loftus admitted. "I anticipated an opening next to the rail on the turn out of the backstretch and again at the head of the homestretch, but every time I was fooled. If I had taken him to the outside an instant sooner he would have won, for he is the gamest and most courageous horse I ever rode. He would have caught Upset in a few more strides and would have gone on a half mile farther [if] I would have urged him to."[23]

Johnny Loftus freely blamed his own mistakes for Man o' War's loss. He did not know yet that many others were blaming him for something worse.

As night settled over Saratoga Springs and racetrackers marveled at the Sanford Memorial Stakes, rumor ran even faster than Man o' War. Certain agents for big bettors, word had it, were boarding fast boats to Europe. *With their winnings on Upset!* suspicious souls said. And why had those fugitives believed that Upset would beat Man o' War? Because, rumor had it, Knapp and Loftus had bet on Upset, then put the race in the bag.

The likely explanation for any betting commissioner exodus was less fun to believe. Agents sometimes wagered more money on a "sure thing"—such as Man o' War—than their bosses authorized. When the sure thing won, the agents secretly kept extra winnings gained with their employers' money. But Man o' War had lost. If the unauthorized deficit was more than certain agents could repay, they wouldn't wait around to be exposed.

Furthermore, in at least one professional's opinion, Man o' War's very short odds played against the notion that any bookies at Saratoga Race Course knew he would lose. "If a bookie had information that a horse was a stiff, he'd always jack up the price to lure more suckers," a bookmaker from Red's era later confessed. "I tell you, talk of a gambling coup and larceny involved in Man o' War's defeat is all a myth."[24] If Loftus and Knapp did bet on Upset—whose odds had closed at 8–1, while the bookies kept Man o' War at 1–2—they had done it with impressive stealth. Word apparently had not leaked before the race.

Rumors of a fix did not make the newspapers. Reporters simply agreed that Man o' War had not deserved to lose. Most of them blamed Johnny

Loftus. The *New York Times*—perhaps impressed by the vigorous final furlong—stood alone in saying, "Man o' War received a fine ride from Loftus, who gave the colt every assistance within his power."[25] George Daley of the *New York World* vouched for "a well-meant but ill-judged effort by Johnny Loftus to save a little ground on the rail."[26] But history wouldn't leave it there.

Although the *Daily Racing Form* noted that Lou Feustel was "not angry"[27] right after the Sanford, Feustel had been stunned. When possible, he simply avoided the subject. When pressed, he allowed, "I wasn't happy with the ride, that's all. . . ."[28] He didn't reveal what Johnny Loftus had said to him shortly after the rumors began.

Forty-one years after Red's defeat, while visiting New York City for the inaugural Man o' War Handicap and warmed by a rush of friendly attention, Feustel told a sports columnist that "Loftus asked him a couple of times after the race won by Upset if he [Feustel] thought he had 'pulled' Man o' War."

"I told him not to be foolish," Feustel said.[29]

In mid-August of 1919, the famous Johnny Loftus knew that his reputation was under attack. No, the stewards did not question him about the Sanford Memorial Stakes. The Jockey Club did not take away his license, as they could do immediately when they caught riders fixing races. But Loftus heard people saying that he had pulled Man o' War. He needed to know: Did Red's trainer believe it was true?

Early in 1962, Feustel relaxed into a confiding mood. While visiting Wayne Capps, a journalist who had become a friend, he picked up the Sanford thread: "You still interested in what I thought about Upset beating Man o' War? Well, promise me you won't print it and I'll tell you." In 1981, eleven years after Feustel's death, Capps finally published the trainer's revelation: "I felt pretty sure that some racketeers got to Loftus and he got paid for throwing the race . . . but there was no way I could prove it . . . no horse alive could beat 'Big Red' in a fair race."[30]

In terms of the best horse winning, everyone knew that the Sanford hadn't been fair. Unproven was any link between unfairness—which could come by accident—and dishonesty. Probing Feustel's memory, Wayne Capps entertained the worst. "Now I asked Lou why it was he hadn't expressed his true feeling about the race hours or days after it was over. 'In those days it wouldn't of done any good,' he sighed. 'Besides, it hurt so much I didn't want to talk about it.'"[31]

No one could prove whether Feustel's guess was accurate. Nor could anyone tell how much of Feustel's 1962 confession was his original gut feeling
and how much might have been the waxy yellow buildup from decades of rumor in the racing world.

For many days after August 13, 1919, rumor fermented reality. Sam Riddle
quickly latched onto two supports: Man o' War, while officially beaten, was
still superior to any rival met so far—Upset did not get him fair and
square—and Johnny Loftus, though guilty of a bum ride, had wanted very
much to win.

Samuel Doyle Riddle was not a naïve soul. As a longtime insider at amateur racing meets, he knew about devious doings in competition. Talking
about his experiences, Riddle gave a knowing wink toward manipulations of
the turf, enjoying the glamour of outlaw behavior politely softened by time.
His audiences laughed with him, enjoying his audacity. But there is an uncomfortable gap between seeing an amusing scam and becoming a victim.
Was this why Riddle wouldn't believe that Loftus might have betrayed him
and Man o' War? When accusations reached him, Riddle would hear none of
it. There was a much kinder explanation for his jockey's poor judgment: Loftus cared too much about winning the Sanford, Riddle maintained, and he
lost his head.

Did the emotional showdown of Riddle versus Jeffords, Man o' War versus
Golden Broom, take Johnny Loftus out of his game? Did he lose his usual
presence of mind?

Sam Riddle had departed this life by the time Jim Ross reached middle age
and published a memoir of racing's "Golden Age." Riddle never read Ross's
description of an ultracool Johnny Loftus that drifts unwelcomely to mind:
"He had, as they say, 'ice water in his veins.' "[32]

I think we can win a bet today.

Before the Sanford, Bill Knapp told Jimmy Rowe that he thought Upset
would beat Man o' War. His belief was far too suggestive to be easily dismissed. For decade after decade, reputable writers and institutions repeated
stories that he and Loftus had fixed the 1919 Sanford. Meanwhile, a likely factor in Red's troubled trip in that race received no publicity. Loftus never used
it in public to defend himself. And any turf writers who heard tell wouldn't
print a revelation that could damage the Sport of Kings, especially soon after
the prohibition of alcoholic beverages had been voted into law.

According to Knapp, his words to Rowe were not sinister, but simply a practical observation. Knapp had been careful the night before the $5,000 Sanford Memorial, turning in around 8:00 P.M. The next morning, he awoke early, as usual, and headed to the barn for work. Knapp's route to the track from his rented house on York Avenue intersected with the road to Saratoga Lake—which was how, around 5:30 A.M. on Wednesday, August 13, Bill Knapp saw Johnny Loftus heading home to bed.

Loftus corroborated Knapp's story in a roundabout way. Eminent sports columnist Bill Corum heard from Red's rider himself that Loftus, "among many others, had been out the night before [the Sanford] celebrating Starter Cassidy's birthday at Tom Luther's lake [house]."[33] Although the exact nature of those celebrations went unrecorded, the all-night revelers had enjoyed to Luther's famously wet hospitality.

The next morning, Bill Knapp told Jimmy Rowe that Upset might well win the Sanford Memorial Stakes—because how sharply could Johnny Loftus handle the boisterous Man o' War, with the remains of something other than ice water in his veins?

9

BUTTERFLIES

THREE DAYS AFTER losing the Sanford, Johnny Loftus redeemed himself at the start of an important race: helping Commander Ross carry off a betting coup with the Spinaway Stakes. Their plan depended on fooling the bookies, the public, and Mars Cassidy.

It began with a private meeting after the races on Tuesday, August 12, when the Commander and "Hard Guy" Bedwell inspected a two-year-old filly named Constancy. Her breeder, A. B. Hancock, of the prominent Claiborne Stud in Kentucky, assured them that Constancy had been tested strenuously at his farm and, even though she had raced twice without showing much, she was lightning fast. To prove it, Constancy then dashed six furlongs in 1:11 1/5. Upset would make the same time the next day, beating Man o' War.

With Bedwell claiming that this was the fastest trial he'd ever heard of for a two-year-old,[1] Ross bought Constancy for about $25,000. Then, tired of bookies reducing the odds on his horses every time they saw his betting commissioners coming, the Commander planned his coup. He exploited two factors: Constancy's secret speed and Johnny Loftus's fame.

Ross entered two fillies, Constancy and His Choice, in Saturday's Spinaway Stakes and assigned Loftus to His Choice. Bookies figured that His Choice, known to have modest ability but toting the star jockey, was the entry's better half. Constancy, who had shown even less, attracted no attention with second-stringer Tommy Nolan aboard. The Commander's betting agents found odds on the Ross entry as high as 20–1 before word got around that a coup was brewing. "My father managed to place his wagers at an average of 15 to 1," Jim Ross later confessed, "and those wagers were sizeable."[2]

Commander Ross had fooled the bookies. Now Johnny Loftus had to fool Mars Cassidy.

Returning to duty two days after the Sanford debacle, Cassidy immediately had cracked down on rowdy riders. There would be no flying starts for Johnny Loftus or anyone else. The *New York Times* revealed the simple beauty of Cassidy's new regime: "Under his plan all horses must be facing the barrier and be standing still before he will order a start."[3]

Seventeen fillies and jockeys tested Cassidy in the Spinaway, skittering around the barrier for eight minutes. Following Bedwell's orders, Loftus pulled His Choice out of line whenever a start looked possible without Constancy perfectly ready. Despite Mars Cassidy's stern warnings, his tactic worked. When the webbing finally flew up, Constancy leaped to the front and never looked back, winning by four supremely easy lengths. And although His Choice started slowly, Loftus even managed to escape without penalty. Fellow jockey Buddy Ensor, trying for a flying start with 50–1 shot Polysanda, drew a suspension from Cassidy.

Constancy's worth was now no secret. As the *New York Herald* reported, the Commander's bets had yielded comfortably more than the $25,000 he'd paid for Constancy. No one reported that Johnny Loftus, for his masterful help, surely collected a bonus from Ross. But nonetheless, Loftus was turning into a marked man.

On Monday, August 18, *The Saratogian* suddenly commented that Man o' War "was beaten here last week in the Sanford Memorial through the abominable riding of Jockey Loftus. . . ."[4] The following day, Loftus got an actual black eye. It happened because jockeys, unlike airplane pilots and race-car drivers, did not wear safety goggles.[5] As Loftus hustled Commander Ross's good colt Damrosch into the homestretch, a clump of mud hit him squarely in the eye. While Damrosch floundered to the finish in fourth place, spectators didn't realize that his rider couldn't see. "Damrosch had to steer his own course through the stretch," a *New York Times* reporter later explained, "and this accounted for what appeared to be a very weak ride on the Ross horse."[6] The black eye, obvious soon after the race, helped Loftus prove his own honesty. It could not help his reputation, though, on Friday, August 22.

*   *   *

Once a suspicion begins, it is difficult to erase. Nine days after Man o' War's defeat, Johnny Loftus inspired another controversy.

Loftus received much praise for his first ride of the day, cleverly steering The Porter to a ground-saving victory in the Plattsburg Handicap. His only other mount, a well-bred two-year-old filly named Beaming Beauty, was thought to be "the surest winner of the afternoon."[7] In her three previous races, Beaming Beauty had suffered from poor starts and traffic troubles. Any strong faith in her winning this maiden race for green and developing two-year-olds, however, depended as much on hope as history. Last time out, she had emerged from "close quarters"[8] to miss victory by less than three lengths but had "tired in the closing strides."[9] That promising but insufficient effort now made her a top-heavy favorite.

This time, many bettors counted heavily on Beaming Beauty showing her class. Unfortunately, she showed temper instead when another filly kicked at her during the post parade. ". . . Loftus . . . did a bronco breaking act in front of the club house," reporter George Daley noted. "Beaming Beauty on which he had the mount was in an ugly mood and no cow pony ever resorted to more tricks to dislodge a rider. The boy finally was unseated but held tight to the reins and landing on his feet prevented the filly from running away. He then remounted with the utmost coolness and avoiding the use of the stirrups for a moment or two, with 'safety first' in his mind used his whip in a way to convince the horse that he was master."[10] Loftus earned an ovation for this performance, but Daley commented with bitter disappointment, "On the way to the post, however, he turned from Dr. Jekyll to Mr. Hyde."

Beaming Beauty's post parade escapades were not a good sign, and her barrier behavior wasn't much better. "Breaking slowly from an outside position, she was a good four lengths back of the pacemaker when straightened away," Daley observed, "but Loftus rushed her up and into a long lead of four or five lengths in the first quarter, riding her as if his life depended on getting to the head of the stretch in front." Daley failed to note, however, that Loftus might have been trying to overcome problems that had beaten Beaming Beauty before: getting trapped in traffic or being left too far behind. The race was only five furlongs long.

Beaming Beauty rounded the far turn well ahead of her nearest rival, but George Daley didn't like what he saw as she entered the homestretch and her lead began to shrink. ". . . [Loftus] went to the whip even while three lengths in front and at the same time let her bear out to the middle of the track," Daley complained. "This kind of riding was enough to stop a much better horse than Beaming Beauty, and she fairly staggered in outside the money." It looked all the worse to suspicious-minded spectators because, while Beaming Beauty finished fourth, a 50–1 shot won the race. But Daley and others who condemned Loftus overlooked an innocent possibility: that Beaming Beauty had beaten herself.

The so-called "surest winner of the afternoon"[11] was, after all, an excitable and rather green individual. When Loftus urged her forward to recover from her slow start, she may have overreacted and gone too fast too soon. Rather than fight with her to slow down, Loftus may have tried to let her settle into stride and hoped for the best. He may have gone to the whip while she still led by three lengths because she showed signs of quitting. *Daily Racing Form*'s chart would say that Beaming Beauty "began slowly and, displaying excellent early speed, raced into a long lead [midway through the race], but quit badly in the last eighth."

That night, the Saratoga crowd argued about Johnny Loftus—"some shouting his praises," George Daley noted, "[and] others not mincing their words in expressing contempt."[12] Loftus himself may have felt that the next day's racing would clear his slate. The next day, he would ride Man o' War in the Grand Union Hotel Stakes.

In a strange way, with his misjudged ride in the Sanford Memorial Stakes, Johnny Loftus had done Man o' War a favor. As turf writer David Alexander later observed, that defeat served as a "vital defect"[13]: the touch of vulnerability that lets an overpowering champion become beloved. But in 1919, Red's fans and handlers did not appreciate the defect. Instead, they looked toward Saturday, August 23: Red's first chance for revenge. With a $10,000 purse, the Grand Union Hotel Stakes offered twice as much money as the Sanford. As a chance to trounce Upset, it offered satisfaction beyond price.

Nine challengers to Man o' War stepped forward, encouraged by Upset's success. Several carried 112 or 115 pounds to Red's now customary 130. Blazes, who had won three sprints in a row, toted 122. Upset picked up ten pounds from his Sanford success, carrying 125.

For five minutes, Evergay and Hasten On delayed the start. Loftus settled Man o' War in post position two, with only a long shot, Evergay, to his inside. No rush today. Red had only to break clean and hold his advantageous place. Then Cassidy triggered a fair break.

Phil Musgrave gunned Evergay forward, aiming to control the race from the start. But Upset vaulted forward first, Knapp clearing the pack from six lanes out, seeking running room inside before they reached the turn. He would fail. Man o' War, though third away, quickly found his stride.

Man o' War, Upset, Evergay—these three surged and converged, with Evergay rippling to the lead, then Red overwhelming him, with Upset pressing from the outside. Now Blazes cruised forward, positioned to pounce, but Red dared anyone to match his speed. In the Sanford, Golden Broom and Upset had dictated the pace, while Man o' War got in trouble from holding back. This time, Loftus let Red fly. First quarter, :22 and three—a burning burst of energy, but worth it. Rocketing into the turn, clear of interference, Red held the inside track.

He wasn't alone for long. Lugging fifteen pounds less than Man o' War, Evergay relaunched his challenge from the outside. Rounding the far turn, it was Red by a head over Evergay—but their race wasn't as close as it seemed. Content with his position, Loftus was giving Red a breather. Even so, the first half-mile—:46 2/5—was Red's fastest opening yet.

Rounding the turn, with Evergay stuck at Red's side, it looked like a contest. Entering the stretch, the truth broke through. As Red passed the quarter pole, Evergay was tiring. Upset, running wide for half a mile now, was leveling out but couldn't gain. Straightening for home, Loftus kept Red close to the rail, with no room for anyone to slip through inside, then let him go again.

Evergay was gone, fallen far behind. Knapp was driving Upset hard, and Upset was game, but Red floated free of company. A furlong from the finish line, Loftus glanced back over his right shoulder, then his left. No one threatened. Satisfied, Loftus tightened the reins. Man o' War resisted forcefully. "To make the colt shorten his stride," a reporter noted, "the great jockey had to stand almost straight in the stirrups and use all the strength his arms possessed."[14] Red neared the finish line with spectators shouting at Loftus to let him go.[15] Johnny ignored them. Winning was what counted. Energy saved now could be used on another day.

Red loped past the post, with Upset driving hard about two lengths behind. The margin fooled no one. Man o' War, said the *New York Times,* "could have made it five had he tried all the way to the wire."[16]

Although Red cantered the last quarter in :25 3/5, he finished in stakes record time of 1:12 flat. For the third race in a row, he had run remarkably fast: equaling a stakes mark in the United States Hotel, beating one in the Sanford (though Upset got the credit), and now owning one outright. Red had revealed a rare dimension: groundbreaking yet casual speed. "He looked better than ever today as he came back to the stand for Loftus to weigh in," a reporter observed, "his appearance, as he stopped and stood with head up and ears pricked, being more like that of a colt going to the post than one that had just won a $10,000 race in record time."[17]

Loftus remarked that Red should have gone off at 1–20 instead of 1–2.[18] "Don't know how fast he would've run had I allowed him," he told *Daily Racing Form*. "There was no reason for his best speed, as he had the others seemingly well spent to live up to his pace during the first three eighths and the rest of the race was only a canter."[19] He also called young Man o' War the greatest colt he had ever ridden.[20] Loftus had let a final layer of caution fall away.

For others as well, old limits on Red's value curled off like an outgrown cocoon. Sam Riddle announced that he had been offered nearly $100,000 for Man o' War—twenty times his purchase price!—but never would sell him. "He is a great race horse, probably one of the greatest we have seen in a decade," Riddle affirmed, "and I look for great things from him as a three-year-old."[21]

Diplomacy softened Riddle's pride. By calling Red "probably one of the greatest we have seen in a decade," he drew a line at 1909. Two of the new century's greatest runners, Colin and Sysonby, had last raced in 1908 and 1905. Colin earned immortality by going undefeated in fifteen starts, but Sysonby—also owned by James R. Keene—had been far more than a warm-up act. Through his first four starts, Sysonby had toyed with his opponents. Then, heavily favored in the rich Futurity, he ran a dull third. Soon afterward, a groom caught with a thick wad of bills admitted to sedating the colt in return for a bribe. Sysonby raced ten more times and never lost again.

While Sam Riddle sidestepped a direct comparison, many racetrackers agreed that Man o' War was "the best two-year-old seen since Colin and Sysonby. . . ."[22] This made his earlier unfair defeat seem all the worse. Many owners would fire a jockey who lost in such a way with such a horse, but Riddle exercised the opposite form of damage control: announcing that he, Feustel, and Loftus were, as *Daily Racing Form* rephrased it, "a combination which would not be broken for a long time."[23]

Two targets remained for Man o' War in 1919: the Hopeful Stakes at Saratoga and the Futurity at Belmont Park. Not pointing for the Hopeful or any other two-year-old target was Golden Broom. By August 25, Mike Daly had shipped him down to Berlin for a healing rest.[24]

No one interviewed Sarah Jeffords about this setback with her expensive colt, or reported whether she and her uncle Sam compared her misfortune to his prodigious gain. The facts were plain enough: Man o' War was now worth more than five times what Golden Broom had brought only twelve months before.

Meanwhile, Sam Riddle's proclamation that Red was not for sale seemed to inspire Commander Ross. Two days after Red's Grand Union romp, the *New York Times* reported that Ross had offered Riddle $130,000. The next day's *New York World* gave an even higher price. "It is thought that Commander Ross made the biggest offer for a two-year-old ever known," the *World* confided, "when he suggested he would give $150,000 for Man o' War."[25] Whatever Ross had offered, Riddle didn't budge.

Shortly afterward, either the Commander pursued a different star or another high roller tried to outdo him. An anonymous party offered Sam Hildreth $300,000 for three-year-old Purchase—the biggest price that anyone could remember for a Thoroughbred horse in the United States,[26] and twice as much as any offer yet made for baby Man o' War.

Because racehorses are a fragile commodity and American dollars were on much sounder footing than the lightly raced Purchase, Hildreth's decision came as a surprise. "I refused the offer," he told the *Times,* "not because I thought Purchase was worth that much money, great colt as he is, but because I would only get a portion of the sum under the present Government tax."[27] Federal income tax, hiked up dramatically during the recent World War and still at those high rates, would have taken more than half of Hildreth's profit. Before the war, his tax on the same income would have been less than 7 percent. The same conditions would hold true for Sam Riddle and any price he took for Man o' War.

Hefty taxes might have discouraged well-off owners from selling a top horse, but sentiment reinforced the financial logic. Sam Hildreth owned Purchase in partnership with Standard Oil tycoon Harry Sinclair, who, as the *New York Herald* noted, "likes as well as anybody to own a good horse [and] has money enough to enable him to enjoy that pleasure. . . ."[28] Sam Riddle spoke of owning Man o' War as a special trust. "He will always remain my property," Riddle promised after the Grand Union Hotel Stakes. "I feel that a great horse like this is in a way public property. The turf has a claim on him, and when he has finished his racing career I shall use him as a sire."[29]

As the Saratoga meet entered its final week, Bill Knapp found that beating Man o' War hadn't brought him any lasting respect. On Tuesday, August 26,

Knapp drew criticism for finishing a very close third on a 1–2 shot named Abadane after steering him wide in the homestretch. Later on the same card, he rode Purchase in the Huron Handicap. Sam Hildreth specifically chose "Old Man" Knapp instead of his expensive young first-call jockey, Laverne Fator, because Purchase needed a strong rider. Despite lugging 134 pounds, Hildreth's big horse won impressively. Even so, his rider came in for a ribbing. Dismounting from Purchase, Knapp told nearby trainer Henry McDaniel, "Anybody could have won with that fellow." Laughing, McDaniel answered, "You have proved it."[30]

This week at Saratoga did offer something more than comic relief. On Thursday, August 28, a little colt from Harry Payne Whitney's barn, sired by the great stallion Broomstick, finished second in a 5 1/2-furlong dash for maiden two-year-olds. "It was John P. Grier's first effort and he ran green but gamely," the *New York World* reported. "He was up in the fighting early, only to drop back and then come again."[31] Even seasoned racehorses rarely regain the lead once they've fallen back off it. John P. Grier, brand-new to competition, came close.

He wouldn't be ready for the August 30 Hopeful Stakes, but Jimmy Rowe could run Upset in that. For John P. Grier—given two more weeks of development—Rowe was thinking Futurity.

Jim Ross would remember Saturday, August 30, the last afternoon of Saratoga's 1919 meet, as "a day of blistering heat, the air heavy with stormful threats. . . ."[32] Even so, more than twenty thousand people crowded Saratoga Race Course. They wanted to see Man o' War battle four other colts and three fillies, including Upset and Constancy, in the $30,000 Hopeful Stakes. Again carrying 130 pounds, the champion would spot his challengers anywhere from five to 18 pounds.

As storm clouds sailed toward the track, Elizabeth Dobson Riddle celebrated Saratoga's closing day in an eye-catching way. "She had more faith in Man o' War than her husband and was more sportily inclined," a reporter observed. "She made a fair sized wager on the colt, while Mr. Riddle bet his limit, which is only $50."[33]

Trying to beat the weather, the jockeys galloped their mounts to the starting place.[34] But they were still forming a line behind the barrier when the dark clouds burst. For twelve minutes, they struggled at the start—shouting, slipping, backing up, rushing forward, pounded by rain. Man o' War broke through the webbing four times, each time sprinting about fifty yards down the track[35] and coming back to the start, as *Daily Racing Form* said, "considerably used."[36] Some horse—maybe Upset, maybe Man o' War—kicked the filly Ethel Gray. One reporter said that Upset kicked Ethel Gray and Man o' War kicked Cleopatra. From their grandstand perch, staring into sheets of rain, reporters couldn't really see what was happening on the other side of the track. Mars Cassidy was having trouble enough only a few feet from the action.

Twelve minutes of chaos—and suddenly, the start for real.

"Come ON!" yelled Mars Cassidy through the downpour, and Constancy shot to the lead. Loftus snugged Man o' War into second place and let her go. Constancy left Red two lengths in her wake, her first quarter reported as a sparkling :23 flat. Though Red had gone faster in the Grand Union Hotel Stakes, this matched his United States Hotel pace, which had been set without near-blinding rain. Curving around the far turn, Constancy's half in :47 shaded Red's United States Hotel opening of :47 and one.

Sam Riddle, watching, hadn't made it through the rain to his clubhouse box. Instead, he had ducked under the grandstand, where he shared a bench with farm manager Barry Shannon and journalist M. M. Leach, an Englishman who wrote under the pen name "Exile." It was Leach who, after the Saratoga Special, had called for "time and patience" in comparing Golden Broom with Man o' War. That call had gone unheeded, but in general his viewpoint drew attention. In both England and America, "Exile" had seen many of the best horses that had ever run.

This time, Leach's opinion seemed doomed to form from misty impressions. "From where we sat it was impossible to see much of anything," Riddle explained. "About all there was to it was we knew when they finally got off, they were just a confused blur as they ran up the back stretch and around the turn, but as they reached the home stretch something jumped out in front of the others and ran away from them. . . ."[37] Jim Ross, rooting for pacesetting Constancy, remembered that moment most gracefully: "If horses think, and I believe they do, she must have wondered just what manner of animal this was when Man o' War ranged up beside her and drew away so easily while she herself was still flying."[38]

In the final furlong, a picture became clear: Man o' War splashing home alone, ears flicking up with ease, Loftus "looking back for the nearest contender"[39] and beginning to pull him up as they approached the finish post. Even so, four lengths separated Red from his nearest foe. Light-weighted Cleopatra slogged past the tiring Constancy, another four lengths back in third. Despite the downpour and "a wet, slippery track,"[40] Red's official time was a more than respectable 1:13.

A reporter saw Sam Riddle celebrating "like a seventeen-year-old lad. He hopped and skipped about the clubhouse and paddock," the reporter noted, "and congratulated his trainer and jockey over and over again."[41] Lou Feustel seemed equally delighted but also grounded by his training responsibilities, saying that he would now start worrying about Man o' War's next race: the Futurity.

"Louis, you worry too much," Sam Riddle interjected. "You don't have to worry over this colt. Let the owners and trainers of the other colts and fillies do the worrying."[42]

Popular opinion indicated that Riddle was right. That evening, the reporter known as "Exile" would bring him a handwritten note: "Please accept my best congratulations. I am convinced that Man o' War is as good a two-year-old as I ever saw run."[43] The next day, the *New York World* pronounced, "There are those who call him the greatest colt ever brought out in this country, and if he trains on and lives up to the name now earned, his fame will spread the world around."[44]

"Samuel D. Riddle's chestnut colt, Man o' War . . . is one of the best two-year-olds that ever raced on this continent," the *New York Herald* proclaimed.[45] As a special honor, the *Herald* displayed a complete listing of Red's nine races between its headlines and racing report. The article voiced one regret: "On August 13 Man o' War was beaten half a length by Upset in the Sanford Memorial Stakes after a stormy journey, a race he should have won as easily as the others." Red's owner, however, said that his only regret was being too heavy to ride Man o' War in the Hopeful Stakes. "If I could only do that," Samuel Doyle Riddle declared, "my delight at owning such a beautiful horse would be complete."[46]

Anyone who had enough money and luck might buy a high-powered race-horse and watch him win. Riddle craved involvement beyond trophies and acclaim. In his youth, he had jockeyed in hunt club steeplechases. In middle age, he still galloped through winter countryside in foxhunts. Man o' War did more than reveal Riddle's race-winning ambitions: He promised unsurpassed speed and thrills that Sam wanted to feel for himself.

The person who might best understand Riddle's hunger was short enough to be a jockey but too old and round. A skilled rider, he limited his daring exploits to polo matches. He was August Belmont.

10

RIGHT WAY,
WRONG WAY

Nᴇᴀʀʟʏ ᴛʜɪʀᴛᴇᴇɴ ᴍᴏɴᴛʜs after sending Man o' War up to
Saratoga for sale, Maj. August Belmont finally found time to watch him race.
He had seen, of course, many newspaper articles and several photographs de-
picting Man o' War at the track. But during the afternoon of Saturday, September 13, Major Belmont stood in the paddock at Belmont Park and studied
the colt he remembered as a suckling, a weanling, and a yearling. While
Feustel and his helpers groomed and saddled Red for America's most important juvenile race, Belmont praised his sturdy bones, well-developed muscles,
and overall fitness. One reporter speculated that Man o' War's breeder,
beneath his obvious admiration, also felt regret: "Back of it all there must
have been a momentary feeling of disappointment that he could not have had
the pleasure of seeing the horse race in his own colors."[1]

Belmont himself showed no regret. In her memoir, Eleanor Belmont
wrote, "If my husband was disappointed that this great horse did not race
under his colors he never indicated it to me or to anyone. . . . He was always proud that as a result of his careful selection, his stable had produced
the sire Fair Play, the dam Mahubah, and their great colt Man o' War."[2]
Being the creative mind behind such successful choices may have been
enough for August Belmont . . . or very nearly enough. Thanks to Thomas
Edison, anyone with the right price could buy a bright lightbulb, but only
one man had found the most effective formula to produce it. Belmont knew
that his own formula had produced a very bright light. Now his main concern was not owning that light for himself, though he did hope to profit

from it. His main concern was focusing that light to make New York racing shine.

Futurity day helped Belmont see just what wattage he had.

A crowd estimated as high as a record thirty thousand swarmed Belmont Park for the Futurity. They would see a race worth $26,650 to the winner: enough to buy a dozen luxury automobiles or eighty pounds of gold. Even the most successful and blasé horsemen coveted this race. Johnny Loftus thought the occasion so special—and felt so confident of winning with Man o' War—that he brought his mother from Chicago to New York to watch.

Margaret O'Dowd Loftus saw her second son ride out first in the post parade, wearing black-and-yellow silks, controlling an eager red colt taller than any other on the track. She saw him as any person would wish to be seen, at the height of possibility.

Few in the crowd thought that Man o' War could lose. Contrarians favored Sam Hildreth's fast colt Dominique, a son of the notable sprinter sire Peter Quince, or Harry Payne Whitney's triple entry of Upset, John P. Grier, and Dr. Clark. With 127 pounds up, Red spotted Dominique five pounds, Upset seven pounds, and John P. Grier ten. Even so, the bookmakers and wagering public made him the odds-on favorite at 1–2. After Dominique at 4–1 and the Whitney trio at 6–1, Red's five other challengers started at 20–1 and more.

Ten two-year-olds paraded past Belmont Park's stately grandstand and down the straight course, reaching the barrier at 3:46 P.M. John P. Grier and Cleopatra promptly began kicking and popping out of line, while Man o' War worsened the delay. "He drew No. 8 position," the *New York Herald* observed, "but was not content to occupy it. He was everywhere, behind and in front of the gate, alternating dashes across the track with visits to the inside and outside rails, and only a strong jockey such as his rider, Loftus, was could have curbed his impetuosity."[3] Loftus, in fact, had remarked while in the paddock that he felt very anxious about Man o' War's performance that day—"Not about the race," Loftus told a friendly reporter, "but at the barrier."[4]

Monitoring Mars Cassidy and his rival jockeys, Loftus drew a fine line between eagerness and control. He would not let Red be caught sideways, backing up, or flat-footed. He would not let other riders outmaneuver him. Once Red leaped through the barrier, making the crowd jump up and yell, "They're off!"[5] Mars Cassidy decided enough was enough. An assistant starter latched onto Red's bridle, anchoring him. Then ten two-year-olds left the barrier in a nearly perfect line.

Onlookers couldn't tell much else. From the grandstand, clubhouse, and infield, they could only see ten small dots rushing head-on from the far side of the training track several furlongs away. Even the professionals had no one positioned to catch the field's early progress. *Daily Racing Form* would not chart the first quarter mile.

For three furlongs and more, the youngsters ran well bunched, anybody's race. Reporters guessed that Miss Jemima or Dominique held a narrow lead. "Just before reaching the half," turf historian John Hervey would write, "Dominique, which had set a fast pace against a stiff head wind, began to feel its effects and John P. Grier passed him, taking command."[6] Now Loftus shook his whip for Red to see and Man o' War changed gears. "Dominique did not falter, as so many of the Peter Quinces do," the *New York Times* reporter pointed out. "He did not have time to falter before Man o' War was on his way, leaving the others to fight it out among themselves."[7]

John P. Grier threw the strongest punch. Nearing the grandstand, he had opened about five lengths on Dominique. But Man o' War, seemingly without effort, stayed about three lengths ahead of Grier. Roughly one furlong from the finish, the many spectators who didn't have strong binoculars recognized the champion—"running so easily that there was no question about the finish"[8]—and a cheer swept through the crowd. In the Riddle box, the polite ideal of losing as if you liked it and winning as if you didn't care fell away. "Mr. Riddle patted, almost slapped, his wife on the back as man does to man to express deep emotion or devotion," a reporter noted, "and her own shout, or better perhaps, scream of joy, could be heard above those around her."[9]

Eddie Ambrose hustled John P. Grier for all he was worth, Grier "swerving under pressure"[10] but game to the end. Unhurried, Red floated ahead. "There was nothing spectacular about the finish," reporter George Daley declared, "but there was something commanding about the way in which he raced to victory, with his ears pricked as if out for an exercise gallop. The crowd recognized this and almost to a man shouted approval as only a racing crowd can shout."[11] If her eyes were indeed on Man o' War, Johnny Loftus's mother saw that "just before going over the finish line Loftus was looking back to see how much he had to spare."[12] Officially, it was Man o' War by two and a half, then John P. Grier by four over Dominique, fast-closing Cleopatra a neck farther back in fourth, and Upset a half length behind her. Red's official time was 1:11 3/5—the fastest Futurity since the race had moved in 1913 to Belmont Park.

For a surreal moment, as Red galloped out around the clubhouse turn, confetti suddenly poured from the sky. A Curtiss airplane dipped low over the track, sending "great clouds of handbills" falling onto the course and spectators' heads. "It was a particularly dangerous stunt," the *Thoroughbred Record* complained, "but the aviator, whoever he was, had no regard for the danger. He continued to scatter the bills over the returning horses and the crowd. . . . He was safe from pursuit in the air and probably continued to drop the bills until he was out of material. Needless to say he will be unwelcome if he attempts any such a performance at any other of the tracks."[13]

Perhaps Sam Riddle and Lou Feustel hardly noticed. Cheers and applause, spreading throughout the clubhouse and grandstand, plus the trackside band playing "Hail to the Chief,"[14] drowned out the airplane sound.[15]

Quickly rebounding from John P. Grier's defeat, Harry Payne Whitney became one of the first to reach and congratulate Riddle. "Like all others," a reporter noted, "he had words of the highest praise for horse and trainer."[16] These words competed with an "ovation [that] lasted fully five minutes," plus the exuberant flinging, loss, and destruction of many straw hats.[17]

The inspiration for this demonstration turned counterclockwise and trotted back toward the judges' stand, "scarcely puffing,"[18] looking "fit and ready to do it all over again. . . ."[19] As the band played in tribute and fans continued "clapping and applauding uproariously,"[20] a newsreel camera pulling in soundless black-and-white footage of the pandemonium caught Sam Riddle patting his horse and praising his horse's handlers, "his face wreathed in smiles. . . ."[21] "Thus, inadvertently, he got himself in the moving pictures," a reporter noted, "and if that smile of his is reproduced it will make many a man and woman in audiences all over the United States smile with him. His face was the picture of the keenest joy and satisfaction."[22]

Satisfaction spilled over into the paddock as Feustel supervised Red's cooling out. A crowd swarmed after them, reluctant to let the moment slide away. "It is a great satisfaction to own such a wonderful horse," Sam Riddle said before rushing away to board his Philadelphia-bound train. "To me he is worth his weight in gold. He has run his last race for this year as he has done quite enough, but he will be back next year, barring accidents, to continue, I hope, the great career he has begun so well. My trainer, Louis Feustel, deserves the highest credit for the skill in which he has trained and handled the horse."[23] As far as anyone knew, Feustel had just become the youngest man to train a Futurity winner,[24] but he aimed the credit back to Man o' War. "That fellow speaks for me," Lou told reporters seeking his thoughts. "He is so full of health and spirits and has such a happy disposition that it has been a pleasure to handle him. Few men are lucky enough to get such a horse to train."[25]

The horse himself was blooming in plain sight: sleek as a sea lion, with nostrils wide as teacups to inhale great streams of air.

Returning to the jockey house and changing clothes for a fancy dinner on the town,[26] Johnny Loftus stepped away from a summit of his own extraordinary career. After this race, he had posed for motion-picture cameras several times and told reporters that Man o' War was the best horse he had ever ridden.[27] And to cap it all, his mother had met him when he came back to the paddock, throwing her arms around him and sobbing with delight. In such moments, the terrible Sanford Memorial Stakes seemed to disappear.

Sam Riddle, retiring Man o' War for the season, seemed to have let that one bad experience dissolve. "I've accomplished the dream of my life," he remarked. "I have won the Hopeful and Futurity with the same horse and I am content to rest on my laurels."[28]

Having watched Man o' War win New York's richest race, August Belmont spent the night at his Hempstead, Long Island, house. When he went back to his Manhattan apartment, evidence of his Futurity pride remained behind. On Wednesday, September 17, Belmont wrote to his Hempstead chambermaid Nora Cloherty, "I left on Sunday in my room, a portion of all the Sunday papers containing account of Man o' War's race. Hope you have not thrown them away. Save them for me when I return this evening."[29]

August Belmont, the most powerful man in a sport that attracted powerful men, sometimes misplaced valuable objects. Moving between his far-flung homes, offices, and farms, he found himself missing a pair of tortoiseshell-framed spectacles, a gold fountain pen, a silver matchbox. A note to his vigilant staff usually solved these problems. At the racetrack, however, Belmont tried to corral forces beyond his control.

Thirty minutes after Man o' War's smashing Futurity win, Major Belmont endured the ridicule of a pet project. The inaugural Jockey Club Stakes, a twelve-furlong event to promote top-class distance racing, was supposed to reinforce Belmont's ideals for the sport. Unfortunately, it flopped. Commander Ross took Sir Barton to Maryland for a richer race, and Sam Hildreth's formidable colt Purchase scared off the remaining contenders. So, with jockey Clarence Kummer aboard, Purchase galloped around the course alone.

Watching a single horse approach the barrier, then start running as if he had someone to beat was too much for some spectators. "A laugh went up from the crowd when Purchase went on his way," the *New York Times* noted. For two minutes and forty-one seconds, the crowd waited while Purchase made one dawdling lap of the course. They had no suspense, no bets to win, and no record time to cheer. Walkovers were bad news for a race meet—and this autumn, Belmont Park spectators had endured two of them.

Some horsemen and reporters blamed August Belmont for this shortfall, making horses at Belmont Park run clockwise like many European courses instead of counterclockwise like all other American tracks. More horses would have run in the Jockey Club Stakes, they said, if Belmont Park ran the American way. Trying to encourage versatile Thoroughbreds that could bend right as well as left, August Belmont pushed against relentless disapproval but still acted as if he could prevail. He practiced such discipline everywhere, from his Jockey Club office to his Long Island farm. Belmont required stable boys at the Nursery, whether Protestant or Catholic, to attend the appropriate church services. They also had to obey their earthly lord.

One day in June 1903, apprentice John H. Freit, about fourteen years old, failed to tip his cap to Mr. Belmont. A sharp rebuke followed. Five years later, in court, Freit testified that Belmont "shook him roughly and called him a 'jackass.' "[30] Summoned to the witness stand, Belmont responded, "I don't recall the exact language I used, but it was proper language intended for the purpose of a reprimand. I often reprimanded my boys for lack of courtesy."[31]

Any reprimands that Lou Feustel received while working for Belmont had been swallowed, not made public. John Freit, however, had proven that a mere employee could make Belmont pay. At first, Freit had apologized for his hat-tipping failure and stayed on at the Nursery, but within months his situation went sour. The following year, Belmont posted a notice in the *Racing Calendar,* an official Jockey Club publication distributed to racing officials and horsemen, stating that Freit had left his employment without permission and "owners and trainers are hereby warned not to employ or harbor him."[32] Freit eventually sued Belmont for $100,000 in damages, claiming that this blackballing notice cost him a lucrative jockey career. Belmont admitted in court that the Rules of Racing didn't require him to publish such a warning, but he claimed that the announcement was not malicious—it simply protected the racing establishment from Freit's disregard for authority. Said Belmont, "I felt it was a flagrant case of insubordination."[33] The jury agreed.

Ironically, while punishing his former employee for insubordination, Belmont also actively supported New York State's groundbreaking Workman's Compensation bill.[34] With his endorsement, many employers became financially responsible for physical injuries that their employees suffered on the job. Injuries to reputation, however, remained far harder to prove. In October 1909, shortly before Freit's appeal would have gone to trial, Belmont settled the rider's $100,000 complaint for $3,500.

In 1920, presiding over The Jockey Club, he would endorse far more costly choices.

Moving his stable to Maryland in early autumn instead of staying at Belmont Park, Commander Ross enjoyed remarkable success. While Purchase drew catcalls for his walkover in Belmont's $5,000-added Jockey Club Stakes, Sir Barton returned to glory in Havre de Grace's $10,000-added Potomac Handicap. In his Kentucky Derby style, he shot to the front and stayed there, easily beating Billy Kelly by a length and a half while carrying 132 pounds to Billy's 125. Taking a conservative tone, the *New York Times* noted that Sir Barton ran "with much of the ease and grace which marked his races in the early part of the season."[35]

With Sir Barton fit, Bedwell kept him busy. On September 24, eleven days after his Potomac win, Sir Barton went off as favorite in the Graw's Record Purse. For the first time, he would race against older horses—a challenge much like a college senior ballplayer facing mature professionals. A top-notch three-year-old might outclass most of his older rivals but fail to beat the very best.

The Record Purse didn't offer all-star competition, but its small field included four-year-old stakes winner The Porter, who had easily beaten Exterminator on September 11 while racing one mile and 70 yards. Now Sir Barton would face him going one mile.

Because Johnny Loftus couldn't make Sir Barton's weight assignment of 110 pounds, Earl Sande took over. Sir Barton handled his jockey change and the track surface rated "heavy," but in the homestretch The Porter cruised past him to win by five lengths. Sir Barton, under strong urging, finished well clear of the rest. He had run like a good three-year-old but not the May and June superstar.

Sir Barton's loss, however, was far from the week's worst shocker. On a fast track in race six that Friday, September 26, jockey Andy Schuttinger had

Dolina in second place, when, unaccountably, she tripped. Dolina hadn't broken down, but she was falling, flipping down onto the track. Three horses close behind—Silk Bird, Artist, and Cain Spring—collided with Dolina, who rolled over onto jockey Schuttinger. As the dust cleared, Schuttinger lay "badly cut and bruised,"[36] suffering from a broken leg and dangerous internal injuries. Not far away, the horse Cain Spring also had a broken leg. His life could not be saved. Schuttinger would be laid up at the Havre de Grace Hospital in such precarious condition that some newspapers reported him dead.

One more life shivered in the balance. When Phil Musgrave fell with Silk Bird into the scramble of horse bodies, a hoof thwacked him on the head. The Havre de Grace infield became his emergency room. For forty-five minutes, doctors tried to treat his fractured skull. But Musgrave was beyond help.

If Johnny Loftus was shaken by the news of this awful accident, it didn't show while he was on the job. The following day, he rode two stakes winners at the Graw for Commander Ross. First came a canny performance with Billy Kelly, getting up to win the Susquehanna Handicap by a neck over a horse carrying 30 pounds less. Then came the $10,000-added Havre de Grace Handicap, with Cudgel giving three and five pounds, respectively, to Exterminator and Sir Barton. There was no room here for sentiment. Loftus rode Cudgel because Bedwell thought that his five-year-old warrior—not his three-year-old celebrity—would beat Exterminator, one of the very best older horses in America. Only four months earlier, Loftus had scored wire-to-wire wins with Sir Barton in the Kentucky Derby and Preakness. Now he watched J. Metcalf sprint along early with Sir Barton and showed no mercy when unleashing Cudgel's stretch run. He drove Cudgel past Exterminator to win by a half length in track-record time, while Sir Barton finished third, losing second place by only a nose.

The result might well have been different. "[Bill] Knapp got into difficulties with [Exterminator] in the final furlong and twice had him blocked," the *New York Times* noted. "When finally free, Exterminator made a game effort, but it was too late."[37] It was the Sanford stretch run in reverse, with Loftus outfoxing Knapp. "Cudgel" the *Times* concluded, ". . . was in receipt of an excellent ride by Jockey Johnny Loftus."

Loftus soon would give another Ross star a far more problematic ride.

II

DONE WITH MIRRORS

By LATE SEPTEMBER of 1919, Johnny Loftus had struck a balance that few jockeys ever found. While his typical riding weight rose to an off-putting 118 pounds, his winning average for the year remained a mighty 36 percent. Loftus got the best of everything, it seemed. Not only could he indulge in being heavy but he also was on course to become far and away the year's highest-earning jockey in purses won—a feat that he also had accomplished when his career first hit high gear, in 1913. In 1919, however, his mounts would earn more than three times as much.

Riding the year's two most successful racehorses gave Loftus a fat bankroll and a leading role in their duel for number one. Man o' War had ended his season with earnings of $83,325. Sir Barton, still active in Maryland's autumn circuit, had earned only $8,875 less. Commander Ross wanted him on top. And so, while Man o' War enjoyed light training at his Eastern Shore haven and bunked in "a special fireproof stable"[1] that Sam Riddle had built for him, Sir Barton aimed for the October 4 Maryland Handicap at Laurel Park—a notable race, paying $7,750 for first place. He would have to get by a talented new challenger, though: Mad Hatter, a three-year-old son of Fair Play that Sam Hildreth leased from August Belmont.

Hildreth had been cautious with this late-developing colt, who shared three of four grandparents with Man o' War.[2] Now Mad Hatter was progressing impressively. After finishing second in his September racing debut, he quickly scored two wins. As his name suggested, Mad Hatter could be temperamental, but he also showed two of Man o' War's useful traits: a large capacity for hard work and a ravenous appetite.

When Sir Barton met Mad Hatter in the Maryland Handicap, bettors found it hard to choose between them. The newcomer lacked experience, but Sir Barton would carry 133 pounds to Mad Hatter's 106. Racing ten furlongs, that was an advantage to take seriously.

With his jockey trying to wear out rivals carrying higher weights, Mad Hatter sailed to the front and set a burning pace—:22 and two, :46 and three—even quicker than Sir Barton's sharpest openers. Sir Barton settled into fourth place, even briefly sliding back to fifth. Midway through the race, Mad Hatter slowed down and Thunderclap poked his head in front. But Mad Hatter only needed a breather. Rounding the far turn, he edged ahead again as Thunderclap, spotting him 12 pounds, tired.

And Sir Barton waited. Then, with slightly more than a quarter mile left, it was time. Ignoring his high weight, Loftus steered him outside around the far turn—no risk of being pocketed. Mad Hatter hit the mile two-fifths faster than Laurel's track mark, yet suddenly Sir Barton was closing fast. Rushing up at Mad Hatter's outside, Sir Barton was only half a length behind.

For about one furlong, lanky Mad Hatter and stocky Sir Barton matched strides, a question of 27 pounds balancing between them. Halfway down the stretch, the balance fell. Mad Hatter had run a tremendous race, but he had done too much too soon. His sensational early pace was no help now. Inside the final furlong, Mad Hatter faltered and Sir Barton pulled away.

In the final yards, Sir Barton widened the gap, winning by two elongating lengths from Mad Hatter, three and a half from Audacious, four from Thunderclap, and six from Be Frank. He made them look ordinary, and that was not the case. Seven days later, Thunderclap would set an American record at a mile and a half. Fourteen days later, Be Frank would easily win the 2 1/4-mile Latonia Cup while getting 12 pounds from dominant long-distance runner Exterminator. Although *Daily Racing Form*'s chart would say that Sir Barton won the Maryland Handicap "easily," his official time of 2:02 2/5 was only two-fifths slower than Laurel Park's track mark. With 133 pounds up, he had run the final quarter mile in :24 and change—even though, somewhere during the race, his shelly feet had lost two shoes.

Struck by the breezy way that Sir Barton had thrashed Mad Hatter, Sam Hildreth said, "There is a real race horse."[3]

Jim Ross treasured another tribute born from this race. Johnny Loftus later called Sir Barton's Maryland Handicap the best effort by any horse he had ever ridden. It also was the last major race that Loftus would win.

During October 1919, while Johnny Loftus relaxed in his success, a tremor in the Midwest started a slow, strong wave that would saturate the sports world. While Sir Barton regained his prestige and rested from his sparkling Maryland Handicap, major-league baseball felt the first tremble of losing its good name. Though the news wouldn't break through for months yet, the damage happened in Ohio and Illinois between October 1 and 9. It happened in the World Series, as the heavily favored Chicago White Sox surrendered to the Cincinnati Reds.

Talk of the World Series fix quickly became an open secret and baseball administrators stubbornly deflected the rumors. Dishonesty in baseball's ultimate games would match The Jockey Club's worst nightmare and then some. Unlike Thoroughbred racing, professional baseball had no interstate governing body that could punish wrongdoers and represent integrity. A World Series travesty, if proved true, could kill their lucrative business. And so individual team owners took a tone of indignation and denial. Meanwhile, Thoroughbred racing couldn't be smug. The man rumored to be behind the World Series fix also frequented the clubhouses at Saratoga and Belmont Park. Whispers were spreading about Arnold "the Brain" Rothstein.

From The Jockey Club's Manhattan headquarters, August Belmont could see how much ground racing had gained in the past few years and how very much it stood to lose. The public tolerated, even enjoyed, a certain amount of reckless behavior. But it could not approve if fixers infiltrated the highest level of the sport.

For now, the public did not seem concerned. In New York, record crowds had gathered to see Sir Barton and Man o' War. In Maryland, purse monies drawn from swelling pari-mutuel pools made New York tracks look miserly. And in Kentucky, two days after the World Series ended, the inaugural Latonia Championship offered three-year-old Thoroughbreds a whopping $50,000—more money than the starting lineup of the Chicago White Sox received for the whole year. "Hard Guy" Bedwell spared Sir Barton the quick train trip from eastern Maryland to central Kentucky for this landmark race, but Sam Hildreth shipped Mad Hatter. Chasing Sir Barton one week earlier had strengthened his stamina and sharpened his speed.

Soaking rain turned Latonia's track muddy, but Mad Hatter seemed comfortable and his rider stayed cool. For a mile, a mile and an eighth, a mile and a quarter, Laverne Fator kept Mad Hatter in third place, under a strong hold, "though," a reporter noted, "it was all he could do to keep the racer from getting away from him."[4] Finally released, Mad Hatter bounded off to win by eight lengths.

Sam Hildreth declared that Mad Hatter was as good as any three-year-old in America. "Now that the brown colt has been one mile and three-quarters in the Latonia championship [sic] at speed," one reporter confided, "Hildreth questions whether there is a 3-year-old about that can give Mad Hatter any weight at all."[5]

Three and a half weeks later, Sir Barton would give him 21 pounds.

November saw Maryland racing move from Laurel Park to Pimlico, from a small town roughly halfway between Baltimore and Washington, D.C., to a site actually within Baltimore city limits. The earnings duel could be settled there. Sir Barton needed less than twelve hundred dollars to pass Man o' War. The November 5 Pimlico Autumn Handicap, worth $3,650 to the winner, provided a promising opportunity.

Although Sir Barton hadn't raced for thirty-two days, the public expected another tour de force like his Maryland Handicap. A *Washington Post* columnist asserted that, "Sir Barton, even with 132 pounds up, looks to have a mortgage on the race."[6] After all, Mad Hatter was in with 111 pounds, five more than when Sir Barton trounced him. Bettors made Mad Hatter the second choice, at roughly 2–1, and Sir Barton the odds-on favorite.

Track conditions didn't do justice to the rematch. Rain had drenched Pimlico during the weekend, and Monday's cloudy weather kept the running surface from completely drying out. On Tuesday afternoon, as their mounts paraded to the start of the Pimlico Autumn Handicap, the more observant jockeys knew that every path around the track was not equally good. Water continued draining toward the inner rail, making the inside path deeper and more tiring.

Lining up behind the barrier, Mad Hatter had drawn the soggy rail. Sailor, Bridesman, Milkmaid, and Sir Barton rolled out to his right. From his middle position, Bridesman leaped into the early lead, pressed by Milkmaid. Fator rated Mad Hatter back into third place, with Sir Barton tracking him,

floating over to the inside. Giving 21 pounds to Mad Hatter, Loftus grabbed
the shortest route around. The same strategy had worked brilliantly in the
Maryland Handicap. But on that day, the inner path had been dry.

Turning for home, Bridesman scampered in front with his 107 pounds.
Then his advantage vanished. Fator let Mad Hatter fly down the firm-footing
middle of the track, and in no time they were all alone. At the wire, it was
Mad Hatter by four, Bridesman chasing in second place, and Sir Barton going nowhere. Somewhere in the final furlong, hopelessly beaten, Loftus
stopped making him try. Sir Barton finished a distant third, eight lengths behind Bridesman and twelve lengths behind Sam Hildreth's new star.

Instead of scoring a popular victory, Johnny Loftus rode back to a furious
"Hard Guy" Bedwell. Curious spectators saw them arguing in the paddock,
for anyone nearby to hear. Most reporters, however, either missed the fight or
chose not to write about it. Months later, one politely noted that Bedwell
"was displeased with the ride and said uncomplimentary things about the
jockey."[7] But overall, most journalists treated the dispute like dirty under-
wear that should be hidden in a hamper rather than displayed. The general
public did not need to know what Bedwell and Loftus had said.

The impact of those angry words, however, soon became clear. Only two
days after his floundering defeat, Sir Barton faced three tough opponents[8] in
Pimlico's Fall Serial Weight-for-Age Race No. 2. Spurning Loftus, Bedwell
gave the leg up on Sir Barton to twenty-year-old Clarence Kummer, winner
of a gold stopwatch as the leading jockey at Empire City's autumn meet.
Breaking sharply and showing what *Daily Racing Form* called "a high flight of
speed from the start,"[9] Sir Barton easily won the one-mile race and jumped
past Man o' War on the annual earnings list. Perhaps the uniformly fast track
surface and carrying 12 pounds less than in his recent defeat helped, but the
dramatic turnaround looked startling. "It is hard to explain the race in the
light of Sir Barton's previous performance," said the *Washington Post.* "Then
he had no speed at any time. Kummer instead of Loftus rode him, and perhaps this made the difference, but to the casual onlooker, the sudden improvement is difficult of explanation."[10]

Sir Barton paid an unusually generous $7.20 for each two dollars bet on
him to win.

Johnny Loftus, who had guided Sir Barton to victory in five classic races,
left the track and started his winter vacation in New York City and Chicago.
Commander Ross no longer wanted him.[11]

* * *

During the autumn of 1919, as his weight pushed the upper limits for an American jockey, Johnny Loftus attracted rumors that he either would retire from the saddle in 1920 or move to a country with higher racing weights. One journalist wrote that Loftus "has been almost overwhelmed with offers from English, French and Spanish noblemen of late . . . but it remained for a representative of a native Indian mogul—said to be the Rajah of Cashmir [sic]—to make an offer for Loftus' services that just about clinches his determination to try his luck in Europe next year."[12] The rajah's two-year contract reportedly offered a $25,000 annual retainer, plus victory bonuses that could add roughly $10,000 per year. All Loftus had to do was spend the warm months riding in England and the winters in India. In late November, however, Loftus proved that he would neither move abroad nor retire. Instead, he renewed his contract to ride first call for Glen Riddle Farm, with a one-year salary said to be as high as $15,000,[13] plus a substantial signing bonus.[14] Replacing Commander Ross with second call would be prominent New York owner Morton L. Schwartz.[15]

During the early spring of 1920, while living at Sam Riddle's Eastern Shore estate and regularly exercising Man o' War, Johnny Loftus made known his master plan. He would spend one more year as a jockey, then retire from the saddle and take out a trainer's license.[16] One more year of making weight, risking his life, building his bankroll, and winning races with the greatest horse he had ever known. Then it would be time to stop.

Bill Knapp, wintering in New Orleans and returning to New York in early March, formed a similar plan. "Unless he changes his mind," the March 6 Daily Racing Form noted, "Knapp will do little or no riding this year, devoting his time to the training end of the sport."[17] Knapp did, in fact, change his mind in late March and submit his jockey application. Still, he had survived the jockey's life for nearly twenty years. It was nearly time.

The Jockey Club's License Committee passed judgment on a more problematic figure in mid-March of 1920, when they began reviewing the annual applications from riders and trainers. As he had done every year since 1913, Cal Shilling tried to regain his jockey license. If successful, he would handle Commander Ross's best horses in major races. Guy Bedwell, who held Shilling in highest esteem, would see to that. But as far as The Jockey Club was concerned, it never would be time for Carroll Hugh Shilling to resume his jockey career. "For the best interests of racing," that door would remain tightly closed.

This phrase "for the best interests of racing" had become The Jockey
Club's blanket to cover great and petty sins, leaving outsiders to guess at each
specific cause. Such discretion might protect the accused as well as the accus-
ers, but New York turf reporter Toney Betts would perceive something else:
Algernon Daingerfield, The Jockey Club's confidential secretary, had a horror of bad publicity. Six bland words, "for the best interests of racing," hid
the sport's most controversial incidents from public view. Journalists complained. The public complained. The Jockey Club quietly applied its considerable leverage and the accused remained, publicly, silent.

Daingerfield's discreet phrase got a workout early in 1920, after The Jockey
Club's License Committee rejected nine jockey applications in its March 11
session. Six of these refusals became public the following day. The other three
required further confidential debate. And so, on Wednesday, March 17—
Saint Patrick's Day—the Stewards of The Jockey Club held a special meeting
to discuss one potential outcast: John Patrick Loftus.

Around the racetracks, there had been speculation that Loftus might be in
trouble. People who got their racing news only from major newspapers had
no clue. The March 18 announcement fulfilled some racetrackers' prophecies
and shocked many casual fans: Johnny Loftus would be denied a license to
ride.

The decision was sensational enough. Making it worse, no one said *why*.
The betting public was supposed to assume that removing Loftus from action
would benefit them. Yet this jockey had won *37 percent* of his races during
1919. For anyone who trusted consistency, there was no better bet right now
than Johnny Loftus—very few better, in fact, in all of racing history.

"The discretionary power of The Jockey Club is almost too Czar-like,"
one reporter declared.[18] "There is considerable difference of opinion as to the
justice of the decision," a *New York Times* editorial asserted.[19] Most reporters
expressed doubt that there had been foul play. "Loftus has had so much at
stake," turf columnist Skipper Sinnott wrote, "has been in a position to make
so much money legitimately and was so near the end of his brilliant career in
the saddle that it is hard to understand his being tempted and yielding to the
persuasion of those who would put over crooked work on the track."[20]

As he had done when Loftus had his license delayed in 1919, reporter
George Daley pointed out another danger: Official silence fed harmful rumors. While figuring that The Jockey Club must have a valid reason for punishing Loftus, Daley noted that "this fact should be pointed out—there is

quite a difference between denying a license to ride or train and in ruling off the turf. Loftus has not been ruled off, which is a plain indication that he was not charged with sharp practice or dishonest riding. The offense, no doubt, was of a minor kind, which leads to the hope that in due time he may be restored to good standing and allowed to continue in his chosen profession."[21]

Johnny Loftus had wanted one more season of race riding and then a graceful transition to a trainer's job. Why couldn't The Jockey Club let him be a jockey for nine more months?

Loftus launched an appeal.

Shortly before The Jockey Club stewards convened on Thursday, April 8, Samuel Doyle Riddle appeared on their doorstep. "It was presumed that he had come up from Philadelphia to speak a good word in the boy's behalf," the *New York World* reported. The public would not learn what kind of hearing Riddle received. Racing insiders might have guessed that Jockey Club officers did not give him any confidential information and certainly could not let him join their final discussion. Sam Riddle owned Man o' War, but he was not a member of The Jockey Club, never mind its most private committee. Riddle may have been as surprised as anyone when their verdict arrived: "The stewards of The Jockey Club refused to reopen the case of ex-Jockey J. Loftus."[22]

Two letters, e-x, slammed the door on an eleven-year career.

At the same time, the stewards made an announcement that would convince many people, over years to come, that Johnny Loftus lost his license because of a Sanford Memorial Stakes conspiracy. They revealed that Loftus would have new company on the ground: Bill Knapp. The same secrecy prevailed. Thoroughly surprised, the *New York Times* defended Knapp's honor with a backhanded compliment: "As the [1919] season advanced, his riding fell off and toward the end he had lost much of his early fame. However, this was due apparently to declining ability and no charge of dishonesty was ever made against him."[23]

What could the specific reason be? Digging through the recent activities of Johnny Loftus, journalists examined incidents of rough riding, warnings about keeping bad company, losses with heavy favorites, and insubordination. Nothing seemed to fit completely.

If foul riding were the reason, why wouldn't The Jockey Club say so openly? Typically, they publicized rough-riding bans, emphasizing their own vigilance. This didn't seem likely at all.

Keeping company with certain bookmakers and professional gamblers could lead a jockey toward exile. The *New York Evening Telegram* carefully aired a rumor that "outside associations with whom [Loftus] has been identified in a social way have had much to do with bringing him into the sort of disrepute which would warrant any such action."[24] But reporters refrained from naming names, and so the public could not judge how credible this rumor might or might not be. Finger wagging against "bad company" may have been a generic warning that the stewards drilled into every rider—a reminder that *we're watching you.*

By late August of 1919, some horseplayers had started complaining that Loftus was suffering too many questionable-looking losses with heavy favorites. Reporter O'Neil Sevier went so far as to write, "It is only fair to Loftus to say that he might satisfactorily explain all of his seemingly queer rides on these well-backed horses. The chance should be given him. His erratic work is assuming the dimensions of a public scandal."[25] But only a year earlier, another reporter had noted, "As he is a jockey of sterling honesty, his mounts are always well backed."[26] From 1918 through 1919, a clear pattern had emerged: The more dominant Johnny Loftus became, the higher public expectations for him rose. His occasional poor ride could look all the worse precisely because a great jockey, rather than a good one, performed it. Bettors who paid special attention to Loftus and wagered more heavily on his mounts could feel all the more deeply wounded by his inevitable human failures.

Some observers believed that such a highly skilled rider as Loftus could not lose with the seemingly best horse unless he chose to do so. Many others agreed with George Daley, who wrote after the Mount Vernon Handicap, ". . . he is not so stupid as to deliberately 'pull' [Sun Briar] in what appeared to be such a flagrant way, even if he had been inclined."[27] Thoughtful spectators might have noticed an honest trait that would fit the Loftus losses with Sun Briar, Man o' War, Beaming Beauty, and Sir Barton: overconfidence. While aware that each horse had limitations, he had handled them as if they outclassed their competition.

Losses with heavy favorites might have gotten Loftus into trouble, but was that enough for him to lose his license? The owners of Sun Briar, Beaming Beauty, and Man o' War had kept employing him after those defeats. There had been, however, one notable case of insubordination.

People who came to believe that Johnny Loftus and Bill Knapp conspired to help Upset beat Man o' War might then have considered what the two men did after losing their jockey licenses. That summer, Bill Knapp would apply for a trainer's license and then hire a lawyer to fight for him when The Jockey Club turned him down. Knapp's objection wouldn't make it to court, but he would try to protest officially. Johnny Loftus, galloping horses for trainer Lewis Garth and hoping to regain his jockey license in 1921, would remain silent.

Sir Barton, not Man o' War, was the key.

Most newspapers didn't touch the Johnny Loftus story that leaked out of New Orleans in late November 1919. They also refused to touch another story broken by the same publication earlier that fall, a story printing the names of eight Chicago White Sox players who had taken bribes to lose the World Series. They ignored the reporting done by a sporting paper called *Collyer's Eye*, which had survived since 1915 by giving gamblers uncensored information on baseball, boxing, horse racing, and other sports. Late in 1919, its November 29 issue ended up on August Belmont's desk.

"Quite a furore [*sic*] was created this week," Bert Collyer wrote, "when horsemen arriving from Maryland reported that strenuous efforts looking to the banishment of Trainer Sam Hildreth and Jockey Loftus were being made."[28] It all traced back to Mad Hatter beating Sir Barton. "After the race," Collyer noted, "Bedwell accosted and openly accused Loftus of 'pulling' Sir Barton. Later he took Hildreth over the verbal derby route claiming that he was responsible for Loftus' ride. In a word Hildreth stood accused of 'influencing' the rider for the Ross establishment. According to the well informed it is understood that Commander Ross will 'leave no stone unturned' in order to bring retribution home to those responsible for the defeat of his horse. Color is lent all this by the absence of Loftus—in the saddle—since that time."

To explore this story, August Belmont would rely on his own private eyes: Pinkerton detectives, whose logo showed a wide-open eye with the motto, We Never Sleep. He would file the copy of *Collyer's Eye*, with its banner across the top of page one shouting, "Bedwell Accuses Hildreth of Influencing Loftus," with one word circled in pencil: "Hildreth."

If Bedwell's accusations were correct, Hildreth and Loftus could be ruled off the turf. Never again could they hold any kind of job at any racetrack using Jockey Club rules. But The Jockey Club would not swallow Bedwell's story whole. Samuel Clay Hildreth—the trainer whose skill August Belmont admired most, now allied with oil tycoon Harry Sinclair—would keep receiving his trainer's license, year after year, until his death in 1929. And so, it seemed, The Jockey Club did not believe that Hildreth had bribed Loftus. But something stuck.

Bedwell's charges did not have to be completely right. The Jockey Club's action might not prove that Johnny Loftus actually had committed a racing sin. It could result from what certain prominent persons believed.

Johnny Loftus had an answer to Bedwell's accusations all right—an answer that, if true, would embarrass a powerful sportsman so thoroughly that The Jockey Club could never let the public know.

Arguing with Johnny Loftus in the Pimlico paddock on November 5, 1919, "Hard Guy" Bedwell destroyed his relationship with a young man whom he had helped raise up to championship level. Here was the same young man who had followed him to South Carolina in 1912 and become a leading rider with his support; who had helped him win four big stakes with Sir Barton only five months back; who had given Sir Barton one of his most brilliant rides only thirty-two days ago. And now Bedwell blasted him, in public, with the worst words that a trainer could aim at a jockey: You pulled my horse.

Trainers expected a jockey to swallow any criticism they gave. Employees weren't supposed to disagree with the boss. But Bedwell showed that he didn't know Johnny Loftus that well after all. A trainer couldn't expect a jockey who had dared disagree with A. K. Macomber's trainer to simply tip his hat and accept an attack on his integrity. When Bedwell accused Loftus of pulling Sir Barton, Johnny fired back his own reason why the champion "had no speed at any time."[29] He accused Bedwell of giving him a cold horse—that is, running Sir Barton without hop.[30]

There was no drug testing to prove or disprove Johnny's claim. There would be no descriptions in the next day's newspapers of Sir Barton's body language, whether or not he had looked especially alert or lethargic while going to the post. It would be safe to say that Loftus, a veteran jockey who had ridden Sir Barton many times, knew how hopped horses acted and how Sir Barton compared. There was no chemist waiting to prove or disprove what he said, but Loftus qualified as an expert witness.

In the Pimlico paddock on a November afternoon, America's leading trainer and jockey attacked each other's reputations without mercy. Bedwell claiming that Loftus had pulled Sir Barton was deadly enough. Loftus retorting that Bedwell had withheld Sir Barton's hop used equally deadly force. Then Loftus stepped even further past any respect for the trainer's authority. "What's more," a spectator heard him warn Bedwell, "I'm going to tell Commander Ross."[31]

And he did. America's leading jockey went to the nation's most successful owner and told him that his most celebrated horse, the champion cheered by so many thousands at the track and featured in newsreels across the land, had run those great races with hop. Did Loftus expect Ross to fire Bedwell? Outsiders could not know. Apparently, he did expect the Commander, who had treated him most considerately during their association, to believe his testimony.

But the Commander did not. Ross refused to believe that Bedwell ever gave any of his horses hop. Perhaps he did not want to face what could happen if what Loftus said was true. The Jockey Club's own Rules of Racing clearly stated the penalty for giving a horse any drug or stimulants before a race. If The Jockey Club believed what Loftus said—that Sir Barton often raced "hot"— they would have no choice but to ban "Hard Guy" Bedwell from Thoroughbred racing permanently. And if, upon investigation, they discovered that the Commander had approved of hopping his horse, they could ban him, too.

Instead, four months after telling Commander Ross that Sir Barton ran a poor race without drugs, John Patrick Loftus lost his right to ride racehorses. As years passed and barely publicized details slipped from sight, many people would assume that Loftus had been grounded for dishonesty. The general public would not be allowed to consider what a few insiders suspected at the time: that Johnny Loftus lost his jockey license by offering more honesty than the sport could stand.

Although grounding a jockey was fairly easy, The Jockey Club performed a delicate dance with more influential powers. While its stewards demoted Johnny Loftus to an exercise rider, the club's confidential secretary helped an underworld leader break into racing with style: In the spring of 1920, Arnold Rothstein would launch his own stable, with his jockeys wearing silks designed by Algernon Daingerfield. The design shouted opulence with a golden horse depicted on the jacket's front and back, but the maroon color of the jacket and cap could remind spectators of August Belmont's famed maroon-and-scarlet silks. At a glimpse, onlookers could attach The Jockey Club chairman's prestige and power to runners owned by the Big Bankroll.

Rothstein had barely claimed owner status, however, when he felt a

restraining gesture. On May 15, the New York season's opening day, August
Belmont barred "ten well-known professional gamblers"[32]—including
Rothstein—from the clubhouses of racetracks operating under Jockey Club
rules. The ten still could watch races from the grandstand, but The Jockey
Club stewards were making a gentle objection . . . to Arnold Rothstein, good
friend of bucket-shop operator Charles Stoneham, good friend of New York
Governor Alfred E. Smith.

12

UP FOR GRABS

IN 1920, NEW YORK horsemen still called Kentucky "the West," as if it belonged to the wild frontier. The Kentucky Derby, staged in early May, had seemed until recently like a last hurrah in the hinterlands before the more prestigious New York season opened. But now Kentucky tracks, with their pari-mutuel machines, could turn gambling revenue into prize money, while New York tracks had to pretend that all bets were private transactions and let the bookmakers keep all profits. Churchill Downs chairman Matt Winn used this advantage to build the Kentucky Derby's status. In 1910, the Derby had offered the winner a modest $4,850. Nine years later, Sir Barton had collected an impressive $20,825 for his victory. For 1920, Churchill Downs dangled $30,000 and drew 107 Derby nominations. But Sam Riddle did not enter Man o' War.

The lengthy train trip to Louisville, with possible illness or accident, was one drawback. The Derby distance was another. Riddle reckoned that early May was too soon to race immature three-year-olds at a mile and a quarter. He may have pictured Harry Payne Whitney's champion filly Regret, who brilliantly won the 1915 Derby after shipping down from New Jersey and then didn't race again until August. Simply working too hard too soon could damage a young, growing horse. Why gamble Red's entire season for one race far from home? Riddle planned to enjoy his marvelous colt for many races within day-trip range of Philadelphia and across the street from his Saratoga cottage. He wanted his friends to see Red win a string of New York classics named for influential racing men: the Withers, Belmont, Dwyer, Travers, and

Lawrence Realization.[1] This schedule also pleased August Belmont—and The Jockey Club chairman's approval could only benefit Samuel Doyle Riddle.

On February 7, Riddle announced that Man o' War would skip the Kentucky Derby.[2] He made this decision even though at that time he had Johnny Loftus—a two-time Derby winner—living at his Maryland farm and riding Red regularly. "It just so happened that we didn't want to risk making the long trip to Kentucky," Lou Feustel would recall. "Besides, Man o' War was off his feed then and I wanted to bring him along for the summer . . . so that's the real story."[3] Exactly when and for how long Red lost his appetite went unrecorded.[4] A dozen years later, Feustel stated that, "Man o' War turned in some nice moves" during spring training, "but he also began to tuck up some about the flanks and that wasn't so good."[5]

In any case, the Kentucky Derby clearly wasn't Sam Riddle's priority. Instead, he nominated Red for the Suburban Handicap at Belmont Park—a historic ten-furlong event, like the Derby, but run four weeks later and worth about $25,000 less. Again, Riddle supported August Belmont's goals. In 1908, just before the antigambling movement severely crippled New York racing, winning the Suburban had been worth nearly $15,000 more than winning the Derby. Nominating Man o' War for the Suburban while passing the Derby, Riddle seemed to say that the impoverished New York classic had more intrinsic value.

Matt Winn, vigorously promoting Churchill Downs, felt snubbed. Without Man o' War, the Kentucky Derby remained a popular spectacle but couldn't claim to be a championship race. Instead, Red's humbled challengers would participate. Harry Payne Whitney would bring Upset and John P. Grier. Sarah Jeffords would bring Golden Broom.

Shipping their runners from Maryland's Eastern Shore to the Bluegrass State in early April, the Jeffordses quickly learned why Sam Riddle had reason to be cautious. Shortly after arriving, one of Walter's fillies died of "intestinal trouble."[6] Fortunately, Golden Broom stayed sound and thriving. After he worked a strong six furlongs at the Lexington track, *Daily Racing Form* proclaimed, "No horse in the big race is more likely to win it than this one."[7]

Golden Broom remained, however, overshadowed by Man o' War. His own trainer couldn't praise him without poking at the Riddle champion. "As a yearling Golden Broom could beat Man o' War, and in the early part of last year he could beat him," Mike Daly avowed. "I am of the opinion that he still can beat him."[8]

His first chance would come on May 18 at Baltimore, in the Preakness Stakes. Meanwhile, the reigning Preakness winner trained at Havre de Grace, preparing to prove that he might still be Horse of the Century.

By mid-April, Sir Barton seemed to be spoiling for a race. "I will give $500 to anyone that can find a blemish on him," Guy Bedwell declared. Sir Barton signaled his vigor by ripping a sweater and shirt from a stable boy's back and trying to eat an electric lightbulb high up in his stall.[9] But exuberance would not help him win his April 19 debut while giving his opponents up to 30 pounds. After pressing the early pace, Sir Barton finished fourth of six starters in the Graw's six-furlong Bel Air Handicap. The *Washington Post* called it a good effort, saying that the champion obviously needed a race to be fully fit.[10] When Sir Barton carried 133 pounds to victory in the six-furlong Climax Handicap only five days after losing the Bel Air, that assessment seemed right. The Climax did not, however, live up to its name. Three days later, Sir Barton raced again.

Stretching out to a mile and a sixteenth in the Marathon Handicap, hauling 135 pounds on a muddy track, while his opponents toted 110 and 106, Sir Barton was being worked like an iron horse. Bedwell's tactics made some sense: He had to push this lazy colt with fake races in the morning, anyway, so why not run for purse money instead? But in morning breezes, Sir Barton didn't spot his sparring partners 25 or 30 pounds. As a four-year-old in handicap races, his superiority had to weigh him down.

Three-year-old Wildair dominated the Marathon, easily opening a clear lead with his 110 pounds. Sir Barton rallied desperately in the homestretch, then gave up. He finished, as one reporter noted, "a distant and distressed last."[11]

Sir Barton had now raced three times in nine days. Bedwell didn't let up. Three days later, Sir Barton entered Havre de Grace's closing-day feature, the Philadelphia Handicap. Burdened with 133 pounds, he ran a close fourth to a long shot toting 100.

Now Maryland racing moved downstate to Baltimore. Sir Barton took a train trip but not a vacation. Four days after the Philadelphia Handicap, he carried 132 pounds in Pimlico's one-mile Rennert Handicap Purse—his fifth race in sixteen days.

Sir Barton emerged from the Rennert seeming less formidable, less magical, than he had appeared seventeen days before. He had won the race, successfully conceding up to 32 pounds, but weakened his reputation, going flat out to beat horses that didn't really belong in stakes races. He had earned two wins this year but shown no brilliance. Then Bedwell found a problem: a wrenched ankle.[12] Sir Barton would not race again in May, June, or July.

Exactly one week before the Kentucky Derby, Golden Broom made his three-year-old debut in Lexington's nine-furlong Blue Grass Stakes.[13] For a colt that never had raced farther than six furlongs, this was a bold step. Furthermore, five of his six opponents already had competed that spring. But Mike Daly apparently believed that Broom's condition and class would prevail.

Golden Broom got his customary streaking start. Fending off all rivals, he hit the first six furlongs in 1:11 3/5—only two-fifths slower than Lexington's track record. But on the far turn, Golden Broom began to tire. Peace Pennant passed him along the rail, Donnacona passed him wide, and Damask edged into third place. With one furlong remaining, Golden Broom trailed the leader by only one length and two heads—but he was through.

Peace Pennant beat Donnacona by a half length, with Damask a nose back in third. Four lengths later came By Golly, then Patches another three lengths back. Golden Broom trailed home two lengths behind Patches, beating only one horse. Although listed in the entries on Derby eve, he would not make it to the post.

Neither would John P. Grier, who was progressing more slowly than his stablemates. Instead of giving Grier his Derby eve workout, Jimmy Rowe scratched him from the race. Even so, Harry Payne Whitney's entry of Upset, Damask, and Wildair would be favored in the seventeen-horse field.

Stolen goods became a theme of the 1920 Kentucky Derby. By mid-afternoon, track police had arrested more than thirty pickpockets. The race itself became vulnerable to a different kind of theft, by a speedy horse that thrived without wet earth flinging back onto his body and spattering into his eyes. When the Derby field left the saddling paddock, the track had been soaked with rain and was just beginning to dry out. It suited a 16–1 shot named Paul Jones. Sailing away to a clear lead, the little gelding copied Sir Barton's style and pace. But where Sir Barton's Derby had turned into a cakewalk, Paul Jones faced a ferocious challenge from the colt who once got the jump on Man o' War. In the homestretch, Upset reached his girth, his neck. Half a furlong out, Paul Jones kept his lead by a nose.

"It was then to be a test of courage between these two," the *New York*

Times reported, "for by this time the pair had drawn away from the balance of the field and were in no danger of a surprise from the others. But Paul Jones never slackened his speed for a single stride, and hanging on gamely he finally outstayed Upset and gained the victory by a head."[14]

Horsemen could only guess whether Man o' War could have beaten them.

Sam Riddle wasn't in any hurry with Man o' War, even suggesting to Lou Feustel that the champion's three-year-old debut could wait until Belmont Park opened late in May. By the first week of March, however, Feustel had felt definite about returning in the May 18 Preakness Stakes at Pimlico. "I always thought Man o' War was a good colt," Feustel told *Daily Racing Form,* "but I never thought he would develop into the great horse he is."[15] Spurning any prep race for Pimlico's nine-furlong classic, Feustel showed smashing confidence. At the same time, he knew that, because large horses put more pressure on their bodies as they work to become racing fit, he had to bring Man o' War along gradually. As the *Washington Post* would observe, "Every person who knows anything about racing is keenly alive to the difficulty of preparing a great, gross three-year-old by work alone for a grueling struggle under big weight with a group of track-seasoned colts and fillies."[16] Feustel himself noted, "There is always the danger in these early races of knocking a horse out in training before the season is well under way."[17]

Fortunately for Feustel, Man o' War was large but not inclined to be fat. Unlike Sir Barton, he loved to exercise as much as he loved to eat. The real questions were his current fitness and the Preakness distance. Despite winning with as much as 130 pounds up, Red never had raced farther than three-quarters of a mile. His pedigree indicated that he should succeed going long—but, then again, his hotheaded sister Masda had found her niche in sprints.

Seventeen days before the Preakness, the Riddle racers moved up to Belmont Park and Red's serious preparations began. Into the preseason calm of Belmont's spacious grounds, Red brought his own radiant energy. Along the backstretch, horsemen watched his every move. When he took to the training track for a gallop or breeze, dozens stopped to admire him. "He is nearly three inches taller than when he went into winter quarters and he has thickened materially," the *New York Telegraph*'s turf editor wrote. "Now in looking him over one finds it difficult to get away from the impression that he is a four-year-old and one of immense power and masculinity, at that."[18]

Feustel concentrated on other measurements. Aiming toward a nine-furlong race, he needed to give Red long drills. On Wednesday, May 5, Sam Riddle visited Belmont Park to watch Red's first trial. *Daily Racing Form* reported a nine-furlong work in a dawdling 1:57 3/5, "accomplished in the easiest possible manner."[19] In fact, it had been too easy. "To our surprise," Riddle later exclaimed, "when he had gone six furlongs it seemed as far as he cared to go!"[20] Was his champion a sprinter—a terrific one, but a sprinter—after all?

Owner and trainer held, as Riddle put it, "a council of war." Should they skip the Preakness? Perhaps it was too soon to tell. Feustel knew that a horse's minor complaints could stay hidden until strong exercise brought an incubating problem to a head. Riddle went home to Glen Riddle with this pacifier from Feustel: They would try again in three or four days. In exchange, he left Feustel with an urgent request to tell him right away what happened in Red's next workout. Wanting no delay and sparing no expense, he authorized Feustel to contact him with a long-distance phone call.

Saturday, May 8, brought the test. Several hours before Paul Jones and Upset dueled in the Kentucky Derby, Man o' War breezed around Belmont Park's training track. Afterward, Feustel dutifully picked up a telephone and told Sam Riddle that Red had easily galloped a mile in 1:41.[21] Perhaps it was fortunate, however, that Riddle hadn't been there to watch. Although Red didn't spit out the bit this time, he seemed to be tiring toward the end. Some horsemen began guessing that he might prefer shorter races. But roughly 1:41 for a mile wasn't a bad workout time, especially over Belmont Park's deep training track. By rule of thumb, Red now should be ready to race eight furlongs in a solid 1:39 or less.

Feustel started cranking him now. Late Monday afternoon, Red worked not eight furlongs, not nine, but ten. About forty-eight hours after Paul Jones took two minutes and nine seconds to win a rain-soaked Kentucky Derby, Man o' War exercised only four-fifths of a second slower on a drying-out surface with his rider holding him back.[22] "The time was not remarkable and is far from a record," the *New York Times* noted, "but the trial was very impressive to those who watched it, as the son of Fair Play ran the last furlong in 12 seconds flat."[23]

Any high-class three-year-old could sprint a furlong in twelve seconds, but how many could deliver that twelve after working a mile and an eighth? Feustel told reporters that Man o' War would win the Preakness Stakes.

* * *

As Man o' War's railroad car neared Baltimore on Thursday, May 13, a small scandal rippled through Pimlico: Trainer Silas Veitch found a sponge in his horse Little Nearer's nose. The hard-knocking gelding had run the previous day, despite Veitch's protest. "On the day of the race the stewards were informed that Little Nearer had been tampered," the *Washington Post* revealed, "but a veterinarian reported that he could find no evidence of anything wrong."[24] Little Nearer went off as favorite and finished more than a dozen lengths behind Wodan, who paid $21.30 to win. Unsatisfied, Veitch pressed for another vet exam. This time, the sponge appeared.

And so, as Lou Feustel shepherded Man o' War to his Pimlico stall, tampering talk swept through the backstretch. Chatting with reporters, Feustel stuck to mundane information, announcing that Red's final workout was scheduled for Saturday afternoon, and suggesting that Lavelle "Buddy" Ensor might ride him on Preakness day. He also posted a twenty-four-hour guard around Man o' War.

Meanwhile, Sarah Jeffords and Mike Daly had abandoned hope of sending Golden Broom after the Preakness. Instead, he ran in the May 15 New Albany Handicap at Churchill Downs. The six-furlong sprint should have been right up Broom's alley. After all, two weeks earlier he sizzled the first six furlongs of the Blue Grass Stakes. Fans agreed, sending Broom off as favorite. But they didn't count on five-year-old Blue Paradise, with 107 pounds up to Broom's 119, beating him to the early punch, then pressing him neck and neck through the first half mile. At the quarter pole, Golden Broom had given way to fellow three-year-old Brookholt—one of the previous summer's speed sensations, in now with 103 pounds—and four-year-old Linden, who finished first, in with 102. They beat him by four lengths and four and a half lengths, respectively.

Perhaps Mike and Sarah saw some spark in Broom's performance. They wheeled the colt back on two days' rest, sending him out on Monday, May 17 in Churchill's $1,600 Louisville Hotel Handicap. This gave Golden Broom a chance for victory at the mile-and-a-quarter Kentucky Derby distance, and charging down the same long homestretch where Paul Jones had fought off Upset nine days before.

As if echoing Paul's Derby, the track surface was muddy. Furthermore, two Derby starters were there for redemption: Peace Pennant, sixteenth of seventeen that day, and Sterling, who had run last of all. This time, Sterling burst into the early lead, while heavily favored Peace Pennant bided his time.

Broom lagged behind the pace, trailing by three lengths, two—then six, ten, and more. He finished last of three starters, beaten fourteen lengths by Peace Pennant, eight lengths by Sterling. He would turn up unsound, and fail to stand training as Mike Daly tried to bring him back. Within a few months, it would become clear that he would never race again.

Golden Broom's retreat signaled a new direction for Sarah Jeffords. With her own favorite colt out of action, she might as well enjoy Man o' War. As the season wore on, Sam Riddle would happily note that Red had become something of a "party horse,"[25] equally beloved by himself, his wife, Elizabeth, and Sarah and Walter Jeffords.

On Friday, May 14, the *Baltimore Sun* announced that Man o' War "will work out between the races tomorrow."[26] The next day, a record crowd of 19,340 people squeezed into Pimlico's old-fashioned facilities. An astonished reporter observed that, "viewed from the infield, the grandstand and bleachers were like incredible cans of animated asparagus tips—not room enough between stalks to insert a match-stem without breaking a stalk."[27] He also noted the striking number of women in the crowd: ". . . not worldly looking women who might be classed on sight as followers of a game of chance, but young girls—the stenographer type, the homebred girl, the young wife; and some were just as obviously mothers of families, and some were grandmothers, or had every right to be." These women weren't merely watching the races. Hardened gamblers said that "never, in all the years they have followed racing, have they seen women who were brand new to it, picking horses and betting in such numbers. . . ." Meanwhile, the diligent reporter discovered, "At the 'hot-dog' stand mustard jars were overturned five times as the crowd struggled fiercely for sandwiches."

The rambunctious crowd enjoyed two bonus entertainments. First, Derby winner Paul Jones paraded between the third and fourth races, with his rider wearing racing silks. He could not run in Tuesday's Preakness because only colts and fillies that might produce offspring—and perhaps improve the breed—were eligible. His owner could, however, bask in Paul's new prestige. But Paul Jones soon seemed like a pleasant warm-up act. Between the fourth and fifth races, Man o' War moved onto the track for a workout, and surging spectators, keen to watch him go, broke the paddock fence.[28]

The Pimlico mob saw what New York horsemen had been admiring for the last two weeks: a coppery-coated colt who did not look like either a great sprinter or a great long distance horse. He looked like both. His extra-wide bodybuilder's chest promised sheer strength, while his deep and well-rounded rib cage promised exceptional lung capacity. His straight hind legs said rapid propulsion, while the long cylinder of his torso stretched over a lot of ground—all the better to cover any distance with fewer strides. The famous Albert Einstein might have described him in a formula for massive power meeting minimum resistance.

With retired jockey Clyde Gordon in the saddle, Red would run the actual Preakness course with the official weight of 126 pounds on his back. He stepped out that clear afternoon onto a slow track surface still drying out after three days of rain. About forty-five minutes before his work, a six-furlong claiming race had been won in a tortoiselike 1:18 1/5. Red hit six furlongs about ten lengths faster than that without Gordon letting him loose. He loitered the fourth quarter mile in about 27 seconds, then picked up speed through the homestretch. Red ran the final furlong in a peppy :12 and two or three-fifths despite slowing down near the wire. Feustel was satisfied.

Most horsemen figured they had just seen the Preakness winner, but a few hoped that Man o' War would tire before the wire. They pointed to his string of solid one-mile works with 30-second quarter miles tacked onto the end and said that he might lack stamina. Billy Garth declared that his quick colt Blazes, sixth in the Kentucky Derby, might pull an upset. It was worth hoping. Many two-year-old champions did not keep their dominance at age three, when the top races got notably longer and pure speed no longer was the main ingredient for victory. Maybe longer races would undo Man o' War. Or maybe Billy Garth and a few other rival trainers did not want to believe their eyes.

Up at Belmont Park, expert trainers with no Preakness runners did not need wishful thinking. "Sam Hildreth, Tom Healey, Sandy McNaughton, Billy Karrick, Tom Welsh, Andrew Joyner—all predict that the great-hearted chestnut will, with reasonable luck, win the Preakness and, after the Preakness, keep on beating the 3-year-olds of 1920 as he beat the 2-year-olds of 1919," Sunday morning's *Washington Post* reported. "These experienced and clear-headed horsemen seem to be of the opinion that Feustel has Man o' War in such excellent condition that he should be capable of making the weight concessions that will be required of him to some of the Preakness runners and of spotting to all any advantage that may have been gained by 3-year-old racing experience."[29]

On Monday morning—Preakness eve—Red went to the barrier and started his morning breeze as if it were a race. "He broke none too well," the *Washington Post* remarked, "but he stepped the quarter in 23 seconds, the three furlongs in 34 4-5 and pulled up the half mile in 48 seconds."[30] This sharp work deterred several Preakness hopefuls. Three days earlier, the *Post* had predicted up to fifteen probable starters. Only nine, including Man o' War, would actually enter.

Assessing Red's chances, the *Post* mixed confidence with caution. "The track will be as fast as the Pimlico track can be, if no rain falls. . . . If he gets far away from his field in the early part he can stop some in the last furlong."

All that the champion needed now was a jockey. With Johnny Loftus grounded, Feustel and Riddle had to decide who could handle Man o' War.

Red was not a complicated horse to ride. He was not malicious or scatter-brained. He was, however, extremely powerful and eager to go. This posed a problem whenever he carried a jockey-weight rider for speedy work. In early March, Lou Feustel had told *Daily Racing Form,* "He is so frisky in the mornings that I am afraid to trust anyone but Loftus on him. I think he would carry a little boy through the windows of the stable."[31] Since then, Clyde Gordon had proven that he could handle Red in workouts, but Gordon was too heavy for race riding. For the Preakness, Feustel turned to a rising star who had breezed Red a few times the previous autumn when Johnny Loftus wasn't available. Riddle and Feustel just needed permission to borrow him.

Canadian owners Mrs. Wilfred Viau and Commander Ross had first and second call on the rider they wanted. Securing him depended upon good sportsmanship and luck. Mrs. Viau could afford to be generous because most of her racers were two-year-olds, too young to run against Man o' War. Fortunately for Glen Riddle Farm, Commander Ross didn't need two riders in the Preakness. His only starter, King Thrush, would be guided by Earl Sande. And so a Long Island blacksmith's son got his breakthrough opportunity. But until Preakness day, the Glen Riddle team did not reveal his identity. "I have a good boy," Riddle explained on Preakness eve, "but I do not care to name him. Man o' War stands out and the public should not worry about the rider."[32] Riddle did not want crooked gamblers worrying about Red's rider, either.

On Preakness morning, the world learned that twenty-one-year-old Clarence Kummer would ride Man o' War. His sudden promotion supported the dream that any triumph is possible in the racing world. During Kummer's first two years as a jockey, the prize money earned by his mounts had totaled only about $8,000. During his third and fourth years, his winning rate climbed to 15 percent, then 20, while his earnings soared. Now, after two seasons of solid success, Kummer would ride one of the best horses in the world. Photographs showing him in jockey gear hinted at the journey he had made to get there. Along with a jockey's typical stoic pose and trace of defiance, the camera often caught a plaintive look in his blue eyes.

The look hinted at the struggle of where he had come from and how he came to ride. Although Clarence Kummer hailed from the Long Island town of Jamaica, his mother and all four of his grandparents had been born in Germany. When Clarence entered the world on February 5, 1899, roughly 10 percent of the United States population either had emigrated from Germany or been born to German immigrants.[33] Few would have guessed how unpopular their heritage soon would become across America. Not long after Clarence Kummer graduated from knee pants to trousers, the United States entered the Great War and sauerkraut became "liberty cabbage," the Metropolitan Opera stopped producing any works by German composers, and advertisements for a popular cigar showed a satisfied soldier saying, "Bullets and bayonets are the only kind of lingo a Hun can understand!"[34] It made for uncomfortable situations, even when a boy had long since left mainstream life and committed to the racetrack.

Clarence could have been drawn into his father's horse-shoeing business, but while still a boy in knickerbockers, he accompanied his father to the racetrack and that was it: Clarence had to ride. Younger brother Eddie would remember that Clarence "begged"[35] trainer Sandy McNaughton to teach him, and McNaughton agreed. The United States census taken in April of 1910 would show that eleven-year-old Clarence Kummer already had left his parents' home. A jockey career, however, did not come quickly. It was not until 1916, at the unusually late age of seventeen, that Clarence Joseph Kummer finally got his Jockey Club license. At that same age, Johnny Loftus already had ridden in two Kentucky Derbies.

Talent, however, was there. At age nineteen, Kummer blossomed. "Kummer's best asset is his quickness at the starting gate," turf writer O'Neil Sevier observed early in 1918. "He seems to be always ready. Moreover, he is as courageous as they make them. He never takes the outside if there is anything resembling a hole by the rail through which he can slip. He is not as patient as [Joe] Rodriguez, but, being an intelligent lad, he gives heed to advice, and he will learn."[36] Kummer had learned all right. He also had been blessed with a strong physique for reining in Man o' War's speed, and that turned out to be the bottom line. "Clarence was husky," Lou Feustel would recall, "and he was the only one who could really rate him."[37]

Man o' War's new jockey would get his chance on a racing day rife with perspiration, anticipation, audacious sunshine, the constant clicking of pari-mutuel machines, and jostling elbows. On this Tuesday afternoon, more than 23,000 people—the biggest gathering at Pimlico since a renowned match race in 1877[38]—came to see Man o' War in Maryland's version of the Kentucky Derby. They waited through three races, simmering in the heat, until the Preakness starters reached the paddock. Many didn't know what trouble Man o' War faced in getting there. Choking the road between his stable and the saddling area were dozens of automobiles. With policemen blazing a trail for him, Man o' War snaked between the metal contraptions and joined the paddock mob.

"This was the only time I ever saw him much upset before he went into a race," Sam Riddle would recall. "It was eight months since he had gone to the post and he was so nervous that he broke out [in a sweat] three times and was upset to that degree that I really don't think it was possible that he was in his best form."[39] In fact, seeing his colt so keyed up, Riddle decided that a stable hand should lead him to the barrier. This would be the most certain way to guide Red and his new rider safely past the vast crowd.

Clarence Kummer, however, didn't want a special escort. For a jockey, having someone else lead his horse to the post seemed like riding a bicycle with training wheels. "No," he told Riddle. "I can manage all right!"[40]

Riddle then presented Kummer with his blunt opinion. "Clarence," he insisted, "Loftus was the only man who could do that."[41] But this kind of comparison was not the way to win a debate with a highly skilled and confident jockey. Kummer would not take a backseat to Loftus for his first public appearance with the famous Man o' War. He set to persuading Sam Riddle that he could take Red out alone and it would be all right.

"Very well," Riddle agreed at last. "But be mighty careful for he is a very powerful colt and may get away from you."[42]

Kummer *knew* how powerful. Unlike Riddle, he had galloped Red around a track.

At four o' clock, with the sun beginning to slant westward, Man o' War took his usual place leading the post parade. Eight other colts ventured out to take him on. Two of them, Blazes and On Watch, shared his top weight of 126 pounds. Upset received a slight break, with 122, while the rest—Wildair, King Thrush, Donnacona, *St. Allan, and Fairway—carried only 114. Competing for the first time in eight months, with a new jockey and no experience with deflecting challengers in a middle-distance race, Man o' War held no advantage except his talent. Most bettors figured that was enough. Pimlico's pari-mutuel odds, established by how much money the public placed on each horse, favored him at 4–5. In other words, a five-dollar win bet on Man o' War could earn only four dollars of profit.

Stepping onto the track, into clubhouse and grandstand view, Red heard a vast surge of sound: *"Here's Man o' War!"* In a flash, before Kummer could react, he bolted down the track. "He's running away!" some spectators shouted. Others, delighted to see a spirited champion in the flesh, only cheered. Their careless noise could have startled Red beyond control, but amid the din something communicated between jockey and horse. Kummer later would say, "He was not so nervous or fretful as he was anxious to get off and do what he was out to do."[43] Within several strides, Red relaxed enough for Kummer to contain his speed, reaching the barrier with his energy unspoiled. Sam Riddle's nightmare had not quite come true.

Red approached post position seven, with speedy Blazes two spots to his inside and speedy King Thrush by his outside. Ten times he had started a race with Johnny Loftus urging him to anticipate the break. Now Clarence Kummer sent similar signals and Red helped to delay the start for about six minutes, breaking through the barrier once. Meanwhile *St. Allan, assigned to post position one, misbehaved so tenaciously that starter Jim Milton finally sent him to the far outside. Then came the official break. Red missed a flying start—Upset, Blazes, and On Watch got away faster—but lost little ground. "In a few jumps and before the crowd had ceased saying 'Man o' War got away badly,'" a reporter noted, "he was in front, over next the rail, and stepping along at a dizzy pace."[44]

Kummer had passed the most vital part of his test. He had Red on the lead, in the clear, the inner rail streaming past their left shoulders. King Thrush, who had dominated a few sprints in Maryland that spring, ambitiously gave chase—"and was made to look foolish," a reporter scoffed.[45] Red led King Thrush by several feet at all times, never letting him close the gap, while Upset lurked up into third place.

After six furlongs of futility, King Thrush was through. Turning for home, Upset made his serious move, cutting into Man o' War's margin and opening daylight on the pack as Wildair advanced into third. But Red raised the ante, reaching the mile four-fifths of a second faster than Pimlico's track record. Upset charged at Red as he had charged at Paul Jones in the Kentucky Derby, but the mile split was too much. His momentum stalled.

Keeping a steady half length of daylight between his rump and his nearest challenger, Red ran his last three furlongs at an unusually even pace, :13 2/5 each. His final time of 1:51 3/5 missed the track record by only three ticks. At the finish line, Kummer's still posture and Red's long, loping form gave the impression of power in reserve. They had beaten Upset by a length and a half, with five more lengths back to Wildair—and while those rivals trailed home under the whip, Kummer had not even waved the stick at Man o' War.

Sam Riddle may have imagined winning the Preakness, but he could not have known how it would feel on a hot day with a record crowd and a performer like Man o' War. Now the noisy, messy reality engulfed him. "Not only did the immense crowd cheer the splendid colt to the echo—it also nearly annihilated his owner in the endeavors to get near enough [to] Mr. Riddle to shake hands with him," a reporter observed. "When he emerged from the human maelstrom he was badly mussed."[46]

Catching up with Man o' War's owner, another reporter found "a plainspoken, unassuming man, with gray hair that he wore slicked down and parted at one side, and distinguished only by the fact that he wore a shirt and collar with pink stripes and sported a buff-colored topcoat."[47] The unassuming man did not brag about his own part in Red's success. "I'm from Quaker and Irish stock and that spells 'modesty,'" Sam Riddle told the *Baltimore Sun*. "I didn't win the race. Man o' War won it and young Kummer helped him do it."[48] The reporter then asked, "Was he running his best?" Riddle "tossed his head" and answered, "I should say not. Pulled in all the time. All the time." At this point, pride overtook modesty. Before leaving the reporter, Samuel Doyle Riddle described the wonders of his Berlin farm, the training ground that had fostered Man o' War.

Clarence Kummer didn't claim any modesty for himself or his mount. "I have been on [Kentucky Derby winners] Sir Barton, Omar Khayyam, Exterminator and many other good horses," Kummer reminded the Preakness reporters, "but Man o' War is the greatest one I have ever ridden. . . . The track, on the back stretch [*sic*], passing the half, was deep and rough and gave way under his feet, but that did not bother him, for it was right there that he opened up such a gap on the others that they were beaten from that moment. He pulled up with plenty of breath, and acted as if he had enjoyed the race. To me he seemed in perfect physical condition."[49] Spectators praised Red's sensational Preakness pace, how he ruled the race without being set to a drive, how close he came to track record time. "It was the opinion of all horsemen present," the *New York Sun and Herald* claimed, "that if he had been compelled to do his best all the way he would have clipped several seconds from the old mark of 1:51."[50] But Man o' War's victory hadn't been as easy as it looked.

Twenty hours after the Preakness, Lou Feustel attended the races at New York's Jamaica track and spent "most of the day accepting congratulations from the crowd."[51] Chatting with reporter Henry V. King, Feustel admitted that Red came back to the barn a tired horse because the track surface had been especially demanding on Preakness day. "The rain last week soaked it," Feustel explained, "and the sand on top which made it fast was kicked off and the heavy clay which was at the bottom brought to the top."[52] This quite naturally took a toll on Man o' War. "He didn't have any too much left at the end, and he was under only slight restraint throughout," Feustel frankly told King (who called the young trainer "modest about Man o' War's feat"). "But he would have smashed all records if the track had been fast."

Two days after his victory, Red arrived home at Belmont Park. "He shipped in fine style," King noted, "and Louis Feustel said he wanted to run as soon as he took him off the train."[53] Meanwhile, Clarence Kummer also had reason to feel frisky: Sam Riddle had given him a one-thousand-dollar bonus.

Although Riddle had no reason to think that Kummer would be willing to make Red lose, he couldn't take anything for granted. Celebrity made Man o' War a most tempting target for race fixing and other larceny. The *New York Times* now told the world that "Man o' War . . . is regarded as the most valuable horse in the country. . . ."[54] Perhaps with Riddle's blessing, the same article also noted, "During his preparation for the Preakness Man o' War was guarded like a king. A bodyguard was placed at his stall and he was watched every hour of the day. The bodyguard consists of four men, two to a shift. It is Mr. Riddle's intention to thus safeguard his colt throughout the season."

Sam Riddle could do no less for his horse's sake, his own peace of mind, and a wife whom *Daily Racing Form* described as "even more enthusiastic about Man o' War than her husband. . . ."[55] Six days after Red's Preakness win, Riddle reflected, "How does it feel to own as good a horse as Man o' War? Fine, only I don't believe I would want many more like him, strange as that may sound. He is too much responsibility. I have always tried to regard him as though he was just an ordinary horse, but my friends and the public at large, to say nothing of my own people, won't let me do it."[56]

For Sam Riddle, Man o' War now stretched Thoroughbred racing far beyond simple fun. Everywhere he turned, Riddle found his private hopes entangling with other people's good and bad dreams. He couldn't escape the fervent wishes of his wife, the heightened expectations of his barn crew, or the possibility that someone might sabotage his *big horse*. Six days after Red's successful three-year-old debut and its chain reactions, Riddle seemed grateful for a resting place. "Now that he has won the Preakness we are all breathing easy," he told *Daily Racing Form,* "and the future, barring accidents, seems serene."[57]

13

SPEED MIRACLES BEGIN

LEGEND HAS IT that "the first supreme thoroughbred [*sic*] racehorse"[1]—an unbeaten stallion named Flying Childers, who raced in England during the early 1720s—could run a mile in one minute flat. Although the accuracy of his mile-a-minute clocking was suspect from the start, Flying Childers would be rightly remembered as a horse of rare quality. Two hundred and fifty years later, an historian wrote, "In his own time and for long afterwards he was reckoned not only the best horse ever seen, but the best ever likely to be seen: an unrepeatable phenomenon."[2] Flying Childers sparked a phenomenon that would be repeated many times, however: public enthusiasm for sensational racehorse speed.

No one expected Man o' War to run a one-minute mile, but racegoers knew what they considered fast. In the spring of 1920, a mile in 1:36—eight furlongs averaging twelve seconds each—was a barrier very rarely breached. Salvator had been the first to break 1:36, running against the stopwatch on August 28, 1890, at New York's Morris Park over a straight, slightly downhill chute nicknamed the "toboggan slide." Smashing the American mile record from 1:39 1/4 to 1:35 1/2, Salvator became an icon. Soon 1:35 1/2, sensational as it was, barely seemed to do him justice. Dwelling in the fertile country of *what if,* Salvator's trainer speculated that the gelding might have reached 1:33 flat if the jockey hadn't let him run too fast during the first half mile.

In the thirty years since Salvator's stunning performance, only three horses in the world officially had beaten 1:35 1/2. Two of them did it on a straight course at Lingfield, England, with a slight downward slope. Salvator's third successful challenger did it on the level and around one turn, in a sanctioned time trial at Saratoga on August 21, 1918. Setting a runaway pace for the first half mile but buoyed by the Spa's extremely fast new track surface, Roamer chopped the American mile record down to 1:34 4/5. That previously unthinkable mark taunted the connections of the brilliant three-year-old colt named Sun Briar.

Fifteen days before Roamer's successful contest with the watch, Sun Briar and the quick Saratoga surface had delivered an American record for a mile in competition: 1:36 1/5. Exactly three weeks after Roamer's 1:34 and four, Sun Briar returned to the Saratoga track and dunked the time trial mark to 1:34 flat. Unfortunately, however, the race meet had ended and The Jockey Club had not sanctioned the troop of clockers that gathered for Sun Briar's exhibition. Roamer's time remained in the record book. Most horsemen, however, believed Sun Briar's "unofficial" clocking. They perceived 1:34 as the actual frontier.

To most Americans in their everyday life, speed like Roamer's was out of reach. For automobile drivers, the average legal limit was twenty miles per hour. Residents of California and New York were allowed to reach a thrilling thirty miles an hour. Galloping racehorses reached thirty-five and more. Only in railroad cars could most people get any idea how that much speed felt. They might see a horse push forty miles per hour, however, watching Man o' War in the one-mile Withers Stakes at Belmont Park on Saturday, May 29.

Early that morning, Feustel sent Red out for a pipe opener, one furlong at high speed. At the end, his stopwatch showed a startling :10 3/5—a forty-two-mile-per-hour burst. The Riddles were elated. Sam told friends and reporters that Red uncorked this incredible furlong "under the strongest pull of which his boy was capable and literally fighting for his head."[3] Racetrackers and reporters accepted :10 3/5 at face value. And yet Man o' War's accepted workout times, even his official racing times—like those of any other horse—were not completely accurate. The stopwatch rounded micromoments up or down into fifths of a second, and the results shown by each watch also depended upon the reflexes of the person triggering it. No one could prove whose stopwatch—if any—captured the absolute truth.

Most people didn't care. That day at Belmont Park, they might see Man o' War break the official Withers Stakes record of 1:38 2/5. He might even approach the official track record, 1:36 3/5. A sharp opponent would be pressing him: Harry Payne Whitney's colt Wildair, who had beaten older horses in the one-mile Metropolitan Handicap five days earlier, "easing up,"[4] in the good time of 1:38 and four. "Man o' War may set a new [stakes] record this afternoon and beat Wildair by a couple of lengths," a turf columnist predicted, "in spite of the fact that the Whitney entry may be up to 1:38."[5]

One of the largest crowds in Belmont Park's history turned out for the Withers Stakes, "and among the thousands," the *New York Times* would note, "were many who had come to the track just to see the great horse they had read so much about."[6] When the Withers entrants appeared to be saddled, "a wild scramble" of spectators converged on the paddock. "Man o' War was there," a reporter noted, "and it seemed that every one of the thousands present were eager to inspect him."[7]

They saw "a colt of heroic proportions with no surplus flesh anywhere,"[8] who "walked so rapidly beneath the trees that his groom was on his toes. . . ."[9] While Man o' War did not seem to react to the crowd, his slightly damp body on an afternoon no warmer than sixty-five degrees betrayed his excitement. His glistening coat also revealed small dark spots scattered over his muscular rump—a legacy from his great-grandsire, Epsom Derby winner Bend Or.

Nearby, holding court from a shaded bench, Sam and Elizabeth Riddle didn't hide their exuberance. Everyone who approached heard them describe Red's lightning-fast furlong that morning, reliving their amazement again and again.[10] The Riddles easily could predict that Man o' War would win this race—he had only to beat Wildair, whom he had thrashed in the past, plus the nonthreatening colt David Harum, who had been entered to collect the third-place money—but even they hadn't guessed that Red possessed such extravagant speed.

Meanwhile, because all three Withers colts would carry a moderate 118 pounds, Man o' War's odds sank to a one-dollar profit for every seven dollars bet. The Withers was becoming not a race but a spectacle. Another clue came from the saddle strapped to the champion's back, as spectators noticed something flashing in the sun. Clarence Kummer, dressed for this ride in "his very best racing toggery,"[11] had bought a special accessory for appearing with Man o' War: stirrups plated with gold.

The most difficult problem seemed to be actually getting Man o' War out of the paddock. Spectators packed around him so tightly that his handlers needed help opening a passage through the crowd. Then, "Tugging at his bit, but not acting meanly,"[12] Red led his two opponents onto the course. Applause welcomed him, the effect reminding one reporter of "the star of a play making his first entrance."[13] Parading leftward past the stands and around the clubhouse turn to where the barrier sat facing three furlongs of backstretch, Red occupied outrider "Red Coat" Murray with his occasional "quick nervous jumps as if," *Daily Racing Form* noted, "he were eager to be away and show the world his matchless speed."[14]

Red didn't have to wait long. For a minute, he poised behind the barrier, with Wildair at the rail to his right, David Harum to his outside. Then he vaulted to the lead, quickly opening two lengths on Wildair, setting an honest pace. But even more was happening than the great crowd waiting across the track could see. Man o' War was flying into the mythmaking dimension of time.

Tradition said that inside this Alice in Wonderland territory, where fractions loom supernaturally large, a galloping racehorse travels one body length during each fifth of a second. Even after 1960s science discovered that actual racehorse speed ranges closer to six or seven lengths per second, working in fifths would remain a popular rule of thumb. One-fifth equaling one length provided an easy ballpark figure, helping fans to visualize a standard space between imperceptible fragments of time. But while people with stopwatches clocked horses in fifths of a second and drew firm conclusions, the horses actually moved in hundredths, thousandths, and fractions too tiny to name. Flying Childers, Salvator, Roamer, and Man o' War inhabited instants impossible to perceive and more fluid than stopwatches could show.

And so, from the first quarter mile of Man o' War's Withers mile, clockers didn't agree. Officially, Red traveled it in an unhurried :24 flat. Unofficial clockers reported a slightly more brisk :23 and three. One could only guess at his precise speed. The concrete fact was Man o' War skimming the inner rail, keeping a half length to a length of daylight between his heels and Wildair's nose. Stretching to save the image, a *New York Times* reporter wrote, "He ran with an ease and grace that suggested that he was bounding along like a rubber ball rather than running."[15]

Although Kummer kept him in check, Red built momentum along the long, straight backstretch run. One unofficial clocker said that he ran those first three furlongs in a sprightly :35. That was tame compared to what seemed to happen as Red entered the far turn. Several unofficial clockers would claim that he seared the fourth furlong, curving through the first half of the bend, in :10 flat. "It was a furlong the like of which had never been heard of before," reporter Henry V. King marveled, "for it was at an express train speed of forty-five miles an hour."[16]

Kummer did let Red fly into the turn, but the ten-second furlong apparently was a mirage created by eager human reactions and problematic vantage points from the opposite side of Belmont Park's huge track. The same unofficial clocker who caught Red's first three furlongs in :35 made his fourth furlong as a quick but not outlandish :11 3/5. *New York Tribune* reporter W. J. Macbeth noticed that, rounding the turn, Man o' War did not lose touch with Wildair, his "extended tail appearing to brush Wildair's nose."[17] However fast Red actually traveled the fourth furlong, he did so with Wildair at his heels.

Kummer throttled Red back through the second half of the turn, hugging the rail as they entered the homestretch, then gave him a bit of rein. Man o' War shot away from Wildair, opening what reporter Macbeth called "a gap of fully six lengths." The official watch said six furlongs in 1:11, only two-fifths of a second slower than the track mark. Henry McDaniel, trainer of Sun Briar and Exterminator, caught Red's six furlongs in 1:10 and seven furlongs in 1:22—tying the track record set by the formidable sprinter Roseben, known as "the Big Train."[18]

Glancing back and seeing Wildair far behind, Kummer began easing Man o' War down. Red motored past the grandstand about three lengths ahead of Wildair, cheers enveloping his progress. Wildair drove after him, "his tail [flying] straight out"[19] from his effort, game but not gaining. Red officially reached seven furlongs in 1:22 4/5. Now momentum, math, and myth were on his side. Complete the final furlong in less than fourteen seconds—almost trotting-horse time—and he would tie Stromboli's 1:36 3/5 track record for one mile. If he could open up like Feustel said he had done that morning—a furlong in :10 and change—he would finish in just over 1:32. But about 100 feet from the wire, heeding Feustel's orders not to let Red run unnecessarily fast, Kummer drew in tightly on the reins. Man o' War won slowing down, leading the still-driving Wildair past by the post by two comfortable lengths, with David Harum another fifteen lengths behind.

A record was about to become real. But which time would it be? Wooden block by wooden block, a track official hung the answer on an infield board. The first two digits were no surprise. The third brought history to its knees:

1:35 4/5.

Man o' War had decimated the Withers Stakes record by the rough equivalent of thirteen lengths. Stromboli's track record, standing since 1914, fell
approximately four lengths behind. Sun Briar's 1:36 1/5 American mark for a
mile in competition had been trimmed by two.

But comparisons only started there. A private clocking caught Red in 1:35
1/5, and similar testimonies quickly poured in. "Scores [of] other timers, including veteran horsemen who have clocked thoroughbreds [*sic*] for years,
made his time much faster [than 1:35 4/5]," reporter Henry V. King announced. "Some caught him in 1:34 2-5 and none slower than 1:35."[20]

Unofficially, Red drew within kissing distance of Roamer's magical 1:34
and four.

That wasn't all. Though Kummer had Red geared down at the finish,
Daily Racing Form noted that "opposite the club-house, when Kummer went
down for a fresh hold of the reins to pull him up Man o' War leaped away
once more like a whippet from the leash as fresh apparently as though the
race had only begun."[21] As a result, some clockers standing near the rail said
that Red charged through a ninth furlong in twelve seconds flat—startling
speed after running a fast mile. Added to the official 1:35 4/5, this would give
Man o' War a sensational mile and an eighth in 1:47 4/5. The world record
was 1:49 and two.

Racetrackers, racing fans, and reporters would not stop at what Man o'
War actually had done. They began wondering what he could do if allowed
to run hard. Despite setting a new American record for one mile in competition, Red pulled up with ample energy in reserve. "When the colt returned to
the paddock after his race he seemed as fresh and strong as when he left
it," Henry V. King declared. "He wasn't taking a long breath. . . ."[22] Even
the more cautious *New York Times* noted, "In view of the fact that Man o'
War was being eased down at the finish, in fact all through the last sixteenth
of a mile, it seems reasonable to presume that he might have come close to
the time made by Roamer had he been extended or even permitted to run it
out."[23]

"There never was a horse like him," Clarence Kummer said. "He didn't
appear to be running at all. From the jump he fought for his head and my
arms are tired from trying to hold him in. I let him loose for a furlong in the
middle of the race and he fairly flew over the ground. So fast was it that I
thought it might tire him and I began to ease him up."[24]

How good was Man o' War? Perhaps the real question was, How good was

Wildair? Doing his level best, he had finished only two lengths behind Man o' War. According to the official timer and conventional measurements, Wildair had just tied Sun Briar's American mark. For a colt who had beaten good older horses while winning three stakes that season, such an excellent time over Belmont Park's state-of-the-art track seemed impressive but quite possible. If Man o' War actually had run a blistering 1:35, however, did Wildair make 1:35 2/5? On an afternoon when Belmont's track proved a bit dull, Wildair had won the Metropolitan Handicap "easing up" in 1:38 4/5, under 107 pounds. Five days later, had he run roughly fifteen lengths faster while carrying 118? Veteran clockers knew what their watches said, but no one could prove exactly where the truth lay.

With the obvious ease of Man o' War's performance taking hold of their minds, excited witnesses leaned away from doubt. "A host of trainers who clocked the race said that Man o' War ran so fast the official timer wouldn't believe his own watch and was afraid to hang out the correct time," Henry King declared. ". . . And every one of the huge throng at the track agreed that if he had been allowed to race at his best clip he would have made 1:33 and smashed all world's records to smithereens."[25]

Red's true competition wasn't Roamer, but the ghost of Salvator. *Salvator's trainer thought the horse might have done 1:33 flat if the jockey hadn't let him run too fast for the first half mile.* When a trainer talks that way, speculation can lodge in listeners' minds as if it were a fact. Salvator—*1:33*. A *what if* version of reality.

In the dreamlike aftermath of Man o' War's Withers win, Clarence Kummer provided the clincher: "If Mr. Feustel had told me to let him run all the way I know he would have hung up 1:33."[26]

Four decades later, Lou Feustel claimed, "I've always had a hunch that even on the tracks of those days he could have turned a mile in 1:32 flat."[27]

Leaving the *what if* Salvator roughly five lengths behind.

The Withers Stakes revealed Man o' War as a sorcerer's stone for turning racing's image into gold. "There was no gambling angle in the flood of feeling over the performance," testified John E. Madden, the man who had bred and raised Sir Barton. "The odds were prohibitive and I do not think there was $1,000 bet on him. The reformers who seek to stifle the foremost outdoor recreation might have drawn a profitable lesson from the ovation which greeted Man o' War's supreme racing excellence."[28]

Madden was right about the emotion that the supreme horse inspired, and he was right that very little money had been bet on Man o' War's race. He missed, however, an inevitable irony: Man o' War's popularity ultimately would support gambling. His presence, drawing large crowds to the track, also would draw more people to the bookmakers or pari-mutuel machines. His own body, whether directed by Sam Riddle toward seemingly sure things or far beyond the typical boundaries for a young American racehorse, would become the world's most famous gambling tool.

Already, in the wake of Red's record mile, sophisticated horsemen were searching their experience for situations big enough to hold his rare power. "A marvelous performance and a wonderful horse," Jockey Club steward Joseph E. Widener enthused. "Could win the English Derby next Wednesday in a walk if he were over there in the condition he showed to-day."[29] Well-traveled trainer Thomas Welsh, who had worshiped the French champion Sardanapale, now called Man o' War, "As good as any horse I ever saw."[30]

One minute, thirty-five and four-fifths seconds had transported Samuel Doyle Riddle far beyond his own comfortable place and time. That suddenly, Man o' War began making American challenges seem small. Send him to England for the Ascot Gold Cup, racing connoisseurs said. Send him to France for the Grand Prix de Paris. Prove that he is indeed the horse of the world.

August Belmont remained one of the few experts showing any restraint. He did not compare Man o' War with other great horses and he even reserved higher honors for a colt that had won several major English races under his silks. "I always thought Tracery the best horse I ever bred," Belmont maintained, "but this colt appears to be a wonderful performer. Having bred him, I cannot praise him as highly as others might."[31]

At least for now, Sam Riddle would not send Man o' War chasing after Tracery. There were plenty of challenges to get through at home.

One challenge for Riddle to accept or reject was racing Red against older horses. Man o' War had been nominated for Belmont Park's prestigious Suburban Handicap, and track official Walter Vosburgh paid the high compliment of assigning him 114 pounds. Although that was 15 pounds less than older champion Sir Barton would carry if he ran, a three-year-old had never won the Suburban carrying more than 110 pounds. Racing a mile and quarter in early June, any extra weight could work against an immature colt—even such a strong individual as Man o' War.

And so Sam Riddle pushed the compliment away. The Suburban would take place only seven days after the Withers Stakes and make Red face accomplished older horses such as Boniface, a good earner for Commander Ross, and Exterminator, a rising champion. The Belmont Stakes, on the other hand, would give Red a two-week break between races, pit him only against fellow three-year-olds, and offer more money. It also might, however, play into the plans of Jimmy Rowe. Rather than bowing down after the Withers Stakes, Rowe had sworn that he would "take one more crack"[32] at beating Man o' War. Racetrackers figured that he would take this crack with the still-improving John P. Grier.

Experience had taught James G. Rowe, Sr., that he was, above all, a winner. To start with, he had trained more champion racehorses than anyone else in American history—twenty-eight champions, and counting. Back in 1881, when only twenty-four years old, Rowe had become the youngest trainer ever to win the Kentucky Derby. At ages fourteen through sixteen, he had been top jockey in the United States. Before that, he had been daring enough to make his living as a trick rider in a circus.

For nearly forty years, Jimmy Rowe had enjoyed a training career so good that it seemed imaginary. He had developed Luke Blackburn, who lowered the American record for 1 1/2 miles by nearly three seconds, and Hindoo, who won 18 of 20 starts at age three. He had trained Miss Woodford, the first American racehorse to win more than $100,000. He had won 14 of 15 career starts with Sysonby and 15 of 15 with Colin. He had trained the champion filly Regret to do something that no female horse had done before: win the Kentucky Derby. He had trained eight winners of the Belmont Stakes. And he had sent Upset to victory over Man o' War.

And so when Man o' War spanked his good colt Wildair with a record mile, Jimmy Rowe did not admit that Man o' War looked unbeatable. He did not suggest that young Lou Feustel had gotten hold of a horse as special as his own Hindoo, Sysonby, or Colin. Rowe did not seem to acknowledge that supreme good fortune might bypass his barn this time and settle in with someone else. Perhaps his force of habit had grown far too strong. In June of 1920, the years from Jimmy Rowe's first Kentucky Derby win to the present day stretched out longer than Lou Feustel's entire life.

Rowe did not seem to dislike Feustel personally. He could respect a solid young horseman who had grown up in August Belmont's system—who had learned, in fact, from Rowe's best friend: former Belmont trainer Andrew

Jackson Joyner. Rowe could hear experienced trainers all around him saying what a good job Feustel was doing with Man o' War and know that it was true. This could not, however, erase another truth: When Lou Feustel first began learning about Thoroughbred racing, Jimmy Rowe had already been a star. Before Feustel saddled his first winner, Rowe had managed Colin. For Rowe, it might have seemed surreal that Man o' War threatened to become even more popular than Colin and, even stranger, that a relatively obscure trainer handled him. Yes, Feustel came from the Belmont farm, but Rowe—trainer of twenty-eight champions—could not think of him as his peer.

In nine racing seasons before Man o' War's debut, Lou Feustel had enjoyed the privilege of training one champion racehorse. Back in 1913, he had prepared August Belmont's colt Rock View for victory in the Withers Stakes, Brooklyn Derby, Travers, and Lawrence Realization, developing him into the year's champion three-year-old. Then the wizardly Sam Hildreth had come back from France and taken over his job.

Feustel did not hold a grudge against Belmont—"the best man I ever knew,"[33] he would say—for hiring Hildreth. He did, perhaps, understand how bad it felt to suddenly lose one's grasp on a good situation. Feustel would show such empathy at a pressure-filled time, five days before Man o' War's date with the Belmont Stakes. During the morning of Monday, June 7, twenty Thoroughbreds owned by Walter and Sarah Jeffords arrived at Belmont Park. In the rearrangement caused by the arrival of the Jeffords string and perhaps other horses from wealthy owners, a trainer with three horses was told to pack up and leave the track. The evicted man drew Feustel's attention, even though he did not ask for Feustel's help.

When Samuel Jay Bush joined the racing world in 1905, the famous Jack Joyner had been among the trainers who gave him a start galloping horses and found that the kid had the makings of a jockey. Yet there was one crucial obstacle: Bush was, in the terminology of the era, a Negro. Few owners and trainers in New York were willing to give him a chance.

Following the lead of Jimmy Winkfield and other talented black jockeys, Bush moved to Russia in 1909. World war buffeted him back to the United States, but Bush returned with a specialty: riding and training steeplechase racers. Blending opportunity with skill, he won the 1917 and 1918 renewals of the International Steeplechase Handicap at Belmont Park. But on June 7, 1920, Belmont Park officials didn't offer Sam Bush any help in relocating the three jump racers in his care. Instead, Lou Feustel stepped forward and said he had three stalls empty that he didn't need. Bush could take them.[34]

"Sam couldn't believe such good luck, and it was with difficulty that Feustel made him accept the invitation," a reporter observed.[35] Finally, Bush thanked Feustel in eloquent racetrack fashion: urging him to bet on a sure winner he would ride that afternoon. No one recorded whether or not Feustel bet, but Bush's mount won by six lengths.

Sam Bush's problem had triggered something that people of all ranks found in Louis Feustel: a basic decency. August Belmont recognized it in a horse-breeding business letter that he sent to Sam Riddle early that year. "I am greatly interested in Feustel's success," Belmont noted before signing off. "I have always liked him and was confident that he would make his mark in the course of time."[36]

One could say that the Belmont Stakes ran in Man o' War's family or that Man o' War's family ran in the Belmont Stakes. His paternal great-grandsire Spendthrift started the trend, with a quick and easy six-length win in 1879. Spendthrift's son Hastings continued the theme in 1896, running "a brilliant race"[37] to catch Handspring in the stretch and win by a head. Fair Play, son of Hastings, did not win in 1908, but had pressed Colin nearly to the breaking point . . . and now, in 1920, the world would see what Fair Play's son Man o' War could do. "That," a *Daily Racing Form* reporter wrote the day before the race, "will be something to tell our grandchildren about. . . ."[38]

As many as thirty thousand people turned out on Saturday, June 12, to watch Man o' War perform in an exhibition called the Belmont Stakes. The throng pressing to see him saddled for the race was so thick that August Belmont himself stood "many rows back of those who crowded the paddock. . . ."[39] "All strata of society that associates with thoroughbred [*sic*] sport were there," a reporter noted, "[and] the silk-gowned clubhouse lady of the ultra exclusive was not abashed to brush skirts with the shop girl for a fleeting peep at Man o' War's classic head, alone visible above the circle of humanity crowded close on all sides."[40]

They would not see Man o' War struggle to win this race. Jimmy Rowe, who had trained eight horses to win the Belmont Stakes, would not try for nine this year. He had sent Upset to Kentucky to run in that afternoon's Latonia Derby, which would pay the winner $16,300—more than twice what the Belmont Stakes winner would earn—and he was keeping Wildair and

John P. Grier in the barn. Apparently, Rowe did not fancy their chances against Man o' War racing a mile and three-eighths while carrying equal weight of 126 pounds.

David Harum had been entered in the Belmont Stakes but bailed out that morning and left the champion facing a walkover. Sportsman George Loft promptly entered his handsome colt Donnacona—an especially generous gesture, because Donnacona had raced twice during the previous five days.[41] There was no way that he would threaten the fresher and more talented Man o' War. But Donnacona would give the crowd something to compare Man o' War with, and his presence also meant that Man o' War would collect the full winner's share of the purse. In a walkover, the lone horse completing the course would receive only half of the advertised first-place prize.

Even a token opponent, while miles better than a walkover, wouldn't satisfy the thirty thousand people who filled Belmont Park this afternoon. Few of them were betting on Man o' War, at odds of 1–25, and very few fancied Donnacona at 20–1. Most people chose to wager on a different question: Would Man o' War beat Sir Barton's record time? Throughout the crowd, 1–1 odds said that he could. "The big doubt," a reporter noted, "was whether Donnacona would be able to keep close enough to the champion to spur him to a record breaking performance."[42]

Lou Feustel apparently heard the talk and accepted the challenge. "The crowd wants to see this fellow do something," Feustel told Kummer in the paddock, "and I don't want them to see a gallop. Let him race, and we'll please them and incidentally get a record."[43] It was clear to Feustel that Red would do this from his own desire for speed. He had told Kummer not to use the whip.

Meanwhile, while waiting in the paddock, Sam Riddle turned down an offer from fellow Philadelphian Joseph L. Murphy: $260,000 for Man o' War.

Then it was time. Navigating safely through the crowd, stable foreman George Conway walked at Red's shoulder, holding the chin strap of his bridle. His gold stirrups flashing in the sun, Kummer sat and waited for freedom while Red led Donnacona past the grandstand and toward the same distant chute feeding into Belmont Park's training track, where Fair Play had chased Colin twelve years before.

For about one minute, two colts hovered behind the barrier. Then Mars Cassidy let them go and Man o' War jumped ahead. As a two-year-old, Red sometimes had let someone else set the early pace. Now, thanks to his growing impatience and more developed body, a different tactic was becoming his habit: sprint to the lead and let the others try to match his powerful strides.

Spectators with binoculars saw a distant black-and-yellow dot cruise about two lengths in front of the other dot, along the backstretch of the training track and into its far turn. Then both dots disappeared behind a screen of trees, lost to sight for about half a mile. Because of the oddly shaped and partly obscured course, the official clocker perched at the finish line took no fractional times. He would only announce the time elapsed from Man o' War's first leap to his meeting with the finish line.

After forty-some dead seconds, a horse shape shot clear of the trees: Man o' War, with Donnacona straining to draw alongside. There was no daylight between challenger and champ as they swung onto the main track's far turn. But now Red's saved energy came into play. "Kummer looked back and, seeing Donnacona, he gave Man o' War his head," noted the *New York Times*. "The son of Fair Play developed a new rate of speed in half a dozen strides. He began to move away from his rival as though the latter was anchored."[44] Straightening into the homestretch, the point where Colin had led Fair Play by a length and a half, Man o' War led Donnacona by four.

It was victory, easily. It was not enough. The crowd shouted at Kummer: Let him out! Let him *go*! And, with Feustel's orders supporting their demand, Kummer did. "Instead of taking a pull on his mount, as he had done in his previous race," the *Times* reporter observed, "he let Man o' War step along all through the stretch, although at no time urging him. He simply let the colt run freely, and then it became evident how much he outclasses the others of his age."

Red had galloped onto the clubhouse turn, pulling up, when Donnacona finally passed the finish line. His official winning margin was stupendous: twenty lengths. But Sir Barton's record was what the crowd cared about. The previous year, they had cheered 2:17 2/5, a new American mark, a remarkable show of speed. The world record was 2:16 and four, set by Dean Swift at Liverpool, England, in 1908, some spectators knew. But Man o' War had run nowhere near those times.

His official time was 2:14 and one.

"As the timekeeper hung out the fateful numbers a pin could have been heard to drop," reporter W. J. Macbeth wrote. "First a '2,' then a '1,' and breathing itself stopped. With the first flash of a '4' such a wild, tumultuous roar thundered up above the handclapping and cheers that the thoroughbreds in their stalls a mile away must have heard and wondered. But when the fraction '1-5' was tailed on the wild acclaim literally raised the roof. Man o' War had been crowned the champion of all champions in the hearts of some thirty thousand thoroughbred [*sic*] admirers. History," Macbeth concluded, "will do the rest for him."[45]

Returning to the stands, Red was not even breathing hard. Instead, the *New York Times* could barely catch its breath. RIDDLE'S SPEED MIRACLE SHATTERS ALL PREVIOUS MARKS FOR MILE AND THREE FURLONGS, its racing headlines exclaimed. WINS BELMONT BY A BLOCK. The first paragraph threw caution completely away, calling Man o' War's performance "beyond a doubt the greatest exhibition of speed ever witnessed on any race track. . . ."[46] And because Kummer had sat still, without urging or restraint, horsemen believed that Red could have gone faster had he been "in the least extended." The *Times* reporter guessed that "perhaps one touch of the whip would have taken another two-fifths from the time." Fair Play, Hastings, and Spendthrift had been done proud.

"The race left no doubt in the minds of all turfmen present that they had seen the greatest horse of this or any other age," the *New York Times* declared. "Up to this time they had been content to say that he was America's finest product, but after he crossed the line in the Belmont and his time was flashed there were none among the veterans of the turf who could think of a horse that compared with him. It is safe to say that Man o' War is the superhorse for all ages as far as records go back; a horse the like of which will probably never be seen by the present generation of horsemen."

The man who had bred the superhorse finally relaxed his reserve. "I will now concede that Man o' War is the best horse I have ever seen," August Belmont told friends at the track. "The manner in which he ran, the speed displayed and the amount of reserve force he had at the close of the race was amazing. He looked as though he could have gone on for two miles and he has now done enough to convince me that he is the best horse we have had in this country."[47]

Horsemen and reporters seemed about to run out of superlatives. One journalist compared Man o' War with Alexander the Great, "seeking new worlds to conquer. . . ."[48] The champion would not conquer new territory, this scribe concluded, by continuing to race against his fellow three-year-olds. Red's only challenge might lie in rewriting the speed-record books, inserting his name at a variety of distances. But already a small undercurrent of dissatisfaction drifted through the sports pages. "We hail Man o' War's astonishing performance in the Belmont," a turf columnist known as "Daniel" wrote, "but what a disappointing race it turned out to be!"[49] Man o' War's extreme dominance had raised a fundamental question: What was Thoroughbred racing supposed to be about? Was sheer speed enough? If everyone dodged Man o' War, could his one-horse exhibitions count as sport? Or was a racehorse not truly tested until he met worthy opponents? Would Man o' War need to measure himself against other flesh and blood champions, even if that search took him out of his age group or far from home?

While these questions gradually emerged, the Belmont Stakes had made one thing immediately clear: Sir Barton was no longer Horse of the Century—unless "Hard Guy" Bedwell could find a way for him to outperform Man o' War.

14

BREATHER

Two days after the Belmont Stakes, New York racing reopened at the Jamaica track and most trainers rejoiced. Although Jamaica lacked Belmont Park's prestige, a simple difference made it more popular: The horses bent to the left around its turns rather than to the right. "Now we have come back to a track where the horses run the American way," a turf columnist proclaimed, "and we are bound to see a big improvement all around—better and truer races and bigger fields."[1] This might not hold true, however, for races featuring Man o' War. Red's astonishing Belmont Stakes performance pushed horsemen into a self-fulfilling prophecy: Man o' War is too great to be beaten, so I won't start my horse and try to beat him. And so the superhorse would have less competition than ever.

Jim Maddux kidded Riddle: "Sam, if you don't retire Man o' War you'll break up racing!"[2]

But Riddle wanted to keep Red running. The question was, What next? Red was eligible for Aqueduct's historic Brooklyn Handicap, to be run twelve days after the Belmont Stakes. On the plus side, the Brooklyn would pay its winner nearly $6,000. Unfortunately, even for a horse as hardy as Man o' War, running a world-record eleven furlongs used up energy stores that took time to replenish. Exercise rider Clyde Gordon noted that Red lost weight after the Belmont Stakes, and nearly a month later, Feustel still was taking care to keep him built up.[3] Even if Red won the Brooklyn Handicap, the effort could set him back. The field would include tough older horses, and Walter Vosburgh assigned Man o' War 118 pounds—the highest weight he ever had given a three-year-old racing more than a mile against older horses in June.[4] Riddle declined this challenge, and whether he made the right choice would remain open for debate. Sam Hildreth would win the Brooklyn with four-year-old Cirrus, carrying only 108 and finishing just three-fifths of a second slower than the world record while beating major stakes winners Boniface, Mad Hatter, and Exterminator. This speed seemed well within Man o' War's reach, but the mature competition put his three-year-old rivals to shame. Wildair, whom Red had beaten so handily in the Withers Stakes, finished last.

Riddle and Feustel decided to race Red two days sooner than the Brooklyn but give him an easier spot: Jamaica's one-mile Stuyvesant Handicap, restricted to three-year-olds. Because of the less demanding conditions, however, Red's weight assignment would be more extreme. Back in January, the *New York Times* had estimated that three-year-old Man o' War "will probably never be asked to carry more than 132 pounds in any race."[5] But that was before Red reeled off two American records. In the Stuyvesant, he would carry 135.

And so, avoiding the older horses at this unfavorable time, the Glen Riddle team let Man o' War carry 17 pounds more than he would have toted in the Brooklyn, while running for $2,000 less. On Stuyvesant morning, the entries showed that Red would give nine pounds to Sam Hildreth's classy colt Dominique; fourteen to On Watch, who had run third in the Kentucky Derby; twenty-five to Irish Dream, a winner who had shown speed in stakes races; and twenty-eight to Krewer, another Hildreth trainee. It was a tantalizing scenario. With four lively challengers and weight concessions up to twenty-eight pounds, the Stuyvesant was shaping up as Man o' War's most competitive race since the Preakness.

But while the public learned of these entries and commuted to the Jamaica track, Man o' War's expected challengers were dropping out. The next day, the *New York Times* would scold, "If the owners did not intend to start the horses they should not have named them merely to make the list of entries appear better."[6] The truth, however, was that Man o' War's prerace pipe opener changed their minds.

As the Tuesday-morning newspapers appeared, promising an interesting contest in the Stuyvesant, Man o' War stepped out for a three-furlong breeze. The track condition did not promise speed. Rain had drenched Jamaica for the past two days, and Monday's races had been run through several inches of water. Although the rain had ceased by Tuesday morning, the track remained "ankle deep"[7] in mud. Man o' War didn't care. His hooves slapping through the goo, he coasted three furlongs in a time Feustel caught as :34 flat.

This was far more speed than Feustel needed to see. It didn't matter that Red pulled up the fourth furlong in :14, finishing half a mile in a brisk but proper :48. Feustel gave Clyde Gordon an earful. Gordon gave a straightforward reply: He'd been holding Man o' War as hard as he could, and Red "wasn't going half as fast as he wanted to."[8]

As word of this extraordinary work flashed around the backstretch, many trainers doubted that Man o' War actually would race that afternoon. No one, however, cared to test that guess. No one else had a three-year-old who could dash three furlongs, under restraint, on a muddy track in :34.

Because radio and television networks did not yet exist, this backstretch news did not reach the outside world. During the early afternoon, more than 20,000 spectators overflowed Jamaica's 1,000-seat clubhouse and 8,000-seat grandstand, expecting to see Man o' War battle Dominique, Krewer, On Watch, and Irish Dream. Elizabeth Riddle enjoyed noting that many in this abnormally large Tuesday crowd made a special effort to watch her horse. "Coming over on the train this morning," she told a reporter from New York's upscale *Evening Post*, "there were a number of Philadelphians who were making the journey for the sole purpose of seeing Man o' War in action. One of them said he had never been at a horse race in his life but had read and heard so much about the colt that he wanted to see him in motion."[9]

Would simply seeing Man o' War in motion be enough? Jamaica's officials, watching the Stuyvesant entries dissolve as quickly as the patrons arrived, wondered how the multitude would react when Man o' War appeared absolutely alone. Their failure to present any opponents for the champion could make them seem like perpetrators of a bad practical joke.

And so, at the last possible moment, a sportsman brought an offering to the volcano's mouth. Richard T. Wilson, President of the Saratoga Racing Association and owner of record-holding miler Roamer, offered a sacrificial virgin of more than one sort by adding to the Stuyvesant his three-year-old gelding Yellow Hand, who had not yet won a race. Only seven days before the Stuyvesant, Wilson had risked his ownership of the young racer in Jamaica's Highland Selling Stakes. Yellow Hand ran a solid but well-beaten second and remained unsold. Racing in a modest purse just four days later, he got off to a bad start and never got into contention.

Now Yellow Hand, a blaze-faced chestnut with white stockings on all four legs, entered the Jamaica paddock for the third time within a single week. Thanks to his humble résumé, he would tote only 103 pounds. Bookmakers were so sure that Man o' War was more than 32 pounds the better horse that they set his odds at 1–100—a possible one-dollar profit for every one hundred dollars bet. "Veterans of the turf said that the price laid against Man o' War was the shortest they had ever heard of in this country or anywhere else," the *New York Times* reported.[10] In fact, most of the bookies ignored the Stuyvesant. Financially, they could only lose.

Lou Feustel didn't worry about losing the $3,850 winner's purse, but he did feel a concern. The Stuyvesant challenge was not Yellow Hand but the 135 pounds on Red's back and the somewhat heavy track. Heavy weight plus high speed on a poor surface could be dangerous. This was not the day to chase Roamer's 1:34 4/5 time-trial mile, set on a wicked fast track under 110 pounds. Today, Kummer would conserve Man o' War.

But Red did not understand those limitations. Parading over the racing surface, hearing the human cheers and music from the band, he knew what he usually was supposed to do. And as Clarence Kummer guided him into place behind the barrier, across from the judges' stand, Johnny Loftus's training was with him still.

To most spectators the Stuyvesant's start was only a formality, the first step toward a sure thing. Not to Man o' War. His memory of a rider's urgency shattered any sense of tedious routine. He burst through the barrier without permission, causing a splash and fall of crowd sound as Kummer leaned back and hauled on the reins. Gradually, they slowed, turned, and returned to the post. Then Red did it again. "The champion did give the crowd one moment of excitement just at the start," the *New York Times* reported. "He showed them how he takes the tremendous bound which sends him to the front of his field as the barrier goes up. The Fair Play colt was very anxious to be on his way, and when it seemed the two horses were to be sent away he threw himself back on his haunches, made a tremendous leap, and, taking the barrier with him, covered nearly twenty feet in the bound. Kummer could not halt him until he had reached the paddock gate. . . ."[11] Turning and heading back almost a quarter of a mile, Red finally reached the barrier for one more try.

They broke for real on the third attempt, and there was hardly cause for adrenaline. While Man o' War bounded forward, Yellow Hand swerved outward, as if uncertain that this race was for real. Well might he wonder. In less than one-sixteenth of a mile, Red led Yellow Hand by the length of his body and at least two more lengths of open daylight. They took the tight first turn that way, Red cruising around the tip of the Jamaica egg and Yellow Hand groping for his own best stride. Up the backstretch, slanting away from the grandstand and clubhouse crowds, Wilson's gelding inched closer, erasing one of the daylight lengths and edging within the second one. Kummer indulged him, holding Red under double wraps. Half a mile in :49. Still Man o' War, though reined in, reached out. The daylight between Red and Yellow began stretching out even farther than before. Six furlongs, 1:13.

Swooping around the egg-butt turn for home, Kummer finally gave his arms a brief rest and Man o' War left his anchor behind. For twelve seconds, from quarter pole to eighth pole, Red neared high gear. One more furlong like that and, slow track or no, Red would annihilate Purchase's record 1:38 4/5, set in the previous year's Stuyvesant under a mere 129 pounds. But one furlong of near freedom was all Kummer allowed. Galloping neck-bent past the crowd, crossing the finish line at the most leisurely pace that his jockey could manage, Red finished an easy eight or ten lengths ahead of Yellow Hand.

The noncompetitive Stuyvesant had become a Man o' War celebration after all. "As has always been the case, he received a big ovation from the crowd," Henry V. King observed. "The thousands knew he hadn't done his best, but they cheered him anyway, and for the fourth time this season all stamped him as the greatest thoroughbred [*sic*] the world has ever seen."[12]

Officially, the winning time, cantering time, was 1:41 3/5. "The track was slow, but ordinary horses could do that well," the *New York Times* noted almost critically, though adding that "Man o' War was never permitted to get out of a gallop, and Kummer had all he could do to restrain him throughout the running."[13] Extraordinary, though, was the canyon between the seventh furlong in twelve flat and the eighth furlong in *sixteen and three-fifths*. Callahan, on Yellow Hand—knowing that his mount couldn't catch Man o' War, however hard he tried—gave up and allowed that final eighth to go by in literally trotting-horse time.

Reporters veered between admiration at simply seeing such a horse as Man o' War and disappointment at seeing him run so slowly. "It wasn't a horse race," W. J. Macbeth told readers of the *New York Tribune*, "it was a joke. . . . He probably would have run faster in a walkover, for then he might have tried to beat time, at least."[14] Trying to be fair, Macbeth did add, "His owner and trainer cannot be blamed for not sending this wonderful horse against time. The track was not at its best." Acknowledging the slow track and Kummer's constant restraint, reporters tried to be logical. But after his startling speed in the Withers and the Belmont Stakes, spectators wanted something beyond logic from Man o' War. They wanted to see what miracle he could perform next.

By late June 1920, while Lou Feustel worked to keep Man o' War fit without letting him get too thin, most rival trainers did not see any trace of vulnerability. To them, the big red colt was starting to seem like a supernatural creature that drained any other horse who tried to keep up with him. "They say that Man o' War takes the heart out of the opposition," one turf columnist reported, "and it surely looks it."[15]

While other stables veered away from letting Man o' War discourage their young horses, Sam Riddle considered going abroad for new victims. The Niagara Racing Association had been courting him to run his superhorse in the July 8 Canadian Derby.[16] Red's presence could give a huge boost to Canadian racing—which, unlike Thoroughbred racing in the United States, had been shut down during the Great War. Riddle gave them hope, actually nominating Man o' War. If Red made the trip, he would travel to the Fort Erie track in Ontario, across the Niagara River from Buffalo, New York—his longest journey since leaving his Kentucky birthplace for the auction at Saratoga Springs. Five days after Red's Stuyvesant win, a *Daily Racing Form* correspondent claimed that "the [Niagara Racing] association has assurances that the Glen Riddle stable will ship him here for the race."[17]

But Man o' War stayed home. The Canadian Derby's $4,000 first-place purse wasn't worth the risk of shipping him more than 400 miles. Red could earn roughly the same amount by staying on Long Island and running in the Dwyer Stakes at Aqueduct on July 10. This choice, however, played straight into Jimmy Rowe's hand. Having fired Upset and Wildair at Riddle's champion that spring without making a dent, Rowe now lined up his best shot. John P. Grier, a gallant second to Red in the Futurity the previous fall, finally was reaching peak condition.

Man o' War's next race would not be a joke. It would be a showdown for the ages.

15

CRUCIBLE

Bᴇғᴏʀᴇ ᴛʜᴇ sᴜɴ climbed high on Tuesday, July 6, Man o' War stepped out onto Belmont Park's training track to gallop the Dwyer Stakes distance of one mile and an eighth. He stepped out onto famously deep footing more conducive to cardiovascular conditioning than razor-sharp speed, and Clyde Gordon took him under a steady hold. "Don't let him go too fast now," Feustel had ordered Gordon. "He won't have to do much to win that race."[1] But even under restraint, Red hit a speed that would win many races, reaching the mile in 1:38 3/5 and the full nine furlongs in 1:52 and three. Considering the training track's tiring surface, the *New York Times* noted, "This would mean close to record time at Aqueduct."[2] Aqueduct's record time— 1:49 2/5—also was the fastest in the world.

Feustel's confidence soared. Given clear weather and a fast track on Saturday, he told a reporter, he would let Man o' War run the Dwyer in record time.[3]

But that didn't discourage Jimmy Rowe. After losing the Withers and abdicating the Belmont Stakes to Sam Riddle's big red juggernaut, Rowe finally saw opportunity entering his range like a trophy buck oblivious to the hunter. And so, several hours after Man o' War's formidable workout, John P. Grier raced in the eight-and-a-half-furlong Sir Walter Handicap at Aqueduct—his own major tune-up for the Dwyer Stakes.

The Sir Walter was a modest race on a Tuesday afternoon, worth little more than one thousand dollars to the winner, but spectators noticed excitement in the Whitney camp. Harry Payne Whitney brought a special visitor to

the track with him: the human John P. Grier.[4] Clearly, inviting his businessman friend Grier to admire the colt, Whitney felt that he had something well
worth showing off. Meanwhile, in an interesting twist, Jimmy Rowe gave
Clarence Kummer the leg up on the equine Grier because regular rider Eddie
Ambrose was traveling back from Kentucky.[5] Kummer would ride Man o'
War, as usual, in the Dwyer on Saturday. Now, however, he would feel how
seriously to take John P. Grier.

The equine Grier "acted meanly going to the post," the *New York Times*
observed, "and Kummer had some trouble getting him to face the barrier."[6]
Once the race started, however, there was no contest. Hefting 126 pounds
while his opponents carried 120, John P. Grier led all the way and beat Donnacona by three lengths, with Kummer glancing back to check the safety
zone and keeping his mount under wraps. Even so, Grier's official time was
only one second slower than Aqueduct's track record.

Impressed, reporters prodded Kummer to compare his temporary mount
with Man o' War. Kummer "thinks John P. Grier is a fast one," one scribe
noted, "but nobody could get him to admit that the Whitney colt has a
chance to take the measure of the Glen Riddle Farm champion."[7] But no
matter what Kummer thought, Jimmy Rowe had John P. Grier—and Man o'
War—right where he wanted them. While Grier had spent several weeks
training toward this showdown but not going out and beating anyone, Man
o' War had been winning major stakes and accruing weight penalties. Grier,
officially inactive, accrued weight allowances instead. In the Dwyer, Man o'
War would carry 126 pounds, while Grier carried only 108. "No horse in the
world," Rowe declared, could beat John P. Grier, as good as he was right
now, while conceding 18 pounds.[8]

When perhaps the most expert trainer in the United States gave such a
bold opinion, even dedicated Man o' War fans had to pay attention—and
Grier's breezy prep race reinforced his trainer's words. Some began expecting
a real struggle. But reporter Henry V. King, picturing Man o' War's recent
brilliant form, couldn't make himself believe that Rowe's prediction would
come true. "Despite this difference in weight," King told his readers, "it is not
likely that John P. Grier will be able to even press Man o' War at any stage of
the journey."[9]

Two days before the Dwyer Stakes, Samuel Doyle Riddle received one of
Thoroughbred racing's ultimate honors: He became a member of The Jockey

Club. This was a mighty leap for someone who, while successful in horse sports for most of his life, had campaigned steadily at major tracks for only five years. Riddle himself knew that he owed this recognition to Man o' War. "That august body could hardly be expected to elect a horse to membership," he mused in later years, "so they met the situation in a spirit I have always applauded and made me a member instead."[10]

Despite being fifty-nine years old, Riddle would start, of course, as a junior member of the club. He would not be invited to help make policy right away, if ever. But membership did reinforce his status as a distinguished patron of the sport. It also might tighten his sense of obligation to August Belmont, who counted on Man o' War's continued presence on New York tracks. The Dwyer Stakes offered a prime example of Riddle's sacrifice. That same Saturday, the Daniel Boone Handicap at Latonia, in Kentucky, would offer its winner over $11,000—more than twice as much as the Dwyer winner would earn. Harry Payne Whitney would be among the Eastern horse owners hoping to collect this Western jackpot. But Whitney, a Jockey Club member since 1900, also would support New York by facing Man o' War with John P. Grier.

The political process behind Man o' War's racing schedule was a fact of life to Lou Feustel, who, as a professional horseman, never could join The Jockey Club, no matter how much Chairman Belmont liked him. "Mr. Belmont and Mr. Riddle and the rest of them used to have long talks about what we would do with him," Feustel said, "but they all came back to me to find out what the horse wanted to do himself."[11] On Dwyer day, Feustel's ideas of what Man o' War wanted to do would cause lasting speculation.

By Dwyer eve, talk of Man o' War setting a new speed record had gained avalanche weight. Feustel tried to lessen the crushing expectation, telling a reporter that he wouldn't let Red run any faster than was necessary to win. At the same time, Feustel reckoned that John P. Grier might well push Man o' War to a new speed mark. New Yorkers reading the Saturday *Sun and New York Herald* over breakfast or brunch found a tempting prediction from Henry V. King: "A world's record is likely to go to the credit of Samuel Riddle's great three-year-old colt Man o' War this afternoon at the Aqueduct track . . . , if he steps along at his best he is likely to cover the one mile and a furlong route in 1:49. . . ."[12]

Also, for the first time in nearly two months, it looked as if Man o' War would have a real contest. In the Dwyer, he would give ample weight not only to a sharp John P. Grier but also to Sam Hildreth's good colt Dominique and

Belmont Stakes foe Donnacona. "We do not hope for a stoppage of the triumphs of Man o' War," a turf columnist wrote on Dwyer eve, "but we do hope for a race, with at least four in it."[13] Overnight, however, the complexion of the race changed as Donnacona and Dominique dropped out. Dominique, especially, could have entertained Grier with early speed while Man o' War waited to pounce. Instead, Red would duel with Grier while conceding eighteen pounds. Red essentially had run match races in his last two starts and had thrived on grabbing a quick lead and exhausting his foe with a fast pace, but those races had featured either equal weights or weak competition. John P. Grier, with his 18-pound gift, was no Yellow Hand.

Years later, Sam Riddle would claim that Feustel feared the Dwyer weights and tried to make him scratch Man o' War that day. In Riddle's account, Feustel forced the issue by working Red a fast mile in 1:37 on Dwyer morning, then feeding and watering him as if he were not racing that afternoon. "They told me what had transpired when I arrived at the stable about noon," Riddle asserted, "so I went over to Clyde Gordon, who always worked Man o' War, took him aside and said to him: 'What did you do with 'Big Red' this morning?" The morning gallop had been effortless, Gordon assured the boss. No harm done if Red raced that afternoon. "So I decided to run him," Riddle declared, "work or no work, oats or no oats."[14]

Daily Racing Form, however, did not support a key detail of Riddle's story. Reporting Red's brilliant Tuesday work, the *Form* had praised his 1:38 3/5 mile. Reporting the Dwyer day workouts, the *Form* did not list any activity by Man o' War. A mile in 1:37, or anything close to it, should have drawn attention.

It is possible that, despite showing great confidence earlier in the week, Feustel did not want Red grappling with John P. Grier after Dominique and Donnacona dropped out. It also is possible that someone misunderstood Red's normal prerace schedule and therefore gave Riddle a misleading description of Feustel's Dwyer-morning actions. Managing Man o' War's abundant energy, Feustel had designed an unusual routine. "We'd always blow him out the day before a race—usually three-eights [*sic*] or better—and the day of the race itself we'd have him on the track for a good gallop, maybe even open him up for an eighth of a mile," Feustel explained to a reporter in later years. Then he added a few words rarely heard: "We never 'drew' him much. He didn't need it."[15] "Drawing" is the common prerace practice of removing food and water from the stall several hours before a race, so that the horse's gut is light when it comes time to run. Man o' War—so fidgety that he bit his hooves after lying down at night—fared better with a late morning meal and some hay to chew.

Perhaps surprise at this atypical approach—galloped and fed on the morning of a race—fostered the idea that Feustel aimed to scratch Man o' War from the Dwyer Stakes. After all, many horsemen had assumed that Man o' War would drop out of the Stuyvesant Handicap because of his fast work on race morning. Red's extraordinary vigor defied conventional routines.

Whatever Feustel had wanted in those final hours before the Dwyer Stakes, he would deny any urge to scratch Man o' War when questioned a dozen years later. "There were reports Red wasn't fit," Feustel would recall. "I wasn't picturing any such romp for Man o' War as he had enjoyed in his previous efforts. But the colt was never better, and I couldn't see Grier beating him."[16]

That afternoon, roughly thirty thousand people—close to forty thousand, by some estimates—crammed the Aqueduct racing plant, which could seat only eight thousand.[17] They came "from all parts of the East to see Man o' War race,"[18] one reporter noted. "The grandstand was a twentieth century version of the Black Hole of Calcutta," another wrote. "There wasn't a cubic inch unoccupied anywhere."[19] Everywhere, as spectators jostled for position, reporters heard the name Man o' War—and much, much more.[20]

"The air was filled with rumors," Abram S. Hewitt recalled. "Feustel did not want to run Man o' War and had given him a full feed at lunch time; Man o' War had his shoes removed; Riddle, confronted by these obstacles, insisted that Man o' War run anyway. We now regret that we never asked either Riddle or Feustel about the truth of such tales."[21] Track handicapper Walter Vosburgh, a man not given to exaggeration, said, "There was a rumor that Rowe had said 'Grier would trim Man o' War to-day,' and was repeated from lip to lip. Besides, when Mr. Riddle inquired of his trainer how Man o' War was doing, the latter replied that the colt 'wasn't screwed up as tight as he might be.' "[22] But nevertheless, Red's sensational performance in his Tuesday workout showed that he was plenty fit.

The weight spread, however, was undoubtedly serious. Just before the race, Jimmy Rowe told his best friend, trainer Jack Joyner, "I've got that big clown today."[23] Maybe Rowe said "clown," or maybe something that a polite reporter did not want to write down. In any case, thousands of people took Rowe at his word, getting odds on Grier as high as 3–1 before the bookies got wise and chopped Grier's odds down to 8–5. Yet Man o' War remained the strong favorite, closing at 1–5. A great majority kept faith in him.

The truly crowded crowd endured a five-furlong purse for two-year-olds, then a two-and-a-half-mile steeplechase. Third on the card came the Tremont Stakes—won by Man o' War the previous year—which fell to the precocious colt Inchcape by ten lengths, in time only one second slower than the track record. Young Inchcape won so easily, under a pull, that many spectators dared to guess he was a second Man o' War.

But now, coming onto the track for a warm-up gallop, was the real thing: the most gorgeous high-headed copper-coated colt of them all. The man who recently had tried to buy Inchcape for fifty thousand dreamed of owning something approaching this. And here, stretching his deerlike legs, was John P. Grier—another "strapping big chestnut"[24] colt, "the same shade of color"[25] as Man o' War, with a hawklike head and a pugnacious gleam in his eye.

Thousands of hands clapped to welcome Red. Cheers rang through the air for Grier. "As the two famous colts were led back to the paddock for their final grooming thousands followed them," a reporter noted.[26] Earlier that week, the New York Times had remarked, "John P. Grier is the last of the 'White Hopes' of the three-year-old division and it seems to be quite up to him to show whether Man o' War can be defeated by any horse of his age."[27] Now the paddock, hemmed in like a boxing ring, echoed that prizefighter metaphor. Spectators pressed against the rails, pressure escalated, and Sam Riddle rose to one of the generous moments of his life. Walking over to John P. Grier's saddling stall, Riddle took Harry Payne Whitney's hand and said, "I wish you luck. If your colt is better than mine I hope you win."[28]

"This sportsmanlike remark had the true ring of sincerity in it," a reporter noted, "and Mr. Whitney appreciated it. 'That's good of you, I wish you good luck, too. I think you have the better horse and I believe you will win.' And for several minutes these two sportsmen stood with hands clasped wishing each other good luck."[29]

Then Clarence Kummer bounced onto Man o' War's back, Eddie Ambrose onto John P. Grier's, and they followed the red-coated outrider toward the track. Major Treat walked beside Man o' War, creating a handsome picture, which many assumed was only for show. In fact, the Riddle crew was doing everything possible to keep Red calm on his way past the crowd, saving his energy to combat John P. Grier.[30]

Owners and trainers split into their separate social groups—Riddle and

Whitney going up to the clubhouse, Rowe and Feustel over to the infield—as their horses moved onto the track, into waves of applause. Man o' War pranced, while Grier seemed "very tame."[31] At the barrier, however, his attitude would change.

Red and Grier moved away from the main crowd and toward the right rear corner of Aqueduct's oblong track, heading for the chute where the barrier waited. Because the course measured ten furlongs plus fifty-one feet around, a nine-furlong race would have had to start on the clubhouse turn were it not for this extension of the backstretch. The colts moved to the track's far right-hand side, then swiveled leftward to face a long straightaway. Nine furlongs to run, with nearly half a mile before the far turn, the only turn in the Dwyer Stakes.

Back at the grandstand, people who had claimed precious seats on benches earlier that day now stood on top of them to see over the people packed along the rail. Others then "swarmed in and stood in the bench runways,"[32] leaning as close as possible to the action. The luckiest saw the colt in post position two cutting up behind the distant net, prompting one reporter to write, "John P. Grier thought he was a rocking horse and tried to stand on his head."[33] The colt beside the inner rail, however, remained invisible to most. "He was screened from the press box view by the foliage inside the chute . . . ," a reporter noted. If press-box occupants, high in the stands, could not see Man o' War at the barrier, neither could most people on the ground.

Then the webbing flew into the air, snapping two words from several thousand throats: "They're off!" With no track announcer and public-address system to broadcast it for them, the crowd yelled their own signal. And in that moment, unable to see through the distant screen of leaves, most missed what happened at the break as Man o' War pushed off from a wet spot on the track where a water wagon had been kept. "He fell to his knees at the start when the ground broke out from beneath him," Kummer would say afterward. "I thought it was all off."[34]

John P. Grier inherited the lead in those first jumps, and Man o' War sprang after him. Red succeeded so well that in a few seconds, as the two colts streamed out of the chute and onto the backstretch, many spectators could see only Man o' War. One horse shape appeared beside the rail, the big red colt topped with yellow-and-black silks. Future radio announcer Clem McCarthy, standing on a bench and vying for a clear view, remembered voices from all sides: *"Where is John P. Grier?" "Was he left?"*[35] But

Grier was keeping stride, to the outside, his slightly smaller body eclipsed by Man o' War.

Sprinting into Aqueduct's long runway of backstretch, they took the first quarter mile in a brisk but not dazzling :23 2/5. With nine furlongs to unfurl, Kummer aimed to keep a moderate early pace and outkick Grier in the homestretch. Instead, he felt their speed increase dramatically as Ambrose encouraged Grier to edge past Man o' War and Red stubbornly kept his own nose in front. "Ambrose ran at me all the way," Kummer later explained. "I wanted to take back, but he wouldn't."[36] Of course Ambrose wouldn't. To win this race, he couldn't let Man o' War steal off at a comfortable pace. Instead, he would start a speed duel and count on light-weighted John P. Grier having more energy than Man o' War near the end.

They barreled down Aqueduct's long backstretch as if it were a Quarter-Horse track, sprinting past the half-mile track record of :46 2/5 in :46 flat. They hit five furlongs in roughly :57 2/5—track record :57 and four. But for sheer audacity, six furlongs was the apex of their flight. Aqueduct's record was 1:11 flat. Clinging to the far turn, Man o' War and John P. Grier officially flashed by in 1:09 2/5. The world record, set on the trampolinelike surface at Juarez, Mexico, was 1:09 and three.

And nothing separated them. "Rounding the turn," a reporter noted, "they were still so close together that not even the nose of John P. Grier, which was on the outside, could be seen."[37]

Racehorses and riders learn a rhythm of gunning for a finish line once they straighten into the homestretch, pouring every effort into a closing burst. Most racetracks, one mile around, provide nearly a quarter mile[38] from the top of the stretch to the finish line. Big Aqueduct, however, was unusually fair to any horses that lost momentum around a turn—and to front-runners, unusually stern. Its homestretch extended nearly half a mile.[39]

Reeling away from six furlongs in world-record time, two colts left the turn and aimed for the distant finish line. They had gone full throttle since furlong three, a reckless outpouring of energy. They officially flew through a mile in 1:35 3/5—four-fifths of a second faster than Aqueduct's record, and only one-fifth faster than the Withers, which Red had won "cantering." But Man o' War carried eight pounds more this time, while setting a much more demanding early pace. And he was looking John P. Grier in the eye. A racehorse feels more stress when another horse matches his effort and does not flinch.

With one furlong to run, Man o' War seemed to slide back as Grier slipped ahead. Could it be true? John P. Grier skipping forward, Man o' War losing ground—a head, a neck, even a half length behind? In an instant, voices catapulted across the track: *"Grier's got him!"*[40] *"Grier is winning!"*[41]

"You've got him, John!" shouted Harry Payne Whitney, his arms waving wildly and knocking the hat and eyeglasses off his friend Henry A. Buck, secretary of the Turf and Field Club.[42]

"My God, I'm beaten!"[43] Lou Feustel cried.

Clarence Kummer measured the track before him, the horse beneath him, the horse at his side. Reaching back, he struck his whip on Man o' War.

With 220 testing yards left in the Dwyer Stakes, a whoosh and smack was what Eddie Ambrose heard. It sounded like Man o' War's defeat. And so, for a moment, Ambrose steadied Grier instead of letting him sail along.[44] For a mile, now, they had been running hard. Let Grier catch his breath, then power on to victory.

Clarence Kummer would later draw a different conclusion from his experiences riding Grier. "That peculiar animal, when he felt like running, would resent any pull on his head," Kummer said, "and his tendency was to dig his toes into the ground and quit."[45] With about two hundred yards remaining in the Dwyer Stakes, Ambrose had tugged slightly on Grier's reins. ". . . I often wonder what would have happened," reflected Kummer, "had Ambrose paid no attention to my whip and given John P. Grier his head the whole route."

But Eddie Ambrose and Man o' War both reacted to that whoosh and smack. Red hadn't felt that sensation in nearly a year—not since Johnny Loftus had gunned him down the Saratoga homestretch in the Sanford Memorial Stakes. Now, as then, he didn't hesitate. "One lash and the great colt sprang out," said the *New York Times,* "and in two or three strides had taken a lead of three-quarters of a length."[46]

Lou Feustel was sprinting, too, racing through the infield as if his own drive could somehow help his horse, waving his hat and yelling, "Come on, Red! Come on, Red!"[47]

"The race now seemed over," the *Times* reporter wrote, "but it was not. Ambrose lashed John P. Grier, and that colt, responding with amazing gameness, moved up again, made a mighty effort as if fully realizing the importance of the duel and once more came to almost even terms with his rival."[48] But Kummer hit Man o' War again, then again. Red surged forward and Grier could not answer. And *now* Sam Riddle reacted. "He didn't yell and shout quite as loudly as his trainer," a reporter noted, "but he held his breath until his colt got a length in front. Then he let out a whoop that could be heard over a hundred yards away even though 40,000 others were shouting their loudest."[49]

A surge, a whoop, a knot slipping loose. Fifty yards from the finish line, for the first time in more than a mile, daylight opened between Man o' War and John P. Grier. Lou Feustel, galloping through the infield shouting "Come on, Red!" failed to see a small ditch near the finish line and tumbled in.[50] He would climb out asking anxiously, "Did Big Red make it?"

Red had indeed made it, passing the finish line a length and a half in front of Grier. Clem McCarthy, stepping down from his bench, looked to the owners' seats and saw Harry Payne Whitney "leaping over the railings" that separated the clubhouse boxes, rushing to congratulate the Riddles "as heartily as if he's had no interest whatsoever in John P. Grier."[51] On an infield pole, wooden blocks slid together to post the official time. Henry V. King had predicted 1:49. Red made 1:49 1/5. A world record had come true.

"Note that it required 13 1/5 seconds to run the last furlong," Abram S. Hewitt would recall. "Man o' War had not quickened; he, too, was faltering, but not as badly as John P. Grier. Two very good colts had given literally their full reserves of speed and stamina, and Man o' War had a little more left at the end. To Rowe's surprise, Man o' War had proven at least 21 pounds better than John P. Grier, which probably was the next best three-year-old of the year. . . ."[52]

Racing's most distinguished photographer, C. C. Cook, tripped his camera shutter as Red neared the line. His photograph caught Man o' War with ears upright, resembling the body language of easy victory. But a horse's ears turn where his or her attention lies, and Red's ears weren't pointing forward enthusiastically. They were swiveled sideways and back, toward the rider urging him on. John P. Grier, well beaten, held his ears in almost the same position. Both were asking, *Can I stop now?*

With his muzzle dusty from his stumbling start,[53] Red returned to the judges' stand a tired horse. "I picked up Man o' War with the pony as he pulled up after the Dwyer," Clyde Gordon would recall, "and he was blowing like a blacksmith's bellows."[54] Bystanders wondered at the sight. They hadn't seen Man o' War beaten, but they had seen him whipped and obviously working hard. Was this *it*? some speculated. Was this *everything*?

Reporters asked the man who had felt the effort in every stride. "John P. Grier had his head in front for a moment at the eighth pole," Clarence Kummer told them, "but . . . the moment I went after him in earnest the race was over. As to whether Man o' War was all in, well, when horses run like they did from the start something has to crack and while I would not like to say how much Man o' War had left it was enough so that he could have gone on to give another horse a battle had there been a third horse in the race. He ran a hard race, but he was not all in at the end."[55]

Red couldn't say, of course, how much of himself he had used. He and Grier could only recover. Journalist Neil Newman would recall, "Both horses . . . were out to the last ounce. They both had their heads down near their knees when they came to the scales."[56] Back at the barn, while Red cooled out, Lou Feustel made a vow: "They'll never catch me napping again with this horse."[57]

Two days after the Dwyer Stakes, Clarence Kummer's afternoon ended horribly. It happened during the day's last race, in front of Aqueduct's grandstand, as a field of two-year-olds charged for the finish line. Near the inner rail, Kummer and the filly Costly Colours bid for the lead. About 100 yards from the finish, trying to dive between two rivals, Kummer's filly stumbled at full speed. For a moment, the rippling stream of legs and necks sucked their trouble from sight. Then, almost before spectators could understand why one horse was lying on the track, a second horror hit: A colt named Flying Cloud tripped over Costly Colours and fell onto her. His jockey landed clear of the mess and crawled safely under the rail. Clarence Kummer wasn't so fortunate.

Not far from the finish line, two images appeared through the settling dust. One was Flying Cloud, flopped senseless on his side. The other was a filly and jockey sprawled together: Costly Colours and Clarence Kummer, who had fallen with his feet still stuck in the stirrups and now lay pinned against his horse. Miraculously quick dodges by the two riders whose horses were directly behind Costly Colours as she went down had kept Kummer from being trampled.

Men ran to the unconscious colt, the unconscious filly, and the jockey trapped by her side. The fallen horses and riders had no ambulance waiting for them. Instead, the horses' trainers tried to help. Max Hirsch was in luck. Reacting to first aid, Flying Cloud jumped to his feet and walked off the track. Willie Midgeley, urging Costly Colours to stand, gained only a struggle. "She regained consciousness and tried many times to get up," a reporter observed, "but each time she fell back."[58] Then a veterinarian discovered why, and Midgeley's only choice was to let Costly Colours be destroyed.

"She was the gamest filly ever foaled," Midgeley said. "Although suffering untold agony from a broken back she tried to respond to my call to get up.

Such gameness would have won her a host of races if she had lived."[59] Instead, near the Aqueduct finish line came the end to a filly bred by August Belmont, by Fair Play out of Violet Ray, by *Rock Sand—a pedigree only one grandmother different from Man o' War's.

Her jockey seemed to escape from the tragedy. "After what seemed like an hour Kummer got his feet free and, covered with dust and blood, walked to his dressing room," a reporter noted. "When asked if he were hurt he replied that he was a bit shaken up and that his arm was slightly cut."[60] Shaking off the shock—or still soaked in it—Kummer tried to return to normal. There was no doctor intercepting him and no requirement for a medical exam. Finally, however, he sought help. Two hours after Costly Colours went down, her jockey visited a hospital in his home township of Jamaica and learned that he had fractured his left shoulder.[61] Sandy McNaughton, the trainer who had taught Kummer how to ride and still served as his agent, announced that his boy would be hospitalized for at least twenty-one days. To Kummer, hooked on motion and adrenaline, each day without riding would feel like an eternity.

Man o' War, meanwhile, rebounded so well from the race of his young lifetime that Feustel flirted with the idea of running him in the Empire City Derby just one week after the Dwyer. "He said his champion was in grand condition and able to beat any colt of his age in the world," a reporter noted, "but that he would consult Mr. Riddle before announcing his next race."[62] Riddle discovered, however, that if Man o' War entered the Empire City Derby, no one else would run.[63] He decided to let Empire City host a real contest and save Man o' War for Saratoga.

Another question now popped up as a sports page headline: CAN MAN O' WAR OVERTAKE DOMINO?[64] To become America's all-time leading earner, Red had $70,101 to go.[65] The Spa's target-rich meet could significantly help his quest, but he would have to progress without trustworthy Clarence Kummer. During August at Saratoga—the setting of his only defeat—Man o' War would be ridden by someone else.

Three days after the Dwyer Stakes, Lou Feustel found the ticking stopwatch that he had pushed into a suit pocket during Man o' War and John P. Grier's wild stretch drive—still waiting for his signal to stop.[66]

16

ALIGHT IN AUGUST

THAT MAN O' War is a wonder all right," Sam Hildreth told Sam Riddle only two days after Red's grueling Dwyer duel. "I saw him out on the track this morning and the boy had all he could do to stay on his back. He is in a class by himself."[1]

Once again, Man o' War's resilience set him apart from most horses. About thirty-two hours after puffing like a steam engine from his ferocious race, Red bounded around the track like his usual frisky self. His quick physical recovery impressed Sam Hildreth, but the Glen Riddle team saw a more profound change. After a moderately stressful Preakness and then three easy races, Man o' War had been to battle—and ignited his competitive fire. For more than a year, Red had been winning races from the sheer pleasure of moving fast. His victories had seemed almost self-contained, satisfying his own need for speed, rather than connected with dominating another horse. Now John P. Grier's relentless challenge and Kummer's insistent whip had brought racing closer to the instinctive wild stallion level of personal combat. After outwrestling John P. Grier, Man o' War reached not only a new physical peak but a mental awakening, as well. "The shaking up he got in the Dwyer Stakes did our colt a lot of good," Sam Riddle told a friend as July drew near its end. "He was a different horse in every way the day after that contest. It tightened him up as he never had been before, and we are all looking for him to show great form at Saratoga."[2]

This would be the perfect time and place to show great form. At Saratoga, Man o' War could spread his reputation beyond New York, beyond the East

Coast, and beyond recent years. The Spa attracted tourists from Canada, Cuba, Europe, and across the United States. Also, during the elite annual meet, generations of racing aficionados gathered at the track, in bars, and on the long porches of grand hotels, arguing about the greatest horses of the past fifty years. Eastern horsemen who had been watching Man o' War all year believed that he belonged at or near the top, but those about to see him for the first time waited to compare his reality with their own memories and myths. Red's string of speed records meant little to them because, as the *New York Times* noted, "tracks are many seconds faster today than they were when their champions were racing. . . ."[3] Before handing Man o' War the all-time greatest crown, many old-timers wanted to see him take a timeless test of class: racing against the best older horses.

Such talk did not sway Sam Riddle. Red's main target at Saratoga would be the Travers Stakes, one of America's most prestigious races for three-year-olds. Worth more than $9,000 to the winner, the Travers also would pay nearly twice as much as a victory in any of the Spa's major races for ages three and older. Preparing Man o' War properly for the ten-furlong Travers, therefore, would be the Glen Riddle team's most important goal.

Nominating Man o' War for several Saratoga stakes, Riddle and Feustel did keep various paths open. Red might prep for the August 21 Travers by running against older horses in the August 14 Champlain Handicap or against three-year-olds in the August 7 Miller Stakes. The Glen Riddle team ignored, however, Saratoga's opening-day feature: the August 2 Saratoga Handicap, which would attract several older stars. For now, they would bypass exactly the kind of test that stubborn old-timers wanted to see.

On a clear Monday afternoon when the temperature reached eighty degrees, a holiday-size crowd welcomed the annual meet at Saratoga Race Course. The crowd's impressive size surprised reporters. Saratoga's meet had always started gently, when it opened on a weekday, and built toward a grand crescendo. This year, the Saratoga Association's beautification efforts and racing's growing popularity completed a circle of expectation and fulfillment. From its expansive shady paddock to the brand-new fountain sparkling in the infield, Saratoga Race Course called out for people to enjoy its gracious facilities. On this day, in the Saratoga Handicap, they would enjoy an added attraction: Sir Barton would run his first race in three months. He would race ten furlongs, the distance of his maiden victory in the Kentucky Derby and also his most brilliant victory in the Maryland Handicap. Despite his long vacation, he would carry the top weight of 129 pounds—giving three pounds to Exterminator, five to The Porter, nine to Mad Hatter, and 14 to three-year-old Wildair.

The meeting of Sir Barton and Exterminator made an especially interesting contrast. Although each had won the Kentucky Derby, their physiques and personalities were opposite. While Sir Barton acted aloof at best and sometimes even tried to hurt his handlers, Exterminator was relaxed and friendly. Sir Barton easily bulked up his short, stocky frame, while Exterminator stood four inches taller and displayed such long, lean muscles over his skeleton that stable hands called him "Old Slim" and "Old Bones," and one wag nicknamed him "the Galloping Hat Rack." At Saratoga in 1919, a reporter had described Exterminator quite appropriately as "the Abe Lincoln of race horses . . . he has the tall, ungainly, gangling form of an equine backwoodsman, with the amiable, affectionate disposition of a family buggy horse."[4] As the Saratoga Handicap weight assignments showed, five-year-old Exterminator also was rising toward championship level. In early July, his winning time for Aqueduct's nine-furlong Brookdale Handicap on a muddy track had been only four-fifths of a second slower than the track and world record. Man o' War, going all out to beat John P. Grier a few days later on a dry track, had finished one second faster while carrying three pounds less. The statistics suggested that Exterminator might not catch Riddle's champion but deserved a chance to try.

And so the Saratoga Handicap might suggest how the best older horses compared with Man o' War. From the start, they looked sharp. Sending Sir Barton straight to the lead and setting a daunting pace, Earl Sande unfurled a ride that might have made Johnny Loftus nod in recognition. The Porter, then Mad Hatter, took turns trying to keep up with the Ross horse and would end up finishing next to last and last.

Andy Schuttinger let Exterminator fall several lengths behind the early pace, but he knew better than to let Sir Barton steal off completely. Along the backstretch, Exterminator built momentum, inching forward comfortably. Rounding the far turn, Schuttinger aimed for a gap at the rail and Exterminator cut the corner. When Sir Barton straightened into the homestretch, still leading the pack, Exterminator was at his heels—and gaining.

At the head of the lane, "Old Slim" and "Dempsey" galloped side by side. Then Earl Sande called their meeting to an end. One slap of the whip and Sir

Barton accelerated, shooting away, and Exterminator had no answer. For about a furlong, Sande let Sir Barton roll, opening daylight as they streamed past the grandstand. Half a furlong from the finish line, he told Sir Barton to start slowing down, and still, broken free from Exterminator and everyone, Sir Barton won by three lengths. His official time—2:01 4/5—shaved two-fifths from the track record, but it meant more than that. Back in 1913, when Harry Payne Whitney's stallion Whisk Broom II had been credited with the world record of two minutes flat, all of the watch-holding horsemen had caught him at least two seconds slower. That particular race[5] at Belmont Park, like the Belmont Stakes, had used a special finish line several yards beyond the regular one. Many people guessed that the official clocker, forgetting the special finish, had snapped his watch too soon. The fact that Whisk Broom carried 139 pounds while supposedly chopping more than two seconds from the world record supported that assessment. And so, even though Whisk Broom's two minutes flat remained in the record books because August Belmont supported the official timer, most experts believed that Sir Barton had just run the fastest ten furlongs ever known. Many also believed that here was the horse who would seriously challenge—maybe even beat—Man o' War.

"It was more than a record breaking performance," reporter Henry V. King enthused about Sir Barton's Saratoga Handicap. "It was wonderful, little less than phenomenal, and when he stepped past the judges he was unanimously proclaimed the greatest handicap horse in the world, and the equal, if not the superior, of the invincible Man o' War at weight for age."[6]

And so a sound rang through Saratoga as Sir Barton's time was posted. It was a glove slap, the challenge for a duel, from one Horse of the Century to the next.

The morning after Sir Barton's brilliant win, Glen Riddle Farm suffered from plain rotten luck. Their most talented two-year-old—a filly named Tottie, which Elizabeth Riddle had picked out as a yearling and named after a cherished pet dog—was exercising at Saratoga's training track when she reached the wrong place at the wrong moment. With perfectly bad timing, a maintenance cart sprayed water just as Tottie approached. Bolting away from this sudden display, the filly crashed into a fence. In an instant, her promising young life narrowed down to a broken foreleg, now barely attached to her body. Within minutes, the track veterinarian ended her misery.

Fortunately, Elizabeth Riddle did not see this sickening sequence of

events. Unfortunately, someone would have to tell her. They chose to mini-
mize the news with a big red distraction: Man o' War. While Mrs. Riddle
learned that she had lost Tottie, she was part of a large gathering near the
main track's finish line to watch Red tune up for his next race. Her reaction
to the tragedy would be swallowed by the buzz that grew when Man o' War
appeared.

Oblivious to anything but his own energy, Red galloped one lap of the
nine-furlong track in a brilliant 1:49 4/5. Some clockers stationed at the finish
line said he did 1:49 flat. *Daily Racing Form,* endorsing the most conservative
time, still called Red's breeze "The greatest working trial by a horse in this
country known to the oldest horsemen. . . ."[7] Horses simply did not perform
their morning exercise, with a heavy rider in the saddle, in nearly world
record time. Experts who, less than twenty-four hours earlier, had thought
Sir Barton looked unbeatable now wondered where Man o' War's ability
might end.

A few professionals noted that the champion "was being urged slightly
during the last three eighths of the workout"[8] and came back puffing. "Was
he tired at the finish?" a Saratoga reporter asked his readers. "Of course he
was! That was what they made him run that way for. He needed to be tired
out and then freshened up, but he came out of it all in fine shape and will be
ready to race next Saturday. . . ."[9] This small dose of effort vanished into the
vast pool of well-earned admiration. Even the most critical observer noted
that Man o' War "seemingly . . . had speed in reserve."[10]

Asserting that Red "had plenty left at the end" of his nine-furlong jaunt,
Lou Feustel didn't want to hear any more glorification of Sir Barton's
Saratoga Handicap. "Red worked as fast as Sir Barton ran," Feustel insisted.
". . . He could have gone a mile and a quarter in record time if I had sent him
that distance at full speed."[11]

Feustel's challenge rushed back to the Sir Barton camp like a spark striking
a dry fuse. In the wake of Red's great workout, someone asked Commander
Ross whether he would match Sir Barton against Man o' War during the
Saratoga meet, "and he declared," a reporter wrote, "[that] the racing public
was certainly entitled to a treat of that sort."[12] When asked how much prize
money would be needed to make the dream race come true, the Commander
said that he would compete for "a blue ribbon if the Saratoga Association will
offer it."

"Such sportsmanship," the reporter declared, "makes the Canadian breeder a leader among the present day horse owners."

The next day, rumor had it that there would be no special match race. Instead, Sam Riddle would send Man o' War against Sir Barton in Saratoga's closing-day feature, the famous Saratoga Cup at one and three-quarter miles.[13]

"In Sir Barton, Man o' War will be meeting the horse best qualified to search out his weaknesses, if he possesses any," *Daily Racing Form* decreed. "No other horse that could be selected could be depended to carry him along all the way. When Sir Barton is in action he is the picture of the relentless, tireless type of thoroughbred [*sic*] that never acknowledges defeat. With his head and tail on a line and his ears flattened to the disappearing point on his neck, he is a veritable racing machine."

"On the other hand," the *Form* allowed, "there is no denying the fact that Man o' War is a phenomenon."[14]

But, as one columnist noted, something pointed against Man o' War meeting Sir Barton in late summer at Saratoga: Sam Riddle and Lou Feustel had not been eager to pit Red against older horses this year.[15] They realized that a severe race might strain his physical limits before he had finished growing up. "He is only a three-year-old and there is plenty of time in the future for him to go out of his way to meet older horses in special events," Sam Riddle explained. "I am confident that he can beat any and all horses in America at weight for age, over any distance. And when the proper time arrives he will be found on the spot."[16]

Spectators wanted to see Man o' War and Sir Barton run head and head, hell for leather, testing each other to the last ounce. Riddle and Feustel, however, might not want to see their phenomenal colt dueling an older champion for a full mile and three-quarters in the Saratoga Cup. The question wasn't could Man o' War succeed. The question was how healthy he would be afterward.

Preparing for the Travers, Riddle and Feustel played it safe. Forsaking the nine-furlong Champlain Handicap, they entered Man o' War in the slightly longer Miller Stakes. This made more sense than the Champlain in several ways: Its distance was closer to the Travers route of ten furlongs; its earlier date would give Red two weeks rather than one to bounce back; its purse would offer several hundred dollars more; and the three-year-old competition should be less demanding than facing the likes of Exterminator and Mad Hatter. The main drawback would be weight. Already this year, Red had carried 135 pounds while racing one mile. In the Miller, he would race a mile and three-sixteenths while lugging 131. Because weight made more difference over a longer distance, he was entering difficult territory indeed.

Feustel, however, was more concerned about the racing surface. As the week wore on, Saratoga's track became so hard that cheap and infirm horses were running times like stakes horses. On such a surface, Man o' War might move unimaginably fast. Unfortunately, the unusual firmness that fostered extreme speed also could overstress a horse's bones. Red's sturdy legs were built with, as Feustel put it, "bone you couldn't cut down with an axe."[17] But with every stride, those legs would sustain the impact of his 1,150-pound body plus 131 pounds balanced on his back. The extra-hard track could punish his legs even while propelling him to landmark speed. And so, when reporters began asking whether they could expect another record from Man o' War that Saturday, Feustel remained noncommittal.

Adding to Feustel's concern, Clarence Kummer would not be able to help. As expected, Kummer's fractured shoulder had not yet healed enough for race riding. From Commander Ross, the Glen Riddle team borrowed a young rider who had won three Saratoga races in one day earlier that week and was becoming the most popular jockey since Johnny Loftus: Earl Sande. They could trust Sande to give an honest ride. Ironically, however, they needed him to hold Red back. The track remained too hard to risk Man o' War at full speed.

Before the Miller Stakes, an enormous swell of 35,000 people overflowed the antique Saratoga stands and swarmed against the rails to see Man o' War. To reach the paddock, Red needed to navigate past thousands of unpredictable human bodies blocking his path. Twelve Pinkerton guards formed a phalanx around the high-headed horse, pressing through the crowd, then creating a living fence around his saddling area.[18] Many platoons of fans tried to squeeze in near Man o' War for a close-up look while newsreel cameras kept grinding away.

When Earl Sande arrived for his final orders, he found a restless horse and cautious handlers. Feustel and Riddle told him to win comfortably but not chase any speed records. Then, making sure that Red wouldn't run away with his new rider, Feustel had George Conway—identified in the news simply as "a tall, lanky chap"[19]—snap a lead shank to Red's bridle and escort horse and jockey to the starting place in front of the grandstand. Conway indeed had a soothing effect, for a reporter noticed that Man o' War "kept searching in his hand for sugar and acted as playfully with him as a St. Bernard puppy."[20]

As Man o' War stepped onto the track, Saratoga's patrons gave him what the *New York Times* called "the most enthusiastic reception he has received anywhere. . . . "[21] They cheered and clapped for what they had heard about this horse and what they hoped he would be. Some compared his appearance with past golden moments at the track, while others came to this moment brand-new. Old-timers and newcomers were bound by knowing that whatever happened in this race, they were participants in history.

History favored them by letting the race start half a furlong before the finish line, where the vast crowd could see Man o' War's run both begin and end. They saw him line up with Donnacona—getting 12 pounds from the champion—to his left and King Albert—getting 17 pounds—to his right. They saw him try to rush through the barrier the moment he reached it, and after the net flew up they saw him charge into a clear lead before he reached the finish line for the first time. They were seeing the essential Man o' War.

But once Red grabbed a clear lead, Earl Sande's orders kicked in. After moving close to the inner rail, Sande geared Red down to an opening quarter mile in a sedate :24—slow motion, by Man o' War standards—then a dawdling half mile in :48 1/5. This still was enough to discourage Donnacona, who lacked the desire to launch a real challenge. During the third quarter, Red doubled his lead, opening to three lengths even while slowing down to a pace of :24 3/5, then :25 flat. Sande was achieving this by keeping a strong pull on the reins and yelling "Whoa!" to Red all the way around.[22]

Even so, entering the homestretch, Man o' War widened away from Donnacona—four lengths, then five. Sande's efforts now verged on a comedy routine: "pulling at the reins as hard as he could and calling to Man o' War to slow up."[23] Red barely cooperated, covering the final three-sixteenths in a fairly brisk :18 4/5, beating Donnacona by six lengths, and finishing in official time of 1:56 3/5—just three-fifths slower than the track and American record held by Commander Ross's good older horse, Cudgel. The near miss played with Sam Riddle's mind. Before the race, saving Man o' War' legs on the hard track had seemed smart. Afterward, nearing another record with so little effort felt like a gamble lost. With Red returning safe and sound, Riddle said he wished he had told Sande to let him loose late in the race.[24] The jockey, who was clearly tired as he dismounted,[25] surely agreed. "You'll never get me on his back again," Sande privately told Lou Feustel. "He damned near pulled my arms out of their sockets."[26]

In public, Sande downplayed the discomfort. "He wanted to run away with me all the way," Earl told reporters, "and once or twice I thought I would have to let him go."[27] Then he could not help praising Man o' War, not diplomatically but with full, honest force: "I never felt anything like that horse in my life. He is a regular machine. He strides further than anything I ever rode and does it so handily that you would not know he was running at all. I thought we came home several seconds below [slower than] the record. In fact, I thought he was traveling at the rate of a selling plater."[28]

Speaking frankly to the press, the young jockey had unwittingly compared the two best horses he had ridden, the two horses that the world most hoped would meet soon. The next day, one headline about Man o' War's Miller announced, "GREATEST RACE HORSE," SAYS JOCKEY SANDE. Meanwhile, the *New York Times* rotogravure section featured a news photo from earlier in the week: Sir Barton, with Earl Sande up, winning the Saratoga Handicap.

Four days after winning the Miller Stakes with Man o' War, Earl Sande guided Sir Barton to victory in the $10,000 Dominion Handicap at Canada's Fort Erie track. Commander Ross valued this prestigious win in his native land more than any Saratoga race. After capturing the Dominion, however, Sir Barton quickly shipped back to the Spa. While the Ross champion rested up from his race and railroad trip, Guy Bedwell amused himself by teasing Lou Feustel about running Man o' War against Sir Barton. As long as Feustel refused, Bedwell seemed to have the upper hand.

After about four days of ribbing, Red's trainer couldn't stand it any longer. "I'll race you this morning," Feustel dared Bedwell on Monday, August 16, "and I'll bet you $100 or $500 I beat you. If that isn't enough, I think Mr. Riddle will back me for $5,000."[29] Feustel's offer was quite extraordinary from someone not known as a betting man.

Bedwell, the hardened gambler, backed away. That morning would be too soon for Sir Barton, who was still rebounding from his Canada trip. As "Hard Guy" retreated, Feustel called after him, "I'll meet you soon enough. I'll meet you in the [Saratoga] Cup, and if you don't run out I'll show you that you only think you have the greatest horse."

Later that day, Feustel announced that Red definitely would start in the

Saratoga Cup. "The only thing that will keep my horse out is an accident," he declared. "But I'm afraid Sir Barton will not be among his opponents. I don't think Bedwell is overanxious to meet me, and he might have an engagement for Sir Barton in Canada about that time."[30]

Sam Riddle, in fact, might not have been overanxious to match Man o' War against Sir Barton for a $5,000 bet. That very morning, enterprising Kentucky racetrack executive Matt Winn had started trying to entice Riddle and Ross to bring their champions to the Bluegrass State for a special $25,000 race with a golden trophy.[31] "Trainer Bedwell took kindly to the proposition," *Daily Racing Form* noted, "and there is every belief that the proposition will likewise appeal to Mr. Riddle."[32]

Twenty-some hours after Lou Feustel lost patience with Guy Bedwell and promised that only an accident would keep Man o' War out of the Saratoga Cup, his words threatened to come true.

Red worked ten furlongs that Tuesday morning, tuning up for the August 21 Travers Stakes. With his legs wrapped in protective bandages, as usual for his training sessions, he sped the Travers distance of ten furlongs in a rapid 2:03 1/5. Feustel and Riddle were delighted until they saw the colt moving unevenly back toward them. "When he returned he was limping badly, and trainer and owner thought he had broken down," a reporter observed. "When Feustel saw him limp he was scarcely able to talk."[33]

All Feustel could do was hurry to Man o' War's side, placing his hands on the leg that Red didn't seem to trust on the ground. Was a bone or tendon breaking under strain? What Feustel found was the best-possible news: Red had thrown a shoe. One of his hind feet, reaching far under his body to propel him forward, had grabbed the heel of a front plate and wrenched it away from the hoof.

Only time would show whether or not Red was completely in the clear, whether his naked foot was sound or sore. Red limped back to his barn, to be watched and to wait. They found his missing shoe five-eighths of a mile before the finish line.

During the afternoon of August 17, while word spread that Man o' War had gone lame, Clarence Kummer resumed race riding. He had arrived in Saratoga Springs three days too late to see Earl Sande wrangle Red through the Miller Stakes. The public had thought that Kummer would reunite with Man o'

War that afternoon in the one-mile Saranac Handicap. Looking at the entry list, they thought they would see the superhorse carry 140 pounds.

Working Red a fast ten furlongs that morning, Feustel obviously had changed his mind—but the public did not know this. "At 1 o'clock Man o' War did not appear on the list of scratches on the official track blackboard," a reporter complained. ". . . Not until just before the first race, or a quarter to 3 o' clock, was the announcement made that Man o' War would not start."[34] By that time, an unusually large and hopeful Tuesday-afternoon crowd filled the track. The Glen Riddle crew may have been distracted from their clerical duties by tending to Red's sore foot, but this oversight made a poor impression. "Another such disappointment," a reporter noted, "may create hard feelings all around."[35]

The crowd did get to welcome Clarence Kummer back to the races, for he won the Saranac Handicap with Glen Riddle second-stringer Dinna Care. "He did everything a great jockey should do," a turf writer enthused, "and when he returned to the scales he was greeted with vociferous cheering by thousands . . . and his riding showed that his injury did not make him careless or timid."[36] Unfortunately, after riding seven races in two days, Kummer found that he had aggravated both his shoulder and his doctor. He would be grounded for the rest of the Saratoga meet.

Man o' War fared better. Although he had been "somewhat sore"[37] immediately after losing his shoe, Wednesday morning found him perfectly sound. "It is astonishing how much solicitude was displayed on the part of everybody when it was rumored that the champion had shown lameness," the *New York Times* remarked. "Everybody wants to see him go on and achieve even greater triumphs than those with which he has been credited to date, phenomenal as they are."[38]

Actually, not quite everyone wanted to see Man o' War achieve even greater triumphs. Still believing that he could get past Riddle's big red roadblock and take the classic races he was accustomed to winning, Jimmy Rowe prepared a two-pronged assault for the Travers Stakes. "Rowe, you are crazy!" some of his friends had said when they learned that he was not giving up after the Dwyer.[39] By mid-August, however, some experts believed that Rowe's plan—John P. Grier to push Man o' War into a torrid early pace and Upset to come flying past them in the homestretch—could succeed. The weights would help Rowe's cause. Man o' War had to carry 129 pounds: six more than Upset and fourteen more than John P. Grier.

Now the whispers reached Sam Riddle: *Watch out.*

"I will own that this was the only time I was ever nervous, really nervous," Riddle claimed, "about the outcome of a race that Man o' War went into after he had shown us what he was."[40] The tension started while Riddle watched the Whitney colts train sharply and heard about Jimmy Rowe's bold predictions. "I knew of the boasts that he had made, that the day of the downfall of Man o' War was at hand," Riddle confided. "I knew that this was believed by a lot of people who passed for very smart, and that they were backing the Whitney pair down to the shortest odds laid against anything that had started against him since the Preakness, his first start that season. But over and above that," Riddle admitted, "what had worked me up to a very tense nervous state was the fact that people kept coming to me and warning me that 'something was going to happen' and for me to 'look out for it.'" Being at Saratoga, where serious gamblers gathered from all over— Saratoga, the only place where Man o' War had lost—made the warnings all the more ominous.

"I knew of course I had nothing to fear from Mr. Whitney or from Jimmy Rowe except the speed and gameness of their entries," Riddle asserted. "But what might come from some outside quarters—that I couldn't tell."

It's possible that Riddle even wondered what might come from inside his own barn. Although news reports from 1919 and 1920 would say nothing about it, Lou Feustel's obituary fifty years later would claim that the trainer "quit Riddle several times"[41] during Man o' War's racing career. While this statement may have been exaggerated, by August of 1920, Sam Riddle well knew that Lou Feustel was not a yes-man. In fact, Riddle believed that Feustel had gone against his wishes by trying to get Man o' War out of the Dwyer Stakes. A rumor unmentioned in the newspapers claimed that at one point Riddle had actually hired private detectives to investigate the Glen Riddle trainer. If so, this may have happened during the "nervous, really nervous"[42] time leading up to the Travers Stakes. In any case, Sam Riddle did not fire Lou Feustel. Despite their differences, the owner saw the trainer clearly doing exceptional work with a sometimes-difficult horse.

Seeking a Travers jockey, however, the *Watch out* warning preyed on Riddle's mind. With Kummer sidelined and Sande away in Canada riding for the Ross stable, there weren't many riders he could trust with Man o' War. Red needed someone with strong arms, an excellent sense of pace, and, beyond that, someone who would not take a bribe.

Finally, Riddle secured the veteran who had ridden Roamer to a time-trial American-record mile and stolen a match race from Billy Kelly. The answer was Andy Schuttinger, whose abilities would help Red handle the super-charged atmosphere. The *New York Times* would note the common "whispers that Man o' War had had too many fast trials and that he was probably step-ping to his doom. . . . All this," the *Times* concluded, "only increased the in-terest in the event."[43]

The interest percolated through Saratoga Springs on Friday night, with thousands of people pouring into town for Saturday's race. "It is expected," a reporter noted, "that the largest crowd that ever witnessed a thoroughbred [*sic*] contest in this country will be present. Thousands and thousands of tick-ets for the grand stand and paddock already have been sold and hundreds of applications have been made for seats in the clubhouse. Harry Stevens, the caterer of the course, has had to turn down more than 200 luncheon parties because of lack of accommodations."[44]

Buzzing with rumors of triumph or doom, the Man o' War crowd stretched Saratoga Race Course past its limits. Along with leaving no empty space in the clubhouse or grandstand, they pressed into the "apron" between the stands and racing surface so tightly that the track management took special steps to ease the crush. Shortly before the Travers, officials announced that spectators could cross the track and watch from the infield. About five thousand fans ac-cepted the offer, some gathering in groups along the backstretch but most gravitating to the homestretch inner rail. They formed a solid mass from the finish line nearly to the far turn, almost a quarter of a mile, and waited for the truth behind the whispers and warnings to appear.

Sam Riddle feared that Joe Rodriguez and Eddie Ambrose, the jockeys handling Upset and John P. Grier, might try to interfere with Man o' War. "Take him out in front the minute the flag falls," Riddle told Schuttinger in the paddock. "Keep him there and keep him going. Don't let either of them get near you. Just show them up, if anybody thinks they can beat him. That's all, for he will do the rest."[45] Lou Feustel gave more casual instructions. "Use your own judgment and be guided by the running," Feustel told their substi-tute rider. "You are on a good horse, and I have no fears for the result."[46]

Man o' War, though periodically cranking his head as high as possible and gazing across the crowd, likewise seemed to have no fears. "There was noth-ing nervous in his movement," *Daily Racing Form* observed, "and he acted more sedate and quiet . . . than in most of his previous starts."[47] Turf expert John Hervey noted that Red appeared physically better than ever and Upset "also looked very fit" but that John P. Grier "seemed hardly so fresh and rugged as he had looked in the Dwyer . . ."[48] While Man o' War had literally gained stature during the past few weeks, Grier literally seemed to shrink.

One furlong before the finish line, Red took his place beside the infield rail, with John P. Grier next to him and Upset at the outside. Moments later, Sam Riddle's and Jimmy Rowe's strategies came to life: Man o' War charging to the front, Grier charging after him, and Upset dropping half a dozen lengths behind to wait his turn. "A vast subdued roar followed the trio as they raced down the stretch and past the watching thousands the first time," John Hervey would remember. "Man o' War was running freely and easily, though Schuttinger had a strong hold on him, and was clear of Grier, which . . . seemed unable to more than reach the leader's heels."[49]

"John P. Grier instinctively knew his master," Andy Schuttinger would remark after the race, "for even in the early running, when I had a steadying hold of Man o' War and invited John P. Grier's presence alongside my mount, he seemingly refused to run on even terms."[50] Schuttinger was observing a common phenomenon: A horse that remembers being dominated by another horse may quickly submit if they meet again. Grier had run painfully hard in the Dwyer but still lost. Recognizing his rival from that day, he would not make a futile all-out effort again.

Setting sail along the backstretch and discouraging Grier, Red set a brilliant pace, reaching the half mile in :46 3/5 and hammering out six furlongs in 1:10 flat. Saratoga's track record was 1:10 and two. No Travers winner ever had shown such insane early speed.[51] An unofficial watch caught Red's seven furlongs in 1:22 3/5—a full second faster than the track mark. Watching Man o' War draw off from the floundering Grier, a reporter noted that "when he was ready to move away he so easily left the Whitney colt struggling under the whip at the turn into the stretch that it caused those in the stands to gasp."[52]

Two summers before, Andy Schuttinger had guided Roamer around this same track to an American-record mile. Easing away from John P. Grier, Red officially clocked the mile in 1:35 3/5, four-fifths of a second slower than Roamer's mark—but Roamer had carried only 110 pounds and didn't have to carry his speed any farther. Red carried 19 pounds more and still had a quarter mile to run.

Upset now rushed past John P. Grier, aiming for the finish line where he had once beaten Man o' War. Schuttinger glanced back from several lengths in front, keeping his hands on Man o' War's neck, ready to let him loose if needed but allowing Upset to slowly gain ground. The whispers and warnings, all of Sam Riddle's fears, had proved powerless. Man o' War loped the final quarter mile in :26 1/5, with Schuttinger standing "almost upright in his stirrups"[53] at the finish line, content to win by three lengths from Upset and nine from John P. Grier. Even so, Red's early speed had guaranteed a sensation. Never touched by the whip and easing up in the final sixteenth of a mile, he officially equaled the track record of 2:01 4/5 set by Sir Barton nineteen days before. "Had Man o' War been permitted to continue at full stride through the stretch," a *Daily Racing Form* reporter guessed, "there is every reason for belief that he would have reduced the running time by a second."[54]

"There never was a stage that Man o' War was fully extended,"[55] Andy Schuttinger confirmed. A reporter noticed the winner "still prancing when the saddle was being removed, his head in the air, truly a superhorse."[56]

Daily Racing Form proclaimed, "Man o' War Is Invincible."[57]

Man o' War's groom reckoned he never saw anything better. Figuring that Red "could have run it in 1:59 that day," Frank Loftus would remember the Travers as Red's finest performance.[58] Others, however, would point to later efforts even more worthy of that honor.

Seven days after Red's scintillating Travers, Sir Barton lugged 133 pounds through Saratoga's Merchants and Citizens Handicap. His performance was classic Sir Barton: taken straight to the lead by Earl Sande, daring anyone to keep pace. Early challenger Jack Stuart could not stay on, but a colt named Gnome, getting 18 pounds from the Ross champion, charged up in deep stretch. One hundred yards from the finish, Gnome stuck his head in front and seemed about to win. Sir Barton fought back. They passed the judges' stand so close together that only people directly at the finish line could know who had won. Commander Ross and Guy Bedwell believed that their colt had lost. When the placing judges posted Sir Barton as the winner, an unhappy mob of Gnome supporters besieged the judges' stand and spent several minutes agitating that the officials must change their decree.[59] The placing judges had the best vantage point, however, and refused to relent. There was no official photo-finish system to verify the result, but odds are that the judges were right. That evening, former wartime aerial surveillance photographer

C. C. Cook developed his film, which showed Sir Barton's nostril in front at the line.

The result mattered to history books as well as to bookmakers because the Merchants and Citizens winner had set a world record of 1:55 3/5 for a mile and three-sixteenths. Although this was a rare race distance outside the United States, the cachet of a world record—and Sir Barton's bravery—lingered. "Later it was said that Gnome's jockey, [Frank] Keogh, had ridden a very overconfident finish," Jim Ross remembered. "Perhaps that was so, but the fact remains, Sir Barton refused to be denied."[60]

Reporter Henry V. King spoke for the backers of Gnome. "Frankie Keough [sic] did not give him the best of rides . . . ," King declared. "In the final sixteenth he allowed Gnome to bear out a trifle and, in short, Earl Sande on Sir Barton outrode him, and for the latter's victory much credit is due his rider."[61]

Sadly, as time passed, this lesson would be lost on Commander Ross.

Two days after Sir Barton's gallant victory, the world learned that he would not run in the Saratoga Cup and neither would Man o' War. One turf columnist spoke for the disappointed masses when he griped, "It looks as if the owners of Sir Barton and Man o' War are afraid of each other and do not care to risk a meeting."[62]

Ross and Riddle's reasons, however, had as much to do with the humane treatment of two priceless animals as with fear of their champions meeting. Sir Barton had gone all out to win the Merchants and Citizens Handicap on August 28—so why should he race nearly two miles in the Saratoga Cup only three days later? Man o' War, committed to Belmont Park's 15/8-mile Lawrence Realization just four days after the Saratoga Cup, had a scheduling crunch in the other direction. Sticking to the schedule that Riddle had announced for Red back in January, Feustel shipped Man o' War to Belmont shortly before the Saratoga meet closed. The Realization, worth more than $15,000 to the winner, exerted a stronger pull than about $5,000 for first place in the Saratoga Cup.

There was one more reason why Sir Barton and Man o' War did not face off at Saratoga. Matt Winn's proposal for a $25,000 match race in Kentucky with a special gold cup had been followed by a $30,000 offer from Laurel Park in Maryland. If Riddle and Ross put their colts into a regular stakes race, they would lose the possibility of creating a much more valuable blockbuster event.

This left "Old Bones" to waltz away with the Saratoga Cup for the second year in a row. Adding sizzle to the deflated stake, he easily set an American record and reinforced his status as the nation's best runner going fourteen furlongs and beyond. "Exterminator showed by his race," one reporter declared, "that even a Sir Barton or a Man o' War must do his best to beat him over a distance of ground. . . ."[63]

Opportunities awaited them all at Belmont Park. Sam Riddle assured his critics that after Man o' War faced other three-year-olds in the Realization, any older horses who cared to challenge him could do so going twelve furlongs in the Jockey Club Stakes.

Man o' War would indeed break boundaries at the Belmont meet. The ways in which he would do this, however, would surprise everyone.

17

REALIZATION

Two days before the thirteen-furlong Lawrence Realization, Lou Feustel wanted Man o' War to tune up with a solid twelve-furlong work. Clyde Gordon held Red under steady restraint, cruising one lap around Belmont Park's giant oval at what appeared to be an ordinary gallop. Knowing Man o' War, however, the flock of trainers clocking their progress should have known to be surprised at the number their watches would show. And yet they bypassed surprise, going straight into disbelief: 2:29 2/5. Faster than any horse in America ever had been caught running this distance, even sweating through the quickest race. Moreover, when Thunderclap had raced to the mark of 2:29 3/5, he had carried only 108 pounds. When reporters asked Feustel how much weight Man o' War had up, the trainer said about 130 pounds. That Saturday, Red would carry 126.

But the real story, reporters realized, was how easily Red achieved this startling time. How much faster do you think he would have gone, they asked the watching horsemen, if that boy had let him go?

The trainers overlapped Red's image of floating ease with their mental files of racers being squeezed for their best speed. Twelve furlongs was a long way, and if Man o' War went just one-fifth faster for each furlong—maybe two-fifths faster for a few of them—multiplied by twelve . . . *The Sun and New York Herald* told its readers, "Some of them said that the colt could have gone at least three seconds faster without being ridden out."[1]

While Man o' War's workout time was genuinely sensational, Belmont's lively track surface had helped. A few hours after Red's mind-boggling move,

Naturalist won the one-mile Manhattan Handicap under 129 pounds in 1:36—just one-fifth of a second slower than Man o' War's American record set in May under 118 pounds. Naturalist was a very swift horse when he didn't sulk or try to take his jockey over a fence, but horsemen didn't mention him in the same breath as Colin, Sysonby, or Man o' War.

On Friday afternoon, Commander Ross's classy filly Milkmaid clipped one fifth from the track mark for 11/16 miles. Earl Sande, urging her home, also demonstrated top form. "During the battle in the stretch Sande didn't slash her with the whip," a reporter observed. "He shook it at her and tapped her gently on the nose with it and put up a hand ride that caused almost all racegoers to declare it the best they had ever seen."[2]

That same day, Sarah Jeffords gave her well-bred but underachieving three-year-old colt Hoodwink a chance to visit the winner's circle. Still wearing blinkers to keep his mind on business, Hoodwink broke alertly and settled into third place. From the first quarter mile to the finish of the six-furlong race he galloped third, third, third, trailing the leaders by a length and a half all the way. *The Sun and New York Herald* Racing Chart noted, "Hoodwink had no excuse."

"Every person is hoping that Man o' War will be permitted to show his best efforts in the Realization," Saturday morning's *Daily Racing Form* proclaimed. "The horse is at his best just now, and the Belmont Park track is faster than ever before in its history."[3] More than twenty thousand spectators came to Belmont to see for themselves, but compared with the record-breaking Saratoga crowds, this was a slightly disappointing turnout. The problem was that Man o' War wouldn't have an even remotely worthy opponent. The only other horse entered in the Realization, George D. Widener's colt Sea Mint, had accomplished so little at this stage of his life that he would carry only 96 pounds. Word had traveled around the backstretch that such good and promising colts as John P. Grier and Donnacona had a hard time recovering from chasing Man o' War, and owners of other good three-year-olds did not want to dishearten them.

The more than twenty thousand spectators who did show up expected not a real race but an exhibition. "A good many of those who go to the track on days when Man o' War is scheduled to start really do not care whether he is confronted with a contest or a mere gallop," one turf columnist wrote on Realization day. "They want to see him take those twenty-five foot strides, throw back that grand head of his and move along like nothing else which is animal."[4]

To a public fascinated with airplanes, race cars, and other mechanical marvels, Man o' War's obviously outsized stride did seem like a modern wonder. At racing speed, the average Thoroughbred racehorse covers about 22 feet with each bound. The great early 1870s racer Longfellow, whose name had been inspired by his lengthy legs rather than by the distinguished poet ("Never heared much of that feller but that colt of mine's got the longest legs of any feller I ever seen," his owner confessed[5]), was said to have possessed a 25-foot stride.[6] The giant mid-nineteenth-century mare Peytona reportedly had displayed the longest stride known for a prominent American racehorse: 27 feet.[7] Longfellow and Peytona, however, each had stood a couple of inches taller than Man o' War and also had competed during eras when long-distance races demanded efficient stamina above sheer speed. If Man o' War's stride matched or exceeded theirs, he was not only a modern marvel but also a throwback.

Racing official C. J. Fitzgerald decided that the uncluttered Lawrence Realization offered a perfect chance to prove how Man o' War compared with the giants of old. Liking Fitzgerald's idea, August Belmont ordered the track superintendent to brush all hoofprints from the homestretch before the race.[8] Now they needed Sam Riddle's cooperation.

"I sought Mr. Riddle in his box," Fitzgerald would recall, "and asked if Man o' War would be permitted to run his best through the stretch in order to get an accurate measurement of his stride."[9]

Sam Riddle never liked to be pushed, and he wouldn't see Red abused—Kummer wouldn't even carry a whip—but he wanted to hear the crowd cheer his colt home. As *Daily Racing Form* had noted that morning, "Every person is hoping that Man o' War will be permitted to show his best efforts in the Realization. The horse is at his best just now, and the Belmont Park track is faster than ever before in its history."[10] Knowing this, Riddle agreed to let Red run as fast as he wanted down the homestretch. During the last quarter mile, in front of the stands, Kummer would let Red go.

But just about the time this deal was struck, the race became even less cluttered than expected. Only one hour before the Realization post time, Sea Mint was scratched. Sea Mint was a big, good-looking colt, but he had yet to win a race. Perhaps it was better to avoid Man o' War and let him learn that victory was possible.

Word reached the Riddles and Jeffordses. In one hour, Man o' War would go out on the track alone. There had been two walkovers at Belmont Park in recent memory, both received with no enthusiasm and even some scorn. The previous year, the crowd had *laughed* at Purchase, beautiful, popular Purchase, when he went out alone for the Jockey Club Stakes. Would they do the same when Man o' War went out alone? Sarah Jeffords said that would be a shame.[11]

But one hour! How many three-year-olds on the grounds were eligible for this stakes race, which required nomination far in advance? And worse, what owner could be persuaded to start? At the marathon distance of a mile and five-eighths, no one wanted any part of Man o' War.

Then Sarah Jeffords made the Realization: Hoodwink! She told Mike Daly to get her colt ready.[12] And so Hoodwink's good looks and fancy pedigree— the basis for his nomination to elite events, before the real world of racing performance chipped away at those dreams—pitched him into history after all.

Almost exactly twenty-four hours earlier, Hoodwink had chased the leaders through a six-furlong race, giving what speed he could summon. If he had been an automobile, his fuel reserves that afternoon would have been far from full. But suddenly his handlers were leading him to the paddock, tightening the girth around his body, buckling the blinker hood around his head . . . and the crowd learned that there would be an added starter for the Realization.

Thanks to Sarah Jeffords, Man o' War would have an opponent to outrun. He also would collect the full winner's share of the prize money instead of only half. Years later, Sam Riddle would claim that he had promised the Jeffordses that "Kummer would permit Hoodwink to remain within hailing distance of Man o' War."[13] Perhaps they had heard Sam promise Chris Fitzgerald that Man o' War would be allowed to run freely only during the last quarter mile. Elizabeth Riddle heard these orders while they waited with Red in the paddock, moments before the bugle call for riders up. Immediately, she prodded Sam: "Why not let him run all the way? If he can make a record let him do it. The public wants to see him race at his best, and I think he should be allowed to do so."

Clarence Kummer stood beside them, listening, but the boss didn't look at him yet. Riddle turned to Feustel, double-checking whether this could do any harm.

"What do you think, Louis?"

"It suits me," Feustel said. "It won't hurt him. If you say so I'll have him smash all the records on the books."

Riddle turned back to his wife, reassured and reassuring: "We'll let him run all the way." Then Feustel looked at Kummer, the pilot awaiting his flight plans, and gave the magic words: "Let him run."[14] Kummer made no comment recorded by the press, but perhaps he felt relief. Thirteen furlongs, bracing against the force of Man o' War, would have been a punishingly long bout of isometric exercise.

Consent given, Sam Riddle added one caveat: Kummer could turn Red loose but not push him. Especially down the stretch, he must not make the colt perform "beyond his own desire to run. . . ."[15] Hoodwink would run under similar orders. But, unlike fellow figurehead opponent Yellow Hand, he would face a Man o' War unrestrained.

Hoodwink did have one small break as he followed Red toward the track: ten pounds. Because he hadn't won a race in more than a year, the Realization's conditions allowed him 116 pounds to Man o' War's 126.

The crowd now had an extra-good chance to eyeball Man o' War. The Realization started in front of the grandstand, one furlong before the finish line. The start was good, though Man o' War, "a little over-anxious at the barrier," actually broke away after Hoodwink. He took three jumps to catch up. "After that," a *New York Times* reporter wrote, "it was necessary to have two sets of eyes to follow both horses at once. . . ."[16] Leaping into his customary speed, Red dashed the first quarter in :23 3/5. Already, Hoodwink lagged roughly twenty lengths behind.

Red bent rightward into Belmont's giant clubhouse turn, a quarter-mile curve, traveling faster than he'd taken the opening straightaway. By the official watch, his third furlong was the quickest yet, :12 flat—three-eighths in :35 3/5. With almost perfect evenness he hit the fourth furlong in :12 and one, the half in an eager :47 and four. It was too fast—not to outlast Hoodwink, still twenty lengths back and unlikely to speed up, but to seize a long-distance record. At his present rate, Red would clock thirteen furlongs in an impossible 2:36. The world record was 2:42 and two.

Kummer was letting Red roll, but maybe some calm flowed from him to his horse. Straightening into the long backstretch, distant as possible from the boiling crowd, Red began to relax. Half a mile of straightaway faced him. No company. Fifth furlong in :12 and three. Sixth furlong, :12 and three. Slowing slightly, Red ran the first six furlongs officially in 1:13. The previous afternoon, Yung Ching had beaten Hoodwink by one and a half lengths in 1:12 2/5. But now Hoodwink, outclassed from the fourth jump, had little heart for this chase. With six furlongs gone, Man o' War led him by roughly 30 lengths.

Along the backstretch, Red drew away constantly. Seventh furlong, :13 flat. Slowest yet—too slow? But maybe that had been a useful breather. Refreshed, Red sped up again. Eighth furlong, :12 and three. He completed one mile in 1:38 3/5—nearly three seconds slower than his official American record in the Withers. As they rounded the far turn, Kummer was earning his wings, not with extreme speed but with a beautifully even pace: ninth furlong, :12 and two. Tenth furlong, :12 and three.

Turning into the homestretch, Red had left Hoodwink roughly fifty lengths behind.

For the first furlong down the homestretch, Red was slowing down. Another breather, :13 flat. In June, he had flashed a mile and three-eighths in 2:14 1/5. Now he settled for 2:16 and three. But even this was nearly one second faster than Sir Barton's American record from the 1919 Belmont Stakes.

Red would run as he pleased down the stretch, Sam Riddle had told the officials. The last quarter mile, in front of the stands, Kummer would let him go. Kummer did. This final quarter mile would be the stunner after all.

Leaving the turn, bounding toward the stands, Red uncorked the fastest furlong yet in this race, :12 and one. Suddenly, he reentered the realm of speed. If his workout in 2:29 2/5 was a surprise, this official split would have torn the American record apart: 2:28 and four.

With one furlong to go 2:28 4/5 opened radical possibilities.

Deep in the aisle of crowd sound, Red freshened his pace. According to the official watch, he stepped the final furlong in :12 flat. But no one needed a watch to know that this moment was one for the ages. The very *look* of the red horse bounding toward them and flashing past, head high and knees bouncing up toward his chest, was nearly beyond belief. "The most astounding display of arrogant annihilation I ever witnessed on a race track was the day Man o' War won the Lawrence Realization," turf writer B. K. Beckwith would declare. ". . . When he turned for home on that long Belmont Park stretch, collecting [his legs] as high as a kangaroo, he was one of the most magnificent and appalling sights you ever saw."[17]

"He came through the final stages of the race like some great bird in full flight," C. J. Fitz Gerald wrote, "his body beautifully poised and his great muscular legs plying with the precision of pistons, the dirt rising in little clouds where his feet had spurned the earth."[18]

Red's victory margin was so large that *Daily Racing Form,* the sport's most trusted chart maker, rounded it off as 100 lengths. Most reporters said that Hoodwink had about one furlong still to run when Red reached the finish line, and 100 lengths roughly equaled that distance, plus half a dozen feeble strides.[19] Hoodwink's jockey felt the full effect of this fantastic beating. "[Eddie] Ambrose had a sickly and foolish grin on his face as he hammered down to the finish," a reporter observed. "He appreciated to the full the hopeless task to which he had been assigned."[20]

The crowd, however, focused on Man o' War's true opponent. Had Red beaten the watch as badly as he had beaten Hoodwink?

The American mark for a mile and five-eighths was 2:45, set by Sam Hildreth's champion Fitz Herbert while winning the 1909 Realization. The world mark was 2:42 2/5, proudly held by the English turf: War Mint, three years old, Hurst Park, 1912. "But much as the crowd was prepared for a record performance," the *New York Times* declared, "there was a gasp of surprise when the time was announced."[21] On the infield board, wooden blocks spelled out 2:40 4/5.

Beautifully rated early on, running entirely free through the stretch but without demands, Red had beaten the *world* record by roughly eight lengths.

How was this possible? Reporters watched with interest as racing officials measured the distance between Man o' War's hoofprints with a steel measuring tape.[22] "The tape showed that after he had gone a mile and a half each bound measured 24 feet 8 inches," a reporter noted, "and that during the first half mile it exceeded 25 feet."[23] These measurements showed that Man o' War actually used a shorter stride at higher speed.[24] Although his early pace had been leisurely, he had sprinted the final furlong in :12 flat.

As Red returned to the stands, head high and feet prancing, spectators marveled at how lively he looked. "The fact that he was running all alone, and was not put to the strain of outfooting a rival may have accounted partly for the freshness he displayed after the race," explained the *New York Times,* perhaps picturing Red's fatigue after the Dwyer battle with John P. Grier. "However, it was further evidence of his greatness, for he accomplished this remarkable feat without appearing to be doing his best, and at no time was he urged. Kummer let him have his head throughout the race, but never touched him with a whip or made a move to send him along at a faster clip."[25]

"He came back to the scales somewhat warm, but respiring regularly as after a warm-up," another reporter observed. "Hoodwink was panting like a chameleon."[26]

In the newspapers, no one noted that Hoodwink had raced twice in two days.

Man o' War had become the first winner of Belmont Park's "triple crown" for three-year-olds. But of all the Realization's measurements—100 lengths, 25 feet, 2:40 4/5—the last was most meaningful and the first, over the years, most often recalled. The time had timeless merit. The stride was interesting mechanical trivia. The victory margin had no meaning at all.

Man o' War's 2:40 4/5 would remain the American record until 1956, and the Belmont Park track record for more than seventy years, long after most racing fans had forgotten its shocking impact. What posterity remembered was the unthinkable gap between Man o' War and his only opponent, that stupendous official winning margin of not one digit, not two digits, but *three*.

They remembered that Man o' War once won a race by 100 lengths. They didn't remember *why*.

While the Belmont Park spectators still buzzed about Red's record run, August Belmont tried to bring off the match that had eluded everyone at Saratoga: Man o' War versus Sir Barton. His bait was the 1 1/2-mile Jockey Club Stakes, one week after Realization day. If both Sir Barton and Man o' War started, Belmont announced, he would raise the purse from $15,000 to $25,000. "Mr. Riddle and Louis Feustel, his trainer, said Man o' War would start," Henry V. King declared, "but Guy Bedwell and Commander Ross said they would decide about starting Sir Barton early this week."[27]

This decision took Bedwell and Ross only two days. "There will be no meeting between Man o' War and Sir Barton in the Jockey Club stakes . . . unless Commander J. K. L. Ross, who is in Canada, overrules the decision of his trainer, H. G. Bedwell,"[28] Henry V. King reported. Bedwell explained, "I would need a much longer time to get my horse ready for a race with Man o' War than the period which now remains before the Jockey Club Stakes. Sir Barton has been on the [railroad] cars a lot and as he is a gross horse and fills up quickly he requires much more work than any other of my string. He breezed three-quarters of a mile this morning in 1:14 4/5, and after pulling up 'blowed' as though he had run a mile and a half. It is going to take a long time to get him where I think he will be at his best."[29]

Bedwell said nothing of money, nothing of alternate plans for Sir Barton. But when he refused August Belmont's offer and pushed a Man o' War/Sir Barton match back into uncertainty, New Yorkers began venting long-held frustrations in his direction. "Were Sir Barton to start in the Jockey Club Stakes he would shoulder 126 pounds and would have to give away eight pounds to Man o' War," a columnist known as "Daniel" pointed out. "There is not and there never was a horse which could concede eight pounds to the son of Fair Play and hope to beat him. Next year, when they would meet at even weights—for there is no difference in the scale [of weight for age] for four and five-year-olds—Bedwell may see fit to risk a race with Man o' War. And then again, it may be that Sir Barton's connections are angling for a $50,000 offer for a match in Maryland, which already has offered $30,000. In the meantime, New York is 'sore' and it does not care how much Bedwell knows it."[30]

The columnist missed an important point. A $50,000 purse would be equally interesting to the owner of Man o' War.

Meanwhile, Saratoga tourists had indeed boosted Man o' War internationally. One testimony arrived in New York with trainer William Hogan, who had been ruled off the turf back in 1913 for stimulating a horse with whiskey and coffee.[31] Returning from a European sojourn, Hogan brought Henry V. King up-to-date. "He said the racing abroad was good and prosperous and that there were many real high class thoroughbreds [sic] there," King reported, "but none the equal of Man o' War. He said the English, French and Irish know all about Man o' War's successes and that hundreds of sportsmen are going to make the trip here to see him race."[32]

Because the voyage from England to New York City took about five days, European sportsmen who jumped onto an ocean liner right after hearing of Man o' War's Realization victory could have reached Belmont Park in time to see Red run in the Jockey Club Stakes. How many actually did so would remain unknown. More than twenty thousand people went to Belmont Park that Saturday, but reporters guessed that the rich Futurity, with its competitive eighteen-horse field, actually served as the main attraction. Once again, Man o' War would face a single opponent—Harry Payne Whitney's second-string colt Damask—which seemed to have no chance of beating him, especially not under the Jockey Club Stakes conditions of weight for age. Three-year-old Damask, like three-year-old Man o' War, would carry 118 pounds.

Many people believed that August Belmont's own standards had kept the superhorse from facing a meaningful contest: Because geldings were not eligible for the Jockey Club Stakes, Willis Sharpe Kilmer could not enter Exterminator. "With him out of the way," a reporter noted, "there is no distance horse outside of Sir Barton capable of making the champion three-year-old extend himself."[33] And Sir Barton, of course, was waiting for another day.

The truth, however, was that a grandfather clause would have let Exterminator run if his owner had cared to pursue it. When The Jockey Club banned geldings from certain stakes races, they had noted that, "This rule shall not apply to horses gelded prior to February 13, 1919."[34] Exterminator had been gelded at age two, in 1917. Kilmer may have preferred to run his long-distance star in Belmont Park's Autumn Gold Cup—even though the Jockey Club Stakes offered more money—because under the Jockey Club Stakes' weight for age conditions, five-year-old Exterminator would have given three-year-old Man o' War eight pounds. Although weight for age was supposed to address the maturity gap fairly, it was hard to imagine Man o' War needing an eight-pound break from any horse.

Cloudy skies that morning also may have kept the crowd down. Many of those who did show up wore raincoats. The weather eventually cleared, but clear running wasn't guaranteed. Jim Ross wrote, "The Futurity . . . was one of the roughest races I can recall."[35] And Jim paid close attention. His father's colt Hildur had reached the lead, possibly on his way to victory, when a filly named Careful swerved hard into him. Knocked off stride, Hildur faded to finish thirteenth, while a filly named Step Lightly scooted through at the rail to win, beating Commander Ross's colt Star Voter, with Earl Sande up, by one length. The stewards let the result stand, and recently reinstated veteran jockey Frank Keogh stepped back into the spotlight with Step Lightly. The spotlight also landed on Elizabeth Daingerfield, whose brother Algernon served as The Jockey Club's confidential secretary. Their father had been one of the most successful stud-farm managers in Kentucky, and after his death, Miss Daingerfield had followed a career path that few women had held: managing her own Thoroughbred nursery. With Step Lightly, she became the first woman to breed a Futurity winner.[36]

The Futurity winners were still fielding congratulations from well-wishers when Man o' War and Damask came onto the track for the Jockey Club Stakes.[37] For the first time that year, someone else's celebration distracted from Man o' War. Even so, a dozen Pinkerton guards kept the crowd back while he was saddled and newsreel cameramen captured his image.

Once again, the stopwatch seemed to be Red's real foe. "For the honor and glory of the turf and for the reputation of this marvel in the shape of a horse it is the hope of every turfite that Mr. Riddle and Trainer Feustel will let him establish a new record for a mile and a half," urged *Daily Racing Form*. ". . . Man o' War deserves the chance to place the figures where they will remain as long as those who are now living go to the races."[38] But there would be no 100-length romp this time. Feustel had ordered Kummer to keep Red under restraint the whole way. Sam Riddle was considering another race for him the next week, and beyond that, Red had to save something for that special meeting with Sir Barton.

Man o' War and Damask fell into line in front of the clubhouse, positioned for one lap around Belmont's titanic course. Eager as ever, Red made two false starts. At the real break, he leapt ahead in two strides, leading Damask by five lengths around the clubhouse turn, and along the backstretch opening up by ten. But by Man o' War standards, his early pace was a crawl: first quarter in :25 2/5. Kummer let Red release some energy—and rested his own arms—with a second quarter in :24 and one, but then he reeled him back. Only stretching past a mile, when many horses would be getting tired, did Red's steady momentum start becoming fast. He reached ten furlongs in 2:03 2/5—one-fifth faster than his Realization pace.

If Kummer let Red loose through the final quarter mile, he still could pulverize the American record. Instead, with Kummer following Feustel's orders, Red traveled the final quarter in :25 2/5, the same pace at which he'd begun the race, and still beat Damask by fifteen lengths. More than twenty years later, writer Ned Welch would recall that "the colt's chin was on his chest as he swept under the wire—it was one of the finest exhibitions of sheer power on the part of a race horse the world has ever seen. . . ."[39] Despite Kummer's stranglehold, Red finished in 2:28 4/5. Obviously without trying, he had knocked four-fifths of a second from the American mark.

"It was the opinion of all who saw him run," Henry V. King reported, "that he could have beaten the world's mark of 2:25 made by He in England if he had been allowed to race as he wanted to."[40] Sounding sincerely awed and slightly bored, the *New York Times* called it both a "sterling performance" and "another hollow victory."[41]

Many people hoped that after this obviously easy race, Man o' War would meet Exterminator in the two-mile Autumn Gold Cup. "The big three-year-old came out of his contest Saturday kicking up his heels," Monday's *New York Times* noted, "and it was announced that if the weight should not be excessive for the Gold Cup he would be among the starters for Wednesday's big prize."[42] But when the entries were published on Gold Cup morning, Man o' War was not among them. Feustel may have wanted to give him more than four days between races, and Riddle may have thought that the purse was a little lean. Wednesday's Autumn Gold Cup offered the winner just over $4,000 for winning at two miles; Saturday's Potomac Handicap, down at Havre de Grace, offered $6,800 for winning at a mile and a sixteenth. The difference between those purses exceeded the average American's income for an entire year.[43] And beyond the money, Sam Riddle wanted to show off his champion for a Maryland crowd. Some people accused Riddle of being scared of Exterminator. Money and regional pride, however, provided strong motivations for his choice.

There also was the largely unpublicized factor of Riddle's home life. Although Man o' War raced for the entity of Glen Riddle Farm, the public assumed that Samuel Doyle Riddle was his owner and often overlooked Elizabeth Dobson Riddle's influence. By letting Mrs. Riddle inhabit the background like the gracious hostess that she indeed was, they underestimated a woman of pioneering spirit who felt great enthusiasm for Man o' War. Her willingness to take risks for her beliefs was manifested in her extensive collection of Early American antiques—a pursuit she had begun during an era when only European antiques were supposed to have significant value. Henry Francis du Pont, whose tremendous array of American Colonial furniture can be seen at the Winterthur Museum in Delaware, was indeed one of the first major collectors in this field—but when he began, Mrs. Riddle already had been at it for many years.

The racing world knew Sam Riddle as a horseman of strong opinions, and it was easy to blame him when Man o' War's schedule didn't conform with racing fans' hopes. While some suggested that Riddle was a coward for not running Man o' War in the Saratoga Cup or the Autumn Gold Cup, they failed to recognize him as a partner in directing his champion's life. A clue was plain to see before the Realization, when Elizabeth Dobson Riddle prompted her husband to let Red really show what he could do. The colt's devastatingly easy world record seemed to vindicate her instinct. Mrs. Riddle would not draw public criticism for Man o' War continuing to run against three-year-olds rather than his elders, but if she had wanted the Saratoga Cup or Autumn Gold Cup instead of the Lawrence Realization or Potomac Handicap, her determination might well have swayed Sam.

Also, when it came to meeting the likes of Exterminator, the Riddles believed that they had time. With any luck, Man o' War would race at age four. He had only one chance, however, to win the more lucrative three-year-old events. The following year, he could pursue the Autumn Gold Cup—or something even more glorious.

Exterminator took what was offered here and now. Spotting Cleopatra 23 pounds and Damask 32 in the Autumn Gold Cup, he beat Damask by a few inches "in a noble finish."[44] Until that moment, the American record for two miles had been 3:25 3/5. Exterminator whacked it down to 3:21 and four. "While there seems to be little doubt that Man o' War would have too much speed for Exterminator even at two miles," a turf columnist reckoned, "there is no dodging the fact that on work done the star of the Kilmer stable deserves the title of champion stayer of 1920."[45] Man o' War, after all, had raced only twice—albeit brilliantly—at or near the minimum "cup race" distance of a mile and a half. Exterminator had now set American records at one and three-quarter miles and two miles. Man o' War had not yet ventured into Exterminator's most effective range.

The Autumn Gold Cup showed that Exterminator was becoming a crowd favorite. "When he poked his head home in front and again when he returned to the scales he received an ovation like that usually accorded to Man o' War," a reporter observed. "Winners and losers alike admired his great stamina and courage and cheered him for several minutes."[46]

But no one measured his stride.

Before the Belmont meet ended, another measurement—champion against champion—finally moved toward reality as Sam Riddle and Commander Ross discussed their match-race options. Matt Winn already had offered $25,000 and Laurel Park had offered thirty. Realizing what a hot property they held, Riddle and Ross agreed to accept the first offer of $50,000 that came their way.

For Riddle, the simple knowledge of supremacy or a blue ribbon from a racing association wasn't enough. He regretted that August Belmont had not nominated the yearling Man o' War for the Latonia Championship, which in 1920 would give its winner $23,000. Fifty thousand dollars, however, would catapult Man o' War's earnings far past Domino's. This circumstance pushed Man o' War away from Kentucky and New York, toward Maryland, then . . . Canada.

Twenty-four hours before the Potomac Handicap, an announcement in the *New York Times* would scoop the other newspapers: Man o' War and Sir Barton would race one mile and a quarter at Kenilworth Park, in the Canadian province of Ontario. Exterminator had been invited to join them. The three owners would meet soon to discuss the details.

Meanwhile, Man o' War had a train to catch.

Red was returning to Havre de Grace, where his serious training had begun but where he had never raced. He last had been there in the spring of 1919, a baby racer full of uncertain potential. Nineteen races, eighteen victories, six track records, seventeen months, and $162,465 later, a champion returned to his old neighborhood, ready to exhibit everything he had learned.

During the morning of Thursday, September 16, Red galloped a mile at Belmont Park in 1:36, tossing off a time that few racehorses could touch, even though Clyde Gordon held him back throughout the homestretch. Down in Maryland, two days hence, they would ask him to race 110 yards farther, carrying about eight pounds more than he felt with Gordon in the saddle. For the privilege of dodging Exterminator and pursuing the winner's share of a $10,000 purse, Man o' War would have to race under 138 pounds—the highest weight ever given to an American three-year-old.[47] Yet if Red could keep anywhere near the pace he had set that morning, there was no question: He was ready.

That evening, he shared a boxcar headed south with Careful and Step Lightly. Newspapers focused on the celebrity appeal of Man o' War traveling with two fine fillies, one the Futurity winner. But anyone open to omens would have done well to take their names to heart.

18

RIVER OF DREAMS

A RECORD CROWD, starting early and still growing even after the viewing areas seemed full, gathered at Havre de Grace on Saturday, September 18. The infield would be opened to hold them. By Potomac Handicap saddling time, human beings would pad the inner rail from the eighth pole to the finish line and half a furlong beyond. They would lean over the outer rail in a mirror image of the infield line, but several deep, forming a dense corridor of movement and noise. They were here to see perfection in action. They were here for history.

With the track officially listed as fast and the sky clear, casual fans had no hint to expect anything less. Lou Feustel, however, was uneasy. No one had more realistic confidence in Man o' War than he. But as a trainer, Feustel had to pay attention when anything might seriously compromise his horse. Red's weight assignment, while sobering, wasn't the worst of it. Most dangerous was the soil quality of the track itself.

From its hasty opening in 1912 to its autumn 1920 meet, Havre de Grace had seemed loyal to its farmland ancestry. Although combed into a racing oval several years earlier, the thick, rich soil still crumbled under foot like furrow sides in a freshly plowed field. In October 1918, the big, long-striding champion Sun Briar didn't race at the Graw because his trainer realized that the colt had trouble getting traction as the loose soil cupped away from under his feet.[1] As 1920 waned, the Graw's loose "going" remained essentially the same, and Man o' War, another long-striding horse, faced the same problem.

Feustel knew this racetrack's tendency toward cuppy soil, but there are many degrees of any condition. It wasn't until the Glen Riddle team arrived, less than thirty-six hours before the Potomac Handicap, that Feustel knew Havre de Grace was worse than usual. As Saturday morning dawned, he realized that they had no business following through with what they had shipped down from New York to do. The crumbly surface of the track, 138 pounds—instinct and experience insisted that it was too much to ask.

And it wasn't as if they needed this race for Man o' War to set the American earnings record. The match with Sir Barton and possibly Exterminator, worth at least fifty thousand dollars, was close to closure. Why risk defeat or an accident for not quite seven thousand? But the decision didn't rest in Feustel's hands.

Sam and Elizabeth Riddle arrived around midday with a large group of Pennsylvania friends. Before settling into his role as their host, Sam headed for the barn to make certain that all was well with his warrior. On this gala day, Riddle particularly wanted no reason to apologize. Thousands of people who had only read the newspaper reports from New York or seen fast-motion newsreel clips of this phenomenon would see it for real today, and understand. They could validate Riddle's belief that a better racehorse than Man o' War never had been seen. And so Sam Riddle headed for the barn, seeking Lou Feustel's familiar indication that everything was a go.

Yes, Red was everything that he should be again on this day—sound on all four feet and still in brilliant form. But Feustel was cold-water forthright: "If the colt was mine I wouldn't start; the track is very bad."[2]

Riddle didn't tolerate this advice. "It so happens," he reminded Feustel, "that I own him."[3]

On most racing days, with most other horses, Riddle might have accepted Feustel's warning to scratch the horse and wait for a better time. But Riddle had seen the immense crowd and knew why so many had come. Severe weight and an unforgiving track were not supposed to stop Man o' War. Could Riddle disappoint or anger them by forfeiting this race to Wildair, Blazes, or Paul Jones?

Later, Riddle also would acknowledge a second motivation: his own curiosity. "I was determined to find out," he told a journalist, "whether Man o' War was horse enough to overcome the difficulties which beset him."[4]

On many days, this owner had protected—some said overprotected—this horse. On this day, Sam Riddle put the people first.

* * *

As the clock passed 4:15 P.M., the Glen Riddle crew did what they had been ordered to do: buckle Red's bridle into place, guide him out of his stall, and bring him over to the paddock, where Kummer's saddle and a saddlecloth would be strapped over leather pockets containing about 23 pounds of lead. They found the paddock "surrounded by a mass of humanity,"[5] with Pinkerton guards letting only people connected with the Potomac runners inside the enclosure. Meanwhile, a reporter noticed that "the pari-mutuel ring and clubhouse proper were deserted."[6] For this one race, the public did not seem interested in making last-minute wagers. They simply wanted to see Man o' War.

Red's extraordinary 138-pound impost amplified their curiosity, but that alone didn't cause suspense. What made some people doubt that Man o' War could win was the weight spread. He would concede 24 pounds to the Kentucky Derby winner, Paul Jones. Wildair, who had run just two lengths short of Red's American record in the Withers back in May, would get 30 pounds this time. And Blazes, a quick sprinter/miler, would carry 33 1/2 pounds less than Man o' War.

Jim Ross watched from his father's clubhouse box, aware of the rumor that Feustel didn't want Man o' War to run. Trainer Billy Garth tried to bet Sam Riddle at even money—two hundred dollars each—that his quick colt Blazes would beat Man o' War. Riddle agreed to put up the money, but he sportingly insisted that Garth's bet should match Blazes's closing odds. With Blazes going off at nearly 10–1, Garth would risk only about twenty dollars. Hungry for more action, Garth bet two hundred dollars to Jim Maddux's three thousand that no colt could give Blazes 33 1/2 pounds and win.[7]

The barrier waited one sixteenth of a mile to the left of the Graw's finish line, surrounded by cheering voices and waving hands. Only four months ago, Man o' War had made his season debut before another boisterous Maryland crowd and Clarence Kummer had refused any escort. In four months, the world had changed. Kummer did not have to prove himself anymore with Man o' War. Now, as a stable hand led Red to the barrier with his jockey a mere passenger, Kummer was seen smiling "from ear to ear."[8]

Sam Riddle, discovering that Maryland's Senator Smith had no place to sit, ceded his box seat beside his wife and was invited to watch instead from the finish line itself, in the judges' stand.

Red didn't know that every bit of his power might count in this race. He squandered time and energy at the barrier, playing for the flying start that Johnny Loftus had drummed into his brain. Kummer probably hoped for the same. Blazes had the rail position, then Paul Jones, Wildair, and Man o' War at the outside. Kummer wanted to beat Blazes to the clubhouse turn and take over the inside track, giving no unnecessary inch in this two-turn race. Make the one with 104 1/2 pounds go wide.

But Man o' War was so disruptive, "rushing through the barrier"[9] several times, that starter James Milton ordered an assistant to hold his bridle. Finally, he was anchored—and the Potomac field was off in a flash. A reporter noted, "The crowd, which by this time had found standing room at a double premium on every little hump on the lawn in front of the grandstand, clubhouse, and bleachers, on every seat and chair, fences and everything that would hold a human body, let alone the hundreds that lined the infield, let out a whoop that made the water in the Susquehanna shiver."[10]

As the barrier sprang up and the crowd whooped, Red veered away from the restraining hand at his bridle, leaping toward the right, away from the inner rail.[11] Blazes gunned to the lead, gaining perhaps three lengths advantage as Kummer sheared Red leftward and let him go. In a few strides, Red caught the small brown colt and began to edge past him, but Blazes fought back. They each had less than a furlong to reach the clubhouse turn and secure the shortest way around. Blazes was running that furlong in :12 seconds flat; Man o' War took it in :11 and change.

Shooting through the aisle created by the crowd, they curved into the clubhouse turn. Blazes still held the rail, but Red, lapped to his outside, was moving away from him already as they sprinted into the bend. There, Blazes laid his body down. Let Man o' War get an easy lead and it was all done. Billy Garth was right about his colt's speed. Kummer let Red fly, but Andy Schuttinger and Blazes answered, shadowing Red through this second, part-curved furlong in :11 flat. If the watch could be trusted, this was the fastest furlong that Man o' War had run in any race.

Kummer waited, waited, waited, clearing the turn and galloping into the backstretch straightaway before Red opened enough daylight to angle over to the rail. He had won the best position, but at what cost? There were still six and a half furlongs to go.

Thick soil crumbled underfoot, two strides within each second of time. With each stride, Red's hind legs pushed his body away from the earth and a single foreleg landed the load. Red couldn't know that he was balancing an extra 138 pounds on that leg, but his body struggled for traction. *Be patient, patient,* Kummer's hands and posture told him. *Steady now.* He got Red a breather, with the third furlong in :12 and three.

But Blazes caught his breath as well, charging again as Red slightly lagged. With Wildair now only a neck behind him, Blazes pressed Man o' War through the fourth furlong in :12 flat. And this, suddenly, was all that Blazes would take. Even getting 33 1/2 pounds, he couldn't break Red's barrier of steady speed. Switching his tail sharply into the air, protesting Schuttinger's whip, Blazes dropped back abruptly, done.

Kummer kept Red humming, not asking for his most explosive sprint but dealing out three twelves in a row, holding a one-length advantage as they reached six furlongs in a brisk 1:11 3/5.

It was Wildair's turn.

They had two and a half furlongs yet to run, entering the far turn, as Wildair breezed past Blazes, taking aim. Man o' War, although his rolling stride looked effortless, was slowing down. He was running the fourth quarter in :26 3/5, more than three seconds slower than his opening quarter mile. Kummer kept a snug hold, saving his horse for the final yards. And here came Wildair, moving up to Red's flank, running without pressure as they straightened for home—Jimmy Rowe pulling for him to do what Upset had once done, what John P. Grier had nearly done, what no one had come close to doing since.

Four months earlier, this picture had been the Withers Stakes: Man o' War in the lead, Wildair trying to close, both under 118 pounds. Now Red carried 138 to Wildair's 108. Four months ago, Man o' War had won by two lengths, and so obviously under wraps that everyone guessed how many seconds faster he would have gone if allowed to go all out. Now, heading into the home-stretch, Kummer let out a wrap and Red hit the mile in 1:38 1/5—a full second below Havre de Grace's track record even though experts thought the track surface now was "at least two seconds slower than a year ago."[12]

They ran the final sixteenth as if this were the Withers all over again, Red appearing unhurried, Wildair driving a couple of lengths behind. It looked like the patented Man o' War romp—bounding along with his head devil-may-care high in the air, his form overlapping past victories so neatly that the whooping crowd couldn't see the truth beneath—that, this time, victory and a record pace came from courage rather than from seemingly endless un-tapped reserves.

He won from Wildair by about a length and a half, just enough space to be called "daylight." Blazes, worn out by the early chase, finished another fifteen lengths back. Paul Jones, never in the hunt, galloped last across the line. "At no stage in the contest did Man o' War appear to be really running," Jim Ross wrote, "and yet he set a new track record of 1:44 4/5 for the mile and a sixteenth."[13]

The track record had become Red's by one-fifth of a second. A record crowd went home satisfied, bearing witness to the phenomenon. This triumphant result, Red's time of 1:44 4/5 had given Sam Riddle an eternal right to say, *"I told you so!"* And perhaps those very words leapt to Lou Feustel's mind as Red came back to the stands. The big horse had returned in one piece. But while Sam Riddle was bowing to public pressure, Man o' War had been bowing to pressure of another kind.

HEAVY BURDEN FAILS TO STOP MAN O' WAR, a *New York Times* headline proclaimed. "Man o' War cannot be stopped," echoed the *Washington Post.*[14] Reporters didn't know what damage that burden had left behind: a swelling spot on Red's right foreleg, where a bruised tendon now threatened his racing career.

Saturday night, in a stall at Havre de Grace, Glen Riddle hands were wrapping Red's lower leg in cold-water bandages, perhaps even soaking it in a bucket of ice. For these first few hours, no one knew whether the swollen tendon would be deformed permanently. All they could do was draw out the heat, rest the limb. Watch. Wait.

Red's tendons, anchored between bones in his lower legs and responding to the muscles that powered his movements, were like elastic bands that stretched and snapped back into shape with every stride. For nineteen races and many dozen breezes, they had always snapped back to perfect form. This twentieth time out—balancing his heavy load at high speed on a crumbly track—Red had slipped and struck this foreleg with a hind hoof.

That night, Man o' War was treading the line between perfectly sound and "racing sound"—a balancing act performed daily by hundreds of far less famous horses. His injured tendon still might prove to be racing strong, but next time it was unusually stressed, it might become a bit more deformed—and so on and on, gradually or abruptly, until reaching a point of no return.

The public did not hear this news. The next morning, newspapers reported another track record for the superhorse. To the world outside his shed row, Man o' War remained linked with the unbeaten Colin and earnings-champion Domino in the most superficial sense. No one revived the memory of Colin's chronic soreness, or Domino's ever-present support bandages—a flawless record and record earnings gathered on speed-strained legs.

For more than a year, in the public eye, Man o' War had been chasing Colin and Domino. In his stall after the Potomac Handicap, unknown to most, he caught up with them.

Fortunately, during the crucial first few hours, the swelling receded. Man o' War could go on.

Red spent Sunday resting at the Graw. Come Monday, he traveled back up the coast to his familiar Belmont Park barn. Upon arrival, Feustel greeted the press—hiding Red's injury but speaking openly to *Daily Racing Form,* the racing insiders' paper, about the super effort that the Potomac had required. "He didn't have much left at the finish and he was doing his best," Feustel admitted. "Wildair, which was in receipt of thirty pounds from Man o' War, was not as easily beaten as the public would imagine. While Man o' War was not punished he was out to the last ounce."[15]

Those who only read the *New York Times,* the *Washington Post,* or other mainstream newspapers never saw that quote. They learned only of another track record by the invincible Man o' War. They still believed that no weight nor horse nor track surface had ever gotten to the bottom of this "speed miracle," that no one had ever seen anything near the best he could do. And so they missed the most telling aspect of his true ability.

If Man o' War actually had possessed nearly supernatural powers, the Potomac Handicap would have been nothing more than another magic trick. Instead, Red had proved his depth to Riddle, Feustel, Kummer, Frank Loftus, George Conway—those few who knew. On three sound legs and one going wrong, he brought home the weight of everyone's illusions.

19

LIGHTING A MATCH

I'LL RACE YOU this morning," Lou Feustel had dared Guy Bedwell on the Saratoga backstretch, "and I'll bet you $100 or $500 I beat you."[1] Commander Ross had said that he would race Sir Barton against Man o' War for "a blue ribbon if the Saratoga Association will offer it."[2] But Man o' War and Sir Barton would not race for a private bet between their handlers or a simple token of honor. There was too much money at stake.

With $174,465 to his credit, Man o' War needed less than $20,000 to become America's richest racehorse. Now one special event could propel him far beyond that. In one afternoon, Sam Riddle could compensate for racing his star three-year-old in several New York classics that pleased August Belmont but paid poorly compared with Kentucky prizes won by other Eastern sportsmen that year. With a winner-take-all match, Riddle hoped to erase his monetary sacrifice and secure another record for Man o' War. He didn't seem to care whether the best offer came from his own neighborhood, such as Maryland's Laurel Park, or as far away as Kentucky.

But the high bidder turned out to be Abe Orpen, manager of a blue-collar racing plant near the factory city of Windsor, Ontario, on the Canadian side of the Detroit River. It was Orpen, shortly before Man o' War shipped out for the Potomac Handicap, who got Ross and Riddle's attention in New York by offering $50,000 for a match race at Kenilworth Park. Then, before receiving an answer, he appeared at Havre de Grace with a new offer: $75,000 for the winner, plus a $5,000 gold trophy.[3] This was a staggering prospect. Seventy-five thousand dollars would pay one year's tuition at Harvard University for 375 students. Commander Ross told a reporter from his homeland, "I never even dreamed that any track in Canada would offer such a purse."[4]

The purse had increased by 50 percent while Orpen hustled to beat the ever-resourceful Matt Winn. His speed, in fact, ultimately kept Man o' War and Sir Barton from chasing an even more spectacular prize. Hours after Riddle and Ross accepted Orpen's deal, Winn offered them a Kentucky race for $100,000. "Upon learning that he was too late, Winn was deeply chagrined,"[5] Jim Ross recalled. Winn had failed to lure Man o' War to the Kentucky Derby and now, for the second time, the world's most famous racehorse would elude racing's most successful promoter.

Meanwhile, rumors abounded that Orpen had promised to give Riddle and Ross a percentage of the admission revenue. Although no evidence of this materialized, it was easy to understand why such a rumor might ring true. To outsiders unaware that the owners would accept the first offer of at least $50,000, it helped explain why the exalted Sir Barton and Man o' War would race in such an unlikely place.

Kenilworth Park's facilities would, in fact, need considerable renovation before the big race. But Woodbine, the blue blood of Canadian racecourses, had not made an offer, and neither had the leading New York tracks. That omission mystified New Yorkers. "If [the match race were] held at Aqueduct or Belmont Park," the New York Times suggested, "a crowd of 50,000 would seem assured, and at the [admission] prices charged here that would more than provide a purse of $75,000 or $100,000."[6]

As it was, this mighty contest landing at Kenilworth Park made New Yorkers feel as if the World Series were being staged in a sandlot. The more they thought about it, the worse they resented it. Prominent owner Morton L. Schwartz even gathered pledges of $5,000 each from several horsemen to ensure that a New York track wouldn't lose money by hosting the event, but the local racing associations did not budge. Riddle and Ross had made a contract with Kenilworth Park, and that was that. "Mr. Orpen," the New York Times concluded, "has shown New York how to do a big thing."[7]

One New York turf columnist finally tried to make peace, though not without admonishing the local racing czars. "We should not let our feelings dim the lustre [sic] of the meeting of two of the greatest horses of all time— one of them without a doubt the greatest of all time," he wrote. "But it would do no harm if the men who run the tracks in this section really woke to the fact that the war is over, that New York is the biggest city in the world and the biggest racing centre [*sic*] and that the race of a right belonged in New York."[8]

The official announcement came from New York City on Thursday, September 23: On October 12, the holiday commemorating the arrival of Christopher Columbus in the New World, Man o' War and Sir Barton would meet at Kenilworth Park. Furthermore, Exterminator had been invited to join them. But before Americans learned that the "Race of the Century" had gotten away from them, the owners of these three runners had held a summit meeting to negotiate other details. Of course it was an honor simply to participate in such an event, but Willis Sharpe Kilmer, Comdr. J. K. L. Ross, and Samuel D. Riddle each strongly wanted to win. Therefore, each wanted to set race conditions—distance, weight, and jockey—that would benefit his horse.

Orpen had proposed a race of one mile and a quarter, a true tiebreaker because Man o' War and Sir Barton shared a speed record at that distance. Ten furlongs, however, might prove a little short for Exterminator. In the Saratoga Handicap at that distance, Sir Barton had soundly beaten Old Bones while conceding five pounds. Kilmer said that he was willing for Exterminator to compete with Man o' War and Sir Barton, but the distance had to be longer. One report claimed that Kilmer wanted a mile and five-sixteenths[9]—that is, half a furlong more than Orpen's proposal. If front-running Sir Barton and Man o' War dueled through a terrific early pace, this would give stretch-running Exterminator several extra seconds to overtake them. A later report said that Kilmer "insisted that the race be at one mile and a half. . . ."[10] That, of course, would emphasize Exterminator's considerable stamina.

Distance was the first of Kilmer's sticking points; weight was the second. Under the weight-for-age system, five-year-old Exterminator automatically would carry the same weight as four-year-old Sir Barton and several pounds more than three-year-old Man o' War. Instead, Kilmer wanted New York track handicapper Walter Vosburgh, who had seen these particular horses race many times, to assign the weights. Vosburgh would take age into consideration, but his decision would depend on each horse's accomplishments. This could only help Kilmer's gelding. In the Saratoga Handicap, Vosburgh had given Exterminator 124 pounds against Sir Barton's 129, and Sir Barton had whupped Exterminator by three lengths. If these two met again in a handicap race, past experience said that Sir Barton would have to spot Exterminator at least five pounds. And surely Vosburgh would rate Man o' War, who had set so many speed records, several pounds above the standard three-year-old. In a handicap race, even allowing for their age difference, Man o' War might carry the same weight as Exterminator—or slightly more.

In later years, Willis Sharpe Kilmer and turf writers influenced by him and the disappointed Matt Winn would claim that Sam Riddle ran away from Exterminator with Man o' War. Their story seemed plausible because Exterminator, with no stud career awaiting him, continued racking up wins long after Man o' War retired to stud and also deservedly ended up in Thoroughbred racing's Hall of Fame. Four decades after both champions retired from racing, journalist David Alexander would write that Kilmer had "pursued Riddle from track to track and club to club, shaking fifty thousand dollars in his face and demanding he put up the same stake for a race between Man o' War and Exterminator at weight-for-age."[11] It is possible that Kilmer gloated about Man o' War not meeting Exterminator in the weight-for-age Saratoga Cup. When the Jockey Club Stakes and Kenilworth Gold Cup came around a few weeks later, however, Kilmer rejected the weight-for-age conditions that would have made his mature five-year-old spot the champion three-year-old six to eight pounds.

Confident in Red's unusually well-balanced speed and stamina, Riddle and Feustel showed flexibility about the match-race distance. But aware that Man o' War still was not fully mature—and perhaps protecting his recently injured leg—they stood firm about the weights. Although the world didn't know it, the Potomac Handicap had been a near thing. Red would meet Sir Barton and Exterminator only if they carried weight for age.

Sir Barton's camp sided with the Man o' War team. In October, under the weight-for-age system, the maturing Man o' War would carry 120 pounds to Sir Barton's 126. A handicap race, with penalties added on top of the weight-for-age standards, would make both colts carry more than that. Sir Barton might as well carry 126 and be done with it.

Therefore, Kilmer lost the debate about weight, and Saturday, September 25, brought official word that the match race would *not* include Exterminator.[12] Ironically, that very day Old Bones was in Canada winning the Toronto Autumn Gold Cup at ten furlongs, under 132 pounds, in time only one-fifth of a second slower than Woodbine's track record—but Kilmer would not risk him at the same distance under lighter weight against Sir Barton and Man o' War. The Kenilworth Gold Cup would focus on the two champions who had inspired it, after all.

With that much settled, Riddle and Ross took up the issue of jockeys. All season, Clarence Kummer had been riding Man o' War as a freelancer. Mrs. Wilfred Viau still had first call, while Commander Ross held second call. And the fact was, as the *New York Herald* later reported, "the day the match was made . . . both Commander Ross and Trainer Bedwell refused to consent to Kummer riding Man o' War."[13]

The Ross team's refusal was completely legal and strategically sound. Jockeyship could make all the difference in a closely matched two-horse race. Let Riddle and Feustel shuffle for a replacement rider. After Loftus left and before Sande took over, Kummer had won with Sir Barton twice in two rides.

According to Jim Ross, his father had two top choices to ride Sir Barton: Clarence Kummer or—despite their painful breakup—Johnny Loftus. Wishing to reunite Loftus with Sir Barton, the Commander indulged in a remarkable blend of nostalgia and fantasy. His wish ignored the fact that if Loftus magically got his license back, he would give first call to Sam Riddle—the owner who had supported him when Ross and Bedwell threw him out. But even if Loftus would agree to ride Sir Barton rather than Man o' War, racing authorities would not defy The Jockey Club by letting Loftus ride, not even across the border in Canada. And above all, the Commander could not get Loftus reinstated without proving to The Jockey Club that he, rather than Loftus, had been wrong about Sir Barton's alleged drug use. He could not exonerate Loftus without putting Bedwell, and possibly himself, out of racing. Commander Ross had backed himself into a position of checkmate.

So Clarence Kummer was the man, and Ross held a stronger legal right than Riddle to employ him. But Riddle held this weapon: Man o' War did not *have* to run. Was that the leverage powerful enough to pry Ross and Bedwell away from their contract rider? History's richest match race, Canada's own, up in smoke. Although details of this contest of wills remained confidential, reporters learned that Riddle and Feustel "insisted"[14] that Kummer ride Man o' War and the Ross team finally gave in. Instead, Ross and Bedwell fell back on young Jim Ross's hero: twenty-one-year-old Earl Sande.

This should not have seemed like a problem. During the year thus far, Sande had ridden about 28 percent winners, and he had handled Sir Barton beautifully in three stakes victories from three starts during August. Bedwell, however, was uneasy. To Commander Ross, he complained that the boy had a nervous stomach and might perform poorly under intense pressure. Meanwhile, he nagged Sande to be careful and not get hurt before the big event. Under Bedwell's scrutiny, Earl began to worry. Bedwell saw Earl worrying and pointed out the jockey's anxiety to Commander Ross. Another factor also intruded: Earl Sande, who had handled Riddle's champion through one arm-pulling ride, did not seem to believe that Sir Barton could beat Man o' War.

For "Hard Guy" Bedwell, securing the right jockey for Sir Barton became a matter of faith. During the last few days of September, stewards of The Jockey Club received a license request from Bedwell's assistant trainer, the marvelous banned jockey who supposedly could handle three horses in one race: Cal Shilling.[15]

Mere hours after Riddle and Ross agreed to match their champions at Kenilworth Park, America learned that crooked gamblers could interfere with even the most hallowed sports events. An official investigation of baseball's 1919 World Series finally had reached the mainstream national headlines. Amid the uproar that would endure for months, two photo spreads in one New York paper showed how deeply violated the sport of baseball seemed. Under the caption "White Sox Players Who Have Been Indicted by Chicago Grand Jury," eight players appeared. The section entitled "Honest Regulars of the Chicago White Sox" featured only four.[16]

Now the great match race offered a gaudy target for ambitious gamblers . . . and if the World Series had fallen prey to them, could Thoroughbred racing do any better? Many of the same high rollers wagered on both sports—including Arnold Rothstein, who stood accused of turning the Chicago White Sox into "Black Sox" with bribery.

This threatening atmosphere intensified the pressure that Sam Riddle had been shouldering throughout the 1920 racing season, a pressure that grew in proportion with Man o' War's fame. Earlier in the year, Riddle had gone so far as to have Red's railroad car fitted with special doors designed to fool anyone not trained to operate them.[17] But if Rothstein or someone like him could infiltrate a World Series team, how long could special guards and contraptions defend a horse as famous as Man o' War?

Earlier that season, Riddle had reiterated his plans to race Man o' War as a four-year-old. Sometime in late September, his viewpoint changed. Owning Man o' War had become more rewarding than the Riddles ever had dreamed, but for Sam it also had gone far beyond simply having fun. The constant security questions only became more difficult, and Red's mishap from the Potomac Handicap showed how fragile even the strongest racehorse could be. And so, at a time when Man o' War fans looked forward to ever more exotic challenges for the superhorse, Riddle took an enormous step: He planned to end Man o' War's racing career.

On Sunday, October 3, newspapers quietly revealed Sam Riddle's statement that this match with Sir Barton would be Man o' War's final race. Elizabeth Riddle, however, was not fully reconciled to Sam's idea. Perhaps as a gesture toward family harmony, her husband announced that Sarah and Walter Jeffords would choose the location where Man o' War would stand at stud. While Golden Broom always would be dear to Sarah's heart, the Jeffordses adopted the Riddle horse as an integral part of their identity. For decades to come, they would share in the privilege of raising and racing horses sired by him, owning several champions and major winners among his descendants. In tribute, they would display a bronze statue of Man o' War high on the main stairway landing of their grand Pennsylvania home, across from the front door.

Once Man o' War and Sir Barton were bound to meet, their preparations sent opposite messages. Man o' War, having overcome his secret injury, trained openly at Belmont Park. Sir Barton, who had not raced since the previous August at Saratoga, trained in private at Commander Ross's Maryland farm. Most reporters, without access to the farm, had no way to observe his progress. Soon rumors circulated that the Ross horse was not training well or would miss the match race due to lameness.

One man returning in early October from a visit to the Ross farm vehemently tried to squelch the rumors, claiming that Sir Barton never had trained better and certainly was not sore. This witness "predicted that [Sir Barton] would be in fine fettle for the big race and give the three-year-old champion the hardest tussle of his career."[18] In fact, Bedwell was using the Ross stable's fastest sprinters, including multiple-stakes winners Billy Kelly and Motor Cop, to run relays against Sir Barton in the mornings—and Sir Barton was beating them.[19] But would that be enough to keep up with Man o' War?

Exactly one week before the Kenilworth Park showdown, Red stepped into the afternoon sunlight, onto the main track at Belmont Park, for his last serious

gallop at the track where he had set four American records. Feustel wanted
the colt to strike a brisk, steady pace for the match-race distance of one mile
and a quarter. He wanted Red to come back with his right foreleg cool and
hard.

Clockers and trainers gathered, watches ready, not realizing that soundness
had been an issue. They did know, by now, that any major work by a fit Man
o' War meant rare speed.

Running well within himself, Red turned the first half mile into a string
of perfectly matched pearls—:12, :24, :36, :48. He hit six furlongs in 1:12, then
seven in 1:24. If Red could run three more :12's—just three more—he would
make ten furlongs in two minutes flat. Whisk Broom's mythical official mark
might become Man o' War's reality.

Could he?

Following orders, Gordon let Red "race along as he desired"[20] without
pushing him. The official watch said one mile in 1:37—only one second behind record pace. Then, one furlong from the finish line, Gordon began gearing him down. As Red slipped past the winning post, the official watch froze
at 2:02 3/5. Some clockers said as fast as 2:02 flat. Not a record, after all, but
precious few races had been run so fast. Only Whisk Broom, Sir Barton, and
Man o' War had officially beaten 2:02. Then, capping a performance that
needed no embellishments, Clyde Gordon estimated that Red "could have
gone two seconds faster if he had pressed him during the last half mile."[21]
This brought Red's potential speed close to two minutes flat. With that sub-
traction for unused effort, a Man o' War mark that could have been blew
kisses past the cheek of Whisk Broom's magic standard that never was.

Down in Maryland the next morning, carrying 126 pounds as he would
against Man o' War, Sir Barton also worked the match-race distance. Though
his time was not impressive—2:16 flat—Sir Barton had been running well
within himself and the track surface at the Commander's farm wasn't so
lively as that at Belmont Park. "His time was very satisfactory," testified Jim
Ross, "but he was not as sharp, to my thinking, as he had been at Saratoga.
Several racing columnists who were present were of this opinion, too."[22]

At noon, a train conveying Sir Barton and Guy Bedwell left Laurel, Maryland. Six hours later, a train left New York bearing Man o' War, Major Treat,
Lou Feustel, Clyde Gordon, a large group of Glen Riddle stable hands, and
several Pinkerton detectives supervised by New York's foremost racetrack op-
erative, Capt. Clovis Duhane. The "Pinks" had been given the mission to

guard Man o' War and—once he arrived in Canada—jockey Clarence Kummer. Because bookies were giving Man o' War shorter odds, a Sir Barton victory would be more profitable for gamblers . . . and with Man o' War monitored around the clock, the easiest way for crooked gamblers to fix the race could be to bribe his rider. Yes, Sam Riddle was paying Kummer an extraordinary five thousand dollars for the ride against Sir Barton—but that might only give crooks a sum to surpass.[23]

Crooks, however, didn't stand much chance of corrupting Clarence Joseph Kummer. "They called him 'Fool Proof,'" Glen Riddle stable hand Fred Ford would recall, "because he was unapproachable. No one could touch him with money."[24] Ford would note that before the match race, "we were almost certain that gamblers approached him, attempted to work their way into his confidence in an endeavor to break his iron resolution." Some of Sam Riddle's friends warned him to "keep an eye on the boy."[25] Their concern about Kummer took Man o' War's owner by surprise.

"On that kid?" the startled Riddle responded. "I would not worry about him if all the gamblers in the world were dogging his footsteps."[26]

Although Riddle did not have to worry about Kummer's honesty, Red's jockey might need more protection than the Pinkertons could provide. When he refused to take a bribe, Kummer officially became an obstacle. His honesty could activate plan B: sabotage.

The trains carrying Sir Barton and Man o' War entered a land where expectations turned upside down. They traveled north of the United States border and yet stopped south of the great city of Detroit—a trick accomplished because of the winding Detroit River, with the American metropolis occupying its northwest side and the Canadian city of Windsor nestling onto its southeast bank. The journey also emphasized the chasm between modern mechanical progress and the old-fashioned frontier. Detroit encompassed roughly a million people and most of America's automobile industry. Windsor's manufacturing plants and railroad hub quickly gave way to—as cosmopolitan young Jim Ross saw it—"wilderness."[27]

The racing journalists who swarmed here for the "Race of the Century" were ill prepared for what they found. A *New York Times* reporter would be struck by Kenilworth Park's location "on a prairie out of sight of any habitation . . ."[28] A less dramatic description noted that the course was "set out in the woods about three miles from [downtown] Windsor. . . ."[29] No one described the setting as beautiful, nor could they wax poetic about the barns where Man o' War and Sir Barton would stay. The special living quarters that had been built for the visiting superstars, set apart from the track's regular barns, projected a grim defensiveness. An eight-foot-high fence topped with barbed wire discouraged unwanted guests, and inside the enclosure body-guards kept watch around the clock. Compared with the relative freedom at Havre de Grace, Saratoga, or Belmont Park, it was like being in jail. But as the *New York Times* explained, "This precaution . . . was deemed all the more necessary because of the stories that grew out of the recent baseball investigation at Chicago."[30]

The Glen Riddle team would employ its own additional precautions, as leading turf historian John Hervey observed:

> Armed men guarded both Man o' War and Sir Barton night and
> day. In addition to the regular stable force from Glen Riddle,
> headed by trainer Feustel and assistant George Conway, with
> Mikey Daly always at hand and Frank Loftus, Man o' War's
> groom, never relaxing their vigilance, several friends of Mr.
> Riddle, gentlemen well-known in the turf world, constituted
> themselves volunteers to protect the American colt, relieving each
> other from the time he took his quarters at Kenilworth. As always
> both his food and water were brought with him and kept where
> they could not be tampered with, and special orders were given
> that no stranger, on any pretext, be allowed to approach him.
> Nor did this caution cease until the race was over.[31]

Sir Barton arrived at his special barn shortly before Thursday's first race went off. About ninety minutes later—as Sir Barton stepped onto the track for a loosening-up gallop, with Cal Shilling aboard—Man o' War checked in. Engulfed by reporters and curious fans, Feustel remarked that Red "stood the journey West without fretting a moment and kept his appetite with him all the way."[32] A reporter observed that "Man o' War . . . was as playful as a kitten while he was being taken to his stall."[33] Red did have a genuine playful side—fetching his groom's hat or indulging in a boxing match—but Feustel also noticed threatening behaviors as the colt with a strong nervous drive began maturing into a competitive full-grown stallion. "He'd peel the shirt off you if you weren't looking," Red's trainer would recall, "and he began to savage other horses even before we retired him."[34] Trying to grab people and other horses with his teeth, Man o' War showed his growing urge to dominate those around him. The public, had they known, might have found this image less charming than the "playful as a kitten" colt but also might have reckoned that it fit. After twenty races, Man o' War had grown into his name.

Five days before the Kenilworth Gold Cup, Kenilworth Park looked like a construction zone. Already the grandstand had been lengthened by nearly 800 feet. Crews still labored over temporary infield and homestretch stands, rushing to accommodate Abe Orpen's projected 45,000 spectators. Setting the admission fee at five dollars per person and eliminating complimentary tickets, he was hoping to net $225,000. In other words, with luck, Orpen would nearly double the money he was investing in the giant match-race purse and track improvements.

Orpen's event planning reached well beyond extra seating. He had the track surveyed, certifying that three feet out from the inner rail it was exactly one mile around,[35] and also designated five backup clockers in addition to the official timer.[36] If Man o' War or Sir Barton set a world record at Kenilworth Park, that record would stand beyond dispute. Furthermore, fourteen motion-picture cameras would be spaced around the course so that, for the first time in history, cinemagoers could view an entire two-turn race. Anywhere that offered a movie theater, Orpen might charge people to watch the battle between Sir Barton and Man o' War.

Man o' War, for his part, promised something worthy of being filmed. On Friday morning, four days before the match, Feustel sharpened him up with a quarter-mile blowout that proved his speed was intact. The *New York Herald* reported that Red went in :22 3/4 and, according to Feustel, "wanted to go faster."[37] Other reliable sources reported his time as :22 1/5—a burning pace, slightly faster than Red had run that distance in any race.[38] Such a quick move would flatter any horse, but racetrack legend would make it even more fantastical. Broadcaster Clem McCarthy would be among those later spreading the story that shortly before the big match—in some versions, on the very morning of the race—Man o' War breezed a quarter in :20 1/5.[39] This story revealed little about what Red actually did and much about what people wanted to believe.

That same morning, Sir Barton worked a sedate half-mile in :49 and Bedwell claimed to be satisfied. "Whether he can beat Man o' War, remains to be determined Tuesday," Bedwell told the *New York Times*. "I am now only concerned in getting the horse into the best possible condition."[40] He refused to guess who would win.

The public, banned from the track during morning workout hours, was still guessing whether Sir Barton had his spark. They missed seeing the Ross colt on Saturday morning, with Cal Shilling in the saddle, "fighting for his head throughout the workout"[41] as he outran two stablemates for ten furlongs in 2:09 flat—two-fifths faster than the track record. Kenilworth Park had seen nothing near this quality of horse before. The public was invited, however, to watch Man o' War exercise in the early afternoon. Fifteen minutes before the first race, Red entertained an exceptionally large crowd of almost 25,000 people with his own ten-furlong workout. With Clyde Gordon keeping a strong hold most of the way but letting him loose through the homestretch, Red covered the final quarter mile in :23 3/5 while the crowd clapped and cheered.[42] He beat Sir Barton's 2:09 by one and three-quarter seconds—as horsemen reckoned time, nearly ten lengths—but Red had sprinted his final quarter while Sir Barton was kept under a hold. The difference really was minimal.

The footing, however, would change between Saturday and Tuesday. Primping for a world record, Orpen had hired a large crew to scrape down the track cushion, then drag heavy rollers over the dirt and press it firm.[43] The *New York Times* estimated that "the ground will be at least two seconds faster to the mile on the day of the match race."[44]

On Sunday night, less than forty-eight hours before the big race, special-event energy converged at Kenilworth Park. Earl Sande and Clarence Kummer embodied the serious professional athletes, aiming to perform at the top of their game, like gunslingers anticipating high noon. Commander Ross, traveling with a jovial crowd in a luxurious railroad car, brought a much-needed infusion of party mood. Even so, Jim Ross seemed hardly able to believe where they had landed: "A bleak and gloomy wilderness on the outskirts of the industrial city of Windsor . . . a low, skeleton-bare racing plant with a hard-surfaced mile track; this was Kenilworth Park, the setting for a spectacle."[45]

That evening, still ignorant of their bleak destination, Sam and Elizabeth Riddle left Philadelphia in their own special railroad car with "a big party of friends"[46] and jockey Kummer. Their entourage also included Mrs. Lou Feustel and Mr. and Mrs. Ed Buhler—Mr. Buhler being the person who had signaled the successful bid on the long-legged, light-footed Fair Play–Mahubah colt at Saratoga two summers before.

The night passed. On Monday morning, Man o' War and Sir Barton took gentle exercise.[47] That afternoon, the Riddle train arrived at Kenilworth Park. Reporters caught up with Sam Riddle and Commander Ross as the two owners visited the track, pressing them and their trainers for predictions. Henry V. King mapped out their responses:

> Mr. Riddle said that his pet will gallop to an easy victory.

> Louis Feustel, his trainer, said Man o' War will gallop Sir Barton to death in the first mile and win by ten lengths.

> Commander Ross said his colt will race Man o' War head and head for a mile, wear him down and win easily.

> Guy Bedwell . . . said his charge will beat Man o' War as he did all three-year-olds last year—in a canter.[48]

Commander Ross's public response did not quite match his private opinion. Jim Ross later wrote that his father "did not deceive himself into thinking he could beat the Riddle horse. . . ." At the same time, Jim maintained that the Commander "had the utmost faith in Sir Barton. He believed strongly that Sir Barton, especially after his mighty August races, could give Man o' War the race of his career, the race which everyone longed to see."[49]

Bedwell's words and actions were more badly disconnected. The gambling man who had saddled more winners in recent years than any other American trainer couldn't fool himself into thinking that this race felt right. Sam Riddle learned the truth, after arriving at Kenilworth Park, when Bedwell corralled him for a private conversation. Riddle would not publicize what Bedwell had to say. Months later, it would become Jockey Club business.

Steering clear of predictions, Abe Orpen attended to a pesky detail. An undistinguished colt named Wickford would be entered in the Kenilworth Gold Cup, then withdrawn—a maneuver made necessary after Exterminator dropped out. The truth was, two-horse match races were illegal in Canada.

* * *

Twenty-four hours before the Kenilworth Gold Cup, track workers prepared two special boxes, side by side, across from the finish line—one draped in black and yellow for Glen Riddle Farm, one in orange and black for Commander Ross. John E. Madden and August Belmont, whose breeding programs had produced Sir Barton and Man o' War, also had been invited to occupy box seats. Ironically, a Canadian vacation would detour Belmont from seeing the race. "Mrs. Belmont and I very grateful to you for your invitation," Major Belmont telegraphed Abe Orpen from New York that Monday. "Just returned from Canada. Was detained two days longer than expected. Am much distressed unable to get away. Have to be at my office [in Manhattan] today."[50]

Meanwhile, Pinkerton detectives thoroughly patrolled the course. A reporter noticed that during Monday afternoon's racing program, the Pinks "warned away more than a score of men who do the sport no good."[51] Through it all, promoting Tuesday's showdown, the specially made gold cup stood on display at the track. "A brief announcement was made to the crowd, and it was stated that there was no inscription on the cup because no one could tell which horse would be the winner," a reporter noted. "This announcement was greeted with a loud cry for Sir Barton."[52]

Clarence Kummer didn't ride any races on the Monday card, instead staying close to Lou Feustel and strategizing about Tuesday's match. "It was said that Kummer would get into the saddle weighing nearly 118 pounds," the *New York Times* noted, "so that there would be only two pounds of dead weight in the saddle which is considered something of an advantage."[53] Some racing experts believed that a rider's weight, shifting with the horse as needed, functioned better than lead weights hanging mindlessly around the saddle.

The Ross team, on the other hand, seemed to be running out of possible advantages. "When my father and I arrived from Montreal and the two of us went out to the stable," Jim Ross recalled, "Bedwell immediately expressed his concern about Sande."[54] Commander Ross refused to decide before watching Sande ride Sir Barton's race-day-morning workout. But he got an unsettling preview on Monday afternoon as Sande rode the Commander's three-year-old filly His Choice in the sixth race. She went off as a solid favorite but, in *Daily Racing Form*'s words, "was in close quarters until in the last sixteenth and had a very rough race. . . ."[55] His Choice missed winning by only one length. Had Sande's ride—a performance that looked hesitant to many observers—made the difference between victory and defeat?

While Earl Sande tried to heed Bedwell's warnings not to get hurt before the match race, his employers quietly tried to work around him. Staying true to the position it had held for eight years, The Jockey Club had refused to give Cal Shilling a jockey license. And so, on Monday afternoon, Commander Ross telephoned Algernon Daingerfield, The Jockey Club's ever-capable assistant secretary, requesting special permission for Shilling to ride Sir Barton in the Kenilworth Gold Cup. He hit a bureaucratic wall. Daingerfield could not make policy, and the Jockey Club stewards, who could take up the Commander's request, would not be meeting again within the short time left before the big race.[56] Cal Shilling, the rider whom Bedwell trusted more than any other, would stay on the ground.

If he knew of his father's efforts to reinstate Shilling, Jim Ross did not mention it in his memoirs. Instead, he would discount rumors that Bedwell "had been drinking heavily" in the days before the match. "For many years he had been a total abstainer," Jim claimed. The young Ross did notice, however, that Sir Barton's trainer seemed more nervous than ever as the confrontation with Man o' War finally drew near. "When I saw him the day before the race he was thin and haggard and in a state of hypertension," Jim observed. "It has always been my feeling that the strain and worry was too much for Bedwell on this particular occasion and that his judgment was not as reliable as usual."[57]

Meanwhile, jockey Frank Keogh had arrived at Kenilworth Park but didn't know exactly why. On Saturday afternoon, Keogh had been riding at Laurel Park in Maryland. That evening, his contract holders gave surprise orders: Go to Canada tomorrow—and when you arrive, report to Mr. Orpen at the Kenilworth track. Keogh knew there was one general reason for heading in that direction. As one reporter noted, "He thought he was being sent here to be on hand in case Sande met with an injury or was taken ill."[58]

There was, in fact, something festering in the desperate environment at Kenilworth Park. "Before the race was over," Jim Ross would write, "I had reason to feel that the track's dinginess was in many respects quite appropriate."[59]

20

BLOW

Since arriving at Windsor, Sam Riddle had been asserting that Man o' War would beat Sir Barton easily. During the evening of Monday, October 11, enjoying their last dinner before the big race, the Riddle party shared an absolutely confident mood. Even though Sam had speculated publicly that the Kenilworth Gold Cup would be Red's final start, his guests were so carried away with the expected conquest that they began planning future triumphs for Man o' War. *After Sir Barton—then what?* The noblest challenge beckoned across the Atlantic Ocean: England's Ascot Gold Cup, at the deeply testing distance of two and one-half miles. Most of the dinner guests, including Sarah and Walter Jeffords, were all for it. Only two were opposed: Leander Riddle and his brother Sam.

The Ross party did not spend Monday evening discussing the Ascot Gold Cup for Sir Barton. They worried about Tuesday afternoon. Not trusting Earl Sande's nerve and denied Cal Shilling's cool control, Commander Ross and friends spent the evening arguing about who should ride Sir Barton. They let young Jim Ross stay up with them, even let him voice his opinion, but the boy felt its futility. "It was an animated, anguished debate through which, as a youth among adults, I sat for the most part silent," Jim recalled. "Several times I spoke out, and spoke out for Sande; I longed to say more, but in that group my pleadings were largely ignored. I felt as though this were a jury room and that a friend of mine were being tried."[1] The group finally adjourned, deadlocked, until morning.

* * *

As fog dissolved in the early-morning light, spectators began gathering out-side Kenilworth Park. Many were so anxious to claim a perfect spot for watching the big race that they arrived without eating breakfast.[2]

Sheltered from the waiting public, Man o' War and Sir Barton took to the track for gentle exercise. Feustel had often let Man o' War run a very fast fur-long or two on a race-day morning, but today Red didn't go out for speed. Instead, Feustel had him gallop one mile at a pace the *Daily Racing Form* judged "very slow."[3] Afterward, Sam Riddle guided his guests behind the barbed wire to Red's stable. Nerves poked through Riddle's confident facade as he told a *Racing Form* reporter that "the best horse" would win, without using Man o' War's name. Sam was standing at the edge of soul-shaking vul-nerability. During the past sixteen months, Man o' War's phenomenal power had become Riddle's own. With every race, his dominance had increased. But today, Sir Barton might take it away.

Sir Barton's people, however, seemed like hikers confronted by a towering cliff face, rather than mountaineers staring down from the pinnacle. After an uneasy night, the Rosses, father and son, joined Bedwell and Sande for Sir Barton's morning exercise. Jim strained for any sign that all would be well, that Sir Barton would run for Sande as for no one else and his father would override Bedwell. Nothing was certain yet. A few firm words from Commander Ross, and Sande's actions in the race could invalidate Bedwell's disapproval.

Sande positioned Sir Barton for a quarter-mile dash from the Gold Cup starting point. Sir Barton never had been a brilliant workhorse, everyone knew. If the lazy colt galloped poorly, Jim hoped his father wouldn't hold it against the young man who telegraphed tension even from many yards away.

Sir Barton got his quarter in a moderate :24 4/5. "Sir Barton didn't seem ra-zor sharp," Jim observed, "but he moved very well. Sande, on the other hand, was in an extreme state of anxiety." Even Jim had to admit that the jockey he idolized looked bad. Still, he tried to change his father's mind, arguing, "Once Sande was in the saddle for the race he'd throw off his nervousness. . . ."[4]

But if Sande was shaking that morning, how could he be less nervous by afternoon, riding into the noise blizzard of thirty thousand spectators? How could he be less nervous following Man o' War onto the track?

Conflicting images flooded the decisive moment: Andy Schuttinger flus-tering Sande two years before, stealing the match from the Commander's beloved Billy Kelly (*two years before,* when Earl was only nineteen); a Saratoga triumph that summer, with Sande marshaling Sir Barton past Gnome by a nose in the Merchants and Citizens Handicap; a Saratoga detour, with Sande hauling the lines in the Miller Stakes on Sir Barton's archrival, Man o' War, and his admiring words afterward: "I never felt anything like that horse in my life. He is a regular machine." But the crucial image was Sande's ride less than twenty-four hours earlier on His Choice—a ride that, to Commander Ross, looked timid and nerve-wracked.

Frank Keogh was available, cool-blooded, recently riding with the best. It was too much, finally, for Commander Ross to endorse someone who acted so uneasy when another rider seemed unshakable. As Jim Ross would painfully recall, "eventually my father, with excruciating reluctance, gave in to Bedwell."[5]

"You've been unlucky lately," Commander Ross reportedly told the stunned Sande.[6] Earl, heartbroken, cried like a child.[7]

Though he would not relent, Commander Ross didn't want the unexpected switch to damage Sande's reputation. Shortly before the race,[8] he delivered a written statement to the astonished press corps, trying to protect Sande from any suspicion that dishonesty had cost him the ride. "My action is taken without prejudice to Sande and in making the change I am only exercising my prerogative as owner of Sir Barton," Ross wrote. "I would rather win this race today than all the other races in which Sir Barton may participate. Keogh is at the top of his form at present, and I want to take advantage of it so there will be no excuse after the contest is won or lost. I have the utmost confidence in Sande but feel that I would be doing myself and Sir Barton an injustice if I did not send him to the post with every avenue safeguarded."[9]

Only six weeks earlier, replacing Earl Sande with Frank Keogh would have seemed ridiculous. As the public read after the Merchants and Citizens Handicap, when Sir Barton nosed out Gnome, "Frankie Keogh did not give him the best of rides. . . . In the final sixteenth he allowed Gnome to bear out a trifle and, in short, Earl Sande on Sir Barton outrode him, and for the latter's victory much credit is due his rider."[10]

When the gates of Kenilworth Park opened at 9:00 A.M. on October 12, 1920, a boisterous festival began. A pari-mutuel clerk named Willie Charlton, who would process wagers at a betting window that afternoon, arrived early with his wife and one-year-old son. To the Charltons' surprise, they literally had to push their way inside and then navigate through an impromptu carnival. "There were three-card monte games going on to fleece the crowd," Willie noted, "and a character called Wheel Grease had a pair of twins from London, Ontario, working as shills for his shell game."[11] Willie noticed a large influx of even more notorious characters: "There were bootleggers and gangsters in from Detroit, Buffalo and Chicago, where there was no racing at that time." He also noticed Kenilworth Park's response: "There were track police everywhere."

Kenilworth Park had prepared to hold 45,000 spectators. Around noon, special trains began delivering most of the multitude that would attend. Eventually, track manager A. M. Orpen announced an official crowd of 21,000—less than half of what he had dreamed, but nonetheless a new record for Canadian racing. Better yet, the crowd had more than covered Orpen's audacious $75,000 purse and special trophy. With each patron paying at least five dollars for admission, Orpen collected more than $100,000.

As the temperature climbed to sixty degrees, two Pinkerton guards hovered near the trophy, which sat in full view: a golden Tiffany cup fourteen inches high, fifteen inches across, and eight inches deep, specially crafted to honor Sir Barton or Man o' War. Sam Riddle could see it as he reached his box with a bevy of friends. Other box holders included Foxhall Keene, whose father owned Sysonby and Colin, and opera star Enrico Caruso. Newspapers would describe the gleaming gold cup and list the VIPs. Willie Charlton, busy working at his betting window, noticed something else: Lonnie Trayne, "the biggest gambler I ever saw," who sometimes would "go home with $8,000, $10,000 a day."[12] Today, Trayne's big chance for profit lay with Sir Barton, who would go off at odds of 5 1/2–1. Man o' War would go off at a miserly 1–20.

Three ordinary races, appetizers, preceded the big match. About two minutes past three o'clock, Algonquin won the third race. Immediately after the field dispersed, Sir Barton appeared on the track. Bedwell wanted to give him a slow, easy warm-up. And so Sir Barton jogged one complete circuit, one mile, limbering his muscles but not wasting energy. "Man o' War came out of his barn a few seconds later but he didn't have any warming up exercise gallop," a reporter noted. "He was walked to the paddock, where he was groomed by Mr. Feustel and walked around the ring."[13]

Unlike the scene before the Potomac Handicap, Feustel wouldn't urge Riddle to keep Red in the barn on this afternoon. Track maintenance men had spent the entire night making certain that the surface was in "perfect condition"[14]—perfect for world-record speed, that is. Perfect for a thin-soled, brittle-hooved horse like Sir Barton—that was another story. Jim Ross ruefully noted "the cement-like condition of the track" and "Sir Barton's antipathy to the hard going. . . ."[15]

Bedwell, more nervous than ever, knew that Sir Barton needed to go straight for the lead. It was all over if that big red battleship stole off at a lazy pace. Hard Guy ordered Keogh not to hesitate: "Shake him up all the way. Give him the whip hard and often and keep him going at his best all the way. If you can get to the front do so. The colt is game and he'll do his best if you urge him."[16] And so Sir Barton's imminent fate—the lash, from the first stride he took—was sealed.

As he saddled Man o' War and gave final instructions to Clarence Kummer, Lou Feustel seemed palpably more secure than Bedwell. His words proved his trust in Red's rider: "Ride as you would in any selling race.[17] Go to the front if you can, but don't get excited."[18]

Then Lou Feustel and Sam Riddle burst out with an overlapping, final message: "Don't worry about being beaten, Clarence. If he beats you it will be all the same. We know you'll do your best so don't worry about us being peeved at you if the unexpected happens."[19]

Kummer's response was jockey-perfect: quick, economical, confident. "Thanks," he said. "I'll win."[20] Then he raised his left leg for Feustel to boost him onto Red's back.

Jim Ross would remember the parade from paddock to starting post, and everything that followed, as noise, unceasing noise. So much sound that Sir Barton versus Man o' War became practically a pantomime, color and motion swimming through the din. Tall, gaunt George Conway taking hold of a leather shank clipped to Man o' War's bridle and leading him onto the track. Chunky little Sir Barton falling into line behind. Miniature gold-and-black ribbons, braided into Red's mane and tail, flashing in the sun. Yellow in his silks, orange in Sir Barton's, in harmony with the dying autumn leaves. From the stands, hundreds of flags—the American Stars and Stripes and the Canadian Union Jack—rippling red, white, and blue.

Navigating through the human noise, Man o' War remained unusually calm. Kenilworth Park had no brass band playing to put him on edge. Sir Barton, however, acted "nervous, anxious and strung-up, giving Keogh plenty to do to restrain him."[21] Suspicious-minded observers might wonder whether Bedwell had given Sir Barton artificial courage.

Both colts radiated star quality. A *New York Herald* reporter thought that if Sir Barton "had been parading with a host of other thoroughbreds [*sic*], excluding Man o' War, [he] would have been proclaimed a wonder. But beside the champion of champions he looked rather insignificant."[22] Floating past the crowd on Red's back, Kummer perched nearly four inches higher in the air than Keogh on Sir Barton. In front of Kummer's knees, Red's neck stretched up like the Eiffel Tower, making him look even more dominant. Red's closing odds, 1-20, echoed that impression. Few doubted that this was anything but his coronation. And yet stranger things had happened in racing—even once, at Saratoga, to Man o' War.

At the end of the backstretch, just before the far turn, the barrier waited. The two colts approached the starting place, their heads rising just above the crowd massed along the infield rail. Kummer and Keogh settled into sharp concentration. Earlier that day, starter Harry Morrissey and special judge Malcolm N. MacFarlan had told them that there would be no official start for this race unless *both* horses were standing *still.*

Behind the webbing, the two champions aimed for equal terms, Sir Barton at the rail, Man o' War to his right. For fifty-five seconds, they balanced toward the perfect starting moment. Twice, Red leaped prematurely at the barrier; twice, Kummer quieted him. Then Man o' War, stopping beside Sir Barton, pressed his four feet flat against the earth.

And up the barrier flew.

The two colts leaped into the far turn's curve, Sir Barton at its shorter side, and the first jump turned preconceptions upside down: *Sir Barton* had the lead! His lightning break left Man o' War one full length behind. The *New York Times* joked that Red was "apparently not accustomed to starting without being in motion."[23] But motion, once gained, was on Red's side.

Sir Barton hugged the inside path, skimming around the turn, Man o' War at his heels. For several seconds, Jim Ross believed he was seeing "a duel of the first magnitude."[24] For several seconds it was as if time had melted and a long-legged yearling churned behind a close-coupled classmate who had uncorked a Quarter-Horse start. Around the turn, Red gained no ground. One length Sir Barton grabbed at first jump, and one length he held while Man o' War built momentum along the wider path outside.

Then the turn relaxed into a straightaway and the duel evaporated. In two or three strides, Red caught Sir Barton and suddenly took the lead. Tearing toward the finish line that first time around, Red sprang a body length ahead, then opened daylight. Two more turns remained to run, and Kummer wouldn't be caught outside again. Three lengths on Sir Barton now, as Red glided toward the ground-saving inner path while Keogh whipped Sir Barton, while cheers at Red's audacious move rose over the constant noise, while two horses flew past the finish and attacked the clubhouse turn. Despite Keogh lashing him, Sir Barton did not gain. "Then it was I noticed," said Jim Ross, "that Sir Barton seemed to sulk. In any event, he was not striding out in his usual manner."[25]

Commander Ross would make two remarks, and two remarks only, during the race. The first came at the clubhouse turn, as Keogh flogged Sir Barton while Man o' War sailed clear: "He's not himself. I think his feet are hurting him, but he certainly is game!"[26]

Official clockers had caught the first quarter in :23 flat. Man o' War, spotting Sir Barton a length at the break and running wider on the first turn, had hustled it in :22 and change. Now the half hurried past in :46 and two. This was the speed battle that everyone expected, the same game Sir Barton and Man o' War each had played so many times, breaking a rival's will. Only once had Red run a faster opening half mile: with John P. Grier staring him in the eye.

Sir Barton, flat out, shaded :47. He was not gaining. Man o' War, head high in Kummer's hands, loped his fifth furlong in :13 2/5. But here Red did what Sir Barton so often had done in races: He threw a shoe. Seven furlongs remained to run. Seven furlongs with one of his hind feet, his propulsion feet, bare. Sir Barton pushed him through the next furlong in :12 flat.

Six furlongs in 1:11 4/5. Four more furlongs at this pace, and Whisk Broom's disputed world record would be unmistakably broken by Man o' War. Sir Barton goaded him on, unable to close ground but never more than three lengths behind. All along the backstretch Sir Barton persevered, holding steady until he galloped past the starting place, into the far turn. "Then suddenly Man o' War began to move away from Sir Barton so rapidly that the distance between the horses increased from three lengths to five in the space of a hundred yards," a *New York Times* reporter reckoned.[27] Spectators yelped with astonishment. But they didn't know that Red's sudden move was not fresh speed—it was Sir Barton's collapse. Delivering, in fact, his slowest two furlongs yet, Red clocked the mile in 1:37 2/5. He had fallen more than a second behind Whisk Broom.

But that slowdown was not all Red's fault. He had been forced to move several feet wider than the innermost path when a sloshing sea of humanity, "hundreds of men and boys,"[28] sprinted across the infield to catch the backstretch action. Dozens wiggled under the rail, actually crawling onto the track. "There were more than fifty special police officers in the infield," a reporter noted, "but they proved wholly inadequate for the occasion."[29] Kummer steered Red away from the invaders, keeping him safe but inviting another problem. "That placed me in an awkward position," Kummer later told reporters, "for if Sir Barton had had speed enough he could have slipped through on the rail and stolen a march on me."[30]

Glancing over his shoulder periodically to make sure that Sir Barton was not sneaking up along the rail, Kummer cautiously swung Red wide around the final turn, wide into the homestretch, six lengths free of Sir Barton's humbled form. "And among the thousands who yelled and screeched as loudly and as sincerely as the unschooled and rough stable lads were men prominent in the social and financial world," a reporter observed. "Mr. and Mrs. Riddle and their guests and Mr. and Mrs. Feustel and their friends became so excited and enthused that they nearly toppled over."[31]

Straightening for home, holding victory safe, Kummer let Red run freely. "Man o' War came through the stretch with great bounds . . . ," said the clearly awestruck *New York Times*. About half a furlong from the wire, Kummer began to wrap it up, shortening the lunge of Red's stride, leaving Red "tugging at the bit as he flashed over the finish line,"[32] decelerating through a fresh swell of noise. Sir Barton panted home, Keogh no longer whipping him, seven lengths behind.

Watching the finish, Commander Ross had three words for the horse who had left his champion in the falling dust. "What a marvel!"[33] he exclaimed.

Jim Ross looked away from Man o' War and Sir Barton to his father, the man who had just lost the race he'd wished to win more than any other. "For a few moments my father just stood and shook his head incredulously," Jim would remember, "and then he quickly turned towards Mr. Riddle, and with a broad smile grasped him warmly by the hand."[34] Their arms entwined, Sam Riddle and Commander Ross walked downstairs, into the loudest celebration of their lives.

Simply by being a famous opponent for Man o' War, Sir Barton apparently had satisfied the crowd. Cheers greeted him as he returned to Bedwell for unsaddling. But as Man o' War reached the stands, the happy mob forgot Sir Barton, even forgot their international rivalry. While Sam Riddle stood in front of the judges' stand and felt the Tiffany gold cup settle into his hands, thousands shrieked and hurrahed and clapped, even Canadian citizens waving American flags. They whooped and waved while Commander Ross shook Sam Riddle's hand again for the movie cameras, while Riddle promised again that Man o' War would take the first triumphal drink from his beautiful cup, never stopping until Man o' War finally returned to his barn.[35]

Man o' War fell short of his most perfect performances in only one obvious way: His official time, 2:03, was not a world record. Thanks to the unruly crowd making him run wide, it also was one-fifth of a second slower than the Canadian standard. But even so, Red had lowered Kenilworth Park's track mark by six and two-fifths seconds.

Though both Man o' War and Sir Barton had run faster at Saratoga, turf experts were willing to call this Red's best ten-furlong race. Perhaps underestimating the speed of Kenilworth's newly scraped-down surface, they figured that the track had been "at least three seconds slower than Belmont Park and Saratoga...."[36] Even "Hard Guy" Bedwell and Commander Ross agreed that, keeping the track difference in mind, Man o' War's 2:03 was as good as Whisk Broom's mythical 2:00 flat.[37] They also doubted that anyone else could get the better of Man o' War. "I can't beat him with anything I've got," Bedwell declared, "and no other man has a horse that can beat him. He's got a Royce Rolls [sic] engine inside of him."[38]

Bedwell and Ross did not know what Sam Riddle was about to find out: Man o' War might not be able to race again.

Reaching Red's barn, the gold cup cradled in his arm, Sam Riddle expected more celebrations. Instead, he entered a Potomac Handicap flashback. For the second race in a row, Man o' War had struck his right front leg with his hind foot. When Riddle walked into the stall, he saw Red's lower foreleg bruised and swelling. That quickly, the gold cup became meaningless. The universe shrank down to Samuel Doyle Riddle sitting in the straw, watching a few trusted handlers treat Man o' War's injury.

Minutes later, a voice brought Riddle back to the outside world: "Has Man o' War had that drink out of the Gold Cup yet?"

"No, he hasn't," Riddle replied, "but he's going to right now!" Then Sam realized that the $5,000 Tiffany trophy was gone.

"You'll never see that cup again!" Jim Maddux exclaimed. "You've dropped it somewhere and it's been picked up and got away with!"[39] Maddux wanted to call the police, but Riddle insisted on searching the stall. They found the gold cup drifted down in deep straw, buried in a corner where Sam had dropped it when he realized Man o' War was hurt.

And so the photographers got their moment. One caught Red in profile, a Glen Riddle Farms sheet cinched around his body and leather "boots" covering his lower forelegs. With his neck stretched forward almost in a flat line and his muzzle deep in the Tiffany cup, the champion of champions looked uncharacteristically tired and subdued.

Later that evening, transported to Sam Riddle's private railroad car, the gold cup was filled not with water but with "a most potent punch" and passed from guest to guest, including Sir Barton's owner. Commander Ross suggested that Man o' War should go to England next, for the Ascot Gold Cup. "But Mr. Riddle stated emphatically," Jim Ross recalled, "that we had seen Man o' War run for the last time."[40]

The following day, Sam Riddle and rival owner Willis Sharpe Kilmer each received a telegram from the ever-persistent Matt Winn. Winn guaranteed $50,000 for a Kentucky race of Man o' War versus Exterminator, at the distance of one and a half miles.

If Red's leg healed properly, could Riddle be tempted? World-record earnings belonged to an English champion, Isinglass: $280,675. American-record earnings now belonged to Man o' War: $249,465 (including the gold cup's $5,000 value). In terms of money won, Red ranked fourth in the world. Racing Exterminator for fifty thousand dollars, winner take all, he could become the global number one.

On Wednesday, October 13, as ex-jockey John Patrick Loftus celebrated his twenty-fifth birthday somewhere unmentioned in news reports, the Glen Riddle Farm crew began a triumphal procession home to the United States. Man o' War, traveling with his equine buddy Major Treat and most of Riddle's stable hands, headed back to Belmont Park. After a layover there, he would reach Glen Riddle, Pennsylvania, the following Tuesday for a special tribute in Sam Riddle's hometown.

Riddle's private railroad car traveled directly to Glen Riddle, arriving on Thursday, October 14—two hours behind schedule, "owing to the enormous crowds that lined the railroad at many stations on the way down from

Harrisburg [Pennsylvania]. . . ."[41] When Sam Riddle finally disembarked, holding the gold cup and a parrot in a golden cage, he found many houses in his village decorated with yellow and black, and American flags flying everywhere.

Savoring the scene, Riddle spoke to the waiting crowd about Red's past and future. A Canadian breeder had offered $400,000 to buy Man o' War and stand him at stud in Canada. "There is not enough money in existence to take Man o' War out of the United States,"[42] Riddle assured his flag-waving neighbors. "The United States soil is good enough for Man o' War. I don't know at this particular time whether or not Man o' War will ever race again on any track."

Several hours before the Kenilworth Gold Cup, *Daily Racing Form* had noticed that Sam Riddle was nervous. Now Riddle's words, reported by the *New York Times,* sounded as if there had been no such moment. "We were confident the horse would perform as he had before and felt sure that he would finish the year an unbeaten three-year-old," Riddle told his neighbors. "His record was too well known to us for distrust, and his capabilities were not overestimated in the least." Then he touched his parrot's golden cage. The bird called out, for all to hear, "Come on, Man o' War! Come on, Man o' War!"

Clarence Kummer quickly resumed his regular routine. On October 13, he rode the train from Ontario to New York, and on the following day he was riding races at Jamaica, guiding Ten Lac to victory in the Hiawatha Handicap. Business as usual—although the crowd, feeling Man o' War's glory still cloaked around Kummer, greeted his performance with more than usual applause.

Afterward, talking with a *New York Herald* reporter, Kummer casually dropped a bombshell: while he was pulling up Man o' War after the match race, one of his stirrup webbings broke. If it had happened during the race, the break could have caused a life-threatening accident. Kummer found it strange that this problem had happened with a new saddle, which had been used only twice. He told the reporter that he hadn't spoken up sooner because "he didn't want to cause Mr. Riddle or Trainer Feustel any annoyance or worry."[43]

The accident reeked of sabotage. In later years, when asked who could have done it, Lou Feustel shot back, "Well, who do you *think?*"[44] He was indirectly pointing toward Frank Keogh, who, of course, had been inside the jockey room before the race. But Feustel may have been wrong. The culprit could have been almost anyone, rider or valet, who was allowed inside the jockey house that afternoon and was not above taking a gambler's bribe.

In the end, the tampering with Kummer's saddle would become an often-forgotten footnote in Man o' War's career. Remembering it did not benefit anyone. As years passed, those closest to the incident treated it like a lucky escape that could be safely buried . . . unlike the only race where Man o' War actually met defeat.

Throughout the United States, Man o' War's "cantering" triumph over Sir Barton had made front-page news. Most people thought the superhorse was just warming up. Surely he could vanquish the long-distance star Exterminator in another rich match race this year, then invade England and win the Ascot Gold Cup next June. In the country where Thoroughbred racing had been born, Man o' War would prove that the United States had produced the most marvelous Thoroughbred ever known.

Sam Riddle knew differently. Red's swollen leg wouldn't let him meet Exterminator anytime soon. He might bounce back for a 1921 campaign, but sail to England? Like his sire, Fair Play, he might hate the experience. Like his great-grandsire Spendthrift, he might become ill during the voyage and lose his racing ability. But Riddle had to convince two determined people very close to his household and heart: Sarah Jeffords and his own wife, Elizabeth.

"Mrs. Riddle has her heart set on that Ascot Cup," Lou Feustel told a reporter several hours after Man o' War beat Sir Barton.[45] Elizabeth Dobson Riddle, who had gambled five thousand dollars to buy Man o' War and also had bet more money on him than her husband ever dared, now pictured him beating the best European horses and also surpassing the great English racer Isinglass as the world's leading money winner. Feustel had told her that, in his opinion, the drawbacks outweighed the possible gains. "I think Man o' War has won quite enough glory and that he can stand on his laurels," he explained. "A trip to England means a lot of wasted time. It would take months to acclimate Man o' War to English weather and English racing ways."[46] When Mrs. Riddle persisted, however, Feustel made it clear that he would support the Riddles' decision as best he could. "I work for the stable and its interests," he told his boss's wife, "and if I am ordered to England with Man o' War I shall go." If Feustel ever had tried to quit Sam Riddle, as a later story claimed, he was not willing to desert Man o' War at this crucial time. The injured Colin had shipped to England, over Jimmy Rowe's protest, without the trainer who knew him best. Feustel would not let that happen to Man o' War.

"Personally I prefer not to go," Feustel told a reporter. "But if I do take him over there you may rest assured he will bring back the cup."[47]

While Sam Riddle evaluated his options and figured out whether or not he could overrule his wife, racing fans enjoyed a surge of anticipation. "England prides itself that when it comes to the turf it still stands in the foremost position," one turf columnist explained. "It is willing to admit with a groan that it has been ousted from the top in the [boxing] ring, on the lawn tennis court and on the athletic field. But on the turf it still thinks itself supreme. If Man o' War goes over Britain will get another jolt. But it will get a great privilege in seeing this greatest of all horses run."[48]

Meanwhile, the American public hoped for a more immediate treat. Championing the proposed showdown with Exterminator, the October 14 *Daily Racing Form* announced, "Man o' War is reported to have come out of his race with Sir Barton in excellent fettle and it would require little or no effort to keep him in good trim for another special race."[49] Unreported, remaining truly unknown to those outside Red's inner circle, was the first-aid scene in Red's stall after the Kenilworth Gold Cup.

Red's legs had carried him through twenty-one races, eight of them at record speed and several under heavy weight. Now one leg had been compromised. Two successive injuries picked away at its resilience. The next time Man o' War raced—if he *could* race—would he hurt it again?

With a less valuable horse, many owners and trainers would try to keep earning purse money. Let the horse recover as much as possible, then return him to competition. If the horse had lost a step from his previous ability but still might be profitable at a lower level, that would be considered a practical strategy.

But to watch Man o' War—superhorse, marvel, speed miracle—lose a step?

Many people believed that they had never seen the extreme limit and duration of his speed. That was left to their imaginations, combining his most brilliant furlongs from a score of races into a supreme display that never had happened and never would. Journalists fed the fantasy. In the October 15 *Daily Racing Form,* "Exile" reported, "Man o' War came out of the big race in perfect fashion, though he lost a shoe in it."[50] Either the columnist didn't know better or that was a friendly cover-up.

Six weeks later, the truth emerged. "Louis Feustel writes from Samuel Riddle's farm at Berlin, Md. that Man o' War is showing no ill effects from his hard campaign last year," the November 30 *New York Herald* reported. "After his victory over Sir Barton in the $75,000 match race at Windsor the great colt's off foreleg puffed up, and for a time it was believed he had seriously injured himself. Under Feustel's care and Dr. McCully's prescription the swelling was quickly reduced and now there is not a blemish on him."[51]

But Sam Riddle didn't wait to see whether or not Dr. McCully's prescription would work before deciding Red's future.

Two days after the Kenilworth Gold Cup, Sam Riddle sat in his Philadelphia office, opening heaps of congratulatory letters and telegrams. He dismissed an invitation for a special dinner at New York's Waldorf-Astoria Hotel that would require guest of honor Man o' War to ride up to the banquet room in a freight elevator. He dispatched a thank-you letter and a bonus check for five thousand dollars to Clarence Kummer. He also chatted with a *New York Herald* reporter who wanted to know whether Red would race Exterminator. "I am considering the offer," Riddle claimed, "but as I have not heard from Mr. Kilmer direct I cannot say as yet whether anything will come of the proposition. You know how long it took to arrange the match race with Sir Barton, and it may not be possible for us to get together on this new proposition before winter arrives. On the other hand, everything may go smoothly and the race may come off in Kentucky."[52] He said nothing about Red's injury.

The reporter didn't know it, but Sam Riddle had given Lou Feustel a mission: to ask Walter Vosburgh, New York's weight setter for handicap races, what impost he would give Man o' War if the colt raced in his domain during 1921. Ironically, even if he stayed home, Man o' War would not avoid English challenges. Vosburgh believed in the English weight standards, under which a four-year-old runner in important races would begin with at least 130 pounds. Each success could raise the weight up through the 130s to 140 pounds and more. As Vosburgh once noted, England's 1 3/4-mile Jockey Club Stakes set its maximum weight at 147 pounds.[53]

This system made champions share the wealth. "If a horse has gone through his two- and three-year-old races successfully," Vosburgh explained, "he must at four give somebody else a chance. The principle is that he has demonstrated his superiority, and his owner has reaped sufficient pecuniary reward, and should be content to carry the penalties or send him to the stud. . . ."[54] Vosburgh thought this plan was only fair. More than once, he had made Roseben, an awesome sprinter known as "the Big Train," carry 148 pounds—and once even gave him 150.

Later on that Friday, October 15, thanks to long-distance telephone, Samuel Doyle Riddle in Pennsylvania heard Vosburgh's verdict from Louis Feustel in New York. "Lou, I can't tell you exactly what weight I'd put on him next year," Vosburgh had explained, "but I'll say this much—I wouldn't start him in his first out at a pound less than 140."[55]

Feustel, in his heart of hearts, thought that Man o' War deserved this. He also could picture Red winning with 140 pounds and marching toward 150. He could be filled with regret but not surprise when Riddle said, "Retire him, he'll never run again."[56]

And Feustel let the reporters know.

August Belmont was not pleased. Retirement meant that Man o' War would never validate American Thoroughbreds at the highest international level. Belmont wanted the English Jockey Club to see, on their own race-courses, that the "impure" American strain in Man o' War's stoutly English pedigree was worthy of the English Stud Book. He did not know yet that Man o' War had been compromised by injury. "It is most unfortunate," he told racing official Chris J. Fitzgerald, "that Man o' War isn't going over to add another laurel to our discredited breed."[57]

But Belmont didn't stagnate in regret. On Monday, October 18, he dictated a letter to Sam Riddle, asking permission to breed several mares to Man o' War. Then, on October 19, Belmont alerted Riddle to another possibility: "Mr. Fitzgerald is authorized to represent me in a proposition in connection with Man o' War, which I trust you will see your way clear to meet."[58]

Fitzgerald found Riddle at the Rose Tree races in Media, Pennsylvania, and made his pitch. On Tuesday, November 2—the day of the presidential election—Belmont Park could host a special program featuring Man o' War running one mile against time. Red would earn $10,000 for the attempt and a $5,000 gold cup if he beat Roamer's 1:34 4/5. "It was my belief," Fitzgerald would say, "that Man o' War, carrying 110 lbs., the same impost as Roamer had in the saddle, could run a mile over Belmont Park in better than 1.34— 1.33 2-5 was the mark I believed him capable of, under the conditions."[59]

Unwilling to give August Belmont a false excuse, Sam Riddle now shared his secret. "Mr. Riddle told me in confidence that Man o' War had bruised one of his tendons in the race at Windsor and would never stand training again," Fitzgerald recalled. "It was a great disappointment to everybody concerned. Had he remained sound and continued on the turf, the total money winnings of Man o' War would probably have surpassed those of any horse ever bred in this country, as the various weight-for-age races would assuredly have been at his mercy. That he could have won the Ascot Gold Cup and other races abroad, the best judges believe would have only been a matter of acclimatization."[60]

With Man o' War officially retired, the Riddles and Jeffordses decided where he would stand at stud. Red would give them a chance to participate in racing as August Belmont or Harry Payne Whitney did: standing an elite stallion and breeding him to their own groups of mares. If they wished, they could corner the market on Man o' War's progeny. There was no guarantee, of course, that Red's offspring would have exceptional talent, but any racehorse breeder would welcome the opportunity to be first in line.[61]

But where should the Riddles locate their new empire? They could hide Man o' War in Glen Riddle, Pennsylvania, or Berlin, Maryland, if they wished, but entrusting him to an expert crew in a place where raising Thoroughbred horses had been elevated to a specialty made the most sense. They settled on the Bluegrass country surrounding Lexington, Kentucky, and chose a farm manager who had become a friend: Miss Elizabeth Daingerfield. "She has a beautiful farm and good help," a reporter acknowledged, "and knows as much about thoroughbreds [sic] as any man in the country."[62]

With Man o' War's future safely organized, Sam Riddle decided to please himself. On Wednesday, October 20, 1920, the world's most famous horse arrived at the Rose Tree Hunt Club's autumn racing meet. His motor van trundled into the small town of Media, Pennsylvania, past the old stone clubhouse where Riddle had presided as the Rose Tree president, and into the stable yard. Soon he would parade for Riddle's neighbors.

As the truck pulled to a halt, several hundred curious bystanders swarmed around. Major Treat, Red's reliable chaperone, strolled sedately down the gangplank. "Man o' War," a *New York Herald* reporter observed, "hesitated when he saw the crowd."[63] Then the human swarm, thrilled to see Man o' War up close, made Red's apprehension worse. They began to cheer.

At that moment, Sam Riddle's pride and joy nearly came to grief. Man o' War leaped sideways off the ramp, launching his body recklessly into space. In that instant beyond anyone's control, Red's life depended on how each of his feet hit the ground. A wrong angle could shatter bone.

The lesson was plain, if Riddle dared to see it. "Riddle's Speed Miracle," no matter how invincible he seemed, still had the instincts of a horse.

In the next instant, danger gave way to relief as George Conway and Clyde Gordon were soothing Riddle's priceless Man o' War, who was standing sound. Thirty minutes later, guarded by a dozen Philadelphia policemen, Red pranced for the adoring crowd. Then came a photo shoot with fellow celebrities. In Rose Tree's paddock, rowing champion Jack Kelly and heavyweight boxing champion Jack Dempsey grinned widely as they walked beside Man o' War. Between the stars, a tall, grim-faced man—George Conway—clung to Red's bridle. Red's wide-eyed expression and exclamation-point ears showed him close to taking flight. Then Sam Riddle took him home.

For not quite a week, the world's most famous horse lingered in Glen Riddle, Pennsylvania. Local children saw him in one of Riddle's barns. For high society, the crescendo came on Saturday, October 23, when Sam and Elizabeth Riddle hosted a dinner party in Man o' War's honor. Here was Sam as jovial host: letting the punch-filled Tiffany gold cup pass from hand to hand, then shepherding everyone out to the garage for a special show. Adults in party clothes strolled across the driveway, chatting into the night, entering the improvised theater. Then a projector whirred into action.

And there, in gray tones over a white surface, glowing daylight bright, was Man o' War—clearly streaking around the hard-packed Kenilworth track despite the film's skipping motion of sixteen frames per second. Sam Riddle's guests marveled at Red's bounding image, focused larger than spectators ever had been able to see him during an entire race, galloping one last oval for all time.

21

SETTLEMENTS

THE NEW REALITY began a few minutes past noon on Tuesday, January 25, 1921. Thickly blanketed against the freezing weather, accompanied by Golden Broom and Major Treat, Man o' War left Sam Riddle's Eastern Shore farm for the last time. With about twenty-five people watching from Holly Grove Road, he boarded his special railroad car and departed for Philadelphia, where a westward-bound express train would deliver him to Kentucky.

The following morning, Red arrived in Lexington. "It was a sad day for me when I took him back to Kentucky for retirement," Lou Feustel would recall. "It was cold and miserable when I unloaded him from the railroad car. There were a lot of people around wanting to strip the blanket off him and take pictures. I guess I wasn't very polite to 'em. I told 'em to get the hell out of there."[1]

Thanks to Sam Riddle's sense of propriety, Feustel got off relatively easy. Lexingtonians had proposed a grand parade through town, with children scattering rose petals in Man o' War's path. Having learned something about his horse's limits from the near accident at the Rose Tree exhibition, Riddle absolutely refused—"and when Mr. Riddle snorted at a proposition," a perceptive turf writer noted, "then that proposition lay dead and partly decomposed."[2] Instead, during the afternoon of January 27, about 2,500 people gathered at the city's old Kentucky Association racetrack. Sam Riddle gave a brief speech. Then, with his lower front legs swathed in cotton wraps and trusty Major Treat by his side, Man o' War galloped down the homestretch with Clyde Gordon, wearing Riddle's black-and-yellow silks, guiding him through the spitting snow.

It was over now. Clyde Gordon dismounted. Lou Feustel and his helpers stripped the tack from Red's back and blanketed him against the chill. Then, handing Red over to his new caretakers, Feustel couldn't help but complain. "When I took him to the van, it was so old and rickety that I said to Miss Daingerfield, 'If you don't get him something better than this to ride in, he'll knock the sides out of it and end up in the road pulling it himself.' She didn't like it, but I was mad. I hated to see him go."[3]

Red's transition from racing to a stud career would be far easier for Sam Riddle than for Lou Feustel. Riddle would own many of Red's babies and could visit him whenever he pleased. Feustel, during every day at the training farm or racetrack, would be aware of Red's empty stall. The routines formed through more than 700 days of interaction had suddenly gone.

The change bothered groom Frank Loftus so much that he begged permission to stay with Man o' War at Elizabeth Daingerfield's Hinata Farm, where Red would reside until Sam Riddle developed his own Bluegrass property. For a few weeks, Frank lived at Hinata and helped to ease the transition for Man o' War. "Frank is seldom out of sight of the colt," a reporter observed, "and spends at least an hour a day playing with him. A boxing match with the colt sparring with his head, ducking Frank's taps and landing mild bucks is the principal sport."[4] But Red soon would need someone different from a racetrack groom—someone experienced with handling stallions in the breeding shed. Frank Loftus would be sent back to the racetrack. Major Treat, whose value as a companion did not change, stayed behind.

Miss Daingerfield brought in John Henry Buckner (better known as "Buck" or "Pork Chop"), who had handled several of Kentucky's most illustrious stallions, to groom and mentor Man o' War in the ways of being a stud. She instituted a routine that included several miles of exercise under saddle six days every week, plus daily free time in a three-acre paddock. This turnout time in his private pasture became Red's chance to let loose without human interference. He had enjoyed the same privilege at Riddle's Maryland farm, and his new handlers at Hinata Farm quickly learned how deeply he enjoyed it. They had one concern: An exuberant ex-racehorse galloping full tilt might slip and run into the paddock's strong wooden fence.

One day not long after Red retired, Miss Daingerfield glanced through her office window and saw him tearing around his enclosure as if it were Belmont Park. Alarmed, she called his groom. "Buck! Don't you see him ripping and running in that paddock? Stop him before he gets hurt!" Buckner answered with airtight logic: "Why, Miss Lizbeth, if all the good horses in New York couldn't catch him, how [do] you expect me to stop Man o' War?"[5]

Two months after Man o' War moved to Kentucky and his former trainer returned to Riddle's Maryland farm, Lou Feustel experienced what a reporter accurately called "the biggest surprise the Jockey Club has handed out in many years."[6] Instead of immediately approving Feustel's application for a trainer's license, the License Committee put it on hold. No one could understand why Feustel, of all trainers—"a righteous honest horseman, living up to both the letter and the spirit of the rules of racing"[7]—would receive such treatment. When a reporter telephoned him with the news, Feustel thought "for many minutes"[8] that the journalist was playing a joke on him.

"I had one or two drinks on the track on a couple of occasions. I wonder if that could be the reason?" Feustel quipped when the truth finally sank in. "There's nothing else," he continued, "unless it is to compel me to testify against a prominent trainer who is likely to lose his license this year."[9] Feustel was correct with his second guess: The Jockey Club wanted him to talk about Guy Bedwell. And if Feustel were reluctant to tell tales on another trainer, his own pending application would provide leverage.

On March 30, Feustel received a trainer's license and Bedwell did not. The reason lay in a confidential letter that August Belmont wrote soon afterward to William P. Riggs, secretary of the Maryland Jockey Club, while Bedwell fought to keep his career going and the Maryland authorities debated what to do with him. "This is for your personal information," Belmont told Riggs. "When we called Feustel and Riddle about the race of Man o' War and Sir Barton in Canada, we found that Bedwell had approached both of them trying to make some arrangement by which he would receive something out of the race."[10] The Kenilworth Gold Cup, of course, had been winner take all. If Sir Barton lost, Bedwell would get nothing except his regular salary. And so, according to the testimony provided by Feustel and Riddle, Bedwell had committed a cardinal sin: asking his opponent to reward him if his horse should lose to theirs.

Because this transgression happened in Canada, The Jockey Club in New York had quietly observed Bedwell's behavior back in the States until they found cause for action within their jurisdiction. The chain reaction didn't take long. Humiliated by the sudden switch to Frank Keogh, Earl Sande asked Commander Ross for his contract soon after the Kenilworth Gold Cup, and the Commander released him. Overnight, top stables launched a bidding war. Sande signed with Sam Hildreth but reserved the right to quit at any time if he became dissatisfied. Earl had discovered his own worth. He wouldn't be terrorized by an employer anymore.

Sande's escape shook the Ross racing stable like a geological fault, and Bedwell took extreme measures to replace him. Ignoring August Belmont and The Jockey Club in New York but winning Commander Ross's support, "Hard Guy" convinced the Maryland State Racing Commission to give Cal Shilling a jockey license. This was a disaster. For flouting their authority, The Jockey Club banned Bedwell from training racehorses in New York State and delayed his licensing in Maryland. Not resting there, August Belmont publicly rebuked Commander Ross for endorsing an outlawed jockey's reinstatement. "He said," a reporter noted, "that Commander Ross was not loyal to the Jockey Club nor to racing itself. . . ."[11]

Amputated from Bedwell, Shilling, and Sande, the fabulous Ross stable started to decline. Ross enjoyed some success, but his days as a dominant force fell further and further away. By 1927, financial troubles had forced Commander Ross to close his racing stable. True to his gambling nature, the Commander reportedly regained several million through the stock market. This was not enough. Late in 1928, trying to become as rich as he had been during Sir Barton's heyday, Commander Ross went bankrupt.[12]

During the 1930s, the Commander migrated to Montego Bay, where he became a steward of the Jamaica Jockey Club and where he was buried at sea in 1951. A few years later, Jim Ross published a vivid memoir of the Ross stable's glory years and dedicated the work to his father: "A true sportsman, who always won without boast and lost with a smile."[13]

"Hard Guy" Bedwell stuck like a barnacle to the Maryland circuit and rebuilt his career. After he spent twenty-eight years in exile from New York, The Jockey Club finally reinstated him—thanks to stubborn support from Sam Riddle, who insisted that Bedwell had suffered long enough. But exile hadn't improved Bedwell's character. When swamp fever made its deadly way through the horse population at New Hampshire's Rockingham Park in 1947, Hard Guy collected life insurance on fourteen racers in his care. Contaminated needles had spread the disease from a single infected horse, scientists figured out. Bedwell lost fourteen by exploiting a new-fangled trend: adding muscle and fire to Thoroughbred geldings by injecting them with testosterone.

Bedwell died on the last day of 1951, ambushed by a heart attack. He had been a ferocious competitor to the end. "Any time he sent a horse out," a Maryland racing official had recently noted, "that horse had a hell of a chance to win."[14] A former Bedwell groom simply remembered the hell. "One day he hauled off without warning and gave me a fancy kick in the rear of my pants. I said to him, 'Mr. Bedwell, have I done anything?' And he replied, 'You haven't done anything, and that's the reason I am kicking you.'"[15]

Earl Sande, on the other hand, always remained one of racing's most popular men. He won the Kentucky Derby twice during the 1920s and retired from riding as a rich man, but then he lost his fortune in 1929 from the stock market crash, plus the expense of campaigning his own stable of racehorses. Emerging from retirement in 1930, Sande rode Gallant Fox throughout a championship season that included the first Kentucky Derby/Preakness/Belmont Stakes sweep since Sir Barton.[16] He then enjoyed success as a trainer but again fell into financial problems. "Money and I are incompatible,"[17] he explained. By the mid-1960s, in poor health, he migrated to the Northwest and died in an Oregon nursing home. Earl Sande died broke but with an unshakable benevolence. Perhaps two international match races—one he wasn't allowed to ride, and another, where he rode the favorite—proved to him that money mattered less than generosity.

On October 20, 1923, Belmont Park had hosted a Yanks versus Brits showdown between Kentucky Derby winner Zev, ridden by Earl Sande, and Epsom Derby winner Papyrus, piloted by England's finest jockey, Steve Donoghue. Thanks to pouring rain, the special $100,000 contest turned into a sad farce. Papyrus, who previously had competed only on grass, faced his first race in the mud. His inappropriately smooth shoes, designed for turf racing, handicapped him even more. While roughly 45,000 people whooped and hollered, Papyrus slid home five lengths behind Zev, unable to show his true ability.

Earl Sande did his own job perfectly that afternoon but knew it had been a hollow win. As the two colts pulled up along the backstretch and the crowd's loud celebration rolled across the track, Sande was deliberately slow in turning Zev toward the winner's circle. Letting the bedraggled Papyrus and Donoghue catch up, he called out, "Let's go back together, Steve."

"It does not sound like much," *Daily Racing Form* wrote, "but was a very big thing, and Donoghue, by this thoughtful act of the best American rider, shared the plaudits of the great throng."[18]

The occasion had a noteworthy effect on someone else who had been at Kenilworth Park on October 12, 1919. Shortly after the race, Guy Bedwell entered the jockey house and found Sande trying to cheer up the disappointed Donoghue. Three years had passed since Bedwell had triggered a chain of events that caused Sande to quit Commander Ross. Three years had passed, as far as racetrackers knew, since Bedwell and Sande had spoken to each other. Now Bedwell took the long step into Sande's presence, offering his hand for a shake while saying, "Congratulations, Earl."

Sande reached across the gap, but reporters left readers to guess at what he felt. He shook hands with the man who had pushed him away from Commander Ross and toward Sam Hildreth, the trainer of Zev—away from a celebrated match race that he could not have won and toward the even richer one that he had just won. Shaking "Hard Guy" Bedwell's hand, Earl Sande simply said, "Thanks."[19]

Unwilling to endure Sam Riddle without the reward of handling Red, Lou Feustel accepted another offer in 1922. He began training for August Belmont, the man who had given him everything that led to Man o' War. Handling several of Red's close relatives, Feustel enjoyed two successful years. He even expected to train Red's progeny that Belmont bred. The oldest would be two-year-olds, perhaps ready to race, in 1925.

But around midday on December 9, 1924, August Belmont felt "a slight pain"[20] in his right arm and went home from his Manhattan office. A few hours later, his severely swollen arm spurred doctors to recommend an operation. This procedure took place at Belmont's Park Avenue home early the following morning but did no good. Around 6:30 that evening, with wife, Eleanor, and son Morgan by his side, August Belmont died. He was seventy-two years old.

Inheriting her late husband's enormous Cape Cod Canal debt, Eleanor Belmont was not financially able to maintain his many homes, farms, and animals. "When in 1925 I had to authorize the dispersal sale of the Belmont Stud and the racing stable," Eleanor wrote, "parting with the cherished thoroughbreds [sic] hurt unbelievably,"[21] Eleanor Robson Belmont, who never remarried, would continue her charity work for the Red Cross and eventually satisfy her love of the arts by serving as a board member for New York's Metropolitan Opera and founding the Metropolitan Opera Guild. August Belmont, Jr., despite his estate dispersal, would enter history as a creative force behind timeless marvels: the New York City subway system, the Cape Cod Canal, and Man o' War.

Lou Feustel swirled away into a long training career that sometimes found him working for prominent owners, including cosmetics queen Elizabeth Arden and movie mogul Harry Warner. But after Man o' War, fate never brought Feustel another champion. Meanwhile, his former foreman, taciturn George Conway, became Sam Riddle's most successful post–Man o' War trainer. In 1937, Conway guided Red's son War Admiral—bred by Glen Riddle Farm—to a Triple Crown sweep.

Johnny Loftus landed further away from Man o' War's legacy. He reapplied for a jockey license in 1921, without success. Early in 1922, he applied for a trainer's license and received it immediately. Loftus enjoyed moderate success and an enviable lifestyle for several years, training for the son of tycoon Thomas Fortune Ryan. His good handling of stakes winner Chestnut Oak took him to England for distinguished race meets during the summer of 1930. During 1938, Loftus took over training War Admiral's former Triple Crown rival, Pompoon, and eked out some good efforts. But then Pompoon went wrong, and similarly good horses did not fill his place. Applying for a Social Security card in October 1942, Loftus listed himself as unemployed. Soon, however, he was working in the Bethlehem Steel Company's Baltimore plant and earning a wartime factory worker's wages. Rather than hustling at the racetrack, trying to trade on his Man o' War fame, Loftus accepted honest work in the mundane world.[22]

Not many miles away, at Glen Riddle, Pennsylvania, and on Maryland's Eastern Shore, Sam Riddle surrounded himself with statues and paintings of Man o' War. Years of Sanford bitterness had done their worst. Riddle reportedly enjoyed showing visitors a handsome likeness of Red with Johnny Loftus up, then huffing, "The greatest regret of my life is that I can't have that—that creature on his back painted out."[23]

After Man o' War retired, Clarence Kummer remained one of America's most successful jockeys. Private life also treated him well, as he married and became the father of a daughter and a son. Professional life seemed to line up perfectly as he became the contract rider for August Belmont and again rode horses trained by Lou Feustel. In one of his most exciting and expert rides, Kummer guided Belmont's homebred colt Ladkin to a narrow victory in a special race at Aqueduct against the great French horse Epinard.

But August Belmont's death, which set Feustel adrift, pushed Kummer onto an even more precarious path. Young William Averell Harriman, son of a powerful railroad executive, acquired many of Belmont's racehorses and also Kummer's contract in 1925. Rider and owner did not get along. The next spring, The Jockey Club refused Kummer's application for a jockey license. "Kummer's riding in general last year was the best of his career," a perplexed reporter noted, "and many are puzzled to know what the charges against him may be."[24]

Like Johnny Loftus, Clarence Kummer was not ruled off the turf. Like Loftus, he did not want to give up race riding. Unlike Loftus, he regained his jockey license within a year but also quickly pursued ventures outside of racing, investing with one of his relatives in a real estate and construction business. "The effort ended disastrously for Kummer," a reporter would note. "He lost all [of his savings] in a couple of years."[25] In fact, 1928 gave Kummer a double whammy. After winning the Belmont Stakes, he offended somebody somehow and The Jockey Club rescinded his license. *Collyer's Eye* reported that, "Residents [of Jamaica, New York] who have known Kummer since childhood and have watched him rise to a foremost position as a jockey are amazed at his recent escapades."[26] The *Eye* alleged that the rider whom Glen Riddle stable hands had called "Fool Proof" had been giving tips to a gambling gang. A more sympathetic source later noted that "away from horses, Kummer fidgeted and developed nerves."[27]

Pressures that did not break Johnny Loftus seemed to consume Clarence Kummer. While the grounded Loftus had steadily toiled as an exercise rider and assistant trainer, even digging postholes while sprucing up his employer's barn, Kummer fell into disagreements with his employers and lacked momentum. From 1928 through 1929, he occasionally worked as an exercise rider but resisted moving on to a trainer's job. Instead, during the summer of 1930, he tried to squeeze back into his former life as a jockey. The effort badly weakened his body. "Clarence was a wizened little old man at the age of 31," a reporter noted. "He was racked by a cruel diet, shriveled and worn."[28] Finally, Kummer admitted that it was time to train horses instead of overtraining himself.

His decision came too late. Several days into December of 1930, Clarence Kummer took sick with pneumonia. After lingering at home in bed for a week, he died.[29] The husky build that had helped make him a strong partner for Man o' War did not let him resume the life he loved. "He always wanted to ride. He was born to ride," Clarence's brokenhearted younger brother Eddie told reporters. "He died because he couldn't give up the saddle."[30]

"He rode a great many horses for me," a stunned Sam Riddle said, "and never gave me a bad ride."[31]

"Clarence Kummer kept a scrapbook of his greatest races," a journalist who visited his house shortly after his death reported. "No one in the family knew where it was today. When he left the track he put the book away. It reminded him too much of the past."[32]

While Man o' War retired with his reputation soaring higher than ever, Sir Barton was not so lucky. Bedwell ran him three more times within a month after the Kenilworth Gold Cup, watching him lose, lose, and lose, before retiring him for the year. Before the 1921 racing season, reckoning that Sir Barton could not physically stand another campaign, Commander Ross retired him for good.

Immortalized as America's first Triple Crown winner but also as the champion demolished by Man o' War, Sir Barton would spend his final years in increasing obscurity. A disappointment at stud, he ended up siring cavalry horses at a United States Army remount station in Wyoming. Even in exile, Sir Barton kept the proud attitude that horsemen call "the look of eagles." The occasional visitor admired his still grand-looking physique and silky soft coat, even shortly before his death at the age of twenty-one. For decades, Sir Barton's remains lay under a piece of sandstone inscribed by the ranch foreman's wife. In 1968, more than thirty years after the Triple Crown became a coveted goal, local Jaycees decided that Sir Barton, the inaugural winner, deserved more attention. They moved his grave to a more accessible site in Washington Park in Douglas, Wyoming, and topped it with a handsome fiberglass statue of a generic horse.[33]

Man o' War, on the other hand, would pose many times during the last several years of his life for a custom-made larger-than-life-sized bronze statue by internationally renowned animal sculptor Herbert Hasletine. He also quickly became a living monument in Kentucky's Bluegrass region. "His name is on all the road directions in this part of the country and on all the 'Seeing Kentucky' programs," farm manager Elizabeth Daingerfield noted three years after Red retired. "Tourists ask first where they can find him and then where they can find the Mammoth Cave."[34] Detailed directions were needed because Sam Riddle's aptly named Faraway Farm, which became

Man o' War's home in 1922, was located several miles from Lexington's major roads. Guidebook writer Robert J. Breckinridge eventually reckoned, "More folks have been lost looking for Man o' War than went down with the Titanic."[35] Enough tourists succeeded, however, that the farm crew soon began keeping guest books for visitors to sign. One early volume may have been inscribed by Man o' War's first stud groom, John Buckner. Inside the front cover, someone penciled in cursive writing: "This is the home of Man O War." And a couple of inches below:

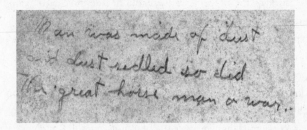

Elizabeth Daingerfield endured nearly ten years in Sam Riddle's employ before resigning in October 1930 to concentrate on her own horse-breeding business. During the late autumn of 1930, a new team, headed by Riddle's friend Harrie B. Scott, began the transition into managing Faraway Farm and Man o' War. John Buckner stayed awhile to initiate Red's new stud groom: Lexington native Will Harbut, a thoroughgoing horseman and church deacon with a "rich, resonant baritone [voice]."[36] Because Riddle allowed the general public to visit Faraway Farm, Harbut's new job involved more than keeping Red clean, fed, and cooperative in the breeding shed.

Harbut's spontaneous wit began amusing the public during the spring of 1931, when record-setting race-car driver Barney Oldfield stopped at Faraway Farm to see the legendary Man o' War. "That baby surely carried some speed in his day," Oldfield reportedly remarked.

"He sure did, Mr. Oldfield," Harbut replied. "If we just had Colonel Lindbergh here right now we would just about have all the speed there is in this world."[37] In a flash, Harbut connected Oldfield and Man o' War with the first airplane pilot to fly solo across the Atlantic Ocean.

A magazine writer, however, transcribed Harbut's words as follows: "If we jist had Colonel Lindbergh here right now we would jist about have all de speed dar am in dis world."[38] As an African-American, Will Harbut stood between two worlds: one appreciating his wit and admiring the horse he tended, another condescending toward his race. Visitors responded positively to Harbut's dignity and charm, but journalists—using conventions that many in their mid-twentieth-century audience expected—usually fell into minstrel-show dialect when they wrote up what he said. A rare exception was equine author and artist C. W. Anderson, who noticed that Harbut didn't say things such as "wasn't nothing" or "dar am."

"He evidently reads quite a bit and his English and grammar are much better than generally portrayed," Anderson observed. "The soft slurred accent so characteristic of the Bluegrass is there, but he does not use the double negatives and more tortured grammar often credited to him."[39]

"Sometimes I get a little sore," Harbut admitted after he had been presenting Man o' War to the public for about ten years. "Seems like some of these newspaper writers don't pay much 'tention to what they write. They come out an' see Red standing like he is now, with his hind quarters on higher ground, an' they write he's old an' sway-backed. Then they make me talk so ignorant. I know my language ain't the best in the world, but it ain't like they make out. They make Red sway-backed an' me ignorant, an' it ain't fair. Why can't they tell things like they are?"[40]

Harbut made a valid point about exaggeration. Although Red developed a dip in his back, just behind his strikingly prominent withers, as he reached the equine senior citizen age of twenty years and more, he never developed a true swayback. Reporters who saw it as such were oversimplifying rather than dealing with actuality. Will Harbut often suffered the same fate.

Even those who caricatured him, however, recognized that Harbut gave the experience of seeing Man o' War the suspenseful rhythm of a theatrical event, showing and commenting on the other residents of the Faraway Farm stallion barn before revealing the greatest star. From 1939 onward, he would save Red's Triple Crown–winning son War Admiral for next to last, describing the Admiral's most thrilling moments with a quiet vigor that could raise the hair on a tourist's neck. "An' so in the Preakness, Wah Admiral went wide, an' let Pompoon run up to him," Harbut would relate. "Then he looked over at Pompoon an' he said, 'Pompoon, my daddy broke John P. Grier's heart. Come *on!*'"[41]

Finally, visitors would see one more stall door open and an imposing high-headed red stallion step forward to the groom's side. They did not have to know anything about racehorses to feel that here was something magnificent. "Man o' War possessed the most impressive dignity of any horse I've ever known," journalist B. K. Beckwith observed. "You would no more have thought of walking up and putting a hand on him than you would of casually poking the Queen of England in the ribs."[42] Harbut, however, shared the monarch's unguarded trust. C. W. Anderson noticed that the mighty Man o' War, while being brushed, often nuzzled his groom or rested his head on his shoulder. "This is what he wants," Harbut told Anderson, reaching to cradle Red's head in his arms. "He's just a big baby. He'd do this all day if I let him."[43]

The general public, peering through the stall door, did not see that Man o' War. Although Red became used to strangers gathering around his stall, he still seemed like a force beyond anyone's reach. ". . . [He] often looks high over the heads of the crowd with that fixed, faraway look horses have, as if seeing something far beyond our vision,"[44] C. W. Anderson noted when Red was more than twenty years old. "Even when he was standing motionless in his stall, with his ears pricked forward and his eyes focused on something slightly above the horizon which mere people never see, energy still poured from him," Joe Palmer wrote. "His very stillness was that of the coiled spring, of the crouched tiger."[45]

With his hushed audience caught by Red's spell, Will Harbut would rest one hand on Red's shoulder and begin talking, as Anderson noted, "in a quiet voice which makes the speech doubly effective. . . ."[46] Except in newsreels, Harbut never had seen Red race. But he studied up on Red's career, and highlights soon found a seductive cadence. Joe Palmer recalled Harbut's commentary as a story "told with rare balance and charm. . . ."[47] Over time, the groom's narrative grew as many verses as any well-tried folk song. By 1941, when he and Red shared the cover of the widely circulated *Saturday Evening Post* magazine, Will Harbut's approach had been refined to a science and elevated to an art. "Although its general substance is always the same," Anderson noted, "it varies according to the audience. When he realizes that no one in the crowd knows if a mile in 1:35 4/5 is good or not, he leaves out a great deal that would be interesting to the more informed."[48]

"But if his visitor seemed to know anything about horses, or just ran his eyes in pure wonder over the great sweeping lines of Fair Play's sweeping son," turf writer Joe Palmer noted, "then Will gave him the full treatment."[49] Palmer, who often guided guests to Faraway Farm, requested the full treatment for British ambassador Lord Halifax. "It lasted something like twenty minutes," Palmer recalled, "and Lord Halifax never took his eyes off the groom, who was unrolling the long glories of Man o' War and his sons and daughters . . . like [the poet] Tennyson on the passing of [King] Arthur." In the barn at Faraway Farm, there was Blockade winning the Maryland Hunt

Cup, War Admiral outdueling Pompoon, and, finally, Man o' War doing everything better than any racehorse had done before.

"He broke all the records and he broke down all the horses, so there was nothing for him to do but retire." Harbut concluded, as Man o' War held a regal pose. "He's got everything a horse ought to have, and he's got it where a horse ought to have it. He's just the mostest horse."

"That" Lord Halifax murmured, "was worth coming halfway 'round the world to hear."[50]

Will Harbut not only made visitors feel that they were seeing a natural wonder but also helped them envision Man o' War running as no horse ever had before or ever would again. Watching the majestic stallion gaze into the distance while Harbut quietly declared, "He's just the mostest hoss that ever was," legions of visitors felt this to be true.

Intensely loyal to Man o' War, Harbut also spread the belief that Johnny Loftus got Red beaten in a crooked race. "He lost one race," Harbut would tell his audiences as a scowl swept across his face, "an' the jockey that rode him—well, he's walkin' now."[51] Throughout the 1930s and well into the 1940s, the old suspicions reached new generations. Loftus became not only that guy who lost on Man o' War; in the minds of multitudes who had been nowhere near Saratoga on August 13, 1919, he was the guy who threw a race on the greatest horse that ever was.

Words, however, could not change the relationship that jockey and horse had forged. After Man o' War had been retired for several years, Johnny Loftus went to visit him at Faraway Farm. Grooms warned him not to approach his old partner, who was "in one of his mean moods." Loftus did not seem concerned. Entering Man o' War's spacious paddock and making a megaphone with his hands, he yelled, "Hey, Big Red!"

Horses have a strong memory for the voices, shapes, habits, and smells of people they have known well. Their reactions, even after months and years apart, reveal what treatment they expect to receive. "Big Red marched right over to Loftus," a reporter noted, "welcomed him with his most lavish display of equine salutation, then true to a habit formed in his youth, poked his nose into Loftus' side pocket looking for sugar cubes."[52]

Loftus did not let him down.

22

EBB TIDE

Sometimes when their lives are about to end, people confess things, let go of guilty secrets or exaggerations. They stop pretending and slide into reality.

To the end of his eighty-nine years, Samuel Doyle Riddle resisted such admissions. With each passing year of Man o' War's long life, he grew more certain of Red's invincibility. He also embroidered his own role, emphasizing that he had always known how brilliant Red would be. Once, he proclaimed, "The greatest day in my life was the day I bought Man o' War." But Elizabeth Dobson Riddle remembered how her own money and decision brought the legend into their lives. "Sam," she chided him, "the greatest day in your life was the day you married me."[1]

Lou Feustel never said whether the greatest day in his life involved Man o' War, but it wasn't hard to guess that it was likely so. When Feustel retired from training and ran a saloon near Pasadena, California, the walls boasted portraits of the high-headed red horse. "I guess like every other trainer in the world, I had sense enough to know I had hold of the tail of a tiger," he recalled, "and, while I could steer him some, I had to do a lot of swinging with him, I had to grow with him and try to out-guess him . . . figure things out with him and let him believe he'd done it for himself. You can't handle a temperamental horse or human being any other way."[2]

Bill Knapp and Johnny Loftus both owed the most infamous day of their lives to Man o' War. Year after year, reporters convinced that Man o' War's Sanford loss was a Loftus/Knapp frame-up kept pestering them to confess.

Until his death in 1972, Knapp swore that he rode an honest race. Two feelings—admiration of a truly great horse and pride in getting the better of him—dueled within him for more than fifty years. Always, Knapp would say that he was proud of his clever ride. Sometimes he would add that Man o' War should have retired unbeaten and that he was sorry he hadn't let him through at the rail.

Johnny Loftus lived with a more disturbing duality. His eyes lighted up whenever someone asked him about racing, but he shrank away when asked about Man o' War.[3] He never could talk about his greatest days without reliving immense pain. "I've explained what happened a number of times," he told a journalist in 1965, "but nobody believes me. I was the goat, so what. It was very unfortunate it happened. Heck, if a ball player makes an error, they forget it. Why me?"[4] He would endure the criticism for nearly sixty years. John Patrick Loftus died in 1976 at age eighty. His obituary appeared in *The Blood-Horse* magazine's issue of March 29—Man o' War's birthday.

The Jockey Club continues to the present day but was forced to transform itself. A horse-owning handicapper named Jule Fink sued the club in 1949, after they refused him a license to race his stable in New York. In 1951, the New York Court of Appeals unanimously ruled in Fink's favor and transferred license-granting power from The Jockey Club to the State Racing Commission. Because license seekers now could sue the license givers, the practice of grounding a jockey without a public hearing disappeared—a justice thirty years too late to help Johnny Loftus.

And Man o' War? People imagined perfection for him: a Speed Miracle that never got tired and always could give something more. In one telling tribute, on April 12, 1947, the First Cavalry Division of the American troops occupying Japan made Man o' War an honorary colonel. When he died, at the impressive age of thirty, the division's three thousand soldiers saluted him in Tokyo.

Weakened by several heart attacks, Red's body gave out at Faraway Farm on November 1, 1947. On November 4, a radio broadcast of his funeral ceremony, including nine eulogies and a bugler playing "Taps," aired throughout the United States. His embalmed remains, interred beneath the marble pedestal of his heroic bronze statue, were moved in 1977 to a spotlighted site near the front entrance of Lexington's popular Kentucky Horse Park. Visitors can view his monument there free of charge. Imagination can carry them back in time, where a red horse is bounding toward the finish line, setting the bar for legends to come.

ADDITIONAL
RESOURCES

APPENDIX A
Man o' War's Records

RACING RECORDS

Because Man o' War's races are described at length in the main text, here is a simple summary of his placings and earnings.

	Starts	1st	2nd	3rd	Earnings
1919—Age Two	10	9	1	0	$83,325
1920—Age Three	11	11	0	0	$166,140
Total	21	20	1	0	$249,465

SPEED RECORDS

1919

At age two, Man o' War did not set any track records, but he did run notably fast for a juvenile. In the 5 1/2-furlong Youthful Stakes on June 21, he finished 2/5 of a second slower than the stakes record while carrying 120 pounds (the stakes record holder, Lord Brighton, had carried 105). In August at Saratoga, his display of record speed began.

Date	Track	Race	Distance	Time	Weight
August 2	Saratoga	United States Hotel Stakes	6 fur.	1:12 2/5	130

(Equaled stakes record set by Garbage under 107 pounds and tied by two-year-old champion Billy Kelly with 127 pounds up.)

Date	Track	Race	Distance	Time	Weight
August 13	Saratoga	Sanford Memorial Stakes	6 fur.	1:11 1/5*	130

(*Finished second to Upset (115 pounds), who lowered the stakes record by 2 1/5 seconds with Man o' War approximately 1/2 length behind him; previous record set by Regret, a future Hall of Fame champion, under 127 pounds and tied by two-year-old champion Campfire with 125 pounds up.)

Date	Track	Race	Distance	Time	Weight
August 23	Saratoga	Grand Union Hotel Stakes	6 fur.	1:12	130

(New stakes record by 2/5; previous record set by Sweep On under 127 pounds.)

Date	Track	Race	Distance	Time	Weight
September 13		Belmont Park Futurity	6 fur.	1:11 3/5	127

(Fastest Futurity since the event moved to Belmont Park (and became several yards longer) in 1913; Thunderer, the next-fastest winner at Belmont, had gone 1/5 slower while carrying 122 pounds.)

1920

At age three, Man o' War set a speed record in eight of his eleven starts—an astonishing percentage. While half of his records were made at Belmont Park, he also was able to set new marks at other tracks in New York, Maryland, and Canada.

Much to racing experts' surprise, three different horses broke two of Man o' War's American records—at one mile and 1 1/8 miles—in the summer of 1921. The greatly improved track surfaces that Man o' War also enjoyed surely played a role in this, but two of the three record breakers carried less weight than Man o' War had done. Furthermore, for most horses, sustaining a record pace is easier over a shorter distance. It makes sense that the eight- and nine-furlong records were the first to fall.

At the other extreme, Man o' War's marks for 1 3/8 and 1 5/8 miles remained America's best over a dirt track for seventy-one years and thirty-six years, respectively. The fact that these distances weren't frequently run contributed to that longevity, but so did Man o' War's exceptional stamina. In the Lawrence Realization, his 2:40 4/5 was not matched until 1960. The horse to do it was another Hall of Famer: Man o' War's great-grandson Kelso.

Date	Track	Race	Distance	Time	Weight
May 29	Belmont Park	Withers Stakes	1 mile	1:35 4/5	118

(American record for one mile in competition by 2/5. Stood until June 1, 1921, when Audacious (118 pounds) lowered it by 1/5.)

June 12	Belmont Park	Belmont Stakes	1 3/8 miles	2:14 1/5	126

(American record by 3 1/5 seconds; world record by 2 3/5 seconds. Broken in 1961 when Wise Ship (113 pounds) went 2:14 flat on Belmont Park's turf course. Stood as American dirt-track record until broken by Timely Warning (112 pounds) in 1991.)

July 10	Aqueduct	Dwyer Stakes	1 1/8 miles	1:49 1/5	126

(American and world record by 1/5. Stood until June 10, 1921, when Goaler (94 1/2 pounds) lowered it by 1/5; tied by Grey Lag (123 pounds), a future Hall of Fame champion, on July 7, 1921.)

August 21	Saratoga	Travers Stakes	1 1/4 miles	2:01 4/5	129

(Equaled track record set by Sir Barton (129 pounds); fastest American and world time except for disputed 2:00 credited to Whisk Broom II with 139 pounds up in the 1913 Suburban Handicap at Belmont Park. Sir Barton and Man o' War's 2:01 4/5 remained Saratoga's track record until Lucky Draw (121 pounds) shaved 1/5 from it in 1946.)

September 4	Belmont Park	Lawrence Realization	1 5/8 miles	2:40 4/5	126

(American record by 4 1/5 seconds; world record by 1 3/5 seconds. Stood until July 25, 1956, when future Hall of Fame champion Swaps (130 pounds)—a great-great-grandson of Man o' War—ran a tremendous 2:38 1/5 at Hollywood Park.)

September 11   Belmont Park   Jockey Club Stakes   1 1/2 miles   2:28 4/5   118
(American record by 4/5. Stood until June 25, 1927, when Handy Mandy (109 pounds) shaved off 1/5; Man o'
War's future Hall of Fame champion son War Admiral (126 pounds) tied Handy Mandy's 2:28 3/5 in 1937.)

September 18   Havre de Grace   Potomac Handicap   1 1/16 miles   1:44 4/5   138
(New track record by 1/5; stood until Jock (112 pounds) shaved 1/5 from it in 1927.)

October 12   Kenilworth Park   Kenilworth Gold Cup   1 1/4 miles   2:03   120
(New track record by 6 2/5 seconds; 1/5 slower than Canadian record. Previous track record set by Christophine
under 102 pounds.)

APPENDIX B

Man o' War's Pedigree

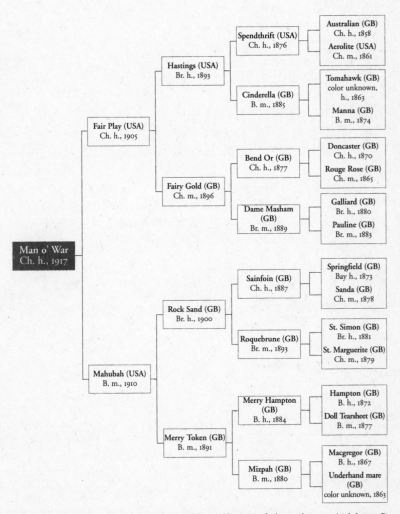

GB=foaled in Great Britain; USA=foaled in the United States. Abbreviations for horse colors appearing below are B. (bay), Br. (brown), and Ch. (chestnut). Males are designated by h. (horse), females by m. (mare).

COMPARING MAN O' WAR
WITH OTHER GREATS

Clearly, any debate about "The Best Racehorse Ever" in North America must include Man o' War. The names most often challenging him for all-around supremacy include Citation, Native Dancer, Kelso, Secretariat, and Spectacular Bid. Experts also might compare his brilliant speed with that of Count Fleet, Dr. Fager, and Seattle Slew; his remarkable consistency with that of Affirmed and Cigar; and his tremendous heart and popularity with that of Seabiscuit.

In-depth comparison of Thoroughbred racing's all-time most impressive champions, however, would require a whole book in itself. Anyone seeking further information on the best American racehorses will find excellent summaries in volumes such as *Champions: The Lives, Times, and Past Performances of America's Greatest Thoroughbreds* (New York: Daily Racing Form Press, 2000, revised edition, January 2006); *Thoroughbred Champions: Top 100 Racehorses of the 20th Century*, by the Staff and Correspondents of *The Blood-Horse* magazine (Lexington, Ky.: Eclipse Press, 2000); and *The Most Glorious Crown: The Story of America's Triple Crown Thoroughbreds from Sir Barton to Affirmed*, by Marvin Drager (Chicago: Triumph Press, 2005; includes a DVD called *Win, Place, Show: The History of Horse Racing*).

Substantial individual biographies are available for Citation, Native Dancer, Ruffian, Seabiscuit, Secretariat, and Whirlaway. Furthermore, the Thoroughbred Legends series from Eclipse Press offers relatively brief but richly detailed portraits of more than two dozen elite racers, including Man o' War.

In this Internet age, Web sites provide quick access to a wealth of racing lore. The only danger is that erroneous information also travels easily. A most reliable source is the Hall of Fame Multimedia section of National Museum of Racing and Hall of Fame site (www.racingmuseum.org/hall/multimedia.asp) and its link to the Hall of Fame pages, which offer career statistics and, when possible, video clips. Another outstanding resource is the Biographies section of the Thoroughbred Champions Web site (www.thoroughbredchampions.com).

To top it off, it's fun and enlightening to watch videos or DVDs of racing's greatest stars. While films and videos can't capture all of the electricity that was in the air as a great race unfolded, they do give some sense of each champion's distinct power.

Happy racing!

NOTES

1. TWO WARS BEGIN

1. "Poor Start in the Brewers' Handicap," *Courier-Journal* (Louisville), June 26, 1910.
2. "Tony Bonero Beats Pinkola at Latonia," *Courier-Journal* (Louisville), June 25, 1910.
3. "Poor Start in the Brewers' Handicap," *Courier-Journal* (Louisville), June 26, 1910.
4. "Latonia Form Chart" for June 24, 1910, *Courier-Journal* (Louisville), June 25, 1910.
5. "Gov. Gray First in Cincinnati Trophy," *Courier-Journal* (Louisville), July 3, 1910.
6. "Horsemen Ruled Off at Latonia," *New York Times,* July 3, 1910.
7. "Latonia Judges Act in the Nadzu Case," *Courier-Journal* (Louisville), July 6, 1910.
8. "Latonia Track Gossip," *Courier-Journal* (Louisville), July 6, 1910.
9. "Spence Is Restored to Good Standing," *Courier-Journal* (Louisville), July 17, 1910.
10. Snowden Carter, "Veteran Veterinarian," *Turf and Sport Digest,* February 1962, p. 12.
11. "Bedwell Still Leads Owners," Louisville *Courier-Journal,* February 19, 1912.
12. Three gentlemen named August Belmont are mentioned in this book: August Belmont, Sr. (1816–1890), August Belmont, Jr. (1853–1924), and August Belmont III (1882–1919). August, Sr., and August III, however, are mentioned only in passing. The man who figures prominently in Man o' War's life was christened August Belmont, Jr. After his father's death in 1890, however, he announced that he would no longer use the suffix *Jr.* (it was, in fact, proper etiquette for a Junior to "graduate" after his father died). This book, of course, begins two decades after that event. Therefore, throughout this book the man who started life as August Belmont, Jr., is simply called August Belmont in most instances. In a few places where he is considered in a wider historical context, his name is given as August Belmont, Jr.
13. Neil Newman, "Colin: Despite Lameness, He Won the Belmont," *The Blood-Horse,* December 27, 1947, p. 848.

14. "Colin the Unbeaten May Not Race Again," *New York Times,* May 29, 1908.

15. "Colin Leads Throughout in Rich Belmont Stake," *New York Herald,* May 31, 1908.

16. *Daily Racing Form* results chart, Belmont Park, May 30, 1908.

17. *Thoroughbred Types 1900–1925: Photographic Portraits of Notable Racehorses, Steeplechase and Cross-Country Horses, Hunters and Polo Ponies,* with descriptive texts by W. S. Vosburgh, Charles D. Lanier, Frank J. Bryan, and James C. Cooley (New York: privately printed, 1926), p. 35.

18. Mahubah produced five foals sired by Fair Play and was never bred to any other stallion.

19. A more accurate spelling would be Marhabah.

20. On March 19, 1923, the *New York Times* printed an item "Giant Colt Is Foaled at Major Belmont's Stud Farm." This colt, by Fair Play from Quelle Chance, stood "42 1/2 inches at the shoulder with a girth of 34 inches."

21. Eleanor Robson Belmont, *The Fabric of Memory* (New York: Farrar, Straus and Cudahy, 1957), p. 100.

22. Ibid., p. 90.

23. Although many future racehorses stayed unnamed until they were at least a year old, the Belmonts wasted no time. A May 24, 1917, letter to The Jockey Club confirmed August Belmont's telephone call reserving names for fifteen foals. Mahubah's colt—first on the list—was not quite two months old.

2. AUCTION AT SARATOGA

1. A telegram found in the Belmont family papers at Columbia University, dated July 15, 1918, and sent to Lt. Raymond Belmont in France, reads, "Operation on Pops successful; no ill effects." In subsequent documents, spanning twelve days, August Belmont, Jr., refers to being hospitalized. By August 6, he clearly was back at home. The nature of his surgery was not disclosed. On July 17, 1918, the *New York Herald* reported in the article "Major Belmont Operated Upon" that "Major August Belmont . . . has undergone a minor operation to correct a slight physical defect and enable him to continue even more active than he has been in the service."

2. Some writers have claimed that Man o' War was originally named My Man o' War. This assumption apparently dates from the list of Belmont yearlings published in the July 20, 1918, issue of *The Thoroughbred Record.* August Belmont's May 24, 1917, letter to The Jockey Club, however, shows that the name originally reserved was simply Man o' War. Letters written by Eleanor Belmont in the 1930s (held by Columbia University) that describe her role in naming the colt do not mention My Man o' War as his name at any point.

3. In 1891, Breslau assumed its present name, Lindenhurst.

4. "Louis Feustal [*sic*] and Man o' War," as told to Lorena M. Frevert, *Long Island Forum,* November 1970.

5. Tape-recorded interview with Louis Feustel, circa 1960s; interviewer unidentified; collection of the National Museum of Racing and Hall of Fame (Saratoga Springs, New York).

6. Charles Robson, *Manufactories and Manufacturers of Pennsylvania of the Nineteenth Century* (Philadelphia: Galaxy Publishing Company, 1875), p. 119.

7. Samuel Riddle had previously married Martha Mercer. She died without bearing any children.

8. Samuel T. Wiley (revised and edited by Winifred Scott Garner), *Biographical and Historical Encyclopedia of Delaware County, Pennsylvania* (Richmond, Indiana, and New York: Gresham Publishing, 1894), p. 164.

9. Bob Finucane, "Flashing Hoofs of Man o' War Carried Riddle to World Fame," newspaper unknown, January 8, 1951.

10. Reports that Samuel Doyle Riddle attended Swarthmore College appear to be mistaken. Chris Densmore of Swarthmore's Friends Historical Library reported to the author on June 23, 2004, "There's an apparently complete list of alumni of Swarthmore published in 1930, with a Samuel Riddle, Class of 1897—identified as living in Louisville, KY at that time. The only other Swarthmore College Riddle [was] Florence Riddle (later Meek), Class of 1916. Swarthmore also had a Preparatory School until 1894. In 1879–80, we have listed Charlotte B., L. Maude, and W. Leander Riddle. No Riddles listed in the other years for the Preparatory School." Charlotte, Maude, and Leander were Samuel Doyle Riddle's siblings. Additionally, Becky Warda of Widener University (formerly Pennsylvania Military College) found Samuel D. Riddle listed in the "Second Class" (sophomore) and "Third Class" (junior) for 1878–1879, but there was no evidence that he was enrolled as a senior or graduated.

11. Finucane, "Flashing Hoofs of Man o' War Carried Riddle to World Fame."

12. Frank Talmadge Phelps, "He Owned Man o' War," *Turf and Sport Digest*, September 1952, p. 35.

13. Feustel gave an approximate date for his visit to the Nursery with Mike Daly when he said, "So then they brought them up to Saratoga six weeks later, and the twelve horses brought a hundred and eight thousand dollars [*sic*]. Six weeks later." Six weeks before the August 17 auction would have been around July 7, 1918. Feustel, Daly, and Pons may have just missed August Belmont, who was back in New York by July 9. Tape-recorded interview with Louis Feustel, loc. cit.

14. Tape-recorded interview with Louis Feustel, loc. cit.

15. Ibid.

16. Part of this area is now incorporated into the Saratoga Race Course property and known as Clare Court, in honor of former track superintendent Tom Clare.

17. "Exile," "Gossip from Saratoga," *The Thoroughbred Record*, August 17, 1918, p. 76.

18. "Billy Kelly Sold to Ross for $30,000," *The Saratogian*, August 10, 1918.

19. John Hervey, "The Turf Career of Man o' War," unpublished manuscript (1933)

later serialized by *Horse* magazine; available through the National Sporting Library (Middleburg, Virginia).

20. Kitty Slater, *The Hunt Country of America*, (South Brunswick, N.J., and New York: A. S. Barnes and Co., 1967), p. 123.

21. Hervey, "The Turf Career of Man o' War."

22. Abram S. Hewitt, "Sire Lines: Part XXXIX: Man o' War," *The Blood-Horse*, November 25, 1974, p. 5200.

23. Hervey, "The Turf Career of Man o' War."

24. Slater, *The Hunt Country of America*, p. 123.

25. "How Man o' War Was Bought," *Daily Racing Form*, August 5, 1919.

26. Slater, *The Hunt Country of America*, p. 123.

27. Frank Talmadge Phelps, "Blacksmith of Champions," *The Thoroughbred of California*, June 1964. This information came from George Tompkins, "who shod Man o' War more often than any other blacksmith." Phelps noted, "Man o' War's right forefoot was larger than his left, which was slightly narrower than normal; hence the foot from which an individual shoe came can be identified." (p. 689) Regarding the quality of Man o' War's underpinnings, Tompkins said, "He had a good foot." (p. 688)

28. Joe H. Palmer (principal author), "Man o' War: Death Ends His Magnificence," *The Blood-Horse*, November 8, 1947, p. 343.

29. Abram S. Hewitt, "Sire Lines: Part XXXIX: Man o' War," p. 5200. Man o' War was indeed slightly Roman-nosed, and his neck appears longer by the end of his two-year-old season than it did in photos taken early that summer.

30. B. K. Beckwith, *Step and Go Together: The World of Horses and Horsemanship* (South Brunswick, N.J., and New York: A. S. Barnes and Co., 1967), p. 58.

31. Hervey, "The Turf Career of Man o' War."

32. Samuel C. Hildreth and James R. Crowell, *The Spell of the Turf*, (Philadelphia & London: J. B. Lippincott, 1926), p. 229.

33. Hervey, "The Turf Career of Man o' War."

34. Hildreth and Crowell, *The Spell of the Turf*, p. 229.

35. Slater, *The Hunt Country of America*, p. 123.

36. Ibid.

37. Ibid.

38. O'Neil Sevier, "Man o' War—De Mostes' Hoss," *Turf and Sport Digest*, December 1947, p. 6.

39. "20,000 Enjoy Thrilling Sport at Saratoga's Fine Racing Park," *New York Herald*, August 18, 1918.

40. *Down the Stretch: The Story of Colonel Matt J. Winn*, as told to Frank G. Menke (New York: Smith & Durrell, 1945), p. 67.

41. Slater, *The Hunt Country of America*, p. 123. Maddux said, "Mrs. Gerry and Mrs. Penn-Smith later told me that they had bid four thousand [on Man o' War], believing they could make a hunter out of him."

42. Eleanor Robson Belmont, *The Fabric of Memory* (New York: Farrar, Straus and Cudahy, 1957), p. 94.

43. Palmer, "Man o' War: Death Ends His Magnificence," p. 343.

44. Beckwith, *Step and Go Together*, p. 58.

45. Wayne Capps, "The Place Where Louie Dwelled," *The Thoroughbred Record*, August 15, 1970, p. 678.

46. Beckwith, *Step and Go Together*, p. 58.

47. "High Price for Yearling," *New York Times*, August 18, 1918.

48. Various totals for the 1918 Belmont yearlings sold at Saratoga would be published. Belmont himself put the figure at $52,250 in an August 27, 1918, letter to his wife, who received 5 percent of the gross.

49. "Society and Turf Patrons at Spa Contribute Largely to War Fund," *New York Herald*, August 28, 1918.

50. "Mrs. Riddle Buys Union Ave. Property," *The Saratogian*, August 27, 1918.

3. LICENSE TO FLY

1. B. K. Beckwith, *Step and Go Together: The World of Horses and Horsemanship* (South Brunswick, N.J., and New York: A. S. Barnes and Co., 1967), p. 58.

2. Horace Wade, "Tales of the Turf," *Turf and Sport Digest*, March 1963, p. 23.

3. Ibid.

4. Ibid.

5. J. A. Estes, "Pedigree Points: The Irascible Hastings," *The Blood-Horse*, February 12, 1938, p 310.

6. Beckwith, *Step and Go Together*, pp. 63–64.

7. Theodore Von Ziekursch, "Before the Barrier," *The Saturday Evening Post*, July 26, 1930, p. 10.

8. In the 1930 *Saturday Evening Post* article "Before the Barrier," Vititoe claimed that Man o' War never threw him. He also claimed that the first time Johnny Loftus got on Red's back, the colt threw the star jockey thirty feet. Unfortunately for historians, some of Vititoe's other claims—such as Man o' War having his head under the infield rail at the start of the Sanford Stakes—clearly are exaggerated or untrue. Without corroboration of Vititoe's stories from other primary sources, it is easier to believe Feustel's simple description of Man o' War throwing Vititoe during the first attempted ride.

9. Beckwith, *Step and Go Together*, p. 59.

10. John Hervey, "The Turf Career of Man o' War," unpublished manuscript (1933) later serialized by *Horse* magazine; available through the National Sporting Library (Middleburg (1933), Virginia).

11. Ibid.

12. Ibid.

13. Ten years after Man o' War retired from racing, Harry Vititoe told *The Saturday*

Evening Post that he bestowed the nickname "Red." Given his need to talk easily with the colt while breaking him to saddle, this is quite possible.

14. "Wicomico Weekly News," *The Democratic Messenger* (Snow Hill, Maryland), November 30, 1916.

15. Hervey "The Turf Career of Man o' War."

16. W. O. McGeehan, "The Golden Stallion," *The Saturday Evening Post,* July 26, 1930, p. 70.

17. The word *furlong* evolved from "furrow long," the typical length of a plowed field.

18. "S. D. Riddle's Man o' War Enjoying a Well-Earned Vacation at Owner's Maryland Farm; The 1919 Juvenile Champion and His Peculiarities and the Stable's Favorite," *Daily Racing Form,* November 30, 1919.

19. Paul Cervin, "Headless Horsemen," *Turf and Sport Digest,* April 1935, p. 75.

20. Charles Hatton, Column in *Daily Racing Form,* September 17, 1958.

21. Adolph Mathis, "Nags Race Well For Old-Time Race Rider," *Collyer's Eye,* January 6, 1923.

22. "Obituary: Johnny Loftus," *The Blood-Horse,* March 29, 1976, p. 1356.

23. "Latonia Turf Chat," *Courier-Journal* (Louisville), June 26, 1910.

24. In the fast-paced racing world, jockey weights and horse imposts are spoken without the words *one hundred.* For example, if Johnny Loftus rode at 110 pounds, racetrackers would say that he made one ten.

25. "East Again Beats West in the Kentucky Derby," *New York Herald,* May 14, 1916.

26. Pronounced MAC-um-ber.

27. Research has not determined whether or not Loftus ever married his daughter's mother. His daughter, Elinor Marie Loftus Farmer, died in 1989. The California Death Index lists her mother's maiden name as Kinsel.

28. "Motor Cop Wins Classic Withers," *New York Herald,* June 2, 1918.

29. "Johren Wins Belmont Stakes," *The Thoroughbred Record,* June 22, 1918, p. 335.

30. Ibid.

31. "Johren Proves a Great Thoroughbred . . . Winning . . . Belmont Test," *New York Herald,* June 16, 1918.

32. "$12,800 Filly My Friend Wins Rosedale Stakes at 5 Furlongs," *New York Herald,* June 19, 1918.

33. J. K. M. Ross, *Boots and Saddles: The Story of the Fabulous Ross Stable in the Golden Days of Racing* (New York: E. P. Dutton, 1956), p. 18.

34. "American Record Set by Sun Briar," *The Saratogian,* August 7, 1918.

35. "Record Succeeds Record on Fast Saratoga Track," *New York Herald,* August 24, 1918.

36. Ibid.

37. A. A. Albelli, "The Horse or the Jockey?" *Popular Mechanics,* month unknown, 1927, p. 916.

38. "Leading Jockeys of 1918," *The Thoroughbred Record,* February 1, 1919, p. 59.

4. WAKE UP, SHAKE UP

1. Emphasizing the fact that he was temporarily out of the racing business, Belmont leased his Saratoga Springs training center, The Surcingle, to Edward F. Simms and J. W. McClelland for the summer and fall of 1919.

2. "Loftus May Ride Again," *New York Times,* April 4, 1919.

3. Ibid.

4. "The Loftus-Lyke Cases: Jockey Club Stewards May Have Found Evidence They Sought; Standing of the Two Riders Not Impaired by the Investigation," *Daily Racing Form,* April 15, 1919.

5. "Loftus May Ride Again," *New York Times,* April 4, 1919.

6. "Jockey Robinson Killed," *New York Times,* April 5, 1919.

7. "Frankie Robinson Dies from Fall in Race at Bowie," *New York World,* April 5, 1919.

8. "Robinson, Jockey, Left Half a Million," *New York Herald,* April 13, 1919.

9. "Current Notes of the Turf," *Daily Racing Form,* June 14, 1919.

10. "Frankie Robinson Dies from Fall in Race at Bowie," *New York World,* April 5, 1919.

11. Instead of saying "fifty-eight and three-fifths" when talking about Dominique's :58 3/5, racetrackers in conversation would use the abbreviation "fifty-eight and three." Although Thoroughbred races now are electronically timed down to hundredths of a second, during Man o' War's era, handheld stopwatches measured increments as small as one-fifth of a second. Such watches, and terminology that began with them, are still in use at the track. "Flat" refers to a time without any fifths (such as Man o' War's :59 in his first race). The phrase "and change" may be used when referring to a time that includes an unspecified number of fifths (for example, Dominique won his race in :58 and change).

12. Samuel C. Hildreth and James R. Crowell, *The Spell of the Turf* (Philadelphia and London: J. B. Lippincott, 1926), p. 224.

13. When a horse's shins "buck," a web of microfractures across the surface of the shinbones make the afflicted area swell outward, giving the bone a convex appearance.

14. On November 30, 1919, *Daily Racing Form* reported, "A remarkable thing about Man o' War is that he never 'bucked.' His shins were perfectly sound all year." Decades later, Frank Loftus told writer Horace Wade ("Man o' War and a warm old man," magazine unknown, circa 1969, p. 34), "Only thing wrong with him that I can remember was that he bucked his shins. It took him seven days to get over that." Man o' War would not have recovered from a serious case of bucked shins in only seven days, but he could have gotten over a mild inflammation in that time.

15. J. K. M. Ross, *Boots and Saddles: The Story of the Fabulous Ross Stable in the Golden Days of Racing* (New York: E. P. Dutton, 1956), p. 132.

16. Ibid., p. 139.

17. Ibid., p. 140.

18. Ibid., p. 18.

19. Ibid.

20. "Hunt for Ross Assets," *Collyer's Eye*, November 10, 1928.

21. Described as "a typical press comment of the day" regarding Commander J. K. L. Ross; cited in Ross, *Boots and Saddles*, pp. 18–19.

22. Henry V. King, "Man o' War Is Winner of the Hopeful Stake," *New York Morning Sun*, August 30, 1919.

23. In his 1956 memoir, J. K. M. Ross recalled the bet as $50,000. The *Daily Racing Form* of February 17, 1919, reported the amount as $25,000 and noted that "the transaction between Commander Ross and Rothstein is one of the largest, if not the largest, ever made in this country, at least in recent years." In his book, Jim Ross downplayed his father's big betting reputation—so it is interesting that he gave such a large figure for the Ross/Rothstein wager.

24. "Obituary: Johnny Loftus," *The Blood-Horse*, March 29, 1976, p. 1356.

25. *Hoofprints of the Century: Excerpts from America's Oldest Journal of Horse Racing and Breeding, the Thoroughbred Record, and Its Predecessor Publications, the Livestock Record and Kentucky Live Stock Record*, as compiled and annotated by William Robertson (covering 1875–1919 and 1966–1974) and Dan Farley (1920–1965); material published by *The Thoroughbred Record*, May 17, 1919.

26. Ibid.

27. "Turf Notes," *The Thoroughbred Record*, May 24, 1919, p. 314.

28. Joe H. Palmer, *American Race Horses, 1947* (N.p.: Sagamore Press, 1948), p. 20.

29. "Flags Leads Home Big Field . . ." *New York Herald*, May 16, 1919.

30. *The Thoroughbred Record*, May 24, 1919, p. 313. Because they need to stand upright much of the time and easily shift their weight in order to maintain healthy circulation and digestion, horses are tricky candidates for major leg surgery. By the mid-1950s, when Hall of Fame champion Swaps survived the difficult recovery period after a leg fracture and surgery, significant advances had been made. Progress continues to this day. Some leg fractures, however, remain irreparable. Without knowing precisely what damage was done to Colinella's leg, one can't guess whether or not she could have been saved by modern medical techniques.

31. Ross, *Boots and Saddles*, p. 153.

32. The record-setting rate was even greater than this statistic suggests. On nine of these 27 racing days, the Saratoga track was rated good, sloppy, heavy, or slow, rather than fast. There were only six days with a fast track during which no records were set.

33. "Belmont Track Is Fastest of All," *Daily Racing Form*, June 4, 1919.

34. Ibid.

35. "Suburban to Corn Tassel; Track Hard on the Horses," *Daily Racing Form*, June 8, 1919. "Before the track was reconstructed this spring, owners complained that the going was faulty and that bowed tendons resulted," *Daily Racing Form* noted.

"Now that it has been made fast, split hooves are prevalent." A track surface that is deep and loose is more conducive to letting tendons overstretch; an especially hard surface is more conducive to fractures and other percussive injuries.

5. LAUNCHED

1. B. K. Beckwith, *Step and Go Together: The World of Horses and Horsemanship* (South Brunswick, N.J., and New York: A. S. Barnes and Co., 1967), p. 57.

2. A photograph of Man o' War early in his two-year-old season shows a braided mane and unbraided tail. Soon, on his racing days, the upper few inches of his tail would be braided, as well.

3. "Man o' War A Whirlwind," *New York Telegraph*, June 7, 1919; cited in John Hervey, "The Turf Career of Man o' War," unpublished manuscript (1933) later serialized by *Horse* magazine; available through the National Sporting Library (Middleburg, Virginia).

4. Because jockeys are short and the stirrups of their saddles are especially high off the ground, an assistant must give the jockey a "leg up" onto the racehorse. Before a race, it is customary for the horse's trainer to do this. The rider will place his left foot, ankle, or knee in the palm of the trainer's hand; with synchronized timing, the rider pushes off the ground with his right leg while the trainer lifts the rider's left leg a few inches, gaining enough height for the rider to swing his right leg over the horse's back. (The word *his* is used here for simplicity's sake. During Man o' War's era, all professional jockeys in sanctioned Thoroughbred racing were men. The profession now includes women, and jockey Julie Krone was inducted into the Hall of Fame in 2000.)

5. Beckwith, *Step and Go Together*, p. 57.

6. *New York Telegraph*, presumably June 7, 1919; cited in Hervey, "Turf Career of Man o' War."

7. Ibid.

8. "Sweep On and Over There Choice for Suburban Handicap at Belmont Park Today," *New York Herald*, June 7, 1919.

9. "War Cloud Rules Favorite for Suburban," *New York Tribune*, June 7, 1919.

10. *New York Telegraph*, presumably June 7, 1919; cited in Hervey, "Turf Career of Man o' War."

11. *Webster's Third New International Dictionary*, 1986.

12. A *New York Times* reporter called the footing "muddy."

13. "Man o' War Sails in an Easy Winner," *New York Times*, June 10, 1919.

14. Henry V. King, "Man o' War Takes Keene Memorial," *New York Morning Sun*, June 10, 1919.

15. "Man o' War First on Sloppy Track," *New York Herald*, June 10, 1919.

16. Margaret Phipps Leonard, "A Derby Winner's Odyssey," *The Horse*, May–June 1938, p. 11.

17. "Sir Andrew Barton," in *The Viking Book of Folk Ballads of the English-Speaking World,* ed. Albert B. Friedman (New York: Viking, 1956).

18. Dr. Frank M. Keller quoted in Snowden Carter, "Veteran Veterinarian," *Turf and Sport Digest,* February 1962, p. 13.

19. David Alexander, *A Sound of Horses* (Indianapolis, Kansas City, and New York: Bobbs-Merrill, 1966), p. 227.

20. John H. Clark, *Trader Clark: Six Decades of Racing Lore* (Lexington, Ky.: Thoroughbred Publications, Inc., 1991), p. 214.

21. "Dope," *The Blood-Horse,* Jan. 24, 1931, letter to the editor by "Roamer" (turf writer Neil Newman), p. 134.

22. "Belmont to Be Run Today," *New York Times,* June 11, 1919.

23. "Sir Barton Only Gallops to Win Belmont Stakes," *New York Herald,* June 12, 1919.

24. "Sir Barton Easily Wins the Belmont," *New York Times,* June 12, 1919.

25. Ibid.

26. "Sir Barton Only Gallops to Win Belmont Stakes," *New York Herald,* June 12, 1919.

27. "Sir Barton Easily Wins the Belmont," *New York Times,* June 12, 1919.

28. "Sir Barton Only Gallops to Win Belmont Stakes," *New York Herald,* June 12, 1919.

29. Dan Lyons, "Johnny Loftus is Conceded to Be Best Rider on Track To-Day," *New York Evening Mail,* June 17, 1919.

30. Ibid.

31. Ibid.

32. "Purchase Defeats Eternal; Loftus Peer of the Riders," *Daily Racing Form,* June 20, 1919.

33. Lyons, "Johnny Loftus is Conceded to Be Best Rider on Track To-Day."

34. King, "Man o' War Takes Keene Memorial."

35. Hervey, "The Turf Career of Man o' War."

36. Later reports would claim that Man o' War, while preparing for the Youthful Stakes, worked five furlongs one afternoon in track-record time. Evidence to support or refute this story did not appear in *Daily Racing Form* or other racing publications during 1919. However, the following spring, Feustel said, "Once he worked five eighths at Jamaica with 133 pounds up in :58 2/5, a whole second better than the track record" ("Man o' War's First Race: Will Make His Three-Year-Old Debut in Rich Preakness; His Trainer Reveals Some Stable Secrets—Glen Riddle Farm Prospects for 1920," *Daily Racing Form,* March 6, 1920).

37. Ed Curley, "Man-o'-War Wins Youthful; Naturalist Captures Stake," *New York American,* June 22, 1919.

38. Henry V. King, "Man o' War Is Easy Victor in the Youthful." *New York Morning Sun,* June 22, 1919.

39. *Daily Racing Form* chart, the Youthful Stakes (Third Race at Jamaica), June 21, 1919.

40. "Naturalist First in Feature Race," *New York Herald,* June 22, 1919.

41. "Hoofbeats," *New York Times,* June 23, 1919.

42. "Naturalist First in Feature Race," *New York Herald,* June 22, 1919.

43. "Man O'War [*sic*] Turns a Regular Somersault," *New York Morning Sun,* June 24, 1919.

44. *New York Morning World,* June 24, 1919.

45. Henry V. King, "Man o' War Is Not an 'Excuse' Horse," *New York Morning Sun,* October 5, 1919.

46. Ibid.

47. Beckwith, *Step and Go Together,* p. 59.

48. "Our Readers Write Us," letter from Louis Feustel, *Turf and Sport Digest,* February 1962.

49. "Current Notes of the Turf," *Daily Racing Form,* June 28, 1919.

50. Cited in Hervey, "Turf Career of Man o' War."

6. PRICKLY HEAT

1. Fifteen and a half hands is written 15.2 and spoken as "fifteen two." Thoroughbred racehorses usually range from about 15.1 to 17 hands, with 15.3 hands considered a medium-size horse and above 16 hands considered a tall horse.

2. *Daily Racing Form* chart: Tremont Stakes (Third Race at Aqueduct), July 5, 1919.

3. "Trompe La Mort Again Home First," *New York Times,* July 6, 1919.

4. John Hervey, "Turf Career of Man o' War," unpublished manuscript (1933) later serialized by *Horse* magazine; available through the National Sporting Library (Middleburg, Virginia).

5. The first published mention I have found of Man o' War as "Big Red" comes from "S. D. Riddle's Man o' War Enjoying a Well-Earned Vacation at Owner's Maryland Farm; The 1919 Juvenile Champion and His Peculiarities and the Stable's Favorite," *Daily Racing Form,* November 30, 1919. The article states, " 'Big Red,' as he is known at home, or Man o' War to the public, is doing well in his vacation quarters at Mr. S. D. Riddle's farm at Berlin, Maryland." It is notable that this publication circulated among racing aficionados rather than the general public.

6. Henry V. King, "Loftus Is Refused a License to Ride," *The Sun and New York Herald,* March 18, 1920.

7. "R. T. Wilson's Colts Run One, Two . . . ," *New York Herald,* August 3, 1917.

8. "Negro Jockeys Shut Out," *New York Times,* July 29, 1900.

9. "Sir Barton Faster Than Ormonde," *Daily Racing Form,* July 2, 1919.

10. "Great Sir Barton Bows to Purchase," *New York Times,* July 11, 1919.

11. "Purchase Beats Sir Barton: J. K. L. Ross' Colt Suffers First Defeat as a Three-Year-Old; Winner Favored by Weight and Track Condition . . . ," *Daily Racing Form,* July 11, 1919.

12. W. S. Vosburgh, *Thoroughbred Types, 1900–1925* (New York: privately printed, 1926), p. 98.

13. "Racing," *The Saratogian,* July 18, 1919.

14. "Order Race Rerun After Odd Episode," *New York Times,* July 18, 1919.

15. "Loftus Admits Bad Ride," *New York Times,* July 19, 1919.

16. "Loftus May Ride Again," *New York Times,* April 4, 1919.

17. "Racing," *The Saratogian,* July 24, 1919.

18. *Daily Racing Form* chart (First Race at Empire City), July 22, 1919.

19. Ibid.

20. "Racing," *The Saratogian,* July 24, 1919.

21. "Report Masda, Beck and Call Cases," *Daily Racing Form,* July 27, 1919.

22. George Daley, "Comment on Sports," *New York World,* July 28, 1919.

23. "Comment on Current Events in Sports," *New York Times,* July 28, 1919.

24. G. F. T. Ryall, "More Surprises at Empire City Track," *New York World,* July 31, 1919.

25. Daley, "Comment on Sports."

26. "Miss Jemima Gets Laurels in Debut," *New York Times,* July 27, 1919.

27. Ibid.

28. Red Smith, *Strawberries in the Wintertime; The Sporting World of Red Smith* (New York: Quadrangle/the New York Times Book Co., 1974), p. 145.

29. Thomas C. Luther, *The Luther Trio Round the World, 1927–28* (Troy, New York: 1928), p. 9.

30. "Racing Opens Three Weeks From Tomorrow," *The Saratogian,* July 10, 1919.

31. "Man o' War Has Yet to Feel Whip: Samuel Riddle's Unbeaten Two-Year-Old Has Won All His Races Without Punishment," *Daily Racing Form,* July 15, 1919.

7. RUNNIN' FOOLS

1. "Man o' War Has Yet to Feel Whip: Samuel Riddle's Unbeaten Two-Year-Old Has Won All His Races Without Punishment," *Daily Racing Form,* July 15, 1919.

2. Peter Chew, *The Kentucky Derby: The First 100 Years* (Boston: Houghton Mifflin, 1974), p. 42.

3. Samuel C. Hildreth and James R. Crowell, *The Spell of the Turf* (Philadelphia and London: J. B. Lippincott, 1926), p. 178.

4. Joe H. Palmer, *American Race Horses, 1947* (N.p.: Sagamore Press, 1948), p. 20.

5. "Cudgel Will Not Be Ready for Handicap," *The Saratogian,* July 28, 1919.

6. "2,200 Horses Now at Saratoga Track," *The Saratogian,* July 30, 1919.

7. "Milkmaid Wins Historic Kenner . . . ," *New York Herald,* August 3, 1919.

8. Ibid.

9. "Man o' War Heads Fine Field at Spa," *New York Times,* August 3, 1919.

10. Ibid.

11. "Milkmaid Wins Historic Kenner . . . ," *New York Herald,* August 3, 1919.

12. *Daily Racing Form* chart, United States Hotel Stakes (Third Race at Saratoga), August 2, 1919.

13. "Man o' War Heads Fine Field at Spa," *New York Times,* August 3, 1919.

14. Henry V. King, "Man o' War Is Winner of U.S. Hotel Stakes," *New York Morning Sun,* August 3, 1919.

15. Ibid.

16. "Man o' War Heads Fine Field at Spa," *New York Times,* August 3, 1919.

17. George Daley, "Man o' War Gets a Bust and Wins Again," *New York World,* August 3, 1919.

18. Ibid.

19. "Valor Runs Mile . . . ," *New York Herald,* August 5, 1919.

20. "2,200 Horses Now at Saratoga Track," *The Saratogian,* July 30, 1919.

21. Henry V. King, "Man o' War Is Not an 'Excuse' Horse," *New York Morning Sun,* October 5, 1919.

22. Charles Hatton, "Frank Loftus Recalls Halcyon Days with Great Man o' War: Big Red's Groom Now Serves in Some Capacity for Nerud, Gallant Man's Conditioner," *Daily Racing Form,* September 17, 1958. Frank Loftus did not specify what he used to protect Man o' War's hooves from the biting. A logical possibility would be "bell boots"—rubber coverings that stretch over the top of the hooves and stay in place while the horse moves around.

23. Ibid.

24. The so-called "check ligament" behind the knee keeps a sleeping horse from falling down.

25. *Hoofprints of the Century: Excerpts from America's Oldest Journal of Horse Racing and Breeding, the Thoroughbred Record, and Its Predecessor Publications, the Livestock Record and Kentucky Live Stock Record,* as compiled and annotated by William Robertson (covering 1875–1919 and 1966–1974) and Dan Farley (1920–1965); material published by *The Thoroughbred Record,* January 4, 1979.

26. "Sun Briar Wins Champlain Handicap . . . ," *New York Herald,* August 10, 1919.

27. Ibid.

28. "Sun Briar Races to Track Record," *New York Times,* August 10, 1919.

29. Ibid.

30. "Exile," "The Saratoga Racing," *The Thoroughbred Record,* August 16, 1919, p. 75.

31. "Golden Broom or Man o' War Best?" *New York Herald,* August 11, 1919.

32. Ibid.

33. Ibid.

34. "Tempting Racing Program This Week," *The Saratogian,* August 11, 1919.

35. "Workouts at Saratoga," *Daily Racing Form,* August 11, 1919. The *New York Herald* (August 12, 1919) reported 1:12 2/5.

36. According to the *New York Herald* (August 12, 1919), Man o' War breezed over a Saratoga track that was in "perfect condition."

37. "Selling Races Costly to Owners," *New York Herald,* August 13, 1919.

38. "Big Crowd for Sanford Memorial," *The Saratogian,* August 13, 1919.

8. THE SANFORD

1. "Jockey Willie Knapp Dies at 84; Defeated Man o' War Aboard Upset," newspaper unknown, Oct. 26, 1972.

2. "Man o' War Best, but Loses Race," *The Saratogian,* August 14, 1919.

3. White Sulphur Spring Hotel's guest register, August 13–15, 1919; Historical Society of Saratoga Springs.

4. "New Starting Gate Is Impracticable," *New York Times,* December 2, 1923. Referring to some "horses [being] unnaturally nervous"—in other words, hop horses—Cassidy continued: "No machine that I have known of can handle the latter as well as a man on the track, as it is necessary often to change the positions of the horses from their original post positions. Such horses would not stand in any box-like contrivance any more than they would stand still on an open track."

5. Charles Hatton, "Delaware Park: Harmonizing Horse to Beat in Sussex Handicap Today," *Daily Racing Form,* July 1, 1961. Glen Riddle Farm exercise rider Clyde Gordon told Hatton that "Loftus said Riddle had instructed him not to try to take the lead from Golden Broom for three furlongs or so."

6. "Sanford Memorial Is Won by Upset," *New York Times,* August 14, 1919.

7. Dunstan, Nelson, "Redcoats, Rascals and Runaways," *Turf and Sport Digest,* July 1935 p. 59. Dunstan observed, "Mars Cassidy had one trick that every jockey on the New York tracks keenly awaited. Just before he pressed the release button, he held behind his back, he would bend his knee, and to the riders that was the 'give-away.' But shrewd old Mars soon knew the jockeys knew, and ever so often would bend the knee and then slap a fine on every rider that bolted or endeavored to 'beat the gate.' And there has never been anything so conductive to good riding habits as a fine for misbehavior. Blaming it on the horse was 'out' with Mars."

8. "Willie Knapp Dead; Hall of Fame Jockey," newspaper unknown, October 26, 1972.

9. Hatton, "Delaware Park: Harmonizing Horse to Beat in Sussex Handicap Today."

10. Joe H. Palmer, *American Race Horses, 1947* (N.p.: Sagamore Press, 1948), p. 21.

11. "Biggest Upset of Season When Upset Beats Man o' War and Golden Broom in Fluky Race for Sanford Memorial at Saratoga," *New York Herald,* August 14, 1919.

12. David Alexander, *A Sound of Horses* (Indianapolis, Kansas City, and New York: Bobbs-Merrill, 1966), p. 126.

13. "Jockey Willie Knapp Dies at 84; Defeated Man o' War Aboard Upset," source unknown, October 26, 1972.

14. Alexander, *A Sound of Horses,* p. 126.

15. "Jockey Willie Knapp Dies at 84; Defeated Man o' War Aboard Upset," source unknown, October 26, 1972.

16. "Biggest Upset of Season When Upset Beats Man o' War and Golden Broom in Fluky Race for Sanford Memorial at Saratoga," *New York Herald,* August 14, 1919.

17. Sports headlines predating the 1919 Sanford Memorial prove that the term *upset* for an unexpected result did not originate with Upset beating Man o' War. For example: "Day of Upsets at Belmont Park: Foul Riding Causes Two Jockeys to Fall, a 2 to 7 Favorite Is Beaten and a Winner Disqualified," *New York Herald,* September 7, 1918; and, "Upsets at Jefferson Park," *Daily Racing Form,* March 16, 1919.

18. "Man o' War's First Race: Will Make His Three-Year-Old Debut in Rich Preakness; His Trainer Reveals Some Stable Secrets—Glen Riddle Farm Prospects for 1920," *Daily Racing Form,* March 6, 1920. Feustel said, "The day he was beaten by Upset he ran three quarters of a mile in 1:10 1/5, being timed separately by myself."

19. "Downcast Over Man o' War's Defeat: Jockey Loftus Tells How the Great Colt Was Beaten in Sanford Memorial Stakes," *Daily Racing Form,* August 16, 1919.

20. Ibid.

21. Ibid.

22. Ibid.

23. Ibid.

24. Lou DeFichy, "Bitter Memories Haunt Man o' War Jock," *Horsemen's Journal,* October 1965, p. 39. The bookmaker quoted in this article remained anonymous.

25. "Sanford Memorial Is Won by Upset," *New York Times,* August 14, 1919.

26. George Daley, "Man o' War Stands Alone Among the Two-Year-Olds," *New York World,* August 18, 1919.

27. "Downcast Over Man o' War's Defeat: Jockey Loftus Tells How the Great Colt Was Beaten in Sanford Memorial Stakes," *Daily Racing Form,* August 16, 1919.

28. Wayne Capps, "Did the Mobsters Get Man o' War Beaten?" *Turf and Sport Digest,* June 1981, p. 22.

29. Ibid.

30. Ibid.

31. Ibid.

32. J. K. M. Ross, *Boots and Saddles: The Story of the Fabulous Ross Stable in the Golden Days of Racing* (New York: E. P. Dutton, 1956), pp. 128–129.

33. Bill Corum, "Sports," *New York Journal -American,* January 9, 1951.

9. BUTTERFLIES

1. "Record Crowd Enjoys Running of Famous Classics at Spa," *New York Herald,* August 17, 1919. In his memoir, J. K. M. Ross wrote that his father had bought Constancy in June 1919, but *Daily Racing Form* charts show that A. B. Hancock owned her during her first two races, on July 1 and July 4 of that year—a fact noted

in the *Herald* article cited above. Jim Ross also described a secret pre-Spinaway workout in which Constancy ran four furlongs in a then unearthly :44 3/5. Since it is unclear whether or not this was part of the private six-furlong workout reported by the *Herald* after the Spinaway, I relied on the contemporary *Herald* report in my narrative for simplicity's sake.

2. J. K. M. Ross, *Boots and Saddles: The Story of the Fabulous Ross Stable in the Golden Days of Racing* (New York: E. P. Dutton, 1956), p. 170.

3. "Hoofbeats of the Racers," *New York Times,* August 19, 1919.

4. "Many Features of This Week's Racing," *The Saratogian,* August 18, 1919.

5. Jimmy "Goggles" McCoy was known for wearing goggles during races as early as 1928, but his innovation did not spread widely until the 1930s. At first, although racetrack stewards determined that McCoy's goggles were safe, most other jockeys thought that the eyewear would impair their field of vision.

6. "Grab Bag Handicap Romp for Blazes," *New York Times,* August 20, 1919.

7. Ed Curley, "3 to 5 Shot Fails at Saratoga," *New York American,* August 23, 1919.

8. *Daily Racing Form* chart (Third Race at Saratoga), August 5, 1919.

9. Ibid.

10. George Daley, "Loftus at Best and Worst in Two Races," *New York World,* August 23, 1919.

11. Curley, "3 to 5 Shot Fails at Saratoga."

12. Daley, "Loftus at Best and Worst in Two Races."

13. David Alexander, *A Sound of Horses* (Indianapolis, Kansas City, and New York: Bobbs-Merrill, 1966), p. 274.

14. Henry V. King, "Man o' War Is Crowned King of Juveniles," *New York Morning Sun,* August 24, 1919.

15. Ibid.

16. "Man o' War Takes Grand Union Hotel Stakes, with Upset Second," *New York Times,* August 24, 1919.

17. "Man o' War Easily Proves His Superiority . . . ," *New York Herald,* August 24, 1919.

18. Ibid.

19. J. L. Dempsey, "Crack Horses in Victory; Man o' War Proves Himself Our Best Two-Year-Old," *Daily Racing Form,* August 24, 1919.

20. "Man o' War Takes Grand Union Hotel Stakes, With Upset Second," *New York Times,* August 24, 1919.

21. Ibid.

22. "Man o' War Easily Proves His Superiority . . . ," *New York Herald,* August 24, 1919.

23. "S. D. Riddle's Man o' War Enjoying a Well-Earned Vacation at Owner's Maryland Farm; The 1919 Juvenile Champion and His Peculiarities and the Stable's Favorite," *Daily Racing Form,* November 30, 1919.

24. "Day of Dull Racing at Saratoga Springs," *New York World,* August 26, 1919.

25. Ibid.

26. "$300,000 for Purchase. S. C. Hildreth Declines to Sell Great Colt for Record Sum," *New York Times*, August 29, 1919.

27. Ibid.

28. Ibid.

29. "Man o' War Takes Grand Union Hotel Stakes, With Upset Second," *New York Times*, August 24, 1919.

30. "Purchase Romps Off with Huron Under 134 Lbs.," *New York Herald*, August 27, 1919.

31. "Hundred-to-One Shot Wins for Father Bill," *New York World*, August 29, 1919.

32. John Hervey, "The Turf Career of Man o' War," unpublished manuscript (1933) later serialized by *Horse* magazine; available through the National Sporting Library (Middleburg, Virginia).

33. Henry V. King, "Man o' War Is Winner of the Hopeful Stake," *New York Morning Sun*, August 30, 1919.

34. Ibid.

35. Ibid.

36. J. L. Dempsey, "Saratoga Meeting Closes: Man o' War Takes the Rich Hopeful Stakes Cantering; Exterminator Takes the Measure of Purchase in the Saratoga Cup Without Much Trouble," *Daily Racing Form*, August 31, 1919.

37. Hervey, "The Turf Career of Man o' War."

38. Ross, *Boots and Saddles*, p. 172.

39. "Two-Year-Old King Takes Rich Stakes," *New York Times*, August 31, 1919.

40. "Man o' War Wins the $30,000 Hopeful Stakes . . . ," *New York Herald*, August 31, 1919.

41. King, "Man o' War Is Winner of the Hopeful Stake."

42. Ibid.

43. Hervey, "The Turf Career of Man o' War."

44. George Daley, "Belmont Park to Open To-Day for Fall Meeting," *New York World*, September 1, 1919.

45. "Man o' War Wins the $30,000 Hopeful Stakes . . . ," *New York Herald*, August 31, 1919.

46. "Some Post Saratoga Reflections: Experts Still Trying to Tell Why Exterminator Defeated Purchase," *Daily Racing Form*, September 2, 1919.

10. RIGHT WAY, WRONG WAY

1. George Daley, "Man o' War Races to Highest Fame in the Futurity," *New York World*, September 14, 1919.

2. Eleanor Robson Belmont, *The Fabric of Memory* (New York: Farrar, Straus and Cudahy, 1957), p. 94.

3. "Man o' War, 127 Pounds Up, Breezes Home with $27,000 Futurity," *New York Herald*, September 14, 1919.

4. Ed Curley, "[First part of headline missing] J.P. Grier 3 Lengths Back," *New York American,* September 14, 1919.

5. "Man o' War, 127 Pounds Up, Breezes Home with $27,000 Futurity," *New York Herald,* September 14, 1919.

6. John Hervey, "The Turf Career of Man o' War," unpublished manuscript (1933) later serialized by *Horse* magazine; available through the National Sporting Library (Middleburg, Virginia).

7. "Man o' War Wins Rich Futurity," *New York Times,* September 14, 1919.

8. Ibid.

9. Daley, "Man o' War Races to Highest Fame in the Futurity."

10. Hervey, "The Turf Career of Man o' War."

11. Daley, "Man o' War Races to Highest Fame in the Futurity."

12. "Man o' War Wins Rich Futurity," *New York Times,* September 14, 1919.

13. "Man o' War Wins The Futurity," *The Thoroughbred Record,* September 20, 1919, p. 134.

14. Henry V. King, "Rich Futurity Is Won Easily by Man o' War," *New York Morning Sun,* September 14, 1919.

15. "Man o' War Wins Historic Futurity in Commanding Style Before 30,000 at Belmont," *New York Tribune,* September 14, 1919.

16. Daley, "Man o' War Races to Highest Fame in the Futurity."

17. "Man o' War Wins Historic Futurity in Commanding Style Before 30,000 at Belmont," *New York Tribune,* September 14, 1919.

18. Ibid.

19. "Man o' War Wins the Futurity," *The Thoroughbred Record,* September 20, 1919, p. 134.

20. Daley, "Man o' War Races to Highest Fame in the Futurity."

21. Ibid.

22. Ibid.

23. Ibid.

24. Henry V. King, "Man o' War Is Not an 'Excuse' Horse," *New York Morning Sun,* October 5, 1919.

25. Daley, "Man o' War Races to Highest Fame in the Futurity."

26. King, "Rich Futurity Is Won Easily by Man o' War."

27. Curley, "[First part of headline missing]; J.P. Grier 3 Lengths Back."

28. King, "Rich Futurity Is Won Easily by Man o' War."

29. Letter from August Belmont, Jr., to Miss Nora Cloherty, September 17, 1919; Belmont Family Papers, Rare Book and Manuscript Library, Columbia University.

30. "Belmont Tells Why He Put Ban on Rider," *New York Times,* October 10, 1908.

31. Ibid.

32. "Stable Boy Failed to Salute Belmont," *New York Times,* October 9, 1908.

33. "Belmont Tells Why He Put Ban on Rider," *New York Times,* October 10, 1908.

34. Belmont, *The Fabric of Memory,* p. 99. Mrs. Belmont wrote, "As a vice president

of the National Civic Federation, he was an active member of the committee which in 1909 secured the passage of the Workmen's Compensation bill for New York State."

35. "Ross Makes Sweep at Havre de Grace," *New York Times,* September 14, 1919.
36. "Jockey Is Killed at Havre de Grace," *New York Times,* September 27, 1919.
37. "Cudgel Is a Winner," *New York Times,* September 28, 1919.

11. DONE WITH MIRRORS

1. "S. D. Riddle's Man o' War Enjoying a Well-Earned Vacation at Owner's Maryland Farm; The 1919 Juvenile Champion and His Peculiarities and the Stable's Favorite," *Daily Racing Form,* November 30, 1919.
2. Fair Play sired both Mad Hatter and Man o' War. Furthermore, Mad Hatter's dam, Madcap—like Red's dam, Mahubah—was a daughter of *Rock Sand.
3. "Sir Barton Wins Maryland Handicap," *The Thoroughbred Record,* October 11, 1919, p. 175.
4. "Mad Hatter Wins Latonia Stakes," *New York Times,* October 12, 1919.
5. "Mad Hatter Peer of Any 3-Year-Old, Says Hildreth," *Washington Post,* October 19, 1919.
6. Colin, "Ahead of the Hoofbeats," *Washington Post,* November 5, 1919.
7. "Loftus Is Refused a License to Ride," *The Sun and New York Herald,* March 18, 1920.
8. Older stakes winners Lucullite and The Porter, plus his distinguished stablemate Billy Kelly.
9. *Daily Racing Form* chart (Fourth Race at Pimlico), November 7, 1919.
10. Harry N. Price, "Sir Barton Runs Improved Race in Winning Serial," *Washington Post,* November 8, 1919.
11. "Jockey J. Loftus Refused a License," *Daily Racing Form,* March 18, 1920. Loftus rode his final two races at Pimlico on Thursday, November 6, 1919: finishing fifth with the Ross filly His Choice in the $5,000-added Walden Stakes, then eighth of ten starters with Mrs. F. Ambrose Clark's The Decision in the Roland Park Claiming Handicap.
12. Lally Collyer, "Loftus Gets Offer of $25,000 a Year to Ride for an Indian Rajah," newspaper and exact date unknown, autumn 1919 (found in Johnny Loftus Boosting and Marching Club scrapbook, presented to Loftus by Ed Curley, Bill Farnsworth, and Moe Druck and passed down to his son and grandson).
13. "Johnnie Loftus, America's Premier Jockey, Is Denied a License by Turf Body," *New York Evening Telegram,* spring 1920 (found in Johnny Loftus Boosting and Marching Club scrapbook). The *New York Times* reported Riddle's 1920 "first call" salary to Loftus as $13,000. In any case, this did not include several thousand dollars that Morton L. Schwartz would have paid for second call, or any fees that Loftus could have earned for freelance rides.

14. "Loftus Is Refused a License to Ride," *The Sun and New York Herald,* March 18, 1920.

15. "Loftus Signs to Ride for Riddle Stable," *New York American,* November 25, 1919.

16. "Loftus Is Refused a License to Ride," *The Sun and New York Herald,* March 18, 1920.

17. "Jockey Knapp Returns to New York," *Daily Racing Form,* March 6, 1920.

18. "George Daley's Sport Talk: More Open Methods Needed in Both Racing and Baseball," *New York World,* March 22, 1920.

19. "Comment on Current Events in Sports. The Unseating of Loftus," *New York Times,* March 22, 1920.

20. James P. Sinnott, "Skipper Sinnott's Column," newspaper unknown, spring 1920 (found in Johnny Loftus Boosting and Marching Club scrapbook).

21. "George Daley's Sport Talk: More Open Methods Needed in Both Racing and Baseball."

22. G. F. T. Ryall, "Racing Stewards Curb an Evil in Selling Events," *New York World,* April 9, 1920.

23. "License Is Denied to Jockey Knapp," *New York Times,* April 9, 1920.

24. "Johnnie Loftus, America's Premier Jockey, Is Denied a License by Turf Body," *New York Evening Telegram,* spring 1920.

25. O'Neil Sevier, "Johnny Loftus's Recent Work in Saddle Arouses Unfavorable Comment at Saratoga," newspaper unknown (dateline Saratoga Springs, August 26, 1919; found in Johnny Loftus Boosting and Marching Club scrapbook).

26. "Jockey Loftus Is Reinstated," newspaper unknown, August 22, 1918.

27. George Daley, "Johnny Loftus Case Still Hanging Fire," *New York Morning World,* July 19, 1919.

28. Bert E. Collyer, "Bedwell Accuses Hildreth of Influencing Loftus; Asserts Sam Played Devious Parts in Sir Barton's Defeat by Mad Hatter," *Collyer's Eye,* Chicago, November 29, 1919 (dateline New Orleans, Louisiana, November 28).

29. Price, "Sir Barton Runs Improved Race in Winning Serial."

30. Ed Curley, "Is Famous Sir Barton 'Hop Colt'?" *New York American,* spring 1920 (exact day unknown; found in Johnny Loftus Boosting and Marching Club scrapbook).

31. Ibid.

32. "10 Gamblers Barred from Track Clubhouse," *Washington Post,* May 16, 1920.

12. UP FOR GRABS

1. "Ambitious Plans for Man o' War," *New York Times,* January 25, 1920.

2. "No Early Racing for Man o' War," *Daily Racing Form,* February 8, 1920.

3. Wayne Capps, "The Place Where Louie Dwelled," *The Thoroughbred Record,* August 15, 1970, p. 671.

4. Man o' War may have been off form in early February, when Riddle nixed the Derby and *Daily Racing Form* ("No Early Racing for Man o' War," February 8, 1920) also explained that Red wouldn't be rushed to make the Preakness.

5. Louis Feustel, as told to Charles Hatton, "Man o' War as I Knew Him," *Daily Running Horse* (New York, New York), December 27, 1932.

6. Walter Jeffords lost a two-year-old filly named Eithne; see *The Thoroughbred Record,* April 24, 1920, p. 307.

7. "Golden Broom Shows His Speed," *Daily Racing Form,* April 13, 1920.

8. "Turf Notes," *The Thoroughbred Record,* April 17, 1920, p. 292.

9. "Sir Barton and Billy Kelly Ready," *Daily Racing Form,* April 17, 1920.

10. "Billy Kelly . . . Scores Handily in the Bel Air Handicap," *Washington Post,* April 20, 1920.

11. "Wildair Displays Derby Form in Mud," *The Sun and New York Herald,* April 28, 1920.

12. "Saratoga Favorites Day," *Daily Racing Form,* August 4, 1920.

13. The race now known as the Bluegrass Stakes originally was run at the old Lexington Association track, enveloped by downtown Lexington, Kentucky. It later moved to Keeneland Race Course on the outskirts of that city, where it remains a major Kentucky Derby prep.

14. "Paul Jones Wins Kentucky Derby," *New York Times,* May 9, 1920.

15. "Man o' War's First Race: Will Make His Three-Year-Old Debut in Rich Preakness; His Trainer Reveals Some Stable Secrets—Glen Riddle Farm Prospects for 1920," *Daily Racing Form,* March 6, 1920.

16. "Trainers Pick Man o' War as Winner of Preakness," *Washington Post,* May 16, 1920.

17. Feustel, as told to Hatton, "Man o' War as I Knew Him."

18. Captain Williams, turf editor of the *New York Telegraph,* quoted in John Hervey "The Turf Career of Man o' War," unpublished manuscript (1933) later serialized by *Horse* magazine; available through the National Sporting Library (Middleburg, Virginia).

19. "Man o' War a Superb Looking Horse: Mr. Riddle's Great Three-Year-Old Cynosure of All Eyes at Belmont Park," *Daily Racing Form,* May 7, 1920.

20. Hervey, "The Turf Career of Man o' War."

21. Some clockers had caught him a bit faster. In "High Lights and Shadows in All Spheres of Sport," *New York Herald,* May 11, 1920, columnist "Daniel" wrote, ". . . Man o' War's tiring in the final furlong of his mile trial in 1:40 3-5 at Belmont Park last Saturday has raised some question as to his being able to go the route."

22. "Mighty Man o' War Fast Tuning Up," *Daily Racing Form,* May 15, 1920.

23. "Man o' War Is Trim for The Preakness at Pimlico May 18," *New York Times,* May 12, 1920.

24. "Sponge Workers Get Busy at Pimlico," *Washington Post,* May 15, 1920.

25. "Match Race to Be Man o' War's Last," *New York Times*, October 3, 1920.

26. "Man O' War [*sic*] at Pimlico," *Baltimore Sun*, May 14, 1920.

27. "Record Crowd of 19,340 Persons Witness Races at Old Pimlico," *Baltimore Sun*, May 16, 1920.

28. Ibid.

29. "Trainers Pick Man o' War as Winner of Preakness," *Washington Post*, May 16, 1920.

30. "Man o' War is a Probable 4 to 5 Favorite in Event," *Washington Post*, May 18, 1920.

31. "Current Notes of the Turf," *Daily Racing Form*, March 10, 1920. Mentioning "windows of the stable," Feustel may have been referring to the wide enclosed aisle that surrounded the stalls at Man o' War's Berlin barn. Riders may have been given a leg up indoors and/or may have walked and jogged horses around this covered shed row on inclement days.

32. C. Edward Sparrow, " 'Tis Preakness Day; It's to Marylanders What Derby Is to Kentuckians," *Baltimore Sun*, May 18, 1920.

33. Dr. Frederick C. Luebke. "Three Centuries of Germans in America" (*American Studies Newsletter* 1, September 1983), http://usa.usembassy.de/etexts/ga-asn0983Luebke.htm (accessed June 6, 2005).

34. Advertisement for White Owl cigars, cited in "History of Advertising in the Early 20th Century" at http://www.trivia-library.com; reproduced by permission from David Wallechinsky and Irving Wallace, *The People's Almanac* series (1975–1981).

35. Jimmy Powers, "C. Kummer: Man-O-War's Old Jockey Succumbs to Pneumonia," newspaper and exact date, unknown (found in Clarence Kummer file at National Museum of Racing and Hall of Fame, Saratoga Springs, New York).

36. "O'Neil Sevier's Maryland Gossip," *The Thoroughbred Record*, April 20, 1918, p. 216.

37. B. K. Beckwith, *Step and Go Together: The World of Horses and Horsemanship* (South Brunswick, N.J., and New York: A. S. Barnes and Co., 1967), p. 59.

38. On October 24, 1877, Parole beat Ten Broeck and Tom Ochiltree in a special contest so hotly anticipated that Congress actually adjourned for the day so that its members could travel from Washington, D.C., to Baltimore to watch it.

39. John Hervey, "The Turf Career of Man o' War," unpublished manuscript (1933) later serialized by *Horse* magazine; available through the National Sporting Library (Middleburg, Virginia).

40. Ibid.

41. Samuel D. Riddle, as told to Neil Newman, "From Man o' War to War Admiral," *Turf and Sport Digest*, June 1938, p. 16.

42. Hervey, "The Turf Career of Man o' War."

43. Quoted in ibid.

44. "Man o' War Is Easy Victor in the Preakness," *The Sun and New York Herald*, May 19, 1920.

45. Ibid.
46. Quoted in Hervey, "The Turf Career of Man o' War."
47. "Record Throng Sees Preakness at Pimlico," *Baltimore Sun,* May 19, 1920.
48. Ibid.
49. Quoted in Hervey, "The Turf Career of Man o' War."
50. "Man o' War Is Easy Victor in the Preakness," *The Sun and New York Herald,* May 19, 1920.
51. Henry V. King "Alcatraz First in Stake at Jamaica," *The Sun and New York Herald,* May 20, 1920.
52. Ibid.
53. Henry V. King, "Alibi Races Like High Class Horse," *The Sun and New York Herald,* May 22, 1920.
54. "Man o' War Is Under Special Bodyguards Night and Day," *New York Times,* May 20, 1920.
55. "Campaign Plans for Man o' War: Will Try Conclusions with the Handicap Division in the Autumn," *Daily Racing Form,* May 26, 1920.
56. Ibid.
57. Ibid.

13. SPEED MIRACLES BEGIN

1. Roger Longrigg, *The History of Horse Racing* (New York: Stein and Day, 1972), p. 55.
2. Ibid.
3. Quoted in John Hervey, "The Turf Career of Man o' War," unpublished manuscript (1933) later serialized by *Horse* magazine; available through the National Sporting Library (Middleburg, Virginia).
4. *Daily Racing Form* chart, Metropolitan Handicap (Fourth Race at Belmont Park), May 24, 1920.
5. Daniel, "High Lights and Shadows in All Spheres of Sport," *The Sun and New York Herald,* May 29, 1920.
6. "Man o' War Sets Record for Mile," *New York Times,* May 30, 1920.
7. Henry V. King, "Man o' War an Easy Victor in Withers Stake," *The Sun and New York Herald,* May 30, 1920.
8. *Daily Racing Form* quoted in Hervey, "The Turf Career of Man o' War."
9. Ibid.
10. King, "Man o' War an Easy Victor in Withers Stake."
11. "Man o' War Sets Record For Mile," *New York Times,* May 30, 1920.
12. Ibid.
13. Ibid.
14. *Daily Racing Form* quoted in Hervey, "The Turf Career of Man o' War."
15. "Man o' War Sets Record for Mile," *New York Times,* May 30, 1920.

16. King, "Man o' War an Easy Victor in Withers Stake."

17. W. J. Macbeth, "Man o' War Shatters World's Mile Record in Capturing the Withers at Belmont Park," *New York Tribune,* May 30, 1920.

18. "Man o' War's Marvelous Speed; Equaled Roseben's 7/8 Record," *Daily Racing Form,* June 3, 1920.

19. "Man o' War Sets Record for Mile," *New York Times,* May 30, 1920.

20. King, "Man o' War an Easy Victor in Withers Stake."

21. *Daily Racing Form* quoted in Hervey, "The Turf Career of Man o' War."

22. King, "Man o' War an Easy Victory in Withers Stake."

23. "Man o' War Sets Record for Mile," *New York Times,* May 30, 1920.

24. King, "Man o' War an Easy Victor in Withers Stake."

25. Ibid.

26. King, "Man o' War an Easy Victor in Withers Stake."

27. *Step and Go Together: The World of Horses and Horsemanship* (New York: A. S. Barnes and Co., 1967), p. 56.

28. Quoted in Hervey, "The Turf Career of Man o' War."

29. "Noted Sportsmen Stamp Man o' War as World's Greatest Thoroughbred," *The Sun and New York Herald,* May 30, 1920.

30. Ibid.

31. Ibid.

32. "Trainer James Rowe Will Try Again," *Daily Racing Form,* June 5, 1920.

33. Beckwith, *Step and Go Together,* p. 56.

34. Henry V. King, "Judges Place Wrong Horse Third at Belmont Park," *The Sun and New York Herald,* June 8, 1920.

35. Ibid.

36. Letter from August Belmont Jr., to Samuel D. Riddle, February 19, 1920; Belmont Family Papers, Rare Book and Manuscript Library, Columbia University.

37. "Names in Pedigrees: Hastings," *The Blood-Horse,* January 14, 1939, p. 65.

38. "Man o' War Under Colors Saturday: Vast Army of Thoroughbred Lovers to See Mr. Riddle's Champion Run in Belmont Stakes," *Daily Racing Form,* June 11, 1920.

39. *The Thoroughbred Record,* June 19, 1920 (story from June 13, 1920), p. 413.

40. W. J. Macbeth, "Man o' War, in Two-Horse Race, Shatters World's Record in Winning Belmont Stakes," *New York Tribune,* June 13, 1920.

41. Donnacona ran third to older horses in the one-mile Little Neck Handicap on Monday, June 7, and easily won a one-mile allowance race against fellow three-year-olds on Wednesday, June 9.

42. Macbeth, "Man o' War, in Two-Horse Race, Shatters World's Record in Winning Belmont Stakes."

43. Henry V. King, "Man o' War Makes World's Record . . . in Winning Belmont by 20 Lengths," *The Sun and New York Herald,* June 13, 1920.

44. "World Record Is Set by Man o' War," *New York Times,* June 13, 1920.

45. Macbeth, "Man o' War, in Two-Horse Race, Shatters World's Record in Winning Belmont Stakes."
46. "World Record Is Set by Man o' War," *New York Times,* June 13, 1920.
47. "Champion of Champions: Man o' War So Hailed After Brilliant Race for Belmont Stakes," *Daily Racing Form,* June 13, 1920.
48. "World Record Is Set by Man o' War," *New York Times,* June 13, 1920.
49. Daniel, "High Lights and Shadows in All Spheres of Sport."

14. BREATHER

1. Daniel, "High Lights and Shadows in All Spheres of Sport," *The Sun and New York Herald,* June 15, 1920.
2. John Hervey, "The Turf Career of Man o' War," unpublished manuscript (1933) later serialized by *Horse* magazine; available through the National Sporting Library (Middleburg, Virginia).
3. Charles Hatton, "Delaware Park: Harmonizing Horse to Beat in Sussex Handicap Today," *Daily Racing Form,* July 1, 1961.
4. Hervey, "The Turf Career of Man o' War."
5. "Ambitious Plans for Man o' War," *New York Times,* January 23, 1920.
6. "Man o' War Sets New Price Record," *New York Times,* June 23, 1920.
7. Henry V. King, "Man o' War Scores Another Victory," *The Sun and New York Herald,* June 23, 1920.
8. Ibid.
9. H. L. Fitzpatrick, "Timely Turf Topics Anent Aqueduct Meet: Personal Notes of Man o' War—How the Horse of the Season Conducts Himself," *Evening Post* (New York), June 28, 1920.
10. "Man o' War Sets New Price Record," *New York Times,* June 23, 1920.
11. Ibid.
12. Henry V. King, "Man o' War Scores Another Victory," *The Sun and New York Herald,* June 23, 1920.
13. "Man o' War Sets New Price Record," *New York Times,* June 23, 1920.
14. W. J. Macbeth, "Handicap Goes to Man o' War in Easy Canter," *New York Tribune,* June 23, 1920.
15. Daniel, "High Lights and Shadows in All Spheres of Sport."
16. "Man o' War Entered for Canadian Derby at Fort Erie," *Daily Racing Form,* June 10, 1920.
17. "Man o' War in the Canadian Derby," *Daily Racing Form,* June 27, 1920.

15. CRUCIBLE

1. Charles Hatton, "Delaware Park: Harmonizing Horse to Beat In Sussex Handicap Today," *Daily Racing Form,* July 1, 1961.

2. "John P. Grier Now Defies Man o' War," *New York Times,* July 7, 1920.

3. Henry V. King, "John P. Grier Gallops to Victory at Aqueduct," *The Sun and New York Herald,* July 7, 1920.

4. Ibid.

5. H. L. Fitzpatrick, "Aqueduct Near End of Meeting," *Evening Post* (New York), July 10, 1920. Ambrose rode Wildair to an eighth-place finish in Latonia's Independence Handicap; another Whitney horse, Dr. Clark, took the $17,950 first-place prize.

6. "John P. Grier Now Defies Man o' War," *New York Times,* July 7, 1920.

7. Fitzpatrick, "Aqueduct Near End of Meeting."

8. Abram S. Hewitt, "Sires Lines: Part XXXIX: Man o' War," *The Blood-Horse,* November 25, 1974, p. 5203.

9. King, "John P. Grier Gallops to Victory at Aqueduct."

10. Samuel D. Riddle, as told to Neil Newman, "From Man o' War to War Admiral," *Turf and Sport Digest,* June 1938, p. 14.

11. B. K. Beckwith, *Step and Go Together: The World of Horses and Horsemanship* (South Brunswick, N.J., and New York: A. S. Barnes and Co., 1967), p. 53.

12. Henry V. King, "Man o' War May Make a World's Record To-day," *The Sun and New York Herald,* July 10, 1920.

13. Daniel, "High Lights and Shadows in All Spheres of Sport," *The Sun and New York Herald,* July 9, 1920.

14. Riddle as told to Newman, "Man o' War to War Admiral," p. 17.

15. Beckwith, *Step and Go Together,* pp. 59–60.

16. Louis Feustel, as told to Charles Hatton, "Man o' War As I Knew Him," *Daily Running Horse* (New York, New York), December 31, 1932.

17. The *New York Times;* generally conservative in their racing reports, estimated that more than 25,000 persons attended the Dwyer. The more exuberant *Sun and New York Herald* said forty thousand, while the moderate *New York Tribune* said "more than thirty thousand." All sources describe the track as being jam-packed.

18. "New Mark Set by Man o' War Before 40,000," *The Sun and New York Herald,* July 11, 1920.

19. W. J. Macbeth, "Man o' War Eclipses World's Record for 1 1/8 Miles in Winning the Dwyer Stakes," *New York Tribune,* July 11, 1920.

20. "New Mark Set by Man o' War Before 40,000," *The Sun and New York Herald,* July 11, 1920.

21. Hewitt, "Sire Lines," p. 5203.

22. Walter S. Vosburgh, *Thoroughbred Racing in America, 1866–1921* (New York: privately printed by The Jockey Club, 1922). p. 241.

23. Horace Wade, "The Trainer Who Couldn't Destroy Man o' War," *National Police Gazette,* August 1969. p. 24.

24. Macbeth, "Man o' War Eclipses World's Record for 1 1/8 Miles in Winning the Dwyer Stakes." Although many stories published in later years would describe

John P. Grier as "little," it may be that his stature seemed to shrink after Man o' War beat him. Right after the Dwyer, another reporter wrote, "Both colts are of the Statuesque sort, but in every detail of conformation Man o' War is just a trifle larger than John P. Grier" (H. L. Fitzpatrick, "Man o' War Race Contest of Thrills," *Evening Post* [New York], July 12, 1920).

25. Fitzpatrick, "Man o' War Race Contest of Thrills."

26. "New Mark Set by Man o' War Before 40,000," *The Sun and New York Herald,* July 11, 1920.

27. "John P. Grier Now Defies Man o' War," *New York Times,* July 7, 1920.

28. "New Mark Set by Man o' War Before 40,000," *The Sun and New York Herald,* July 11, 1920.

29. Ibid.

30. Macbeth, "Man o' War Eclipses World's Record for 11/8 Miles in Winning the Dwyer Stakes."

31. "Man o' War Again Sets World Mark," *New York Times,* July 11, 1920.

32. Macbeth, "Man o' War Eclipses World's Record for 11/8 Miles in Winning the Dwyer Stakes."

33. Ibid.

34. C. J. Fitz Gerald, "Man O' War [*sic*], Turf Idol and Sire," *The Field Illustrated,* July 1925, p. 29.

35. John Hervey, "The Turf Career of Man o' War," unpublished manuscript (1933) later serialized by *Horse* magazine; available through the National Sporting Library (Middleburg, Virginia).

36. Fitzpatrick, "Man o' War Race Contest of Thrills."

37. "New Mark Set by Man o' War Before 40,000," *The Sun and New York Herald,* July 11, 1920.

38. About 390 yards—that is, 60 yards short of a quarter mile.

39. About 770 yards—that is, only one-sixteenth short of half a mile.

40. Hervey, "The Turf Career of Man o' War."

41. Macbeth, "Man o' War Eclipses World's Record for 11/8 Miles in Winning the Dwyer Stakes."

42. H. A. Buck, "A Few Notes on Names," *The Blood-Horse,* March 5, 1938, p. 444.

43. "New Mark Set by Man o' War Before 40,000," *The Sun and New York Herald,* July 11, 1920.

44. "When Man-o'-War Was Whipped," *Turf and Sport Digest* (originally published in May 1927; reprinted July–August 1975), as written exclusively for the N. T. D. by Jockey Clarence Kummer, p. 38.

45. Ibid.

46. "Man o' War Again Sets World Mark," *New York Times,* July 11, 1920.

47. "New Mark Set by Man o' War Before 40,000," *The Sun and New York Herald,* July 11, 1920.

48. "Man o' War Again Sets World Mark," *New York Times,* July 11, 1920.

49. "New Mark Set by Man o' War Before 40,000," *The Sun and New York Herald,* July 11, 1920.

50. Lou Feustel, as told to Pat O'Brien; cited in Edward L. Bowen, *Thoroughbred Legends: Man o' War* (Lexington, Kentucky: Eclipse Press, 2000), p. 98.

51. Hervey, "The Turf Career of Man o' War."

52. Hewitt, "Sire Lines," p. 5203.

53. Fitz Gerald, "Man O' War, Turf Idol and Sire," p. 29.

54. Hatton, "Delaware Park: Harmonizing Horse to Beat In Sussex Handicap Today." The "pony" mentioned by Clyde Gordon would have been Man o' War's favorite companion, Major Treat.

55. "Man o' War Again Sets World Mark," *New York Times,* July 11, 1920.

56. Neil Newman, "Still the King," *The Guild Race Review,* April 1947, p. 29.

57. Hatton, "Delaware Park: Harmonizing Horse to Beat In Sussex Handicap Today."

58. Henry V. King, "Kummer Injured in Spill at Aqueduct," *The Sun and New York Herald,* July 13, 1920.

59. Ibid.

60. Ibid.

61. "Bad Spill Mars Aqueduct Racing," *New York Times,* July 13, 1920.

62. Henry V. King, "Naturalist Wins Stake at Yonkers," *The Sun and New York Herald,* July 15, 1920.

63. Hervey, "The Turf Career of Man o' War."

64. "Can Man o' War Overtake Domino?" *The Sun and New York Herald,* July 25, 1920.

65. After the Dwyer, their earnings stood at Domino, $193,550; Man o' War, $123,450.

66. Robert H. Reed, "Big Red Comes of Age," *Country Gentleman,* April 1938.

16. ALIGHT IN AUGUST

1. "Past and Present Idols: Saratoga Visitors Compare Man o' War to Other-Day Heroes; Mr. Riddle's Champion to Be Big Attraction For Many Who See Racing Only at the Spa," *Daily Racing Form,* August 1, 1920.

2. "Saratoga Awaits First Bugle Call," *New York Times,* August 2, 1920.

3. Ibid.

4. *New York Herald* report, August 1919, cited in Eva Jolene Boyd, *Exterminator* (Lexington, Kentucky, Eclipse Press, 2002), p. 93.

5. Whisk Broom II ran his disputed 2:00 in the 1913 Suburban Handicap.

6. Henry V. King, "Sir Barton Fast with Weight Up," *The Sun and New York Herald,* August 3, 1920.

7. "Man o' War and Sir Barton Rivals," *Daily Racing Form,* August 4, 1920.

8. Ibid.

9. "Man o' War Runs Remarkable Trial," *The Saratogian,* August 4, 1920.

10. "Man o' War and Sir Barton Rivals," *Daily Racing Form,* August 4, 1920.

11. Henry V. King, "Saratoga Track Lightning Fast," *The Sun and New York Herald,* August 4, 1920.

12. "Man o' War Runs Remarkable Trial," *The Saratogian,* August 4, 1920.

13. "Man o' War and Sir Barton May Meet in Saratoga Cup," *New York Times,* August 5, 1920.

14. "Royal Contest in Store: Eager Interest Waits on Meeting of Two Great Horses; Characteristics of Man o' War and Sir Barton and Their Bearing on Saratoga Cup Race," *Daily Racing Form,* August 8, 1920.

15. Daniel, "High Lights and Shadows in All Spheres of Sport," *The Sun and New York Herald,* August 6, 1920.

16. John Hervey, "The Turf Career of Man o' War," unpublished manuscript (1933) later serialized by *Horse* magazine; available through the National Sporting Library (Middleburg, Virginia).

17. B. K. Beckwith, *Step and Go Together: The World of Horses and Horsemanship* (South Brunswick, N.J., and New York: A. S. Barnes and Co., 1967), p. 58.

18. "Man o' War Romps to Easy Victory," *New York Times,* August 8, 1920.

19. H. K. Fitzpatrick, "International Aspect to Saratoga Meeting; Entries From East, South, West, and Canada Feature Racing at Spa," *Evening Post* (New York), August 9, 1920.

20. Ibid. This article also noted that after the race, "realizing that the big stableman was again on the halter lead . . . Man o' War began to snuggle for sugar, and this time he found a lump ready for him."

21. "Man o' War Romps to Easy Victory," *New York Times,* August 8, 1920.

22. Henry V. King, "Man o' War Wins Miller Stakes," *The Sun and New York Herald,* August 8, 1920.

23. "Man o' War Romps to Easy Victory," *New York Times,* August 8, 1920.

24. "Man o' War's Easy Triumph: Takes the Miller Stakes Before a Great Assemblage," *Daily Racing Form,* August 8, 1920. See also Hervey, "The Turf Career of Man o' War."

25. "Near Another Record at Saratoga," *Evening Post* (New York), August 9, 1920. The caption for the so-titled photograph of Man o' War with Clarence Kummer up reads in part, "Jockey Sande, who had the mount, endeavored throughout the race to hold the champion back and was about all in when he returned to the post."

26. Beckwith, *Step and Go Together,* p. 59.

27. " 'Greatest Race Horse,' Says Jockey Sande," *The Sun and New York Herald,* August 8, 1920.

28. Ibid. The word *plater* was a term for horses who ran in cheap races, and "selling races," after which the winner would be auctioned, were similar to modern claiming races.

29. "Man o' War Ready to Meet Sir Barton," *The Sun and New York Herald,* August 17, 1920.

30. Ibid.

31. "Man o' War Versus Sir Barton," *Daily Racing Form,* August 17, 1920.

32. Ibid.

33. Henry V. King, "Dinna Care Is a Worthy Stable Mate of Man o' War," *The Sun and New York Herald,* August 18, 1920.

34. H. L. Fitzpatrick, "Dinna Care's Victory an Impressive One," *Evening Post* (New York), August 18, 1920.

35. Ibid.

36. King, "Dinna Care Is a Worthy Stable Mate of Man o' War."

37. "Man o' War Has Completely Recovered from Lameness," *New York Times,* August 19, 1920.

38. Ibid.

39. Hervey, "The Turf Career of Man o' War."

40. Ibid.

41. "Obituary: Louis C. Feustel," *The Blood-Horse,* July 11, 1970, p. 2072. Feustel died on July 4 in Fremont, Ohio.

42. Hervey, "The Turf Career of Man o' War."

43. "Man o' War Beats Grier with Ease," *New York Times,* August 22, 1920.

44. Henry V. King, "Mad Hatter Goes Mile in 1:37 1/5," *The Sun and New York Herald,* August 21, 1920.

45. Hervey, "The Turf Career of Man o' War."

46. J. L. Dempsey, "Man o' War Is Invincible: Takes the Travers Stakes and Leads All the Way Easily," *Daily Racing Form,* August 22, 1920.

47. "Pay Homage to Man o' War: Champion the Magnet That Attracted Largest Crowd in History of Saratoga's Famous Track," *Daily Racing Form,* August 24, 1920.

48. Hervey, "The Turf Career of Man o' War."

49. Ibid.

50. "Pay Homage to Man o' War: Champion the Magnet That Attracted Largest Crowd in History of Saratoga's Famous Track," *Daily Racing Form,* August 24, 1920.

51. Through August 2005, Man o' War's 1:10 remained the fastest opening six furlongs ever run by a Travers winner.

52. "Man o' War Beats Grier with Ease," *New York Times,* August 22, 1920.

53. Hervey, "The Turf Career of Man o' War."

54. Dempsey, "Man o' War Is Invincible."

55. "Pay Homage to Man o' War: Champion the Magnet That Attracted Largest Crowd in History of Saratoga's Famous Track," *Daily Racing Form,* August 24, 1920.

56. "Man o' War Beats Grier with Ease," *New York Times,* August 22, 1920.

57. Dempsey, "Man o' War Is Invincible."

58. Horace Wade, "Looking Back: Man o' War and a Warm Old Man," source and exact date unknown, 1969.

59. "Sir Barton Sets New World Mark," *New York Times,* August 29, 1920.

60. J. K. M. Ross, *Boots and Saddles: The Story of the Fabulous Ross Stable in the Golden Days of Racing* (New York: E. P. Dutton, 1956), p. 201.

61. Henry V. King, "Sir Barton Wins in Record Time," *The Sun and New York Herald,* August 29, 1920.

62. Daniel, "High Lights and Shadows in All Spheres of Sport."

63. Henry V. King, "Leonardo II Wins Hopeful, Cup for Exterminator," *The Sun and New York Herald,* September 1, 1920.

17. REALIZATION

1. "Man o' War Breaks Record in Workout," *The Sun and New York Herald,* September 3, 1920.

2. Henry V. King, "Milkmaid Sets New Record at Belmont," *The Sun and New York Herald,* September 4, 1920.

3. "Features at Belmont Park," *Daily Racing Form,* September 4, 1920.

4. Daniel, "High Lights and Shadows in All Spheres of Sport," *The Sun and New York Herald,* September 4, 1920.

5. Quote attributed to John Harper, who bred, owned, and trained Longfellow; cited by the National Museum of Racing and Hall of Fame (Saratoga Springs, New York) in its Hall of Fame page entry for Longfellow (accessible at www .racingmuseum.org).

6. C. J. Fitz Gerald, "Man O' War [*sic*], Turf Idol and Sire," *The Field Illustrated,* July 1925, p. 29.

7. Daniel, "High Lights and Shadows in All Spheres of Sports."

8. Fitz Gerald, "Man O' War [*sic*], Turf Idol and Sire," p. 29.

9. Ibid.

10. "Milkmaid Wins Handicap," *Daily Racing Form,* September 4, 1920.

11. Henry V. King, "Man o' War Makes a World's Record," *The Sun and New York Herald,* September 5, 1920.

12. Ibid.

13. Samuel D. Riddle, as told to Neil Newman, "From Man o' War to War Admiral," *Turf and Sport Digest,* June 1938, p. 51.

14. King, "Man o' War Makes a World's Record."

15. "World Mark Again Set by Man o' War," *New York Times,* September 5, 1920.

16. Ibid.

17. B. K. Beckwith, *Step and Go Together: The World of Horses and Horsemanship,* (South Brunswick, N.J., and New York: A. S. Barnes and Co., 1967), p. 58.

18. Fitz Gerald, "Man O' War [*sic*], Turf Idol and Sire," p. 29.

19. One horse length, from outstretched nose to last curve of the rump, equals about eight feet; therefore, 100 lengths equal about 800 feet—one furlong plus 46 yards (138 feet). The average Thoroughbred racehorse has a 21- or 22-foot

stride. Hoodwink was a large horse but also was very tired during the last phase of this race. Estimating his stride at 20 feet and using *Daily Racing Form*'s estimate puts him one furlong plus about six lengths behind Man o' War when Red reached the finish of the Realization.

20. W. J. Macbeth, "Man o' War Shatters World's Record in Winning Realization Stakes by a Furlong," *New York Tribune,* September 5, 1920.

21. "World Mark Again Set By Man o' War," *New York Times,* September 5, 1920.

22. Fitz Gerald, "Man O' War, Turf Idol and Sire."

23. King, "Man o' War Makes a World's Record."

24. Triple Crown winner Secretariat showed the same trait—using a shorter stride at higher speed—when his stride was measured after a very fast sprinting workout several days before the 1973 Preakness. Observers who had heard the legend of Man o' War's 28-foot or 30-foot stride were disappointed that Secretariat's longest stride from this breeze measured "only" 24 feet, 11 inches. Jockey Ron Turcotte pointed out, however, that the champion used a longer stride when running at a moderate pace and shortened his stride when he kicked into high gear. This may be a common characteristic. Back in the 1940s, Hall of Fame jockey George Woolf said that Triple Crown winner Whirlaway was the only horse he had ridden who actually lengthened stride when he hit full speed. (Woolf was angry about this revelation because, riding "Whirly" for the first time, he had misjudged the horse's movement and narrowly lost the race.)

25. "World Mark Again Set by Man o' War," *New York Times,* September 5, 1920.

26. Macbeth, "Man o' War Shatters World's Record in Winning Realization Stakes by a Furlong."

27. King, "Man o' War Makes a World's Record."

28. Henry V. King, "Lion D'Or Defeats High Class Rivals," *The Sun and New York Herald,* September 7, 1920.

29. Ibid.

30. Daniel, "High Lights and Shadows in All Spheres of Sport," *The Sun and New York Herald,* September 8, 1920.

31. "Doped Horse with Whiskey and Coffee," *New York Times,* July 4, 1913.

32. Henry V. King, "Teddy R. Victor in Mineola Stakes," *The Sun and New York Herald,* September 9, 1920.

33. King, "Lion D'Or Defeats High Class Rivals."

34. Amendment to The Jockey Club's Rule 119, as noted in the "Scales of Weights" sections of the *Daily Racing Form* chart books for 1920. The amendment read in full, "No gelding three years old and over shall be qualified to start in any race closing seventy-two hours or more before the date of running, except handicaps and selling races. This rule shall not apply to horses gelded prior to February 13, 1919." The implementation of this amendment was cited in "Important Jockey Club Action: Proposed Amendment Excluding

Geldings from Certain Big Races Adopted," *Daily Racing Form,* February 14, 1919.

35. J. K. M. Ross, *Boots and Saddles: The Story of the Fabulous Ross Stable in the Golden Days of Racing* (New York: E. P. Dutton, 1956), p. 203.

36. Daniel, "High Lights and Shadows in All Spheres of Sport."

37. Henry V. King, "Futurity Upset by Step Lightly," *The Sun and New York Herald,* September 12, 1920.

38. "Man o' War Starts Today," *Daily Racing Form,* September 11, 1920.

39. Ned Welch, *Who's Who in Thoroughbred Racing,* vol. 2 (Washington, D.C.: Who's Who in Thoroughbred Racing, Inc., 1946), p. 28.

40. King, "Futurity Upset by Step Lightly."

41. "Futurity Is Won by Step Lightly," *New York Times,* September 12, 1920.

42. "Good Races Still on Belmont Card," *New York Times,* September 13, 1920.

43. The average American's income for the year 1920 was $2,160.

44. *Daily Racing Form* chart (Autumn Gold Cup) (Fourth Race at Belmont Park), September 15, 1920.

45. Daniel, "High Lights and Shadows in All Spheres of Sport."

46. Henry V. King, "Exterminator Wins Cup and Makes New Record," *The Sun and New York Herald,* September 16, 1920.

47. John Hervey, "The Turf Career of Man o' War," unpublished manuscript (1933) later serialized by *Horse* magazine; available through the National Sporting Library (Middleburg, Virginia).

18. RIVER OF DREAMS

1. "Sunbriar [*sic*] in Cup Race," *New York Times,* October 5, 1919.

2. Walter S. Vosburgh, *Thoroughbred Racing in America, 1866–1921* (New York: privately printed by The Jockey Club, 1922), p. 234.

3. Samuel D. Riddle, as told to Neil Newman, "From Man o' War to War Admiral," *Turf and Sport Digest,* June 1938, p. 51.

4. Ibid.

5. C. Edward Sparrow, "Track Record Falls Before Man o' War's Flying Hoofs," *Baltimore Sun,* September 19, 1920.

6. Ibid.

7. John Hervey, "The Turf Career of Man o' War," unpublished manuscript (1933) later serialized by *Horse* magazine; available through the National Sporting Library (Middleburg, Virginia).

8. Sparrow, "Track Record Falls Before Man o' War's Flying Hoofs."

9. "Heavy Burden Fails to Stop Man o' War," *New York Times,* September 19, 1920.

10. Sparrow, "Track Record Falls Before Man o' War's Flying Hoofs."

11. Vosburgh, *Thoroughbred Racing in America, 1866–1921.* p. 234.

12. Sparrow, "Track Record Falls Before Man o' War's Flying Hoofs."

13. J. K. M. Ross, *Boots and Saddles: The Story of the Fabulous Ross Stable in the Golden Days of Racing* (New York: E. P. Dutton, 1956), p. 206.

14. "Man o' War, Under Weight Impost, Makes Show of Field," *Washington Post,* September 19, 1920.

15. "Man o' War Did His Best: Trainer Feustel Makes Comment," *Daily Racing Form,* September 21, 1920.

19. LIGHTING A MATCH

1. "Man o' War Ready to Meet Sir Barton," *The Sun and New York Herald,* August 17, 1920.

2. "Man o' War Runs Remarkable Trial," *The Saratogian,* August 4, 1920.

3. J. K. M. Ross, *Boots and Saddles: The Story of the Fabulous Ross Stable in the Golden Days of Racing* (New York: E. P. Dutton, 1956), p. 204.

4. "Horse Owners to Meet," *New York Times,* September 22, 1920.

5. Ross, *Boots and Saddles,* p. 204.

6. "Comment on Current Events in Sport," *New York Times,* September 20, 1920.

7. "Comment on Current Events in Sport," *New York Times,* September 27, 1920.

8. Daniel, "High Lights and Shadows in All Spheres of Sport," *The Sun and New York Herald,* September 30, 1920.

9. "Man o' War to Race Sir Barton in Canada," *The Sun and New York Herald,* September 23, 1920.

10. "Man o' War and Sir Barton to Race for $75,000 Purse," *The Sun and New York Herald,* September 25, 1920.

11. David Alexander, *A Sound of Horses* (Indianapolis, Kansas City, and New York: Bobbs-Merrill, 1966), p. 127.

12. "Mr. Kilmer insisted that the race be at one mile and a half, and that it be a handicap affair," *The Sun and New York Herald* stated; see "Man o' War and Sir Barton to Race for $75,000 Purse," September 25, 1920.

13. "Man o' War, Pulled to a Canter, Beats Sir Barton and Drinks From Gold Cup," *New York Herald,* October 13, 1920.

14. Ibid.

15. "Oceanus Handicap Won by Mulciber," *The Sun and New York Herald,* October 12, 1920.

16. "White Sox Players Who Have Been Indicted by Chicago Grand Jury" and "Honest Regulars of the Chicago White Sox," *The Sun* and *New York Herald,* September 30, 1920.

17. "Threatens Injury to Man o' War," *The Democratic Messenger,* March 5, 1921.

18. Henry V. King, "Cleopatra Held by Starter in Stake," *The Sun and New York Herald,* October 3, 1920.

19. "Sir Barton Is Already Fit for Test with Man o' War," *New York Times,* October 5, 1920.

20. "Man o' War Has Fast Trial at Belmont," *New York Herald,* October 6, 1920.
21. Ibid.
22. Ross, *Boots and Saddles,* p. 210.
23. "This sum is one of the largest ever offered to a jockey in this country for riding one race. . . ." *The Sun and New York Herald* noted; see "Kummer to Get $5,000 for Riding Man o' War," September 30, 1920.
24. "Tiny Tales of the Turf," *Collyer's Eye & The Baseball World,* December 27, 1930.
25. Ibid.
26. Ibid.
27. Ross, *Boots and Saddles,* p. 207.
28. "Man o' War Victor Over Sir Barton by Seven Lengths," *New York Times,* October 13, 1920.
29. "Man o' War's Great Test Comes Today," *New York Times,* October 12, 1920.
30. "Great Racers Show Speed in Workouts," *New York Times,* October 9, 1920.
31. John Hervey, "The Turf Career of Man o' War," unpublished manuscript (1933) later serialized by *Horse* magazine; available through the National Sporting Library (Middleburg, Virginia).
32. W. J. Macbeth, "Sir Barton's Time Bettered by Man o' War," *New York Tribune,* October 10, 1920.
33. "Great Colts Arrive at Battle Ground," *The Sun and New York Herald,* October 8, 1920.
34. B. K. Beckwith, *Step and Go Together: The World of Horses and Horsemanship* (South Brunswick, N.J., and New York: A. S. Barnes and Co., 1967), p. 59.
35. "Man o' War's Great Test Comes Today," *New York Times,* October 12, 1920.
36. Henry V. King, "Man o' War Choice in To-Day's Match," *The Sun and New York Herald,* October 12, 1920.
37. "Man o' War Breezes a Quarter Mile in 22 3/4," *New York Herald,* October 10, 1920.
38. "Great Racers Show Speed in Workouts," *New York Times,* October 9, 1920. Eminent turf historian John Hervey, who often saw Man o' War race, also used :22 1/5 in his manuscript "The Turf Career of Man o' War."
39. Old Rosebud, "Odds and Ends: Man o' War's Trial," *The Blood-Horse,* June 29, 1935, p. 766.
40. "Great Racers Show Speed in Workouts," *New York Times,* October 9, 1920.
41. "Crowds Gather to See Turf Classic," *New York Times,* October 11, 1920.
42. "Champion Horses Are Fit for Test," *New York Times,* October 10, 1920.
43. "Man o' War's Great Test Comes Today," *New York Times,* October 12, 1920.
44. "Crowds Gather to See Turf Classic," *New York Times,* October 11, 1920.
45. Ross, *Boots and Saddles,* p. 207.
46. "Man o' War to Be Horse Show Star," *The Sun and New York Herald,* October 3, 1920.
47. On October 11, the day before their match, Man o' War clocked three furlongs

in :41, four furlongs in :54, and Sir Barton clocked five furlongs in 1:04, six furlongs (perhaps pulling up) in 1:21.

48. King, "Man o' War Choice in To-Day's Match."

49. Ross, *Boots and Saddles,* p. 207.

50. Telegram to A. M. Orpen from August Belmont, Jr., October 11, 1920; Belmont Family Papers, Rare Book and Manuscript Library, Columbia University.

51. "Man o' War to Be Horse Show Star," *The Sun and New York Herald,* October 3, 1920.

52. "Man o' War's Great Test Comes Today," *New York Times,* October 12, 1920.

53. Ibid.

54. Ross, *Boots and Saddles,* p. 213.

55. *Daily Racing Form* chart (Sixth Race at Kenilworth Park), October 11, 1920.

56. "Oceanus Handicap Won by Mulciber," *The Sun and New York Herald,* October 12, 1920.

57. Ross, *Boots and Saddles,* p. 211.

58. "Man o' War Victor Over Sir Barton by Seven Lengths," *New York Times,* October 13, 1920.

59. Ross, *Boots and Saddles,* p. 207.

20. BLOW

1. J. K. M. Ross, *Boots and Saddles: The Story of the Fabulous Ross Stable in the Golden Days of Racing* (New York: E. P. Dutton, 1956), p. 213.

2. "Man o' War Victor Over Sir Barton by Seven Lengths," *New York Times,* October 13, 1920.

3. "Man o' War's Mightiness," *Daily Racing Form,* October 13, 1920.

4. Ross, *Boots and Saddles,* p. 214.

5. Ibid.

6. Charles B. Parmer, *For Gold and Glory: The Story of Thoroughbred Racing in America* (New York: Carrick and Evans, Inc., 1939), p. 191.

7. "Man o' War, Pulled to a Canter, Beats Sir Barton and Drinks From Gold Cup," by Henry V. King, *New York Herald,* Oct. 13, 1920.

8. Jim Ross said his father's statement was delivered at noon. The *New York Times* reporter said Ross delivered the statement "an hour before the running of the race"—about 2:30 P.M.

9. "Man o' War Victor Over Sir Barton by Seven Lengths," *New York Times,* October 13, 1920.

10. Henry V. King, "Sir Barton Wins in Record Time," *The Sun and New York Herald,* August 29, 1920.

11. "A Big Day Up North," source unknown, February 1971 (found on file in the Selima Room, Bowie Branch of the Prince George's County Memorial Library System, Bowie, Maryland).

12. Ibid.

13. Henry V. King, "Man o' War, Pulled to a Canter, Beats Sir Barton and Drinks from Gold Cup," *New York Herald*, October 13, 1920.

14. "Man o' War's Mightiness," *Daily Racing Form*, October 13, 1920.

15. Ross, *Boots and Saddles*, pp. 210–11.

16. King, "Man o' War, Pulled to a Canter, Beats Sir Barton and Drinks from Gold Cup."

17. A selling race (or claiming race), in which some or all of the horses in the race are for sale, is the lowest and most ordinary level of competition.

18. King, "Man o' War, Pulled to a Canter, Beats Sir Barton and Drinks from Gold Cup."

19. Ibid.

20. Ibid.

21. John Hervey, "The Turf Career of Man o' War," unpublished manuscript (1933) later serialized by *Horse* magazine; available through the National Sporting Library (Middleburg, Virginia).

22. King, "Man o' War, Pulled to a Canter, Beats Sir Barton and Drinks from Gold Cup."

23. "Man o' War Victor Over Sir Barton by Seven Lengths," *New York Times*, October 13, 1920.

24. Ross, *Boots and Saddles*, p. 215.

25. Ibid., p. 216.

26. Ibid.

27. "Man o' War Victor Over Sir Barton by Seven Lengths," *New York Times*, October 13, 1920.

28. King, "Man o' War, Pulled to a Canter, Beats Sir Barton and Drinks from Gold Cup."

29. Ibid.

30. Ibid.

31. Ibid.

32. "Man o' War Victor Over Sir Barton by Seven Lengths," *New York Times*, October 13, 1920.

33. Ross, *Boots and Saddles*, p. 216.

34. Ibid.

35. King, "Man o' War, Pulled to a Canter, Beats Sir Barton and Drinks from Gold Cup."

36. Ibid.

37. Ibid. "The track over which the race was run was at least three seconds slower than Belmont Park and Saratoga, and it was the opinion of all expert horsemen, including the owner and trainer of the vanquished Sir Barton, that it was the equal of the questionable world's record of 2:00 made by Whisk Broom at Belmont Park in 1913."

38. Ibid.

39. Hervey, "The Turf Career of Man o' War."

40. Ross, *Boots and Saddles*, p. 217.

41. "Refuses $400,000 for Man o' War," *New York Times,* October 15, 1920.

42. Ibid.

43. "Man o' War's Stirrup Broke After Big Race," *New York Herald,* October 15, 1920.

44. Tape-recorded interview with Louis Feustel, circa 1960s; interviewer unidentified; collection of the National Museum of Racing and Hall of Fame (Saratoga Springs, New York).

45. W. J. Macbeth, "Man o' War to Race Abroad Next Summer; Riddle Family Council Decides Champion Shall Try for the Ascot Gold Cup," *New York Tribune,* October 14, 1920.

46. Ibid.

47. Ibid.

48. Daniel, "High Lights and Shadows in All Spheres of Sport," *New York Herald,* October 15, 1920.

49. "Man o' War–Exterminator: Kentucky Offers a $50,000 Prize for the Two Horses to Meet at One and One-Half Miles," *Daily Racing Form,* October 14, 1920.

50. "Exile," "Man o' War's Racing Future," *Daily Racing Form,* October 15, 1920.

51. "Hastings Engaged to Train for Jeffords," *New York Herald,* November 30, 1920.

52. "May Be Another Race," *New York Herald,* October 15, 1920.

53. *Hoofprints of the Century: Excerpts from America's Oldest Journal of Horse Racing and Breeding, the Thoroughbred Record, and Its Predecessor Publications, the Livestock Record and Kentucky Live Stock Record,* as compiled and annotated by William Robertson (covering 1875–1919 and 1966–1974) and Dan Farley (1920–1965); material published by *The Thoroughbred Record,* January 23, 1909.

54. Ibid.

55. B. K. Beckwith, *Step and Go Together: The World of Horses and Horsemanship* (South Brunswick, N.J., and New York: A. S. Barnes and Co., 1967), p. 56.

56. Ibid. Feustel told Beckwith: "What could we do? He wins at 140 and then there's no ceiling. Vosburgh was right, of course. He deserved it. But Riddle says, 'Retire him, he'll never run again.'"

57. Chris J. Fitzgerald, "Man o' War's Romantic Career Marred by a 'Bar Sinister,'" *The Rider and Driver,* November 6, 1920, p. 100.

58. Letter from August Belmont, Jr., to Samuel D. Riddle, October 19, 1920; Belmont Family Papers, Rare Book and Manuscript Library, Columbia University.

59. C. J. Fitz Gerald, "Man O' War [*sic*], Turf Idol and Sire," *The Field Illustrated,* July 1925, p. 50.

60. Ibid.

61. During the breeding season of 1921, the Riddles and Jeffordses used Man o' War as a "private stallion"—that is, breeding him only to mares that they owned.

During 1922 and each year thereafter, they made him available to a limited number of "outside" mares, including a few owned by August Belmont, Jr.

62. "Miss Daingerfield to Take Care of Man o' War," *New York Herald,* October 21,
1920.

63. "Man o' War Narrowly Escapes Breaking Leg," *New York Herald,* October 21,
1920.

21. SETTLEMENTS

1. B. K. Beckwith, *Step and Go Together: The World of Horses and Horsemanship*
(South Brunswick, N.J., and New York: A. S. Barnes and Co., 1967), p. 56.

2. Joe H. Palmer, *This Was Racing* (South Brunswick, N.J., and New York: A. S.
Barnes and Co., 1953), p. 77–78.

3. Beckwith, *Step and Go Together,* p. 56.

4. Henry V. King, "Man o' War, Greatest of Horses, Has Been Placed Under
Charge of Woman," newspaper unknown, February 20, 1921 (found in Johnny
Loftus Boosting and Marching Club scrapbook, presented to Loftus by Ed Cur-
ley, Bill Farnsworth, and Moe Druck and passed down to his son and grandson).

5. Kent Hollingsworth, "What's Going On Here," *The Blood-Horse,* April 13, 1968,
p. 1027. The quote originally appeared as, "Why, Miss Lizbeth, iffn all the good
horses in New York couldn't ketchim, how'n you expect me to stop Man o' War?"
Buckner surely spoke with a southern dialect and may have sounded much like
this. However, many writers during the era of Man o' War's retirement
(1921–1947) used stereotypical speech for any African-American person. Since we
can't assume that the transcription above accurately portrays Buckner's actual accent, writing the alleged quote in plain English seems more clear and fair.

6. "Feustel Refused License to Train," *New York Herald,* March 11, 1921.

7. Ibid.

8. Ibid.

9. Ibid.

10. Letter from August Belmont, Jr., to William P. Riggs, April 27, 1921; Belmont
Family Papers, Rare Book and Manuscript Library, Columbia University.

11. Henry V. King, "Ban to Remain on Jockey Shilling," *New York Herald,* November 16, 1920.

12. "Hunt For Ross Assets," *Collyer's Eye,* November 10, 1928.

13. J. K. M. Ross, *Boots and Saddles: The Story of the Fabulous Ross Stable in the
Golden Days of Racing* (New York: E. P. Dutton, 1956), p. 7.

14. "Obituary: H. Guy Bedwell Dies Suddenly," *The Blood-Horse,* January 12, 1952,
p. 107. Quote attributed to the *Baltimore Sun.*

15. Ibid.

16. In 1930, the Preakness actually was run eight days before the Kentucky Derby.
New York Times reporter Bryan Field used the term "triple crown" (with lower-

case letters and quotation marks) in his Belmont Stakes story to describe Gallant Fox's feat. There was no official recognition at that time, however, of these three races as the Triple Crown.

17. Frank Talmadge Phelps, "Earl Sande: November 13, 1898–August 18, 1968," *The Thoroughbred Record,* August 31, 1968, p. 795.

18. *Daily Racing Form,* July 16, 1924; quoted in John McEvoy, *Through the Pages of Daily Racing Form* (New York: Daily Racing Form Press, 1995).

19. "Race Puts Sande and Bedwell Once More on Speaking Terms," *New York Times,* October 21, 1923.

20. Dan M. Bowmar III, *Giants of the Turf* (Lexington, Kentucky: The Blood-Horse, 1960), p. 93.

21. Eleanor Robson Belmont; *The Fabric of Memory,* (New York: Farrar, Straus and Cudahy, 1957), p. 119.

22. "Obituary: John P. Loftus," *Blade Tribune* (Carlsbad, Calif.), March 23, 1976, courtesy of Carolyn Rodosta. The last job ever held by Johnny Loftus was reported to be "a shipping foreman for the Axel Electronics in New York."

23. "Oddenda," *Thoroughbred of California,* January 1961, pp. 122–123.

24. "Jockey Club Explodes Bomb in Racing Circles by Withholding Licenses of Two Riders; Clarence Kummer, L. M. Fator Denied License as Riders," *Evening Post* (New York), March 24, 1926.

25. Joseph O'Shea, "Kummer Piloted to Victory Many Leading Turf Stars," newspaper and exact date unknown (found in Clarence Kummer file at the National Museum of Racing and Hall of Fame, Saratoga Springs, New York).

26. "New York Stewards War on Race 'Fixers,'" *Collyer's Eye,* July 7, 1928.

27. "Jockey Kummer Dies, Ill Week," newspaper and exact date unknown (found in Clarence Kummer file at the National Museum of Racing and Hall of Fame, Saratoga Springs, New York).

28. Jimmy Powers, "C. Kummer: Man-O-War's Old Jockey Succumbs to Pneumonia," newspaper and exact date unknown (found in Clarence Kummer file at the National Museum of Racing and Hall of Fame, Saratoga Springs, New York).

29. A *New York Times* report on Kummer's will reaching probate court said that he died on December 17; other sources give December 18. He may have passed away during the night of December 17–18. Most newspapers published his obituary on December 19.

30. "Jockey Kummer Dies, Ill Week," newspaper and exact date unknown (found in Clarence Kummer file at the National Museum of Racing and Hall of Fame, Saratoga Springs, New York).

31. "Riddle Lauds Kummer," *New York Times,* December 19, 1930.

32. "Jockey Kummer Dies, Ill Week," newspaper and exact date unknown (found in Clarence Kummer file at National Museum of Racing and Hall of Fame, Saratoga Springs, New York).

33. Marvin Drager, *The Most Glorious Crown: The Story of America's Triple Crown*

Thoroughbreds, from Sir Barton to Secretariat (New York: Charles Scribner's Sons, 1975), pp. 28, 30.

34. Elizabeth Bent, "She Breeds Great Horses," *New York Times,* December 30, 1923.

35. Frank Talmadge Phelps, "He Wuz de Mostes' Hoss," *Turf and Sport Digest,* March 1960, p. 4.

36. Philip Ardery, "The Will of Man o' War," *Spur,* November/December 1984, p. 59.

37. "The Groom's Big Three," *The Blood-Horse* (citing the *New York Times*), June 20, 1931, p. 937.

38. Ibid.

39. C. W. Anderson, *Big Red* (New York: Macmillan, 1943), p. 63.

40. Ibid.

41. Joe H. Palmer, *American Race Horses, 1947* (N.p.: Sagamore Press, 1948), p. 27.

42. Beckwith, *Step and Go Together,* p. 60.

43. Anderson, *Big Red,* p. 60.

44. Ibid.

45. Palmer, *This Was Racing,* p. 77.

46. Anderson, *Big Red,* p. 63.

47. Palmer, *American Race Horses, 1947,* p. 27.

48. Anderson, *Big Red,* p. 63.

49. Palmer, *American Race Horses, 1947,* p. 27.

50. Palmer, *This Was Racing,* pp. 80–81.

51. Palmer, *American Race Horses, 1947,* p. 27.

52. Abe Kemp, "California Turf Gains Glamorous Figure in Loftus," newspaper and exact date unknown, circa 1936 (found in Johnny Loftus Boosting and Marching Club scrapbook).
    This article claims that Loftus yelled, "Hey, Big Red!" Other sources say that, in general, a call of "Hey, Red!" would summon Man o' War. Loftus could have used either.

22. EBB TIDE

1. Abram S. Hewitt, "Sire Lines: Part XXXIX: Man o' War," *The Blood-Horse,* November 25, 1974, p. 5200.

2. B. K. Beckwith, *Step and Go Together: The World of Horses and Horsemanship* (South Brunswick, N.J., and New York: A. S. Barnes and Co., 1967), pp. 53–54.

3. Told to the author by Vicki Fleming of Stealth Productions, who had interviewed Loftus son-in-law Col. C. V. Farmer. During the last five years of his life, Johnny Loftus had lived with his daughter, Elinor M. Farmer, and her husband in Carlsbad, California.

4. Lou DeFichy, "Bitter Memories Haunt Man o' War Jock," *Horsemen's Journal,* October 1965, p. 38. At the time of this interview, Johnny Loftus was employed as a carpenter.

ACKNOWLEDGMENTS

Many times during a decade of researching Man o' War's story, the quest pulled forward by a single shining thread. One good friend from upstate New York, the unsinkable Joan Meyer, helped me happily navigate a move to Saratoga Springs, New York. One Man o' War–oriented classified ad in *The Blood-Horse* magazine drew a response from a brilliant young writer named Laura Hillenbrand, who was developing a book proposal about Big Red's grandson Seabiscuit, and launched a deeply sustaining friendship. One reply from literary agent John A. Ware of Manhattan began years of most valuable feedback, which raised my writing awareness to the level that made this book possible. One enthusiastic editor, Marc Resnick at St. Martin's Press, offered the contract that brought *Man o' War: A Legend Like Lightning* from proposal to fruition. And one relative of a key person in Man o' War's life, Johnny Loftus's daughter-in-law Colleen Andrepont, reached out to the National Museum of Racing and Hall of Fame. Without her contacting the museum, this researcher would not have known that someone with such rare information and insight about Johnny Loftus existed.

While those connections appeared like rope bridges over otherwise-impassable chasms, a great web of connections built the book's frame and filled out much of the story.

In cyberspace, I gathered census and draft-registration information through Ancestry.com and collected vintage Man o' War magazine articles, newspapers, advertisements, and ephemera from vendors throughout North America, courtesy of eBay.

In Virginia, Peter Winants and then librarian Laura Rose at the National Sporting Library in Middleburg opened a path into the life of Major Treat and provided a copy of John Hervey's manuscript, "The Turf Career of Man o' War." The Marshall Historical Society offered additional clues to the lives of Major Treat and Samuel D. Riddle's good friend James Kerfoot Maddux.

In Washington, D.C., the Library of Congress opened its archives from the Pinkerton Detective Agency. The Social Security Administration provided copies of the original Social Security applications filed by Louis Feustel and John Patrick Loftus.

In Maryland, Brian Boseman described the Glen Riddle Farm near Berlin, and the Worcester County Library in Snow Hill provided many additional details. George Mohr remembered Sir Barton and Cal Shilling. The Selima Room in the Bowie Branch Library of the Prince George's County Memorial Library System provided various useful articles. The Baltimore Public Library microfilm collection yielded articles from the *Baltimore Sun*.

In Pennsylvania, Mr. and Mrs. John H. Richards and Mr. and Mrs. Robert Gauthrop graciously guided me into the world of Sam Riddle and the Rose Tree Hunt. The Delaware County Historical Society provided key information about the Riddle and Jeffords families.

In New Jersey, Princeton University's exceptional microforms collection provided access to hundreds of vintage newspaper articles.

In Massachusetts, Robin Bledsoe provided wonderful source materials through her Cambridge bookshop. Many friends at Berklee College of Music gave me wings to venture onward with this book.

In Kentucky, standing in Man o' War's old barn at Faraway Farm made it easy to feel the reverence he inspired. At Keeneland Library in Lexington, so ably overseen by Cathy Schenk, ever-kindly Phyllis Rogers gave essential support with the *Daily Racing Form* archive, photographic collection, and other riches. At Kentucky Horse Park, Bill Cooke happily discussed Man o' War's stride and other wonders. At large, collector extraordinaire Ken Grayson acted as a marvelous guide to Man o' War relics and locales; Tom Harbut, by his conversation and very presence, showed what a perceptive horseman and charismatic person his father must have been; and the remarkable Dr. William McGee related his experiences as a young veterinarian attending elderly Man o' War and confirmed that it was his idea—a most practical one, knowing that the great horse's body would lie in state for a few days—to take the revolutionary step of embalming him.

In Illinois, the University of Illinois at Urbana-Champaign Library provided access to many issues of *Collyer's Eye* (thanks to Bob Carney, scholar of the Black Sox scandal, for sharing his views about the quality of the *Eye's* reporting and helping me locate this unusual resource). The Cook County Clerk's Office provided a copy of the birth certificate for Johnny Loftus.

In New York, Columbia University granted access to the fascinating files of August Belmont, Jr., and Eleanor Robson Belmont. The Black Crow Network of Saratoga Springs suggested running an advertisement seeking interview subjects in a racing magazine. The Saratoga Springs Public Library provided vintage articles from *The Saratogian* newspaper, via microfilm, and additional local lore through its Saratoga Room. At the Saratoga Historical Society, Martha Stonequist unveiled the White Sulpher Springs Hotel registers, which shed new light on the Sanford Memorial Stakes. Tommy and Helen Luther recalled their sojourns at Sam Riddle's Maryland farm. Bill Cherry, who was a young jockey in the 1940s, said old-timers told him that jockey Cal Shilling was "a terrible bunch of talent." The Lyrical Ballad bookstore provided many excellent source materials. Anne and Joe McMahon of McMahon of Saratoga Thoroughbreds enriched my understanding of the life cycle of Thoroughbred racehorses. Living across the street from the property where August Belmont, Jr., brought the yearling Man o' War, and a stone's throw from Saratoga Race Course, brought all of racing's rhythms alive.

Working for seven years at the National Museum of Racing and Hall of Fame in Saratoga Springs became one of the best graduate programs that a Thoroughbred racing writer/researcher could desire. Files on Hall of Fame horses, jockeys, and trainers revealed much compelling information. The boots and saddle that Johnny Loftus used while riding Man o' War brought horse and rider into 3-D. Former Museum historian Tom Gilcoyne, sage of nine decades of racing, never would let me forget that Man o' War lost the Sanford *Memorial* Stakes and memorably described Mars Cassidy as "a squatty little guy who always looked like he wanted to start something" (not necessarily a horse race). Current Museum historian Allan Carter helped to secure many loose ends. Peter Hammell helped me to acquire *Daily Racing Form* chart books from Man o' War's racing years. Field Horne volunteered the Man o' War guest books for perusal. Karen Wheaton shared quality time with her grand horse Killian, a flame red descendant of Man o' War. Kathleen Lippiello gave a good-luck charm. Sharon LaPier always knew that this book would come true. Curatorial professionals Lori Fisher and Beth Sheffer offered all sorts of wise help. Former racing steward Dick Hamilton knows how to keep it real and often make you laugh at the same time.

Within and outside of the racing world, I am especially grateful to Miles and Hally Baker, Brenda Booth, Kate Cravens, Beth Gallagher, Jan Gillespie,

Letitia Grant, Dick Hamilton, Juanita Hodges, Joan Meyer, Kathy Newcomb, Pat Newcomb, Robert M. Ours, Sean Pickard, Nina and Polly Quinn, Michelle and Evelyn Tonkin, and Jeanne Williams for intelligent reading and/or cheerleading, and to Robert, Ann, and Linda Ours for their gifts of history, imagination, and encouragement.

Everyone named here, and many others during life's journey, made a vital impact on this book. A few have influenced this particular project in the highest degree. Special places in the winner's circle belong to Hally Montague Baker, who said, "Intention is everything"; Michelle Tonkin, who held my favorite hat for ransom and said, "You know what to do"; Nina Quinn of Heyday Morgans, who helped me to get a clean break from the gate, give a strong kick to the finish line, and interpret what the horses communicate; John A. Ware, astute agent and champion of clarity in writing; Marc Resnick, insightful editor and cheerful coach through the challenging book-birthing process; Laura Hillenbrand, guru with laugh-out-loud humor; Colleen Andrepont, who gave this story such a powerful infusion of heart and soul; and, of course, the immortal Man o' War. Thank you, Red, for the ride.

Dorothy Ours
Stockton, New Jersey

INDEX

accidents, 94, 188–89, 193, 196
    fatal, 47, 127
Ace of Aces, race with Man o' War, 75
African-Americans
    jockeys, 38, 77, 166–67
    reporters and, 321*n*
Alexander, David, 113, 231
Algonquin, 246
Ambrose, Eddie, 91, 93, 96, 122, 179, 183–87,
    202, 213
Anderson, C. W., 270, 271
Anniversary, race with Man o' War, 63
Aqueduct racetrack, 71, 74, 172, 182
Arden, Elizabeth, 266
Armistice, race with Man o' War, 101
Army, U.S., horses for, 10, 35, 268
Artist, 127
Ascot Gold Cup, 14, 243, 252, 254
Autumn Gold Cup (Belmont), 216, 218, 219
Autumn Handicap, 131

Bain, George A., 29
baseball, major-league, 130, 233
Battalion, 25
Beaming Beauty, 112–13, 136
Beck and Call, 82
Beckwith, B. K., 212, 270
Bedwell, H. G. "Hard Guy," 43, 58, 78, 88,
    90, 110, 132, 133, 143–44, 214, 228,
    232–33, 235, 238–39, 240, 247, 265
    background of, 5–8
    challenges Feustel to a Man o' War—Sir
        Barton match race, 198–99
    Jockey Club investigation and loss of
        license, 262–63
    later life of, 263–64
    possibility of hop accusation, 137–39

switches jockeys for Kenilworth Gold
    Cup, 241–45
trainer for Ross, 50–55
Be Frank, 129
Bel Air Handicap, 143
Belmont, August, Sr., 10, 283*n*
Belmont, August, Jr., 14, 29, 33, 45, 124–25,
    128, 137, 139–40, 142, 164, 180, 209,
    214–15, 220, 241, 257, 262–63, 266–67,
    283*n*
    breeding system, 165–67
    death of, and dispersal of estate, 265–66
    devotion to racing, 8–11
    Nursery farm of, Babylon, Long Island,
        N.Y., 18–19
    Nursery Stud of, in Kentucky, 21
    praise for Man o' War, 170
    sale or auction of 1918 yearlings, 17–18,
        22–25, 31
    sees Man o' War race, 120–21
    sued by Freit, a stable boy, 125–26
    World War I service, 15–18
Belmont, August, III, 45, 283*n*
Belmont, Eleanor Robson, 15–16, 265–66
Belmont, Morgan, 265
Belmont, Raymond, 17
    stable of, 17
Belmont Park, 11, 58–59, 121–25, 142, 166,
    210, 264
    clockwise circuit of, 125, 172
    track records, 158–59
    track surface, 65, 207, 290*n*
    training in, 145
    triple crown for three-year-olds, 214
Belmont Stakes, 11–13, 58, 65–67, 167–68
    See also Man o' War, races
Bend Or, 159

Man o' War
  auctioned at Saratoga Springs, 25–31
  Belmont's decision to sell, 17–18
  betting on, and odds, 163–64, 175
  birth, 15
  called superhorse, 170–71
  career management, 218–19, 222, 228,
    251–59
  death and funeral of, 274
  earnings, 128, 228, 252, 275
  fame of, 1
  first race, 61–62
  guards placed on, 155, 233–34, 236, 237
  illnesses, 73
  injuries to, 199–200, 226–27, 251–52,
    255–56
  introduction to racing, 59
  lack of competition for, 172, 208
  later life of, 268–74
  match with Sir Barton, 230–51, 268
  name and nicknames of, 16, 34, 75, 284n,
    288n
  not a hop horse, 72
  not entered in Kentucky Derby, 141
  offers to buy from Riddle, rejected, 115,
    116, 168, 253
  pedigree of, 279
  photographs and films of, 187, 238, 259
  physical defects of, supposed, 26, 27
  public admiration of, 148–49, 152
  races. See Man o' War, races
  rank of, among great horses, 1
  records set by, 114, 161–63, 169, 187, 204,
    213, 217, 251, 275–77
  resilience of, after races, 172, 190
  retirement planned, 234, 252–58
  retires to Kentucky, 258–62
  running flat out, 210–14
  soundness of, 28, 49–50, 196, 226, 235
  speed of, 36–37, 62, 88, 115, 146, 148–49,
    158–59, 160–63
  stallion nature of, 190, 237–38
  standing at stud, 258, 261–62, 320n
  statue and monument of, 268, 274
  stride of, 209, 213, 314n
  as tourist destination, 268–69

  training of, 32–37, 56, 60, 68–69,
    71–72
  wild behavior (rearing, etc.), 71
  winner-take-all match sought with Sir
    Barton, 228–29
  workouts, 36, 88, 173, 178, 181–82, 194,
    199, 207, 220, 234–35, 238
Man o' War, races
  June 6, 1919, Belmont Park, purse for
    juveniles, 61–62
  June 9, 1919, Belmont Park, Keene
    Memorial Stakes, 62–64
  June 21, 1919, Jamaica, Youthful Stakes,
    69–70
  June 23, 1919, Aqueduct, Hudson Stakes,
    71–72
  July 5, 1919, Aqueduct, Tremont Stakes,
    74–75
  August 2, 1919, Saratoga, United States
    Hotel Stakes, 89–92
  August 13, 1919, Saratoga, Sanford
    Memorial Stakes, 99–109, 135–37
  August 23, 1919, Saratoga, Grand Union
    Hotel Stakes, 113–15
  August 30, 1919, Saratoga, Hopeful
    Stakes, 117–19
  September 23, 1919, Belmont Park,
    Futurity Stakes, 121–23
  May 18, 1920, Pimlico, Preakness Stakes,
    150–55
  May 29, 1920, Belmont Park, Withers
    Stakes, 159–63
  June 12, 1920, Belmont Park, Belmont
    Stakes, 168–71
  June 22, 1920, Jamaica, Stuyvesant
    Handicap, 173–76
  July 10, 1920, Aqueduct, Dwyer Stakes,
    183–88
  August 7, 1920, Saratoga, Miller Stakes,
    197–98
  August 21, 1920, Saratoga, Travers Stakes,
    202–4
  September 4, 1920, Belmont Park,
    Lawrence Realization, 211–14
  September 11, 1920, Belmont Park, Jockey
    Club Stakes, 217–18